A GUIDE TO
SQL/DS

A GUIDE TO
SQL/DS

A user's guide to the IBM product
Structured Query Language / Data System
(a relational database management system
for the VM and VSE environments)
and its major companion products
QMF, AS, CSP, etc.

C. J. DATE

with

COLIN J. WHITE

Codd and Date Consulting Group

ADDISON-WESLEY PUBLISHING COMPANY

Reading, Massachusetts   Menlo Park, California   New York
Don Mills, Ontario   Wokingham, England   Amsterdam   Bonn
Sydney   Singapore   Tokyo   Madrid   San Juan

Many of the designations used by manufacturers and sellers to distinguish their products are claimed as trademarks. Where those designations appear in this book, and Addison-Wesley was aware of a trademark claim, the designations have been printed in initial caps or all caps.

The programs and applications presented in this book have been included for their instructional value. They have been tested with care, but are not guaranteed for any particular purpose. The publisher does not offer any warranties or representations, nor does it accept any liabilities with respect to the programs or applications.

Library of Congress Cataloging-in-Publication Data

Date, C. J.
   A guide to SQL/DS / by C. J. Date with Colin J. White.
      p.   cm.
   Bibliography: p.
   Includes index.
   ISBN 0-201-14688-6
   1. Data base management. 2. SQL/DS (Computer program) I. White,
Colin J. II. Title.
QA76.9.D3D3736 1989
005.75′65—dc19   88-2183
                                                 CIP

ABCDEFGHIJ-DO-898

To Sharon
—better late than never

Preface

IBM currently markets two mainframe relational database management systems: DB2 for the MVS environment, and SQL/DS for the VM and VSE environments. In many respects, the two products are very much alike—in fact, they share a common ancestry—but at the same time they do differ from one another at the detail level in numerous ways (not all of which are immediately apparent, incidentally). The aim of this book is to provide a comprehensive introduction to SQL/DS specifically. The book is directly based on an earlier volume, *A Guide to DB2* (Addison-Wesley, 1st edition 1984, 2nd edition 1988), which performs the same function for DB2; however, it has been revised throughout, and in some places totally rewritten, to reflect the specifics of SQL/DS. It does not assume any knowledge of the earlier book, nor of DB2.

SQL/DS ("SQL/Data System") and DB2 both support the relational language SQL ("Structured Query Language"). That language was originally defined in IBM Research in 1974, and a major prototype implementation called System R was built and evaluated by IBM over a period of approximately five years (1975–79). The technology developed in that prototype was then incorporated, first, into SQL/DS (announced for DOS/VSE in 1981 and VM/CMS in 1983); next, into DB2 (announced for both MVS/370 and MVS/XA in 1983); then into the OS/2 Extended Edition Database Manager (announced for OS/2 in 1987); and, most recently, into SQL/400 (announced for IBM's new Application System/400 in 1988). The fact that these products are all based on the same SQL language means that they can all be regarded as members of the same family (see further discussion of this point below).

SQL/DS was thus IBM's first fully supported relational product. Like all relational products, it supports the *relational approach* to database management; in other words, it permits users—both end-users and application programmers—to store data in, and retrieve data from, a database that is perceived as a collection of *relations* or tables. It provides access to those tables by means of the relational language SQL mentioned above. The relational approach, first proposed in 1969–70 by E. F. Codd (at that time a member of IBM Research in San Jose, California), has slowly but steadily been gaining acceptance, both inside and outside IBM, ever since that time. SQL/DS is now a leading member of a family of mainline products from IBM, all of them relational, all of them based to a greater or lesser extent on SQL, and all of them running on one of the major IBM operating systems (MVS, VM, VSE, PC/DOS, OS/2, and OS/400).

To elaborate on this last point a little further:

- Collectively, IBM's relational products form "the IBM Relational Productivity Family." All of the IBM products discussed in this book—not only SQL/DS (and DB2), but also QMF, CSP, AS, DXT, ECF, etc.—are members of this family.

- In fact, IBM now considers SQL/DS to be a key member of its "Systems Application Architecture" (SAA) product set. SAA was announced in March 1987. It consists of a set of IBM standard interfaces, conventions, and protocols that are collectively intended to provide what IBM calls "cross-system consistency"—i.e., the ability to develop applications in and for all major IBM computing environments in a consistent, compatible, and portable manner. The SQL language is defined as the common database interface within SAA, and of course SQL/DS is the provider of that interface for the VM environment (also for the VSE environment—but VSE is not currently included in SAA).

- What is more, SQL (or at least a dialect of SQL) is now an official industry-wide standard: It was adopted by the American National Standards Institute (ANSI) in 1986 and the International Standards Organization (ISO) in 1987 as a standard interface for interacting with relational databases. And the ANSI/ISO dialect of SQL is quite close to the IBM dialect as implemented in SQL/DS (in fact, certain features were added to SQL/DS Version 2 Release 1 and Release 2 with the specific objective of bringing the SQL/DS dialect a little closer into line with the ANSI/ISO standard).

The major purpose of this book, then, is to present a detailed (and not wholly uncritical) description of the SQL/DS product: what it is and is not, what it is intended for, and how it can be used. The book is aimed at DP management, end-user management, database specialists (including database and system administrators, database designers, and database application programmers), DP students and teachers, and end-users or DP professionals who wish to broaden their knowledge of the database field by studying a state-of-the-art system. The emphasis throughout is on the *user* (where by "user" we mean, principally, either an end-user or an application programmer); treatment of user-oriented material, such as the SQL language, is very thorough. By contrast, details that are of interest only to system programmers or operators, such as details of system commands, are generally omitted or at best treated only sketchily. Readers are assumed to have at least a general appreciation of the overall structure, concepts, and objectives of database systems in general; however, prior knowledge of relational systems per se is not required.

Note: The book overall is at the SQL/DS Version 2 Release 2 level. The product discussions in Part III are all at the level of the most recent version or release of the product in question, namely:

SQL/DS	—	Version 2 Release 2
DB2	—	Version 2 Release 1
QMF	—	Version 2 Release 2
AS	—	Version 1 Release 5 Modification Level 1
CSP	—	Version 3 Release 2
DXT	—	Version 2 Release 3
HDBV	—	Version 2 Release 1 Modification Level 1
ECF	—	Version 1 Release 1
DBRAD	—	Version 1 Release 1

ACKNOWLEDGMENTS

First and foremost, it is a real pleasure to acknowledge the friendship and support I have received from Ted Codd, not only during the writing of this book (and many others) but throughout my professional activities over the last several years. Like so many other people in this field, I owe my career and very livelihood to the work that Ted originally did in the late sixties and early seventies, and I am delighted to be able to acknowledge that debt once again in public here.

Second, as the title page indicates, the present book includes a significant amount of material on the principal auxiliary products (QMF, AS, CSP, etc.) in addition to the discussions of SQL/DS per se. This material, which appears in Part III of the book, has been written by my friend and coauthor Colin White, and I believe it enhances the value and usefulness of the book considerably. I would like to thank Colin very warmly for his major contribution.

Third, I would like to thank the reviewers Jim Doak (IBM), Pam Mc-Farland (VM Software Inc.), Gary Sampson (IBM), and Joe Schmitt (Codd and Date Consulting Group) for their many constructive criticisms. Thanks also to Nagraj Alur of Codd and Date Consulting Group and Brett Mc-Intyre and Bob Sunday of IBM for their help with numerous technical questions. I would also like to acknowledge the help and encouragement I have received from my friends and family—most especially from my friend and colleague Sharon Weinberg, to whom this book is dedicated. Needless to say, however, all remaining errors, whether of omission or commission, are my own responsibility.

Finally, I cannot do better than repeat the following from the preface to *A Guide to DB2:* I am (as always) grateful to my editor, Elydia Davis, and to the staff at Addison-Wesley for their assistance and their continually high standards of professionalism. Once again, it has been a pleasure to work with them throughout the production of this book.

Saratoga, California   C. J. Date
1988

Contents

PART II   THE SQL/DS DATABASE
MANAGEMENT SYSTEM

PART III   THE IBM RELATIONAL
PRODUCTIVITY FAMILY

PART IV   SUMMARY AND CONCLUSIONS

APPENDIXES

APPENDIX B / **The Relational Model**   441

APPENDIX C / **Date and Time Support**   453

APPENDIX D / **Syntax of SQL Data Manipulation Operations**   467

AN OVERVIEW
OF SQL/DS

SQL/DS:
A Relational System

1.1 INTRODUCTION

The subject of this book, SQL/DS ("SQL / Data System"), is an IBM program product for the VM* and VSE environments. More specifically, it is a *relational database management system* for those environments. A relational database management system (relational DBMS for short) is a system that allows users (end-users or application programmers or both) to store data in, and retrieve data from, databases that are perceived as collections of *relations* or tables. Access to those databases is performed by means of some relational language; in the case of SQL/DS, that language is a

---

*Throughout this book we shall use the term "VM" to mean both the VM system product (VM/SP) and the extended version VM/XA ("VM/Extended Architecture"). Every reference in the text to "VM" applies equally to both versions.

dialect of the well-known relational language SQL ("Structured Query Language"). The aim of this book is to describe the SQL/DS product, and the dialect of SQL supported by that product, in some depth.

What does it mean for a system to be relational? To answer this question properly, it would unfortunately be necessary to discuss a good deal of preliminary material first. Since any such discussion would be out of place at this early point in the book, we defer it for now (see Section 1.2 and Appendix B for the details); however, we give a rough-and-ready answer to the question without that discussion, in the hope that such an answer will help to allay any apprehensions the reader may be feeling at the outset. Briefly, a relational system is a system in which:

(a) The data is perceived by the user as tables (and nothing but tables); and

(b) The operators at the user's disposal (e.g., for query) are operators that generate new tables from old. For example, there will be one operator to extract a subset of the rows of a given table, and another to extract a subset of the columns—and of course a row subset and a column subset of a table are both in turn tables themselves.

Fig. 1.1 illustrates these two points. The data (see part (a) of the figure) consists of a single table, named CELLAR, with three columns and four rows. Two sample queries—one involving a row-subsetting operation and the other a column-subsetting operation—are shown in part (b) of the figure.

(a) Given table:

CELLAR	WINE	YEAR	BOTTLES
	Zinfandel	77	10
	Chardonnay	82	6
	Cabernet	76	12
	Riesling	82	9

(b) Operators (examples):

1. Row subset:

```
SELECT WINE, YEAR, BOTTLES
FROM    CELLAR
WHERE   YEAR = 82
```

Result:

WINE	YEAR	BOTTLES
Chardonnay	82	6
Riesling	82	9

2. Column subset:

```
SELECT WINE, BOTTLES
FROM    CELLAR
```

Result:

WINE	BOTTLES
Zinfandel	10
Chardonnay	6
Cabernet	12
Riesling	9

Fig. 1.1 Data structure and operators in a relational system (examples)

The two queries of Fig. 1.1 are in fact examples of the SELECT statement of the Structured Query Language SQL mentioned earlier. SQL is the database language supported, not only by SQL/DS, but also by IBM's DB2, OS/2 Extended Edition Database Manager, and SQL/400 products, and by numerous nonIBM products. A dialect of SQL was adopted by the American National Standards Institute (ANSI) in 1986 and by the International Standards Organization (ISO) in 1987 as an official standard for relational systems. The SQL/DS version of SQL is reasonably close to that standard (see Appendix E). *Note:* The name "SQL" is usually pronounced "sequel," though the official pronunciation is "ess-cue-ell." Likewise, the name "SQL/DS" is sometimes pronounced "sequel-dee-ess" and sometimes "ess-cue-ell-dee-ess." In this book we lean toward the "sequel" pronunciations.

The purpose of the book, then, is to provide an in-depth tutorial and reference text on a specific relational system, SQL/DS (also on its principal companion products QMF, AS, CSP, etc.—see Chapter 3). It is intended for end-users, application programmers, database administrators, and more generally anyone who wishes to obtain an understanding of the major concepts of the SQL/DS system. It is not intended as a substitute for the system manuals provided by IBM; but it *is* intended as a comprehensive, convenient (single-volume) guide to the use of the product. As stated in the Preface, the emphasis is definitely on the user, and therefore on product externals rather than internals, although various internal aspects are discussed from time to time. The reader is assumed to have an overall appreciation of the structure and objectives of database systems in general, but not necessarily any specific knowledge of relational systems in particular. All applicable relational concepts are introduced in the text as they are needed. In addition, Appendix B provides a more formal summary of those concepts, for purposes of reference.

In this preliminary chapter, we present a brief overview of the SQL/DS product. In particular, we give some idea as to what is involved in creating and accessing a database in SQL/DS, and we briefly discuss some aspects of the SQL language. These topics, and of course many others, are amplified in subsequent chapters.

1.2 RELATIONAL DATABASES

SQL/DS databases are relational. *A relational database is a database that is perceived by its users as a collection of tables (and nothing but tables).* An example, the suppliers-and-parts database, is shown in Fig. 1.2. As you can see, this database consists of three tables, namely S, P, and SP.

```
S   S#   SNAME   STATUS   CITY                          SP   S#   P#   QTY
    --   -----   ------   ------                             --   --   ---
    S1   Smith      20    London                             S1   P1   300
    S2   Jones      10    Paris                              S1   P2   200
    S3   Blake      30    Paris                              S1   P3   400
    S4   Clark      20    London                             S1   P4   200
    S5   Adams      30    Athens                             S1   P5   100
                                                             S1   P6   100
P   P#   PNAME   COLOR   WEIGHT   CITY                       S2   P1   300
    --   -----   ------   ------   ------                    S2   P2   400
    P1   Nut     Red       12     London                     S3   P2   200
    P2   Bolt    Green     17     Paris                      S4   P2   200
    P3   Screw   Blue      17     Rome                       S4   P4   300
    P4   Screw   Red       14     London                     S4   P5   400
    P5   Cam     Blue      12     Paris
    P6   Cog     Red       19     London
```

Fig. 1.2 The suppliers-and-parts database (sample values)

- Table S represents suppliers. Each supplier has a supplier number (S#), unique to that supplier; a supplier name (SNAME), not necessarily unique; a rating or status value (STATUS); and a location (CITY). For the sake of the example, we assume that each supplier is located in exactly one city.

- Table P represents parts (more accurately, kinds of part). Each kind of part has a part number (P#), which is unique; a part name (PNAME), not necessarily unique; a color (COLOR); a weight (WEIGHT); and a location where parts of that type are stored (CITY). For the sake of the example, again, we assume that each kind of part comes in exactly one color and is stored in a warehouse in exactly one city.

- Table SP represents shipments. It serves in a sense to connect the other two tables together. For example, the first row of table SP in Fig. 1.2 connects a specific supplier from table S (namely, supplier S1) with a specific part from table P (namely, part P1); in other words, it represents a shipment of parts of kind P1 by the supplier called S1 (and the shipment quantity is 300). Thus, each shipment has a supplier number (S#), a part number (P#), and a quantity (QTY). For the sake of the example, once again, we assume that there can be at most one shipment at any given time for a given supplier and a given part; thus, for a given shipment, the combination of S# value and P# value is unique with respect to the set of shipments currently appearing in the SP table.

This example is of course extremely simple, much more simple than any real database that you are likely to encounter in practice. Nevertheless, it is adequate to illustrate most of the points that we need to make in this book, and we will use it as the basis for most (not all) of the examples in the following chapters. You should therefore take a little time to familiarize yourself with it now.

Note: There is nothing wrong with using more descriptive names such as SUPPLIERS, PARTS, and SHIPMENTS in place of the rather terse names S, P, and SP; indeed, descriptive names are generally to be recommended in practice. But in the case of the suppliers-and-parts database specifically, the three tables are referenced so frequently in the chapters that follow that very short names seemed desirable. Long names tend to become irksome with much repetition.

There are a number of points arising from the example that are worth calling out explicitly:

- First, note that *all data values are atomic.* That is, at every row-and-column position in every table there is always exactly one data value, never a set of multiple values. Thus, for example, in table SP (considering the first two columns only, for simplicity), we have

```
S#   P#
--   --
 .    .
S2   P1
S2   P2
 .    .
S4   P2
S4   P4
S4   P5
 .    .
 .    .
```

  instead of

```
S#    P#
--    --------------
 .     .
S2    ( P1, P2 )
 .     .
S4    ( P2, P4, P5 )
 .     .
 .     .
```

  A column such as P# in the second version of this table represents what is sometimes called a "repeating group." A repeating group is a column that contains *sets* of data values (different numbers of values in different rows), instead of just one value in each row. *Relational databases do not allow repeating groups.* The second version of the table above would not be permitted in a relational system.

- Second, note that the entire information content of the database is represented as *explicit data values.* This method of representation (as explicit values in column positions within rows of tables) is the *only* method available in a relational database. Specifically, there are no "links" or pointers connecting one table to another.* For example, there is a connexion (as already pointed out) between the S1 row of table S and the P1 row of table P, because supplier S1 supplies part P1; but that connexion is represented, not by pointers, but by the existence of a row in table SP in which the S# value is S1 and the P# value is P1. In nonrelational systems, by contrast, such information is typically represented by some kind of physical link or pointer that is explicitly visible to the user. Some consequences of this difference will be discussed later in the book.

- Third, note that each of the tables in the example has a *unique identifier*—that is, a column (or combination of columns) whose value in any given row is unique with respect to the set of all such values appearing in the table. The unique identifier for table S is S#; for table P, it is P#; and for table SP it is the combination (S#,P#). For example, values of the S# column of table S can be used to pinpoint individual supplier rows within that table.

  The formal relational term for such a unique identifier is *primary key*. SQL/DS does not currently enforce the primary key discipline (that is, it does not actually require every table to have a primary key), but users are nevertheless *strongly* recommended to follow such a discipline in practice. We will do so throughout this book. See Chapter 12 for further discussion.

At this point the reader may be wondering why a database such as that in Fig. 1.2 is called "relational" anyway. The answer is simple: "Relation" is just a mathematical term for a table (to be precise, a table of a certain specific kind—details to follow in Chapter 5). Thus, for example, we can say that the database of Fig. 1.2 consists of three *relations*. For the most part, in fact, we will take "relation" and "table" as synonymous in this book. Relational systems have their origin in the mathematical theory of relations; of course, this does not mean that you need to be a mathematician in order to use a relational system, but it does mean that there is a respectable body of theoretical results that can be applied to practical problems of database usage, such as the problem of database design.

If it is true that a relation is just a table, then why not simply call it a table and have done with it? The answer is that we very often do (and in this book we usually will). However, it is worth taking a moment to under-

---

*This sentence does not mean there cannot be pointers *at the physical level*—there certainly can, and indeed there certainly will. But all such pointers are *concealed from the user*. We are concerned here purely with the logical level of the system. See the further discussion of this point in the next section.

stand why the term "relation" was introduced in the first place. Briefly, the explanation is as follows. Relational systems are based on what is called *the relational model of data.* The relational model, in turn, is an abstract theory of data that is based in part on the mathematical theory mentioned earlier. The principles of the relational model were originally laid down in 1969–70 by one man, Dr. E. F. Codd, at that time a researcher in IBM. It was late in 1968 that Codd, a mathematician by training, first realized that the discipline of mathematics could be used to inject some solid principles and rigor into a field—database management—that, prior to that time, was all too deficient in any such qualities. Codd's ideas were first widely published in a now classic paper, "A Relational Model of Data for Large Shared Data Banks" (*Communications of the ACM 13,* No. 6, June 1970). Since that time, those ideas (by now almost universally accepted) have had a wide-ranging influence on just about every aspect of database technology, and indeed on certain other fields as well, such as the field of artificial intelligence and natural language processing.

Now, the relational model as originally formulated by Codd very deliberately made use of certain terms—such as the term "relation" itself—that were not familiar in data processing circles at that time, even though the concepts in some cases were. The trouble was, many of the more familiar terms were very fuzzy. They lacked the precision necessary to a formal theory of the kind that Codd was proposing. For example, consider the term "record." At different times that single term can mean either a record *instance* or a record *type;* a *COBOL-style* record (which allows repeating groups) or a *flat* record (which does not); a *logical* record or a *physical* record; a *stored* record or a *virtual* record; and so on. The formal relational model therefore does not use the term "record" at all; instead, it uses the term "tuple" (short for "*n*-tuple"), which was given a precise definition by Codd when he first introduced it. We do not give that definition here; for our purposes, it is sufficient to say that the term "tuple" corresponds approximately to the notion of a record (more precisely, *flat logical record instance*), just as the term "relation" corresponds approximately to the notion of a table. If you wish to study some of the more formal literature on relational systems, you will of course have to familiarize yourself with the formal terminology, but in this book we are not trying to be very formal, and we will stick for the most part to terms such as "record" that are reasonably familiar. One formal term we will use somewhat, however, is the term "primary key" introduced earlier in this section.

Fig. 1.3 shows the terms we will be using most heavily (table, record, row, field, column, also primary key). For interest it also gives the corresponding formal term in each case. Note that we use the terms "record" and "row" interchangeably, and the terms "field" and "column" likewise.

Formal relational term	Informal equivalents
relation	table
tuple	record, row
attribute	field, column
primary key	unique identifier

Fig. 1.3 Some terminology

Note also, therefore, that we are definitely taking "record" to mean "record instance" and "field" to mean "field type."

1.3 THE SQL LANGUAGE

As already explained, SQL/DS—in common with numerous other products, from IBM and other vendors—supports the relational language SQL ("Structured Query Language"). This language is used to formulate relational operations (i.e., operations that define and manipulate data in relational form). In this section, we present a brief introduction to the SQL language.

First the definitional operations. Fig. 1.2 (the suppliers-and-parts database) of course represents that database as it might appear at some particular instant in time; it is a *snapshot* of the database. Fig. 1.4, by contrast, shows the *structure* of that database; it shows how the database might be defined or described, using SQL "data definition" statements.*

As you can see, the definition includes one CREATE TABLE statement for each of the three tables. The CREATE TABLE statement is, as already indicated, an example of a SQL data definition statement. Each CREATE TABLE statement specifies the name of the table to be created, the names and data types of the columns, and the primary key of the table (probably some additional information also, not illustrated in Fig. 1.4; see Chapter 5).

It is not our purpose at this juncture to describe the CREATE TABLE statement in detail. That detailed description appears later, in Chapter 5. One point that does need to be stressed right at the outset, however, is that CREATE TABLE is an *executable statement.*† If the three CREATE

---

*Throughout this book we show SQL statements, commands, etc., in upper case, for clarity. In practice it is usually more convenient to enter such statements and commands in lower case. SQL/DS will accept both.

†In fact, every statement in the SQL language is executable, except for a few that are used in embedded SQL only (see Chapters 13 and 15).

```
CREATE TABLE S
     ( S#        CHAR(5)   NOT NULL,
       SNAME     CHAR(20),
       STATUS    SMALLINT,
       CITY      CHAR(15),
     PRIMARY KEY ( S# ) )

CREATE TABLE P
     ( P#        CHAR(6)   NOT NULL,
       PNAME     CHAR(20),
       COLOR     CHAR(6),
       WEIGHT    SMALLINT,
       CITY      CHAR(15),
     PRIMARY KEY ( P# ) )

CREATE TABLE SP
     ( S#        CHAR(5)   NOT NULL,
       P#        CHAR(6)   NOT NULL,
       QTY       INTEGER,
     PRIMARY KEY ( S#, P# ) )
```

Fig. 1.4 The suppliers-and-parts database (data definition)

TABLEs in Fig. 1.4 were to be entered at a terminal, the system would actually build the three tables, then and there. Initially, of course, those tables would be empty—that is, they would each contain just the row of column headings, no data rows as yet. However, we could now go on to insert such data rows (possibly via the SQL INSERT statement, to be discussed in Chapter 8), and, in just a few minutes' work, we could have a (probably small, but still useful and usable) database at our disposal, and could start doing some useful things with it. So this simple example illustrates right away one of the advantages of relational systems in general, and SQL/DS in particular: They are very easy to use (ease of "getting on the air" is of course just one aspect of ease of use in general). As a result, they can make users very productive. We shall see many other advantages later.

   Note: Although it really has nothing to do with the subject of this section (namely, the SQL language), it is worth mentioning in passing that SQL/DS is specifically designed to be easy to install as a *system*—by which we mean that, not only is it easy (as indicated above) to "install" or create new data tables at any time, but it is also easy to install the SQL/DS system in the first place. In other words, the process of building the necessary library data sets (files), specifying the required system parameters, defining certain system defaults, etc., is deliberately made as simple as possible. The overall process should typically take a maximum of one to two working days.

   To continue with the example: Having created our three tables, and loaded some records into them, we can now start doing useful work with them, using SQL *data manipulation* statements. One of the things we can do is *data retrieval,* which is specified in SQL by the SELECT statement. Fig. 1.5 illustrates the use of that statement.

A particularly significant feature of most relational systems, including in particular SQL/DS (and DB2, incidentally), is that the same relational language (here SQL) is available at *two different interfaces,* namely an interactive interface (ISQL—"Interactive SQL"—in the case of SQL/DS) and an application programming interface. The two interfaces are both illustrated in Fig. 1.5:

(a) Fig. 1.5(a) shows an example of the interactive interface ISQL. Here, the user has entered the SELECT statement at a terminal, and SQL/DS has responded—through its ISQL component—by displaying the result ("London") directly at that terminal.

(b) Fig. 1.5(b) shows essentially the same SELECT statement embedded in an application program (a PL/I program, in the example). In this second case the statement will be executed when the program is executed, and the result "London" will be returned, not to a terminal, but to the program variable XCITY (by virtue of the INTO clause in the SELECT; XCITY is just an input area within the program).

Thus, SQL is both an *interactive query language* and a *database programming language.* Furthermore, this remark applies to the entire SQL language; that is, any SQL statement that can be entered at a terminal can alternatively be embedded in a program. Note in particular that the remark applies even to statements such as CREATE TABLE; you can create tables from within an application program, if it makes sense in your application to do so (and if you are authorized to perform such operations). SQL statements can be used with programs written in any of the following languages: APL, BASIC, COBOL, FORTRAN, PL/I, Prolog, the REXX procedure

(a) Interactive (ISQL):

```
SELECT CITY -                Result:  CITY
FROM    S -                           ------
WHERE   S# = 'S4'                     London
```

(b) Embedded in PL/I (could be COBOL, FORTRAN, etc.):

```
EXEC SQL SELECT CITY          Result:  XCITY
         INTO    :XCITY                ------
         FROM    S                     London
         WHERE   S# = 'S4' ;
```

Fig. 1.5 A retrieval example

language, and System/370 Assembler Language (see Chapters 2 and 13 for further discussion).

Note: Interactive SQL and embedded SQL do differ from each other on certain points of detail, of course. For ISQL, each statement line except the last must be followed by a continuation character (usually a hyphen; see Fig. 1.5(a) for an illustration). For embedded SQL, each *statement* (not statement line) must be prefixed with EXEC SQL and followed by an appropriate statement terminator (semicolon in the case of PL/I; see Fig. 1.5(b) for an illustration). Likewise, the SELECT statement of Fig. 1.5(b) needs an INTO clause to designate the input area, as we have seen, and the host language variable named in that clause has a colon prefix in order to distinguish it from a database column name. So of course it is not 100 percent true to say that the SELECT statement is the same at both interfaces. But it is broadly true, if we overlook the minor differences of detail.

We are now in a position to understand how SQL/DS looks to the user. By "user" here we mean either an end-user at an online terminal or an application programmer writing in one of the SQL/DS-supported host languages such as PL/I. (We note in passing that the term "user" will be used consistently throughout this book with either or both of these two meanings.) As already explained, each such user will be using SQL to operate on tables. See Fig. 1.6.

The first point to be made concerning the figure is that there will normally be many users, of both kinds, all operating on the same data at the same time. SQL/DS will automatically apply the necessary *locking* controls (see Chapter 14) to ensure that those users are all protected from one another; i.e., SQL/DS will guarantee that one user's updates cannot cause another user's operations to produce an incorrect result.

Next, note that tables, like users, also come in two kinds. The two kinds of tables are called *base tables* and *views*. The difference between them is as follows.

- A base table is a "real" table—i.e., a table that physically exists, in the sense that there exist physically stored records, and possibly physical indexes, in one or more operating system files, that directly represent that table in storage. (An "operating system file" is a VSAM file in VSE, a minidisk in VM.) Tables S, P, and SP in Fig. 1.4 are all base tables.

- By contrast, a view is a "virtual" table—i.e., a table that does not directly exist in physical storage, but looks to the user as if it did. Views can be thought of as different ways of looking at the "real" tables. As a trivial example, a given user might have a view of the suppliers base table S in which only those suppliers in London are visible. Views are

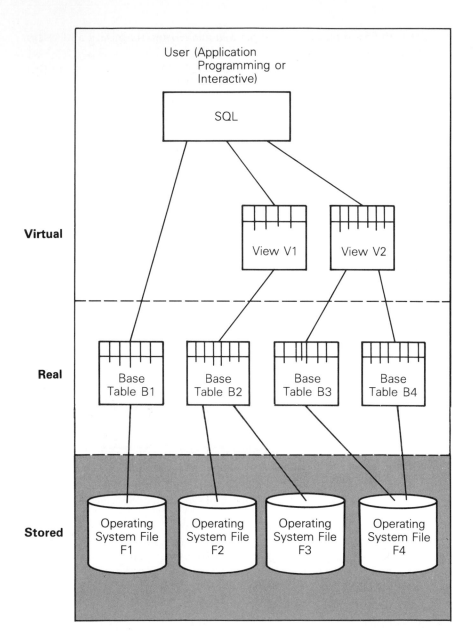

Fig. 1.6 SQL/DS as perceived by an individual user

defined, in a manner to be explained in Chapter 10, in terms of one or more of the underlying base tables.

Note carefully, however, that the foregoing does *not* mean that a base table is *physically stored* as a table—i.e., as a set of physically adjacent stored records, with each stored record consisting simply of a direct copy of a row of the base table. There are numerous differences of detail between a base table and its storage representation (see Chapter 16). The point is, however, that users can always think of base tables as physically existing, without having to concern themselves with how those tables are actually represented in storage. In fact, the whole point of a relational database is to allow users to deal with data in the form of tables per se, instead of in terms of the storage representation of such tables. To repeat from Section 1.2, a relational database is a database that is *perceived by its users* as a collection of tables. It is *not* just a database in which data is physically stored as tables.

Like base tables, views can be created at any time. The same is true of indexes. (The CREATE TABLE statement already discussed is for creating "real" or base tables. There is an analogous CREATE VIEW statement for creating views or "virtual" tables, and an analogous CREATE INDEX statement for creating indexes. All of these statements will be discussed in detail in later chapters.) Similarly, base tables, and views and indexes, can all be "dropped" (that is to say, destroyed) at any time, using DROP TABLE or DROP VIEW or DROP INDEX. With regard to indexes, however, note carefully that although the user (that is, *some* user, probably the database administrator—see Chapter 11) is responsible for creating and destroying them, users are *not* responsible for saying when those indexes should be used. Indexes are never mentioned in SQL data manipulation statements such as SELECT. The decision as to whether or not to use a particular index in responding to, say, a particular SELECT operation is made by the system, not by the user. We shall have more to say on this topic in the next chapter.

The primary user interface to SQL/DS is the SQL language. We have already indicated (a) that SQL can be used in both interactive and embedded environments, and (b) that it provides both data definition and data manipulation functions. (In fact, as we shall see later, it provides certain "data control" functions as well.) The major data definition functions—

```
CREATE TABLE
CREATE VIEW
CREATE INDEX

DROP TABLE
DROP VIEW
DROP INDEX
```

—have already been touched on. The major data manipulation functions (in effect the only ones, if we temporarily disregard some embedded-only functions) are

```
SELECT
INSERT
UPDATE
DELETE
```

We give examples (Fig. 1.7) of SELECT and UPDATE to illustrate an additional point, namely the fact that SQL data manipulation statements typically operate on *entire sets of records,* instead of just on one record at a time. Given the sample data of Fig. 1.2, the SELECT statement (Fig. 1.7(a)) returns a set of four values, not just a single value; and the UPDATE statement (Fig. 1.7(b)) changes two records, not just one. In other words, SQL is a *set-level language.*

Set-level languages such as SQL are sometimes described as "nonprocedural," on the grounds that users specify *what,* not *how* (i.e., they say what data they want without specifying a procedure for getting it). The process of "navigating" around the physical database to locate the desired data is performed automatically by the system, not manually by the user. (For this reason, relational systems are sometimes described as "automatic navigation" systems.) However, "nonprocedural" is not really a very satisfactory term, because procedurality and nonprocedurality are not absolutes. The best that can be said is that some language *A* is either more or less procedural than some other language *B.* Perhaps a better way of putting matters is to say that a language such as SQL is at *a higher level of abstraction* than a language such as COBOL or PL/I.* With a language like SQL,

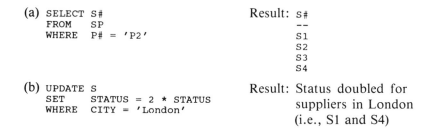

```
(a) SELECT  S#              Result:  S#
    FROM    SP                       --
    WHERE   P# = 'P2'                S1
                                     S2
                                     S3
                                     S4

(b) UPDATE  S              Result: Status doubled for
    SET     STATUS = 2 * STATUS     suppliers in London
    WHERE   CITY = 'London'         (i.e., S1 and S4)
```

Fig. 1.7 SQL data manipulation examples

---

*Or a language such as DL/I, come to that. DL/I is the database language used with the IBM DOS DL/I database management system, a nonrelational—actually hierarchic—system.

in other words, the system handles more of the details than it does with a language like COBOL. Fundamentally, it is this *raising of the level of abstraction* that is responsible for the increased productivity that relational systems such as SQL/DS can provide.

1.4 SUMMARY

This brings us to the end of this preliminary chapter, in which we have sketched some of the most significant features of SQL/DS, IBM's relational database management system for the VM and VSE environments. We have seen in outline what it means for a system to be relational; we have discussed the relational (tabular) data structure; and we have described some of the operators available in SQL for operating on data in that tabular form. In particular, we have touched on the three categories of SQL statement (data definition, data manipulation, and data control), and given examples from the first two of those categories. We remind the reader that:

(a) All SQL statements are executable;

(b) Every SQL statement that can be entered at a terminal can also be included in a program, and that program can be written in APL, BASIC, COBOL, FORTRAN, PL/I, Prolog, the REXX procedure language, or System/370 Assembler Language;

(c) SQL data manipulation statements (SELECT, UPDATE, etc.) are all set-level.

In the next two chapters we will examine the internal structure and principal components of SQL/DS, and we will discuss the environments in which SQL/DS runs. We will also take a quick look at some important SQL/DS-related products.

EXERCISES

1.1 What does it mean to say that SQL/DS is a relational system?

1.2 Given the sample data of Fig. 1.2, show the effect of each of the following SQL statements.

```
(a)  SELECT  SNAME
     FROM    S
     WHERE   STATUS = 30

(b)  SELECT  S#, P#
     FROM    SP
     WHERE   QTY > 200

(c)  UPDATE  SP
     SET     QTY = QTY + 300
     WHERE   QTY < 300
```

   (d) `DELETE`
        `FROM    SP`
        `WHERE   QTY = 500`
        `OR      QTY < 200`

   (e) `INSERT`
        `INTO    SP (S#, P#, QTY)`
        `VALUES  ('S3','P1',500)`

1.3 What is ISQL?

1.4 What is a repeating group?

1.5 Define the terms *relation* and *relational database*.

1.6 (a) Give a possible CREATE TABLE statement for the CELLAR table of Fig. 1.1.

    (b) Write an *embedded* PL/I-SQL statement to retrieve the number of bottles of 1977 Zinfandel from that table.

1.7 Define the terms *base table* and *view*.

1.8 What do you understand by the term "automatic navigation"?

1.9 Define the term *primary key*.

ANSWERS TO SELECTED EXERCISES

1.1 A relational system such as SQL/DS is a system in which the data is perceived as tables (and nothing but tables), and the operators available to the user are operators that generate new tables from old.

1.2 (a) `SNAME`
        `-----`
        `Blake`
        `Adams`

   (b) `S#   P#`
        `--   --`
        `S1   P1`
        `S1   P3`
        `S2   P1`
        `S2   P2`
        `S4   P4`
        `S4   P5`

   (c) `S#   P#   QTY`
        `--   --   ---`
        `S1   P2   500`
        `S1   P4   500`
        `S1   P5   400`
        `S1   P6   400`
        `S3   P2   500`
        `S4   P2   500`

       (Only altered rows shown.)

   (d) Rows (S1,P5,100) and (S1,P6,100) are deleted from table SP.

   (e) Row (S3,P1,500) is inserted into table SP.

1.3 ISQL—"Interactive SQL"—is the SQL/DS component that (among other things) allows SQL statements to be entered and executed interactively. For more information, see Chapter 17.

1.4 A repeating group is (conceptually) a column of a table that contains multiple data values per row (different numbers of values in different rows). Repeating groups are not permitted in a relational database. *Note:* An explanation of, and justification for, this apparent restriction can be found in the book *An Introduction to Database Systems: Volume I,* 4th ed., by C. J. Date (Addison-Wesley, 1986).

1.5 A relation is a table (without repeating groups!). A relational database is a database that is perceived by its users as a collection of relations. *Note:* More precise definitions are given in Appendix B.

1.6 (a)
```
CREATE  TABLE  CELLAR
         ( WINE       CHAR(16)  NOT NULL,
           YEAR       INTEGER   NOT NULL,
           BOTTLES  INTEGER,
         PRIMARY KEY ( WINE, YEAR ) )
```

    (b)
```
EXEC SQL SELECT BOTTLES
         INTO    :XBOTT
         FROM    CELLAR
         WHERE   WINE = 'Zinfandel'
         AND     YEAR = 77 ;
```

1.7 A base table is a "real" table; it has some direct storage representation. A view is a "virtual" table; it does not have any direct storage representation of its own. A view is like a window on to one or more underlying base tables, through which the data (or some subset of the data) in those underlying tables can be observed, possibly in some rearranged structure.

1.8 "Automatic navigation" means that the system assumes the responsibility of searching through the physical database to locate the data the user has requested. Users specify what they want, not how to get to what they want.

1.9 Informally, a primary key is just a unique identifier for a table. For example, the primary key for the parts table P is the field P#; given a P# value $p,$ that value p can be used to identify an individual part record and to distinguish that record from all others appearing in the P table. A more formal definition of the term is given in Chapter 12.

2

◆

System Structure

2.1 MAJOR COMPONENTS AND SERVICES

The internal structure of SQL/DS is quite complex, as is only to be expected of a state-of-the-art system that provides all of the functions normally found in a modern DBMS (including, for example, recovery control, concurrency control, authorization control, and so on) and more besides. The product thus contains a very large number of internal components. From a high-level point of view, however, SQL/DS can be regarded as having just three *major* components, each of which divides up into numerous subcomponents. The three major components are as follows (refer to Fig. 2.1):

1. The *Data System Control* component (DSC), which supports system startup and shutdown, communication with the system operator, communication with other subsystems such as CICS, and similar functions;

21

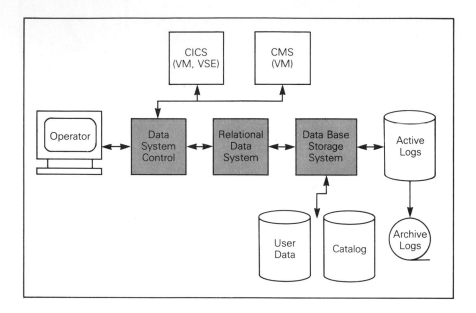

Fig. 2.1 SQL/DS structure

2. The *Relational Data System* component (RDS), which provides the necessary SQL language support;

3. The *Data Base Storage System* component (DBSS), which manages the actual stored database (i.e., it performs all of the basic data searching, data retrieval and update, index maintenance, and similar functions). The DBSS invokes other, lower-level components as necessary to perform detailed operations such as locking, logging, recovery, etc., during the performance of its basic task.

From the user's perspective, SQL/DS provides three major sets of services:

1. *Interactive SQL facility* (ISQL). As explained in Chapter 1, ISQL supports interactive SQL access to the database from an online terminal. It also provides a rudimentary report-writing facility and (in VSE only) supports the copying of data from a DOS DL/I database into a SQL/DS database ("DL/I Extract").

2. *Embedded SQL support.* As explained in Chapter 1 (again), SQL statements can be embedded in programs written in a variety of host languages (COBOL, PL/I, etc.). For each such language, SQL/DS provides a *preprocessor,* whose purpose is to convert such SQL statements

into an *access module.* The access module is stored in the SQL/DS database; it contains a set of internal control structures representing a compiled form of the original SQL statements. See Sections 2.2 and 2.3 for more details (for an explanation of the meaning of "compiled" in this context, in particular).

3. *Data Base Services utility* (DBS utility). The DBS utility provides a number of critical support functions, including data load (loading data from sequential files into SQL/DS tables) and data reorganization (unloading and reloading of SQL/DS tables). The DBS utility is discussed in more detail in Chapter 17.

As far as the base SQL/DS system is concerned, however, each of these items—ISQL, the language preprocessors, and the DBS utility—can be regarded just as a special application program, not really part of the base system itself. Most aspects of the base system are (as already indicated) "transparent to the user." In this chapter (and in this book generally), therefore, we concentrate on just those aspects of the system that the user really needs to understand in order to use the system effectively. Specifically, in Sections 2.2 and 2.3, we explain what is involved in preparing a program for execution in SQL/DS, and we describe what happens to such a program at execution time. We also explain what happens when SQL statements are submitted for execution interactively.

For reasons of completeness, however, before we get into the details of program preparation and execution per se, we give below a quick summary of the major additional functions of SQL/DS (the so-called system service functions). Those functions are as follows:

- Logging

    The DBSS component is responsible for maintaining the SQL/DS *log.* The log is a predefined disk data set (file) that is used to record information for recovering system and database data in the event of a failure. Dual copies of the log can be maintained to allow SQL/DS to recover even if an error occurs on (one copy of) the log itself. To prevent the log from overflowing, log data can be archived (i.e., dumped to disk or tape, thus releasing log space) during system operation or at system shutdown. Log space can also be released by archiving the database itself; again, such archiving can be performed either during system operation or at system shutdown.

- Locking

    The DBSS uses its own internal locking and deadlock management mechanisms to control concurrent access to data. The locking scheme is described in some detail in Chapter 14.

- Data and Buffer Management

  The DBSS is responsible for the physical transfer of data between the external medium and (virtual) storage; in other words, it performs the necessary physical I/O operations. It employs a variety of buffering techniques, such as lookaside buffering, in order to get the best performance out of the buffers under its care and to minimize the amount of physical I/O actually performed.

- Accounting

  The (optional) SQL/DS accounting facility keeps track of the resources (CPU, I/O, and elapsed time) consumed by SQL/DS users, writing appropriate accounting records to a sequential file. The information in those records can subsequently be loaded into SQL/DS tables and analyzed by means of regular SQL statements.

- System Monitoring

  Two commands are provided to enable the system operator to monitor SQL/DS activity: COUNTER, which displays values for certain specified "system counters" (number of I/O's, number of deadlocks, number of RDS calls, etc.), and SHOW, which displays detailed information regarding overall system status (locking information, logging information, buffer information, etc.).

- Backup and Recovery

  SQL/DS provides a set of commands for performing database backup and recovery. More information is given in Chapter 17.

- System Tables

  The RDS component manages a set of system data tables known as the *catalog*. The catalog tables contain descriptor information regarding user data tables, database indexes, etc. They are accessible by means of ordinary SQL data manipulation statements, which can be used (e.g.) to produce reports for use by the database administrator. The catalog is described in more detail in Chapter 9.

2.2 PROGRAM PREPARATION

Before a program can be executed under SQL/DS, it must first be prepared for execution ("prepped," to use the jargon); i.e., it must be processed by the appropriate language preprocessor. (It must then be compiled and link-edited in the usual way, of course.) In this section we examine this program preparation process, first at an overview level and then in more detail. Refer to Fig. 2.2.

- Preprocessing ("prepping")

  The function of the preprocessor is to analyze a host language program (more accurately, host language *module*), stripping out the embedded SQL statements it finds and replacing them by host language CALL statements. From the SQL statements it encounters, it constructs an *access module,* which it stores in the SQL/DS database. The access module contains a set of internal control structures representing a compiled form of the original SQL statements in the source module. In particular, it includes calls on the DBSS component (see "Execution" below).

  Note that the foregoing paragraph amounts to saying that SQL/DS is a *compiling system:* The preprocessor performs a compiling function for embedded SQL statements, much as the host language compiler provides a compiling function for the host language statements in which those SQL statements are embedded. We shall return to this point in Section 2.3.

  Note: Version 1 of SQL/DS genuinely did compile SQL statements into actual machine code. As indicated above, however, Version 2 compiles them into a set of internal control structures (in effect a higher-level intermediate language), not into machine code per se. (Those control structures are then used to drive a set of generalized I/O routines within the DBSS. One advantage of this change is that access modules are more compact in Version 2 than they used to be in Version 1.) For simplicity, however, we will continue to regard the preprocessor as compiling SQL statements into "code," even though that code is no longer true machine code per se.

- Compiling and Link-Editing

  After preprocessing, the source module must be compiled (by the host language compiler) and link-edited in the normal way. These steps are basically standard.

- Execution

  At run time, the host language CALLs inserted by the preprocessor will pass control—indirectly—to the Relational Data System (RDS). The RDS will then load the access module into main storage and pass control to it, and the access module in turn will invoke the DBSS component to perform the appropriate operations on the physical database.

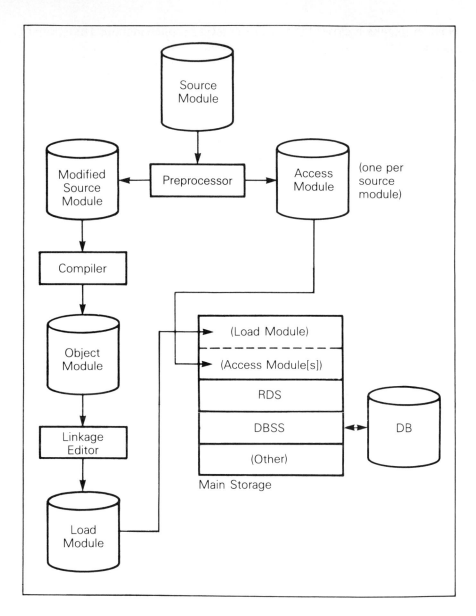

Fig. 2.2 SQL/DS application program preparation and execution (overview)

Now let us take a closer look at this process. Suppose for the sake of the example that we have a PL/I source module *P* that includes one or more embedded SQL statements.*† Before *P* can be compiled by the PL/I compiler, it must be preprocessed by the SQL-PL/I preprocessor (Fig. 2.3). The major functions of that preprocessor are as follows:

▪ Parsing and Syntax Checking

The preprocessor examines the SQL statements in the source module, parsing them and reporting on any syntax errors it finds. It replaces each (valid) SQL statement by a PL/I CALL statement, which—as explained above—will pass control to the RDS when it is executed at run time. A copy of each SQL statement is left behind in the modified source module in the form of a comment. The preprocessor also produces a source listing, showing the original source code, diagnostics, cross-reference tables, etc.

▪ Optimization

SQL/DS—actually the RDS component of SQL/DS—includes an *optimizer* as an (extremely important) subcomponent. The preprocessor invokes that optimizer as part of its task of creating the access module. The function of the optimizer is to choose, for each SQL manipulative statement it processes, an optimal access strategy for implementing that statement. Remember that data manipulation statements such as SELECT specify only what data the user wants, not how to get to that data; the *access path* for getting to that data is chosen by the optimizer. Programs are thus independent of such access paths (for further discussion of this important point, see Section 2.3).

   As an example of the foregoing, consider the SELECT statement shown in the PL/I source module *P* in Fig. 2.3. Even in that very simple case, there are probably at least two ways of performing the required retrieval:

1. By doing a physical sequential scan of (the stored version of) table S until the record for supplier S4 is found;

---

*We take PL/I for definiteness. The overall process is of course essentially the same for the other host languages—at least, it is for the compiled languages (COBOL, FORTRAN, Assembler Language). It is a little different for the interpreted languages (APL, BASIC, Prolog, REXX). Details of the differences are beyond the scope of this chapter.

†If *P* also includes any CICS statements (of the form EXEC CICS ... ;), then it must also be processed by the CICS preprocessor. The SQL preprocessor must be run before the CICS preprocessor.

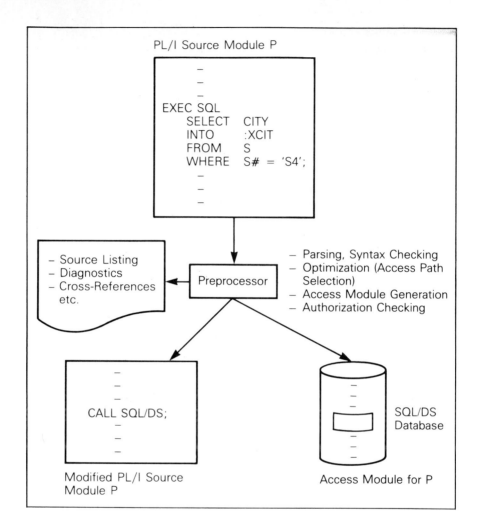

Fig. 2.3 Preprocessing

2. If there is an index on the S# column of that table—which there prob-
    ably will be*—then by using that index and hence going directly to the
    S4 record.

---

*Recall that field S# is the primary key for table S. A SQL/DS table will
always have a UNIQUE index on its primary key. For details, see Chapters 5 and
12.

The optimizer will choose which of these two strategies to adopt. In general, the optimizer will make its choice on the basis of such considerations as the following:

- Which tables are referenced in the SQL statement (there may be more than one)
- How big those tables are
- What indexes exist
- How selective those indexes are
- How the data is physically clustered on the disk
- The form of the WHERE clause in the request

and so on. The preprocessor will then generate code (see the next step below) that is *tightly bound* to—i.e., highly dependent on—the optimizer's choice of strategy. For example, if the optimizer decides to make use of an index called *X,* then there will be code in the access module that refers explicitly to index *X*.

- Access Module Generation

This is the process of physically building the access module. Again, the preprocessor actually performs this function by invoking certain RDS services (details beyond the scope of this chapter). The access module is stored away in the SQL/DS database; it contains the necessary control structures (compiled code) to implement the original SQL statements. As previously explained, the access module will reflect the implementation strategies chosen by the SQL/DS optimizer.

- Authorization Checking

The preprocessor will also check authorization; that is, it will check that the person doing the preprocessing (i.e., the user who invoked the preprocessor) is allowed to perform the operations requested in the source module. We will examine authorization in detail in Chapter 11.

One final point regarding program preparation: As we have seen, access modules are *created* by invoking the appropriate SQL preprocessor. That invocation is performed either via job control statements or—interactively—via the SQLPREP command (see Chapter 17); it is not performed by means of a SQL statement. However, access modules are *destroyed* by means of DROP PROGRAM, which *is* a SQL statement. The syntax is:

```
DROP PROGRAM access-module
```

where "access-module" identifies the access module (not program!) to be dropped. *Note:* An analogous CREATE PROGRAM statement does exist, but only as part of the so-called "extended dynamic SQL facility." See Chapter 15 for more information.

This brings us to the end of our description of the preprocessor functions. We conclude this section with a brief note on the (necessary) compiling and link-editing steps. As mentioned earlier, these steps are basically standard—except that certain IBM-supplied modules, provided as part of the SQL/DS product, must be included in the input to the link-edit process. Further details are beyond the scope of this chapter.

2.3   PROGRAM EXECUTION

In this section we consider what is involved in executing the PL/I program *P* from the previous section. Since the program preparation process has effectively broken the original program into several pieces (one load module plus one or more access modules), those pieces must somehow be brought back together again at execution time. This is how it works (see Fig. 2.4). *Note:* We assume for simplicity that the original program includes just one source module with embedded SQL statements, so that there is just one access module. The extension to the case of multiple source modules (and hence multiple access modules) is straightforward.

First, the PL/I load module *P* is loaded into main storage; it starts to execute in the usual way. Sooner or later it reaches the first call to the RDS. The RDS then retrieves the access module from the database, loads it into main storage, and passes control to it. The access module in turn invokes the DBSS, which performs the necessary operations on the actual stored data and passes results back (as appropriate) to the PL/I program.

Note, however, that the foregoing paragraph glosses over one very important point, which we now explain. First, as indicated in Section 2.2, SQL/DS is a compiling system; database statements are *compiled* (at prep time) into internal form. By contrast, most other database systems—certainly all nonrelational systems, to this writer's knowledge—are *interpretive* in nature. Now, compilation is certainly advantageous from the point of view of performance; it will nearly always yield better runtime performance than will interpretation.* However, it suffers from the following significant drawback: *It is possible that decisions made at compilation time are no*

---

*This claim is (obviously) especially true for repetitive transactions, i.e., transactions that are executed over and over again in a production environment. What is perhaps not so obvious is that compiling can provide a significant performance advantage in the ad hoc query environment also. For further discussion of this point, see later in this section.

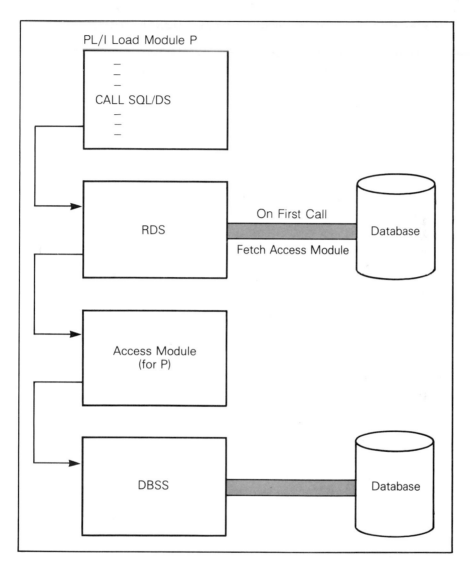

Fig. 2.4 Execution time

longer valid at execution time. The following simple example will serve to illustrate the problem:

1. Suppose program *P* is compiled (prepped) on Monday, and the optimizer decides to use an index—say index *X*—in its strategy for *P.* Then

the access module(s) for *P* will include explicit references to *X,* as explained in the previous section.

2. On Tuesday, some (authorized) user issues the statement

DROP INDEX X

3. On Wednesday, some user tries to execute the program *P.* What happens?

What does happen is the following. When an index is dropped, SQL/DS examines all access modules in the database to see which of them (if any) are dependent on that index. Any that it finds it marks "invalid." When the RDS retrieves such a module for execution, it sees the "invalid" marker, and therefore *automatically produces a new access module*—i.e., it chooses some different access strategy for implementing the original SQL statements,* and then generates a new access module in accordance with that new strategy. In other words, the RDS automatically *recompiles* the original SQL statements. Provided that the recompilation is successful, the new access module replaces the old one in the database, and execution continues. Note that this entire process is "transparent to the user"; the only effect that might be observed is a slight delay in the execution of the first SQL statement in the program (possibly some change in overall program performance also, of course; the point is, however, that there should be no effect on program *logic*).

Note carefully that the automatic recompilation we are talking about here is only a *SQL* recompilation, not a *PL/I* recompilation. It is not the PL/I source code that is invalidated by the dropping of the index, only the access module.

We can now see how it is possible for programs to be independent of physical access paths—more specifically, how it is possible to create and drop such paths without at the same time having to rewrite programs. As stated earlier, SQL data manipulation statements such as SELECT and UPDATE never include any explicit mention of such paths. Instead, they simply indicate what data the user is interested in; and it is the system's responsibility (actually the optimizer's responsibility) to choose a path for getting to that data, and to change to another path if the old one no longer exists. We say that systems like SQL/DS provide a high degree of *physical data independence:* Users and user programs are not dependent on the physical structure of the stored database. The advantage of such a system—a highly significant advantage—is that it is possible to make changes in the

---

*The original SQL statements were saved as part of the access module.

physical database (e.g., for performance reasons) *without having to make any corresponding changes in application programs.* In a system without such independence, application programmers have to devote some significant portion of their time—a figure of 50 percent is quite typical—to making changes to existing programs that are necessitated merely by changes to the physical database. In a system like SQL/DS, by contrast, those programmers can concentrate exclusively on "real work"—i.e., on the production of new applications.

One further point concerning the foregoing: Our example was in terms of a dropped *index,* and perhaps that is the commonest case in practice. However, a similar sequence of events occurs when other objects (not just indexes) are dropped also—likewise when an authorization is revoked (see Chapter 11). Thus, for example, dropping a table will cause all access modules that refer to that table to be flagged as invalid. Of course, the automatic recompilation will only work in this case if another table has been created with the same name as the old one by the time the recompilation is done (and maybe not even then, if there are significant differences between the old table and the new one).

Given the fact that SQL/DS performs automatic recompilations when some existing object (say an index) is dropped, the reader may be wondering whether it will do the same thing if a new object is created. The answer is no, it will not. The reason for this state of affairs is that there can be no guarantee in this case that recompiling will actually be profitable; automatic recompilation might simply mean a lot of unnecessary work (existing access modules might already be using an optimum strategy). The situation is different with DROP—an access module will simply not work if it relies on a nonexistent object, so recompilation is mandatory in this case. Hence, if you CREATE a new index, and you have some existing access module that you suspect could now profitably be replaced, then it is your responsibility to request an explicit "reprep" for that module. See Chapter 17.

We conclude this chapter by noting that SQL is *always* compiled in SQL/DS, never interpreted, even when the statements in question are submitted interactively (e.g., via ISQL). In other words, if you enter (say) a SELECT statement at the terminal, then that statement will be compiled and an access module created for it; that module will then be executed; and finally, after execution has completed, the module will be discarded. Performance tests have indicated that, even in the interactive case, compilation almost always results in better overall performance than interpretation. The advantage of compilation is that the process of physically accessing the required data is done by compiled code—that is, by code that is tightly tailored to the specific request, not by generalized, interpretive code. The disadvantage is of course that there is a cost in doing the compilation, i.e., in producing that tightly tailored code. But the advantage almost always outweighs the disadvantage, sometimes dramatically so. It is only when the query is extremely simple that the cost of doing the compilation may be greater than the potential savings. An example of such a simple query might be, "Retrieve the supplier record for supplier S1"—that is, a request for a single, specific record, given a value for a field that identifies that record uniquely. Notice that this query does not really exploit the set-level facilities of SQL at all.

EXERCISES

2.1 Name the major components of SQL/DS.

2.2 Draw a diagram showing the overall process of program preparation and program execution in SQL/DS.

2.3 List the principal functions of the SQL preprocessor.

2.4 Define *physical data independence.* Explain how SQL/DS provides such independence. Why is physical data independence desirable?

ANSWERS TO SELECTED EXERCISES

2.1 The major components of the base SQL/DS product are the Data System Control, Relational Data System (RDS), and Data Base Storage System (DBSS) components. Other components of the overall product (and in some respects the components that are of more direct interest to the user) are the Interactive SQL facility (ISQL), the high-level language SQL preprocessors, and the Data Base Services utility (DBS utility).

2.2 See Fig. 2.2 in Section 2.2.

2.3 See Section 2.2.

2.4 Physical data independence means that users and user programs do not depend on the physical structure of the database. User requests (i.e., SQL statements) are formulated purely in terms of the logical structure (i.e., in terms of tables and fields); the choice of physical access paths to implement those requests is made by the system (actually by the optimizer), not by the user. As a result, the physical structure of the database can be changed—e.g., for performance reasons—without requiring any user programs to be rewritten.

3

♦

Operating Environments and Related Products

3.1 OPERATING ENVIRONMENTS

SQL/DS applications operate in a number of different environments (refer to Figs. 3.1 and 3.2):

1. VSE online (under CICS)
2. VSE interactive (under ICCF)
3. VSE batch
4. VM online (under CICS)
5. VM interactive (under CMS)
6. VM batch (under CMS)

Note: Except where noted otherwise, the term "application" refers throughout this section both to user-written applications and to the IBM-

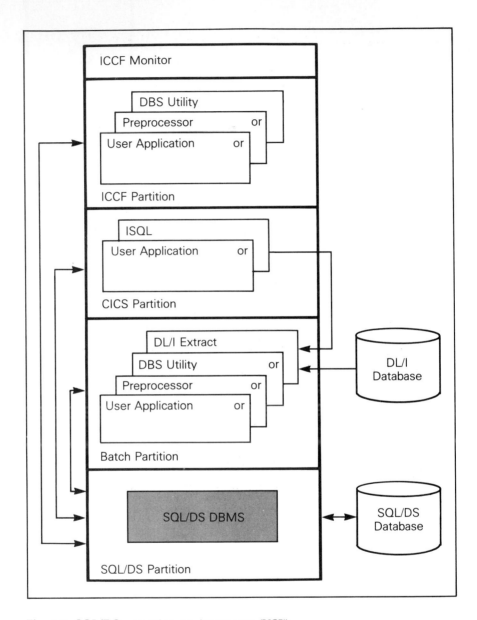

Fig. 3.1 SQL/DS operating environments (VSE)

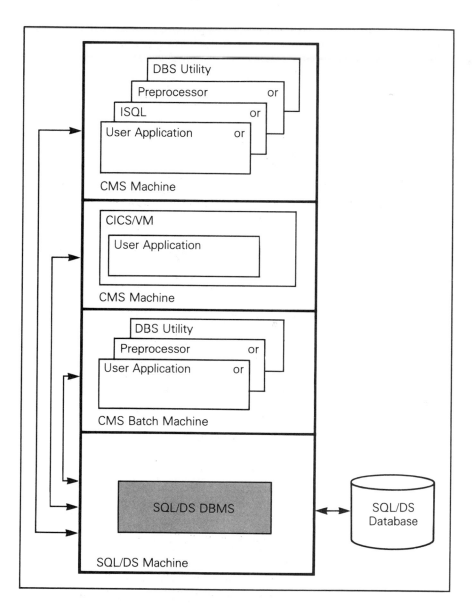

Fig. 3.2 SQL/DS operating environments (VM)

supplied applications provided with the SQL/DS product (ISQL, the DBS utility, and the language preprocessors). The term "VSE" refers to both the VSE system product (VSE/SP) and the Small System Executive (SSX/VSE).

We explain the differences among these various categories as follows:

1. A VSE online application is a VSE application running under CICS (strictly, CICS/DOS/VS) as the necessary *transaction manager.* Such an application is invoked from a CICS terminal; it uses the data communication facilities of CICS to exchange messages with that terminal. ISQL and user-written applications (but not the DBS utility and not the language preprocessors) can run as VSE online applications. User-written VSE online applications can access DOS DL/I data (also VSAM data) in addition to SQL/DS data.

   Note: The combination of SQL/DS with CICS acts as a *full-function database/data communications (DB/DC) system,* in which (as already indicated) CICS serves as the necessary transaction manager component. The reader is warned, however, that the term "transaction" has different interpretations in different systems. See Chapter 14 for an explanation of the interpretation used in this book. For readers who may already be familiar with CICS, we should perhaps stress the point that we are *not* using the normal CICS interpretation here.

   SQL/DS itself serves as the transaction manager component in all other environments (Cases 2–6 below).

2. A VSE interactive application is a VSE application that is invoked from an ICCF terminal (ICCF is a VSE component specifically intended to support the interactive invocation and execution of VSE applications). User-written applications, the language preprocessors, and the DBS utility (but not ISQL) can all run as VSE interactive applications. Such applications use the facilities of ICCF to communicate with the terminal.

   The VSE interactive environment is intended primarily for application development.

3. Conventional VSE batch applications can also operate on SQL/DS data. User-written programs, the language preprocessors, the DBS utility, and the ISQL DL/I Extract facility (see Section 3.2 and Chapter 17 for more information on the last of these)—but not ISQL per se—can all run as VSE batch applications.

4. A VM online application is a CICS/VM application that is invoked from a CMS terminal and uses CMS facilities to exchange messages with that terminal. See Case 5 below for a brief discussion of CMS. Note that, in contrast with the VSE online environment (Case 1 above),

CICS is *not* the transaction manager in this case; actually, CICS/VM runs under the control of VM/CMS. Only user-written applications are supported in this case. *Note:* The VM online environment could be useful for testing an application that is intended eventually to run as a VSE online application (Case 1 above).

5. A VM interactive application is a VM application that is invoked from a CMS terminal (CMS is a VM component intended primarily to support the interactive invocation and execution of VM applications). User-written applications, ISQL, the language preprocessors, and the DBS utility can all run as VM interactive applications. Such applications can use the facilities of ISPF or GDDM or CMS itself to communicate with the terminal.

6. User-written applications, the language preprocessors, and the DBS utility (but not ISQL) can all also run as conventional batch applications under VM/CMS.

For the reader who may be unfamiliar with CICS (CICS/DOS/VS or CICS/VM) and/or ICCF and/or VSE and/or VM/CMS, we offer the following words of encouragement: It is not necessary to be familiar with these products in order to understand and appreciate the capabilities of SQL/DS. All that is necessary is to understand that an application that uses the facilities of SQL/DS must operate as either

(a) an online application (CICS/DOS/VS under VSE or CICS/VM under VM), or

(b) an interactive application (ICCF under VSE or CMS under VM), or

(c) a batch application (VSE or VM/CMS).

It is also important to realize that the various categories are not always interchangeable. That is, an application that is designed to run under (e.g.) CICS/VM cannot be moved to (e.g.) the VM/CMS environment without some coding changes. However, the changes in question have to do with the portions of the application that communicate with the terminal or with the operating system, not the portions that perform database operations; the database operations are the same in all cases.

Before we can conclude this section, there are two further topics that need to be addressed under the general heading of "operating environments": *multiple- vs. single-user mode,* and *database switching.* First, multiple- vs. single-user mode (refer to Fig. 3.3):

▪ In multiple-user mode (the normal case), the SQL/DS system resides in its own partition (VSE) or virtual machine (VM), and multiple applications communicate with the system concurrently from their own parti-

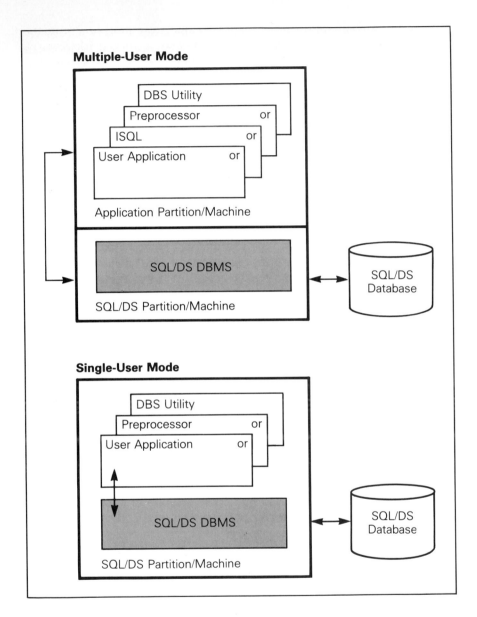

Fig. 3.3 Multiple- and single-user modes

tions or virtual machines. The applications in question can be online, interactive, and batch applications, or any combination; furthermore, they can all be accessing the same data at the same time (SQL/DS automatically performs the necessary locking to protect each application from the effects of all the others). Logging is always enabled in multiple-user mode. ISQL always runs in multiple-user mode.

▪ In single-user mode, there is only one application running, and that application resides in the same partition or virtual machine as SQL/DS itself. Logging may optionally be disabled in this mode. Single-user mode is desirable for certain kinds of processing, such as database loading and unloading and certain batch jobs, because it is operationally simpler and it reduces system overhead.

Second, database switching. At any given time, any given SQL/DS system is connected to exactly one SQL/DS database. However, *database switching* (see Fig. 3.4) allows a given SQL/DS *application* to access multiple databases, either at different times or at the same time (i.e., even within a single execution of the application in question).* More precisely, the database switching facility (which is available only under VM/CMS) allows an application that is executing under one SQL/DS system to connect dynamically to a database that is attached to another SQL/DS system. That second SQL/DS system (and hence second SQL/DS database) may reside at the same physical site as the first or it may be at some remote site. If it is remote, the application communicates with it through the VM Transparent Services Access Facility (TSAF). *Note:* Although database switching thus allows a single application to operate on multiple databases simultaneously, it does not allow a single *SQL statement* to do so.

For the reader who may be familiar with DB2, it is perhaps worth making the following point. In DB2, any number of databases can be attached to the same DB2 system, and any number of databases can be accessed simultaneously within the same application (even within the same SQL statement). However, DB2 does not currently allow an application to access a database on another DB2 system. In SQL/DS, by contrast, each SQL/DS system has exactly one (active) database, and one application can access any number of databases simultaneously (one database on each of

---

*The *first* (or only) database accessed by a given application is specified either when the application is invoked (VM) or when the SQL/DS system is started (VSE). Note that under VM there can be multiple SQL/DS systems (and hence multiple SQL/DS databases) simultaneously active on the same physical machine, whereas under VSE there cannot—unless the VSE system in question is running in its own virtual machine under VM. In this case, VSE applications can access databases that are attached to other (SQL/DS) virtual machines of that VM system.

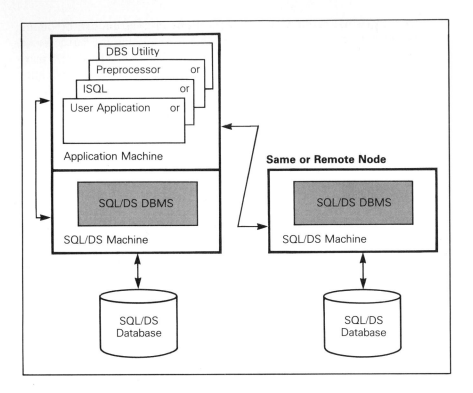

Fig. 3.4 Database switching

any number of SQL/DS systems), but different databases cannot be accessed simultaneously within the same SQL statement.

Database switching is supported for user-written applications, ISQL, the language preprocessors, and the DBS utility.

3.2 RELATED PRODUCTS

The IBM "Relational Productivity Family" (mentioned in the Preface and discussed in some detail in Part III of this book) includes a large number of companion products in addition to SQL/DS (mostly only rather loosely integrated with the base SQL/DS system, however). Of those companion products, the principal ones are as follows:

- DB2 (IBM DATABASE 2)

   As mentioned in Chapter 1, DB2 is a relational DBMS for the MVS environment. It supports a dialect of SQL that is identical in most major respects to that of SQL/DS. To be more precise, data manipulation operations and "logical" data definition operations are basically the same in the two products (except for a few comparatively minor details); stored data formats are not the same, however, and hence "physical" data definition operations are not the same either.* But it is easy to move data from one product to the other, using IBM's "Data Extract" product DXT (see below). *Note:* The major differences between SQL/DS and DB2 are summarized in Appendix F.

- QMF (Query Management Facility)

  QMF is an ad hoc query and report-writing product for both SQL/DS and DB2. It supports (among other things) ad hoc SQL access to SQL/DS and DB2 data; the QMF dialect of SQL is essentially identical to the dialect supported by SQL/DS and DB2. QMF supports SQL/DS in both the VM and VSE environments; however, the VM version includes certain features that are not available in the VSE version. The VM version is described in detail in Chapter 19 and Appendix G.

- AS (Application System)

  AS is an end-user application development facility for both SQL/DS (VM only) and DB2 (as well as for other IBM products). It provides a very wide range of facilities, including query, report-writing, business graphics, statistics, financial planning, and others. AS is discussed in Chapter 20.

- CSP (Cross System Product)

  CSP is an application development system for DP professionals. It supports both SQL/DS and DB2 as well as other IBM products. CSP-generated SQL/DS applications can execute under either CICS or CMS. CSP is described in Chapter 21.

---

*It is not just in the stored data format that the two products differ, of course; numerous other distinctions can be drawn, most of them having to do with the fact that DB2 was specifically designed for the large-system (MVS) environment and SQL/DS was not. For example, the amount of data that can be stored online in a DB2 system is constrained in practice only by the amount of online storage available, whereas SQL/DS is limited to a single online database of 64 billion bytes (theoretical maximum; the practical maximum is somewhat less). Likewise, the DB2 security mechanism is considerably more elaborate than that of SQL/DS, reflecting the fact that there are probably many more users, and many more categories of user, in a DB2 installation than in a SQL/DS installation. But it is not the purpose of this book to spell out all such differences in detail.

- DXT (Data Extract)

  DXT is a generalized data copying program. It allows IMS, VSAM, SAM, SQL/DS, DB2, or other data to be copied to a SQL/DS or DB2 database. DXT can be used to download data from a production system (e.g., from a centralized DB2 system to a departmental SQL/DS system); it might also be used to help in migration from an older system to SQL/DS (or DB2). DXT is discussed in depth in Chapter 22. *Note:* Under VSE, SQL/DS itself provides a set of facilities ("DL/I Extract") for copying data from a DOS DL/I database to a SQL/DS database. See Chapter 17.

- ECF (Enhanced Connectivity Facilities)
  HDBV (Host Data Base View)

  ECF is a set of IBM products with the overall objective of allowing a PC user to access data on a connected mainframe. The data on the mainframe can be managed by a variety of VM and MVS products, including in particular SQL/DS and DB2; it can be copied down to the PC, where it can be accessed via any of several familiar PC products, such as Lotus 1–2–3 or dBase III. ECF and HDBV are described in Chapter 23.

- DBRAD (Data Base Relational Application Directory)

  DBRAD is a directory product for SQL/DS (VM only) and DB2. It stores information regarding application programs, application data objects, etc., together with their interrelationships, in a set of SQL/DS or DB2 tables. DBRAD is intended to help in the development and maintenance of database applications. It can also be used to assist with data and system administration. DBRAD is described in depth in Chapter 24.

In addition to the products listed above, all of which (except DB2) are considered in more detail later in this book, there are a number of others that should at least receive a brief mention here:

- IC/1 (Info Center / 1)

  IC/1 provides ad hoc query, report-writing, graphics, and financial planning functions for SQL/DS (VM only), DB2, and other products.

- TIF (The Information Facility)

  TIF is an end-user application development tool supporting SQL/DS (VM only), DB2, and other products.

- DBEDIT (Data Base Edit Facility)

  DBEDIT provides a "fill-in-the-blanks" interface for the creation and execution of simple forms-based query, maintenance, and data entry applications. It supports both DB2 and SQL/DS (VM only). *Note:* Another product, SQLEDIT, provides essentially similar capabilities for SQL/DS under VSE.

- IBM Expert System Environment

  This product is an expert system shell that assists in the development of knowledge-based applications. It provides interfaces to SQL/DS (VM only) and DB2 that allow such applications to access relational data.

- RXSQL (VM Interpreter Interface to SQL/DS)

  RXSQL allows applications written using the REXX procedure language to use SQL facilities to access SQL/DS data (VM only). *Note:* From a technical standpoint, SQL/DS support for REXX is analogous to SQL/DS support for (e.g.) APL; the difference is, however, that REXX support is provided by a separate product (i.e., RXSQL), whereas APL support is provided as part of the standard APL product.

- OS/2 Database Manager

  The Extended Edition of IBM's new personal computer operating system OS/2 includes a Database Manager that is broadly compatible with SQL/DS and DB2.

- SQL/400

  SQL/400 is a SQL product for the new IBM Application System/400 (the follow-on to the IBM System/36 and System/38, announced in June 1988).

And the list goes on. It can be seen that the problem is not lack of products—rather, it is a problem of choice (how to select the right product set for a given set of needs?). The solution to that problem, of course, is highly dependent on the user's own environment and so is beyond the scope of this book. However, we do present (in Part III of the book) a thorough treatment of the major products in the list, together with a general discussion of requirements, functions, and product categories at a survey level. Part III also provides an overview, more detailed than that above, of some of the other IBM products and also of selected nonIBM products that cooperate in some manner with SQL/DS.

PART

II

♦

THE SQL/DS DATABASE MANAGEMENT SYSTEM

Basic Objects and Operators

4.1 INTRODUCTION

In this chapter we describe the fundamental scalar (i.e., elementary) objects
and operators supported by SQL/DS. The basic data object is the *scalar
value;* for example, the object appearing at the intersection of a given row
and a given column of a given table is a scalar value. Each scalar value is
of some particular scalar data type. For each such data type, there is also
an associated format for writing literal values (i.e., constants) of that type.
Scalar data types and constants are discussed in Sections 4.2 and 4.3, respectively.

Scalar objects can be operated upon by means of certain scalar operators. For example, two numeric values can be added together by means of
the scalar arithmetic operator " + ", and can be tested for equality by means
of the scalar comparison operator " = ". In addition, SQL/DS provides

49

certain scalar functions (e.g., the DATE function, which is used to convert a scalar value to a date), which can also be regarded as scalar operators. Scalar objects and operators can be combined to form scalar expressions. The operators available for each data type, and the corresponding scalar expressions, are discussed in Section 4.4. Section 4.5 then discusses the general operations of scalar assignment and scalar comparison. Finally, Section 4.6 considers the question of missing values or missing information.

Note: "Scalar value," "scalar operator," and "scalar expression" are not official SQL/DS terms. We use them because they are more precise than the official terms, which are simply "value," "operator," and "expression," respectively. On the other hand, "scalar function" is an official SQL/DS term; it is used in order to distinguish such functions from the "aggregate" (or column) functions, to be described in Chapter 7.

4.2 DATA TYPES

SQL/DS supports the following scalar data types.

Numeric Data

INTEGER	Fullword binary integer, 31 bits and sign
SMALLINT	Halfword binary integer, 15 bits and sign
DECIMAL(p,q)	Packed decimal number, p digits and sign ($0 < p < 16$), with assumed decimal point q digits from the right ($0 <= q <= p$)
FLOAT (p)	Doubleword floating point number n, say, represented by a binary fraction f of p binary digits precision ($-1 < f < +1, 0 < p < 54$) and a binary integer exponent e ($-65 < e < +64$), such that $n = f * (16**e)$

FLOAT (p) *Notes:*
1. The symbol "**" stands for exponentiation. The approximate range of magnitudes for n is 5.4E$-$79 to 7.2E$+$75 (see the explanation of float constants in Section 4.3 for an explanation of this notation).
2. Although we use the symbol "**" in our explanations, note that SQL/DS does not in fact support any such operator (see Section 4.4).

3. If $p < 22$ the number n is single precision and occupies a fullword, otherwise it is double precision and occupies a doubleword.

String Data

CHARACTER(n)	Fixed length string of exactly n 8-bit characters ($0 < n < 255$)
VARCHAR(n)	Varying length string of up to n 8-bit characters ($0 < n < 32768$)
GRAPHIC(n)	Fixed length string of exactly n 16-bit characters ($0 < n < 128$)
VARGRAPHIC(n)	Varying length string of up to n 16-bit characters ($0 < n < 16384$)

Date/Time Data

DATE	Date, represented as a sequence of eight unsigned packed decimal digits (*yyyymmdd*), occupying four bytes; permitted values are legal dates in the range January 1st, 1 A.D., to December 31st, 9999 A.D.
TIME	Time, represented as a sequence of six unsigned packed decimal digits (*hhmmss*), occupying three bytes; permitted values are legal times in the range midnight to midnight, i.e., 000000 to 240000
TIMESTAMP	"Timestamp" (combination of date and time, accurate to the nearest microsecond), represented as a sequence of 20 unsigned packed decimal digits (*yyyymmddhhmmssnnnnnn*), occupying ten bytes; permitted values are legal timestamps in the range 00010101000000000000 to 99991231240000000000

Notes:

1. The following abbreviations and alternative spellings are permitted:

INT	for	INTEGER
DECIMAL(p)	for	DECIMAL($p,0$)

DECIMAL	for	DECIMAL(5)
DEC	for	DECIMAL
FLOAT	for	FLOAT(53)
REAL	for	FLOAT(21)
DOUBLE PRECISION	for	FLOAT(53)
CHARACTER	for	CHARACTER(1)
CHAR	for	CHARACTER
LONG VARCHAR	for	VARCHAR(32767)
GRAPHIC	for	GRAPHIC(1)
LONG VARGRAPHIC	for	VARGRAPHIC(16383)

Some of the foregoing were permitted in earlier releases of SQL/DS, others were added in Version 2 for reasons of compatibility with the ANSI standard.

2. If the precision p of a DECIMAL value is specified as an even integer, it is rounded up to the next odd integer ($p + 1$).

3. The GRAPHIC and VARGRAPHIC data types are intended for dealing with double-byte character sets—i.e., character sets with more than 256 distinct characters (e.g., Kanji), in which each character is represented by a 16-bit encoding. (It is in fact possible to mix 8- and 16-bit characters within the same string, but the details are beyond the scope of this book.)

4. If the length n is greater than 254 for VARCHAR or 127 for VARGRAPHIC (or if LONG VARCHAR or LONG VARGRAPHIC is specified explicitly), the value is a "long string" and is subject to severe restrictions. Long strings are intended for the handling of free-format data such as text, rather than simple formatted data such as a supplier number or a shipment quantity. Long string values can be used in assignment operations, either to the database (INSERT or UPDATE) or from the database (SELECT); however, they cannot be used in any operation that would involve a long string comparison. Thus, for example, long strings cannot be indexed, nor can they be referenced in a WHERE clause (except with LIKE) or GROUP BY clause or ORDER BY clause, and so on. (See Chapters 6 and 7 for an explanation of these last two clauses.) For completeness, we list the restrictions here. A long string cannot appear in any of the following contexts:

- any function
- DISTINCT
- WHERE (except in a LIKE predicate)
- GROUP BY
- HAVING (except in a LIKE predicate)
- ORDER BY
- CREATE INDEX

- UNION
- target in SET (unless source is a host variable or NULL)
- source in SET
- source in INSERT . . . SELECT

5. From this point on, we will reserve the term "character string" to mean data of type CHAR or VARCHAR, the term "graphic string" to mean data of type GRAPHIC or VARGRAPHIC, and the unqualified term "string" to mean data of both string types generically.

4.3 CONSTANTS

In this section we summarize the various kinds of literal value or constant supported in SQL/DS:

integer	Written as a signed or unsigned decimal integer, with no decimal point
	Examples: `4` `-95` `+364` `0`
decimal	Written as a signed or unsigned decimal number, with a decimal point
	Examples: `4.` `-95.7` `+364.05` `0.007`
float	Written as a decimal or integer constant, followed by the letter E, followed by an integer constant
	Examples: `4E3` `-95.7E46` `+364E-5` `0.7E1`
	Note: The expression $x\mathrm{E}y$ represents the value $x * (10 ** y)$
character string	Written *either* as a string of characters enclosed in single quotes* *or* as a string of pairs of hexadecimal digits (representing the EBCDIC encodings of the characters concerned) enclosed in single quotes and preceded by the letter X

	Examples: `'123 Main St.'`
	`'PIG'`
	`X'F1F2F340D481899540E2A34B'`
	`X'D7C9C7'`

---

*As usual, a single quote must be represented as two consecutive single quotes within a character string constant.

(the 1st and 3rd of these examples represent the same value, as do the 2nd and 4th)

graphic string

Written *either* as a string of double-byte characters preceded by the "shift out" character X'0E' and followed by the "shift in" character X'0F', the whole enclosed in single quotes and preceded by the letter G,* *or* as a string of quads of hexadecimal digits (representing the internal encodings of the double-byte characters concerned) enclosed in single quotes and preceded by the letter X

Example: G'<string>'

(the shift out and shift in characters have been shown as "<" and ">", respectively; "string" represents the required string of graphic characters)

date

Written as a character string constant of the form *mm/dd/yyyy,* enclosed in single quotes (but see "Notes on Date/Times" below)

Examples: '1/18/1941'
          '12/25/1989'

time

Written as a character string constant of the form *hh:mm* AM or *hh:mm* PM, enclosed in single quotes (but see "Notes on Date/Times" below)

Examples: '10:00 AM'
          '9:30 PM'

timestamp

Written as a character string constant of the form *yyyy-mm-dd-hh.mm.ss.nnnnnn,* enclosed in single quotes (but see "Notes on Date/Times" below)

Examples: '1990-4-28-12.00.00.000000'
          '1944-10-17-18.30.45'

---

*This is the normal format. The format in PL/I contexts is slightly different. See the IBM manuals for details.

Notes on Date/Times:

1. Strictly speaking there is no such thing as a date constant. Instead, there are *character string representations of date values.* If a character string value—in particular, a character string constant—appears in a context that requires a date value, then that character string will be interpreted as a date value, provided of course that it is of the appropriate form (a conversion error will occur if it is not). We will use the term "date string" to refer to a character string that represents a valid date.

2. The remarks of the previous paragraph apply to times and timestamps also, mutatis mutandis. We will use the terms "time string" and "timestamp string" to refer to character strings that represent valid time and timestamp values.

3. Several different character string representations of dates and times are supported: US style, European style, etc. A variety of methods (installation options, preprocessor options, etc.) are available for specifying the style to be used in any particular context. The examples above all use US style. See Appendix C for further discussion.

4. We remark that a peculiarity of US-style time strings in SQL/DS is that they do not include a seconds component, as can be seen from the discussion of "time constants" above. Nevertheless, the internal representation of a time value always does include such a component.

5. Leading zeros can be omitted from the month and day portions of a date or timestamp string and from the hours portion of a time or timestamp string. The seconds portion (including the preceding colon or period) can be omitted entirely from a time string (in fact, it must be so omitted from a US-style time string); an implicit specification of zero is assumed. Trailing zeros can be omitted from the microseconds portion of a timestamp string; the microseconds portion (including the preceding period) can also be omitted entirely, in which case an implicit specification of zero is assumed.

6. The full SQL/DS support for dates and times is quite complex. For this reason we defer detailed discussion of that support to an appendix (Appendix C).

Data Types of Constants

The data type of a given constant is as indicated below:

integer	INTEGER
decimal	DECIMAL(p,q), where p and q are the actual precision and scale specified

float	FLOAT(53)
character string	VARCHAR(n), where n is the actual length specified
graphic string	VARGRAPHIC(n), where n is the actual length specified

Constants are always assumed to have the NOT NULL property (see Section 4.6).

4.4 SCALAR OPERATORS AND FUNCTIONS

SQL/DS provides a number of builtin scalar operators and functions that can be used in the construction of scalar computational expressions. We summarize those operators and functions below, for purposes of reference. *Note:* For a discussion of the builtin *aggregate* functions, see Chapter 7. For more details on the date/time functions, see Appendix C.

- Numeric operators

  SQL/DS supports the usual numeric operators $+$, $-$, $*$, and $/$, all with the obvious meanings. *Note:* The $+$ and $-$ operators can be used with dates, times, and timestamps as well as with numbers (again, see Appendix C for details).

- Concatenation

  The concatenation operator $\|$ can be used to concatenate two character strings or two graphic strings. It is written as an infix operation; e.g., the expression INITIALS $\|$ LASTNAME can be used to concatenate the values of INITIALS and LASTNAME.

- CHAR

  Converts a date, time, or timestamp to its character string representation.

- DATE

  Converts a scalar value to a date.

- DAY

  Extracts the day portion of a date or timestamp (or "date duration"—see Appendix C).

- DAYS

  Converts a date or timestamp to a number of days.

- DECIMAL

  Converts a number to decimal representation (with specified precision).

- DIGITS

  Converts a number (decimal or integer) to character string representation. (Strangely, there is no converse function to convert a character string representation of a number into the corresponding numeric value.)

- FLOAT

  Converts a number to floating point representation.

- HEX

  Converts a scalar value to a character string representing the internal hexadecimal encoding of the value.

- HOUR

  Extracts the hours portion of a time or timestamp (or "time duration"—see Appendix C).

- INTEGER

  Converts a number to integer representation.

- LENGTH

  Computes the length of a scalar value in bytes (or double-bytes, for graphic data).

- MICROSECOND

  Extracts the microseconds portion of a timestamp.

- MINUTE

  Extracts the minutes portion of a time or timestamp (or "time duration"—see Appendix C).

- MONTH

  Extracts the month portion of a date or timestamp (or "date duration"—see Appendix C).

- SECOND

  Extracts the seconds portion of a time or timestamp (or "time duration"—see Appendix C).

- STRIP

  Removes leading and/or trailing blanks (or other characters) from a string.

- SUBSTR

  Extracts a substring of a string. For example, the expression SUBSTR (SNAME,1,3) extracts the first three characters of the specified supplier name.

- TIME

  Converts a scalar value to a time.

- TIMESTAMP

  Converts either a single scalar value or a pair of scalar values, representing a date and time respectively, to a timestamp.

- TRANSLATE

  Converts one string into another by replacing each character in accordance with a specified translation table (useful for, e.g., case-insensitive comparisons).

- VALUE

  Converts a null into a nonnull value (see Section 4.6).

- VARGRAPHIC

  Converts a character string into a graphic string.

- YEAR

  Extracts the year portion of a date or timestamp (or "date duration"— see Appendix C).

Special Registers

SQL/DS also supports a number of "special registers." (*Note:* This is the DB2 term. SQL/DS does not appear to have a generic term for the concept at all. A better term—admittedly rather cumbersome, but at least descriptive and accurate—would be "zero-argument builtin scalar functions.") The special registers currently defined are USER, CURRENT DATE, CURRENT TIME, CURRENT TIMESTAMP, and CURRENT TIMEZ-ONE. A reference to a special register returns a scalar value, as follows:

- USER

  Returns the user ID of the user executing the SQL statement in which the USER reference appears. See Chapter 11 for an illustration of the use of USER.

- CURRENT DATE

  Returns the current date, i.e., the date "today."

- CURRENT TIME

  Returns the current time, i.e., the time "now."

- CURRENT TIMESTAMP

  Returns the current timestamp, i.e., the date "today" concatenated with the time "now."

- CURRENT TIMEZONE

  Returns a "time duration" (see Appendix C) representing (typically) the displacement of the local time zone from Greenwich Mean Time. Note that the value returned by each of CURRENT DATE, CURRENT TIME, and CURRENT TIMESTAMP is based on a reading of the local clock, incremented in each case by the value of CURRENT TIMEZONE.

  For examples of the use of the various CURRENT special registers, see Appendix C once again.

Scalar Expressions

As indicated at the beginning of this section, the scalar operators and functions can be used (in conjunction with scalar operands and arguments) to construct scalar expressions. A scalar expression is an expression whose operands are simple scalar values and whose value in turn is another such scalar.* Generally speaking, such expressions can appear wherever a *constant* of the appropriate type is permitted—for example, as operands in SELECT, WHERE, and HAVING clauses (see Chapters 6–8)—though, regrettably, there are many exceptions to this simple general rule. Such exceptions are noted later at appropriate points in the book.

---

*For details regarding the data type, precision, etc., of the result of a scalar expression, the reader is referred to the IBM manuals.

There are six types of scalar expression, characterized according to the data type of the value they represent: numeric, character string, graphic string, date, time, and timestamp expressions. We give examples here of the first two types only; graphic string expressions are syntactically similar to character string expressions, and date, time, and timestamp expressions are discussed in Appendix C. Note that (as several of the examples below suggest) parentheses can always be used in an expression to force a desired order of evaluation. Note too that the aggregate functions discussed in Chapter 7 can also be used within certain scalar expressions, since they each return a scalar value.

Numeric expressions:

```
STATUS
WEIGHT * 454
SALARY + COMMISSION + BONUS
( QTY + 1500 ) / 75.2
·50 - ( AVG ( QTY ) / 100 )
```

Character string expressions:

```
PNAME
INITIALS || LASTNAME
SUBSTR ( SNAME, 1, 3 )
'NNNN' || SUBSTR ( DIGITS ( QTY ), 8, 2 )
MIN ( COLOR )
USER
```

4.5 ASSIGNMENTS AND COMPARISONS

Assignments

Assignment operations are performed when values are retrieved from the database (e.g., via SELECT) or stored into the database (e.g., via UPDATE). In general, an assignment involves assigning the value of some scalar expression (the *source*) to some scalar object (the *target*). The data type of the source and the data type of the target must be *compatible*. Compatibility is defined as follows:

1. All numbers are compatible with one another.

2. All character strings are compatible with one another.

3. All graphic strings are compatible with one another.

4. All dates are compatible with one another. Dates and character strings are also compatible with one another.

5. All times are compatible with one another. Times and character strings are also compatible with one another.

6. All timestamps are compatible with one another. Timestamps and character strings are also compatible with one another.

7. In Cases 4, 5, and 6 above, the character string in question must be a valid date string or time string or timestamp string (as applicable), unless it is being assigned to, in which case its value is irrelevant. See Appendix C for further discussion.

8. There are no other instances of compatibility.

Note 1: The target of an assignment in an INSERT or UPDATE operation must be represented by an *unqualified* name. See Chapters 5 and 6 for a discussion of qualified and unqualified names.

Note 2: In a date/time assignment, the source can be—for example— the days component of a given date/time (specified by means of the DAY function), but the target cannot.

Comparisons

Comparisons are performed under many circumstances—for example, when duplicate values are being eliminated from the result of a SELECT DISTINCT (see Chapter 6). A comparison is also one kind of *predicate* (though not the only kind); predicates are used in WHERE and HAVING clauses (see Chapters 6–8). Comparisons can be regarded as a special kind of scalar expression, but a scalar expression that evaluates to a truth value instead of to one of the SQL/DS-supported data types. The general form of a comparison is

comparand operator comparand

where:

(a) The two comparands must be compatible, as that term is defined under "Assignments" above. In other words, the comparands must be scalar expressions of the same type—i.e., both numeric or both character string or . . . (etc.). The data types of the two expressions are not required to be absolutely identical, but for performance reasons it is usually a good idea if they are.

(b) The operator is any of the following: =, ~ = (not equals), <, < =, >, > =.*

---

*For typographic reasons we use the tilde (~) to represent "not" in "not equals." SQL/DS actually uses the PL/I-style "not" symbol. SQL/DS also allows "not equals" to be written as < > (for reasons of compatibility with the ANSI standard).

Comparisons are evaluated as follows:

- Numbers compare algebraically (negative values are considered to be smaller than positive values, regardless of their absolute magnitude).

- Strings (character or graphic) compare in accordance with their internal byte encoding. If two strings of different lengths are to be compared, the shorter is conceptually padded at the right with blanks to make it the same length as the longer before the comparison is done—*unless* both strings are varying length. In this latter case, the comparison is performed as follows:

  - Let the strings to be compared be A and B, of lengths a and b respectively;
  - Without loss of generality, assume $a <= b$;
  - Let C be the string consisting of the first a characters of B;
  - Then:
    If $A > C$, then $A > B$;
    If $A < C$, then $A < B$;
    If $A = C$ and $a < b$, then $A < B$;
    If $A = C$ and $a = b$, then $A = B$.

  As an example, let A and B have the values "XYZ" (length 3) and "XYZb" (length 4, with b representing a blank). Then $A < B$.

- Dates and times and timestamps compare in accordance with the obvious chronologic ordering. See Appendix C for further discussion.

Examples:

```
WEIGHT * 454 > 1000
PNAME >= 'C'
REVIEW_DATE < CURRENT DATE
```

4.6 MISSING INFORMATION

To complete this chapter on basic objects and operators, it is necessary to say something regarding missing information. The problem of missing information is one that is frequently encountered in the real world. For example, historical records sometimes include such entries as "Date of birth unknown"; meeting agendas often show a speaker as "To be announced"; and police records may include the entry "Present whereabouts unknown." Hence it is desirable to have some way of dealing with such situations in our database systems.

SQL-based systems such as SQL/DS represent such missing information by means of special markers called *nulls*.* If a given record has a null in a given field position, it means that the value of that field is unknown (or perhaps does not apply) for the record in question. For example, a shipment record might contain a null QTY (we know that the shipment exists but we do not know the quantity shipped); or a part record might contain a null COLOR (perhaps COLOR is irrelevant for some kinds of part). Note carefully that null is not the same as (e.g.) blank or zero; in fact, it is not really a data value at all in the usual sense of that term, which is why we referred to nulls as "markers" above.

In general, any field can contain nulls *unless* the definition of that field explicitly specifies NOT NULL (see Chapter 5). If a given field is allowed to contain nulls, and a record is inserted into the table and no value is supplied for that field, SQL/DS will automatically place a null in that position.

- Suppose, for example, that NOT NULL is specified for field S# in table S. The effect of this specification is to guarantee that every record in table S will always contain a genuine (i.e., nonnull) S# value; in other words, a value must always be supplied for field S# when a record is inserted into the S table, and updating an existing S# value to null will not be allowed.†

- Suppose also, by contrast, that NOT NULL is *not* specified for field STATUS in that same table. Then field STATUS might be null in some S record; in other words, it is possible to insert an S record without supplying a STATUS value, and updating an existing STATUS value to null will be allowed.

Aside: In SQL/DS, a column that can accept nulls is physically represented in the stored database by two columns, the data column itself and a hidden indicator column, one byte wide, that is stored as a prefix to the actual data column. An indicator column value of binary ones indicates that the corresponding data column value is to be ignored (i.e., taken as null); an indicator column value of binary zeros indicates that the corresponding data column value is to be taken as genuine. But the indicator column is always (of course) "transparent to the user."

---

*Also known as *null values*. However, this usage is deprecated, since (as explained subsequently) the whole point of null is precisely that it is not a value.

†In fact, NOT NULL *must* be specified for field S#, because it is the primary key for table S. See Chapters 5 and 12.

We now examine the effect of nulls on scalar expressions. Consider, for example, the numeric expression

```
WEIGHT * 454
```

where WEIGHT represents the weight of some part, P*x* say. What if the weight of part P*x* happens to be null?—what then is the value of the expression? The answer is that it also is considered to be null. In general, in fact, *any* (scalar) numeric expression is considered to evaluate to null if any of the operands of that expression is itself null. Thus, e.g., if WEIGHT happens to be null, then all of the following expressions also evaluate to null:

```
WEIGHT + 454        454 + WEIGHT        + WEIGHT
WEIGHT - 454        454 - WEIGHT        - WEIGHT
WEIGHT * 454        454 * WEIGHT
WEIGHT / 454        454 / WEIGHT
```

Analogous considerations apply to other scalar expressions also.*

Comparisons are also affected by the presence of nulls. Let A and B be two expressions that are compatible for comparison purposes (see Section 4.5). If A evaluates to null or B evaluates to null *or both,* then (in the context of a WHERE or HAVING clause) each of the comparisons

```
A = B        A ~= B
A < B        A >= B
A > B        A <= B
```

evaluates, not to *true* or *false,* but to the *unknown* truth value. The *unknown* truth value is defined by the following truth tables (where T = *true,* F = *false,* and ? = *unknown*):

```
AND | T ? F          OR  | T ? F          NOT|
----+------          ----+------          ---+---
 T  | T ? F           T  | T T T           T | F
 ?  | ? ? F           ?  | T ? ?           ? | ?
 F  | F F F           F  | T ? F           F | T
```

Note in particular, therefore, that (in the context of a WHERE or HAVING clause) two nulls are not considered to be equal to one another. Despite this fact, however, two nulls *are* considered to be equal (equivalently, to be duplicates of each other) for purposes of indexing (UNIQUE—see Chapter 5) and duplicate elimination (DISTINCT—see Chapter 6) and ordering (ORDER BY—see Chapter 6) and grouping (GROUP BY—see Chapter 7).

The question of the effect of nulls on comparisons is discussed further in Chapter 6.

One final point: In certain contexts—but *not* in general scalar expres-

---

*The effect of nulls on aggregate functions such as SUM is discussed in Chapter 7.

sions, and not in a SELECT clause—the special zero-argument function NULL can be used to represent null.* For instance:

```
UPDATE S
SET    STATUS = NULL
WHERE  CITY = 'Paris'
```

Author's note: It is this writer's opinion that nulls, at least as currently defined and implemented in SQL, are far more trouble than they are worth and should be avoided; they display very strange and inconsistent behavior and can be a rich source of error and confusion. (Please note that these remarks apply to any system that supports SQL-style nulls, not just to SQL/DS specifically. An extensive discussion of the problems that can be caused by SQL-style nulls can be found in the book *Relational Database: Selected Writings,* by C. J. Date, Addison-Wesley, 1986.) In this book, therefore, we will generally specify NOT NULL for all fields, unless we are trying to illustrate some specific point involving nulls.

---

*SQL/DS does not actually consider NULL to be a "zero-argument function" (nor is it a constant or "special register"), because it cannot appear in all contexts in which such objects can appear. Exactly what SQL/DS does consider it to be is not at all clear.

5

♦

Data Definition

5.1 INTRODUCTION

In this chapter we examine the data definition statements of SQL/DS in some detail. It is convenient to divide those statements into two broad classes, which we may very loosely characterize as *logical* and *physical*—"logical" having to do with objects that are genuinely of interest to users, such as base tables and views, and "physical" having to do with objects that are primarily of interest to the system, such as physical storage. Needless to say, matters are not really as clearcut as this simple classification would suggest—some "logical" statements include parameters that are really "physical" in nature, and vice versa, and some statements do not fit neatly into either category. But the classification is convenient as an aid to understanding, and we will stay with it for now. The present chapter is concerned only with "logical" data definition.

The principal logical data definition statements are listed below:

```
CREATE TABLE        CREATE VIEW        CREATE INDEX
ALTER TABLE
DROP TABLE          DROP VIEW          DROP INDEX
```

We defer discussion of CREATE and DROP VIEW to Chapter 10; the remaining statements above are the subject of the present chapter.

5.2 BASE TABLES

A base table is an (important) special case of the more general concept "table." Let us therefore begin by making that more general concept a little more precise.

Definition

A *table* in a relational system consists of a row of *column headings*, together with zero or more rows of *data values* (different numbers of data rows at different times). For a given table:

(a) The column heading row specifies one or more columns (giving, among other things, a data type for each);

(b) Each data row contains exactly one data value for each of the columns specified in the column heading row. Furthermore, all the values in a given column are of the same data type, namely the data type specified in the column heading row for that column.

Two points arise in connexion with the foregoing definition.

1. Note that there is no mention of *row ordering*. Strictly speaking, the rows of a relational table are considered to be unordered. (The rows of a relation constitute a mathematical *set*, and sets in mathematics do not have any ordering.) It is possible, as we shall see in Chapter 6, to *impose* an order on those rows when they are retrieved in response to a query, but such an ordering should be regarded as nothing more than a convenience for the user—it is not intrinsic to the notion of a table per se.

2. In contrast to the first point, the columns of a table *are* considered to be ordered, left to right. (At least, they are considered to be so ordered in most systems, including in particular SQL/DS.) For example, in table S (see Fig. 1.2 in Chapter 1), column S# is the first column, column SNAME is the second column, and so on. In practice, however, there are very few situations in which that left-to-right ordering is significant,

and even those can be avoided with a little discipline. Such avoidance is to be recommended, as we shall explain later.

Aside: Of course, rows and columns do have a physical ordering in the stored version of the table on the disk; what is more, those physical orderings can and do have a very definite effect on system performance. The point is, however, that those physical orderings are (in most situations, and ideally in all situations) *transparent to the user.*

To turn now to base tables specifically: A base table is an *autonomous, named* table. By "autonomous" we mean that the table exists in its own right—unlike (e.g.) a view, which does not exist in its own right but is derived from one or more base tables (it is merely an alternative way of looking at those base tables). By "named" we mean that the table is explicitly given a name via an appropriate CREATE statement—unlike (e.g.) a table that is merely constructed as the result of a query, which does not have any explicit name of its own and has only ephemeral existence (for examples of such unnamed tables, see the two result tables in Fig. 1.1 in Chapter 1).

CREATE TABLE

We are now in a position to discuss the CREATE TABLE statement in detail. The general format of that statement is as follows:

```
CREATE TABLE base-table
  ( column-definition [, column-definition ] ...
  [, primary-key-definition ]
  [, foreign-key-definition [, foreign-key-definition ] ... ]
  [  IN dbspace  ] )
```

where a "column-definition", in turn, takes the form:

```
column data-type [ NOT NULL ]
```

The optional NOT NULL specification has already been explained in Chapter 4 (Section 4.6). We defer detailed discussion of "primary-key-definition" and "foreign-key-definition" to Chapter 12; note, however, that although the primary key definition is in fact optional, we will always include such a definition in our examples in this book. The optional specification "IN dbspace" has to do with physical storage matters and is discussed (very briefly) in Chapter 16.

Note: Square brackets are used in syntactic definitions throughout this book to indicate that the material enclosed in those brackets is optional (i.e., may be omitted). An ellipsis (. . .) indicates that the immediately preceding syntactic unit may optionally be repeated one or more times. Material in capitals must be written exactly as shown; material in lower case must be replaced by specific values chosen by the user.

Here is an example (the CREATE TABLE statement for table S, now shown complete):

```
CREATE TABLE S
      ( S#       CHAR(5)  NOT NULL,
        SNAME    CHAR(20) NOT NULL,
        STATUS   SMALLINT,
        CITY     CHAR(15) NOT NULL,
      PRIMARY KEY ( S# ) )
```

The effect of this statement is to create a new, empty base table called *xyz*.S, where *xyz* is the user ID for the user issuing the CREATE TABLE statement (see Chapter 11). Entries describing the table are made in the system catalog. User *xyz* can refer to the table by its full name *xyz*.S or by the abbreviated name S; other users must refer to it by its full name. The table has four columns, called *xyz*.S.S#, *xyz*.S.SNAME, *xyz*.S.STATUS, and *xyz*.S.CITY, and having the indicated data types; column *xyz*.S.S# is the primary key. User *xyz* can refer to those columns by their full names or by the abbreviated names S.S#, S.SNAME, S.STATUS, and S.CITY; other users must always use the *xyz* qualifier. For user *xyz* (only), the "S." portion can be omitted also if no ambiguity results. In general, the rules concerning names are as follows: User names, such as *xyz*, must be unique across the entire database; (unqualified) table names must be unique within user; and (unqualified) column names must be unique within table.* "Table" here refers to both base tables and views; that is, a view cannot have the same name as a base table.

Once the table has been created, data can be entered into it via the SQL statements INSERT and PUT (see Chapters 8 and 13, respectively), the ISQL statement INPUT (see Chapter 17), or the DBS utility (again, see Chapter 17).

ALTER TABLE

Just as a new base table can be created at any time, via CREATE TABLE, so an existing base table can be *altered* at any time by the addition of a new column at the right, via ALTER TABLE:

```
ALTER TABLE base-table
      ADD column data-type
```

For example:

```
ALTER TABLE S
      ADD DISCOUNT SMALLINT
```

---

*In addition, SQL keywords (CREATE, TABLE, SELECT, etc.) cannot be used as names. The first character of any name must be "alphabetic" (A–Z or one of the special characters #, $, @), the remainder if any must be alphabetic, numeric (0–9), or the underscore character. Table and column names are limited to a maximum of 18 characters, user IDs and access module names to a maximum of 8 characters.

This statement adds a DISCOUNT column to the S table. All existing S records are extended from four field values to five; the value of the new fifth field is null in every case (note that the specification NOT NULL is not allowed in ALTER TABLE). Note also, incidentally, that the expansion of existing records just described is not physically performed at the time the ALTER TABLE is executed; all that happens at that time is that the description of those records in the catalog changes. Thereafter, for a given record in the ALTERed table:

1. The next time it is read from the disk, SQL/DS appends a null to the record before passing it to the user;

2. The next time it is written to the disk, SQL/DS writes the physically expanded version (unless the additional value is still null, in which case the expansion still does not occur).

But from the user's perspective, it is as if the records *were* all physically expanded at ALTER TABLE time. There is no way to tell the difference.

ALTER TABLE also allows primary and foreign key specifications to be added to or removed from a given table (see Chapter 12). Note, however, that it does *not* support any kind of change to the width or data type of an existing column, nor does it support the removal of an existing column.

DROP TABLE

An existing base table can be destroyed at any time by means of the SQL DROP statement:

```
DROP TABLE base-table
```

The specified base table is removed from the system (more precisely, the description of that table is removed from the catalog). All indexes and views defined on that base table are automatically dropped also. (All foreign key specifications that refer to that base table are also automatically dropped. See Chapter 12.)

5.3 INDEXES

Like base tables, indexes are created and dropped using SQL data definition statements. However, CREATE INDEX and DROP INDEX are the *only* statements in the SQL language that refer to indexes at all; other statements—in particular, data manipulation statements such as SELECT—deliberately do not include any such references. The decision as to whether or not to use some particular index in responding to a particular SQL request is made not by the user but by SQL/DS (actually by the optimizer), as explained in Chapter 2.

CREATE INDEX takes the general form:

```
CREATE [ UNIQUE ] INDEX index
    ON base-table ( column [ order ]
                 [, column [ order ] ] ... )
       [ other parameters ]
```

The optional "other parameters" have to do with physical storage matters; see the IBM manuals for details. Each "order" specification is either ASC (ascending) or DESC (descending); if neither ASC nor DESC is specified, then ASC is assumed by default. The left-to-right sequence of naming columns in the CREATE INDEX statement corresponds to major-to-minor ordering in the usual way. For example, the statement

```
CREATE INDEX X ON B ( P, Q DESC, R )
```

creates an index called X on base table B in which entries are ordered by ascending R-value within descending Q-value within ascending P-value. The columns P, Q, and R need not be contiguous, nor need they all be of the same data type, nor need they be all fixed length or all varying length.

Once created, an index is automatically maintained by SQL/DS to reflect updates on the base table, until such time as the index is dropped.

The UNIQUE option in CREATE INDEX specifies that no two records in the indexed base table will be allowed to take on the same value for the indexed field or field combination at the same time. For instance, if we assume for the sake of the example that supplier names are unique, we would probably specify a UNIQUE index as follows:

```
CREATE UNIQUE INDEX XSN ON S ( SNAME )
```

Now SQL/DS will reject any attempt to introduce a duplicate value (via an INSERT or UPDATE operation) into field S.SNAME. *Note:* SQL/DS will automatically create a UNIQUE index on the primary key of a table. In the case of suppliers-and-parts, for example, SQL/DS will automatically create UNIQUE indexes on field S.S#, field P.P#, and (composite) field SP. (S#,P#). See Chapter 12 for further discussion.

Indexes, like base tables, can be created and dropped at any time. Note, however, that an attempt to create a UNIQUE index on a table that does not currently satisfy the uniqueness constraint will fail. As mentioned in Section 4.6, two nulls are considered to be equal to each other for UNIQUE indexing purposes.

Any number of indexes can be built on a single base table. Here is another index for table S:

```
CREATE INDEX XSC ON S ( CITY )
```

UNIQUE has not been specified in this case, because multiple suppliers can be located in the same city.

The statement to drop an index is

```
DROP INDEX index
```

The index is destroyed (i.e., its description is removed from the catalog). If an existing access module depends on that dropped index, then, as explained in Chapter 2, that access module will automatically be regenerated the next time it is invoked. Refer back to Chapter 2 if you need to refresh your memory regarding this process.

5.4 DISCUSSION

The fact that data definition statements can be executed at any time makes SQL/DS a very flexible system. In older (nonrelational) systems, the addition of a new type of object, such as a new record type or a new index or a new field, is an operation not to be undertaken lightly: Typically it involves bringing the entire system to a halt,* unloading the database, revising and recompiling the database definition, and finally reloading the database in accordance with that revised definition. In such a system, it becomes highly desirable to get the database definition (and therefore, much more significantly, the database *design*) *complete* and *correct* once and for all, before starting to load and use the data—which means that (a) the job of getting the system installed and operational can quite literally take months or even years of highly specialized people's time, and (b) once the system is running, it can be difficult and costly, perhaps prohibitively so, to remedy early design errors.

In SQL/DS, by contrast, it is possible to create and load just a few base tables and then to start using that data immediately. Later, new base tables and new fields can be added in a piecemeal fashion, without having any effect on existing users of the database. It is also possible to experiment with the effects of having or not having particular indexes, again without affecting existing users at all (other than in performance, of course). Moreover, as we shall see in Chapter 10, it is even possible under certain circumstances to rearrange the structure of the database—e.g., to move a field from one table to another—and still not affect the logic of existing programs. In a nutshell, it is not necessary to go through the total database

---

*We remark in passing that many modern installations simply cannot afford to bring the system to a halt—they require nonstop (24-hour-a-day) operation. For such an installation, the comparative inflexibility of nonrelational systems is a major drawback, possibly a complete showstopper.

design process before any useful work can be done with the system, nor is it necessary to get everything right the first time. The system is *forgiving*.

Caveat: The foregoing should *not* be taken to mean that database design is unnecessary in a system like SQL/DS. Of course database design is still needed. However:

- It doesn't all have to be done at once.

- It doesn't have to be perfect first time.

- Logical and physical design can be tackled separately.

- If requirements change, then the design can change too, in a comparatively painless manner.

- Many new applications—typically small-scale applications, involving, for example, personal or departmental databases—become feasible in a system like SQL/DS that would simply never have been considered under an older (nonrelational) system, because those older systems were just too complicated to make such applications economically worthwhile (in particular, the upfront costs in those systems were prohibitive).

EXERCISES

5.1 Fig. 5.1 shows some sample data values for a database containing information concerning suppliers (S), parts (P), and projects (J). Suppliers, parts, and projects

S	S#	SNAME	STATUS	CITY
	S1	Smith	20	London
	S2	Jones	10	Paris
	S3	Blake	30	Paris
	S4	Clark	20	London
	S5	Adams	30	Athens

P	P#	PNAME	COLOR	WEIGHT	CITY
	P1	Nut	Red	12	London
	P2	Bolt	Green	17	Paris
	P3	Screw	Blue	17	Rome
	P4	Screw	Red	14	London
	P5	Cam	Blue	12	Paris
	P6	Cog	Red	19	London

J	J#	JNAME	CITY
	J1	Sorter	Paris
	J2	Punch	Rome
	J3	Reader	Athens
	J4	Console	Athens
	J5	Collator	London
	J6	Terminal	Oslo
	J7	Tape	London

SPJ	S#	P#	J#	QTY
	S1	P1	J1	200
	S1	P1	J4	700
	S2	P3	J1	400
	S2	P3	J2	200
	S2	P3	J3	200
	S2	P3	J4	500
	S2	P3	J5	600
	S2	P3	J6	400
	S2	P3	J7	800
	S2	P5	J2	100
	S3	P3	J1	200
	S3	P4	J2	500
	S4	P6	J3	300
	S4	P6	J7	300
	S5	P2	J2	200
	S5	P2	J4	100
	S5	P5	J5	500
	S5	P5	J7	100
	S5	P6	J2	200
	S5	P1	J4	100
	S5	P3	J4	200
	S5	P4	J4	800
	S5	P5	J4	400
	S5	P6	J4	500

Fig. 5.1 The suppliers-parts-projects database

are uniquely identified by supplier number (S#), part number (P#), and project number (J#), respectively. The significance of an SPJ (shipment) record is that the specified supplier supplies the specified part to the specified project in the specified quantity (and the combination S#-P#-J# uniquely identifies such a record). Write a suitable set of CREATE TABLE statements for this database. *Note:* This database will be used in numerous exercises in subsequent chapters.

5.2 What are the main advantages of indexes? What are the main disadvantages?

5.3 "Uniqueness" of a field or field combination is a logical property, but it is enforced in SQL/DS by means of an index, which is a physical construct. Discuss.

ANSWERS TO SELECTED EXERCISES

5.1
```
CREATE TABLE S
    ( S#        CHAR(5)   NOT NULL,
      SNAME     CHAR(20)  NOT NULL,
      STATUS    SMALLINT  NOT NULL,
      CITY      CHAR(15)  NOT NULL,
      PRIMARY KEY ( S# ) )

CREATE TABLE P
    ( P#        CHAR(6)   NOT NULL,
      PNAME     CHAR(20)  NOT NULL,
      COLOR     CHAR(6)   NOT NULL,
      WEIGHT    SMALLINT  NOT NULL,
      CITY      CHAR(15)  NOT NULL,
      PRIMARY KEY ( P# ) )

CREATE TABLE J
    ( J#        CHAR(4)   NOT NULL,
      JNAME     CHAR(10)  NOT NULL,
      CITY      CHAR(15)  NOT NULL,
      PRIMARY KEY ( J# ) )

CREATE TABLE SPJ
    ( S#        CHAR(5)   NOT NULL,
      P#        CHAR(6)   NOT NULL,
      J#        CHAR(4)   NOT NULL,
      QTY       INTEGER,
      PRIMARY KEY ( S#, P#, J# ) )
```

Note: We allow field SPJ.QTY to accept nulls purely because it is required to do so by a later exercise—not for any really good reason.

5.2 The advantages of indexes are as follows:
   (a) They can speed up direct access based on a given value for the indexed field (combination). Without the index, a sequential scan would be required.
   (b) They can speed up sequential access based on the indexed field (combination). Without the index, a sort would be required.
   (c) In SQL/DS in particular, UNIQUE indexes serve to enforce uniqueness constraints.
   The disadvantages are as follows:
   (a) They take up space in the database. The space taken up by indexes can easily exceed that taken up by the data itself in a heavily indexed database.

(b) While an index may well speed up retrieval operations, it will at the same time slow down update operations. Any INSERT or DELETE on the indexed table or UPDATE on the indexed field (combination) will require an accompanying update on the index.

5.3 An unfortunate state of affairs. SQL/DS is not quite as data independent as it ought to be.

6

♦

Data Manipulation I: Retrieval Operations

6.1 INTRODUCTION

SQL provides four data manipulation statements: SELECT, INSERT, UPDATE, and DELETE. This chapter and the next are concerned with the SELECT statement; Chapter 8 is concerned with the other three statements. The aim in all three chapters is to be reasonably comprehensive but *not* to replace the relevant IBM manuals. As usual, all examples are based on the suppliers-and-parts database. Also, we assume until further notice that all statements are entered interactively. The special considerations that apply to embedded SQL are ignored until Chapter 13.

Note: Many of our examples, especially those in the next chapter, are quite complex. The reader should not infer that it is SQL itself that is complex. Rather, the point is that common operations are so simple in SQL (and indeed in most relational languages) that examples of such operations tend to be rather uninteresting, and do not illustrate the full power of the language. Of course, we do show some simple examples first (Section 6.2). Section 6.3 is concerned with a slightly more complicated—but extremely important—facility known as *join*.

6.2   Simple Queries

We start with a simple example—the query "Get supplier numbers and status for suppliers in Paris," which can be expressed in SQL as follows:

```
SELECT S#, STATUS
FROM    S
WHERE   CITY = 'Paris'
```

Result:
S#	STATUS
S2	10
S3	30

The example illustrates the commonest form of the SQL SELECT statement—"*SELECT* specified fields *FROM* some specified table *WHERE* some specified condition is true." Notice that the result of the query is another table—a table that is derived in some way from the given tables in the database. In other words, the user in a relational system like SQL/DS is always operating in the simple tabular framework, a very attractive feature of such systems.*

Incidentally, we could equally well have formulated the query using *qualified field names* throughout:

```
SELECT S.S#, S.STATUS
FROM    S
WHERE   S.CITY = 'Paris'
```

The use of qualified names is often clearer (and sometimes essential, as we shall see in Section 6.3 and elsewhere).

---

*Because of this fact, we say that relational tables form a *closed system* under the retrieval operators of a language like SQL. In general, a closed system is a collection (possibly infinite) of all objects of a certain type, say OBJS, and a corresponding collection of operators, say OPS, such that:

(a) The operators in OPS apply to the objects in OBJS, and
(b) The result of applying any such operator to any such object(s) is another object in OBJS.

The practical significance of this point (in the case of relations specifically) is as follows: Since the result of one SELECT operation is another relation, it is possible, at least in principle, to apply another SELECT operation to that result, provided of course that that result has been saved somewhere. It also means, again in principle, that SELECT operations can be nested. See Sections 7.2 and 8.2 and Chapter 10 for illustrations of these points.

For reference, we show below the general form of the SELECT statement (ignoring the possibility of UNION, which is discussed in the next chapter).

```
SELECT [ ALL | DISTINCT ] item(s)
FROM    table(s)
[ WHERE  predicate ]
[ GROUP  BY field(s) ]
[ HAVING predicate ]
[ ORDER  BY field(s) ]
```

We now proceed to illustrate the major features of this statement by means of a rather lengthy series of examples. *Note:* The GROUP BY and HAVING clauses are discussed in Chapter 7. All of the remaining clauses are at least introduced in this chapter, though the more complex aspects of those clauses are also deferred to Chapter 7.

6.2.1 Simple Retrieval. Get part numbers for all parts supplied.

```
SELECT P#
FROM    SP
```

Result: P#
--
P1
P2
P3
P4
P5
P6
P1
P2
P2
P2
P4
P5

Notice the duplication of part numbers in this result. SQL/DS does not eliminate duplicate rows from the result of a SELECT statement unless the user explicitly requests it to do so via the keyword DISTINCT, as in the next example.

6.2.2 Retrieval with Duplicate Elimination. Get part numbers for all parts supplied, with redundant duplicates eliminated.

```
SELECT DISTINCT P#
FROM    SP
```

Result: P#
--
P1
P2
P3
P4
P5
P6

The alternative to DISTINCT is ALL. ALL is assumed if neither is specified.

6.2.3   *Retrieval of Computed Values.*   For all parts, get the part number and the weight of the part in grams (part weights are given in table P in pounds).

```
SELECT  P#, 'Weight in grams =', WEIGHT * 454
FROM    P
```

Result:
```
P#
--  ------------------  ----
P1  Weight in grams =   5448
P2  Weight in grams =   7718
P3  Weight in grams =   7718
P4  Weight in grams =   6356
P5  Weight in grams =   5448
P6  Weight in grams =   8626
```

The SELECT clause (also the WHERE and HAVING clauses) can include general scalar expressions (involving, e.g., scalar operators such as plus and minus and scalar functions such as SUBSTR) instead of or as well as simple field names.

6.2.4   *Simple Retrieval*   (*"SELECT *"*).   Get full details of all suppliers.

```
SELECT  *
FROM    S
```

Result: A copy of the entire S table.

The star or asterisk is shorthand for a list of all field names in the table(s) named in the FROM clause, in the order in which those fields are defined in the relevant CREATE (and possibly ALTER) TABLE statement(s). The SELECT statement shown is thus equivalent to:

```
SELECT  S#, SNAME, STATUS, CITY
FROM    S
```

The star notation is convenient for interactive queries, since it saves keystrokes. However, it is potentially dangerous in embedded SQL (i.e., SQL within an application program), because the meaning of "*" may change if the access module is regenerated and some definitional change has occurred in the interim. In this book we will use "SELECT *" only in contexts where it is safe to do so (basically ad hoc queries only), and we recommend that actual users of SQL/DS do likewise.

Incidentally, it is possible to qualify the "*" by the name of the relevant table. For example, the following is legal:

```
SELECT  S.*
FROM    S
```

6.2.5 Qualified Retrieval. Get supplier numbers for suppliers in Paris with status > 20.

```
SELECT S#
FROM   S
WHERE  CITY = 'Paris'
AND    STATUS > 20
```

Result: S#
      --
      S3

The condition or *predicate* following WHERE can consist of a simple *comparison* (see Chapter 4 for a definition of this term), or it can consist of multiple comparisons and/or other kinds of predicate all combined together using the Boolean operators AND, OR, and NOT, and parentheses if required to indicate a desired order of evaluation. (Additional kinds of predicate are discussed in numerous subsequent examples.)

6.2.6 Retrieval with Ordering. Get supplier numbers and status for suppliers in Paris, in descending order of status.

```
SELECT S#, STATUS
FROM   S
WHERE  CITY = 'Paris'
ORDER  BY STATUS DESC
```

Result: S# STATUS
      -- ------
      S3   30
      S2   10

In general, the result table is not guaranteed to be in any particular order. Here, however, the user has specified that the result is to be arranged in a particular sequence before being displayed. Ordering may be specified in the same manner as in CREATE INDEX (see Section 5.3)—that is, as

```
column [ order ] [, column [ order ] ] ...
```

where, as before, "order" is either ASC or DESC, and ASC is the default. Each "column" must identify a column of the *result table*. Thus, for example, the following is ***ILLEGAL***:

```
SELECT S#
FROM   S
ORDER  BY CITY
```

It is also possible to identify columns in the ORDER BY clause by column *number* instead of column name—i.e., by the ordinal (left-to-right) position of the column in question within the result table. This feature makes it possible to order a result on the basis of a "computed column," which does not have a name. For example, to order the result of Example 6.2.3 by ascending part number within ascending gram weight:

```
SELECT P#, 'Weight in grams =', WEIGHT * 454
FROM   P
ORDER  BY 3, P#
```

The "3" refers to the third column of the result table. Result:

```
P#
--  ------------------  ----
P1  Weight in grams =   5448
P5  Weight in grams =   5448
P4  Weight in grams =   6356
P2  Weight in grams =   7718
P3  Weight in grams =   7718
P6  Weight in grams =   8626
```

6.2.7   Retrieval Using BETWEEN.   Get parts whose weight is in the range 16 to 19 (inclusive).

```
SELECT P#, PNAME, COLOR, WEIGHT, CITY
FROM   P
WHERE  WEIGHT BETWEEN 16 AND 19
```

Result:

P#	PNAME	COLOR	WEIGHT	CITY
P2	Bolt	Green	17	Paris
P3	Screw	Blue	17	Rome
P6	Cog	Red	19	London

The BETWEEN predicate is really just a shorthand for a predicate involving two individual comparisons "ANDed" together. The foregoing SELECT statement is equivalent to the following:

```
SELECT P#, PNAME, COLOR, WEIGHT, CITY
FROM   P
WHERE  WEIGHT >= 16
AND    WEIGHT <= 19
```

NOT BETWEEN can also be specified—for example,

```
SELECT P#, PNAME, COLOR, WEIGHT, CITY
FROM   P
WHERE  WEIGHT NOT BETWEEN 16 AND 19
```

Result:

P#	PNAME	COLOR	WEIGHT	CITY
P1	Nut	Red	12	London
P4	Screw	Red	14	London
P5	Cam	Blue	12	Paris

Like the BETWEEN predicate, the NOT BETWEEN predicate can be regarded merely as a shorthand for another predicate that does not use

NOT BETWEEN. Exercise: Show the "expanded form" of the foregoing example.

6.2.8 **Retrieval Using IN.** Get parts whose weight is any one of the following: 12, 16, 17.

```
SELECT P#, PNAME, COLOR, WEIGHT, CITY
FROM    P
WHERE   WEIGHT IN ( 12, 16, 17 )
```

Result:

P#	PNAME	COLOR	WEIGHT	CITY
P1	Nut	Red	12	London
P2	Bolt	Green	17	Paris
P3	Screw	Blue	17	Rome
P5	Cam	Blue	12	Paris

IN, like BETWEEN, is really just a shorthand. An IN predicate is logically equivalent to a predicate involving a sequence of individual comparisons all "ORed" together. For example, the foregoing SELECT statement is equivalent to the following:

```
SELECT P#, PNAME, COLOR, WEIGHT, CITY
FROM    P
WHERE   WEIGHT = 12
OR      WEIGHT = 16
OR      WEIGHT = 17
```

NOT IN is also available:

```
SELECT P#, PNAME, COLOR, WEIGHT, CITY
FROM    P
WHERE   WEIGHT NOT IN ( 12, 16, 17 )
```

Result:

P#	PNAME	COLOR	WEIGHT	CITY
P4	Screw	Red	14	London
P6	Cog	Red	19	London

Like IN, NOT IN is really just a shorthand. Exercise: Show the "expanded form" of the foregoing example.

6.2.9 **Retrieval Using LIKE.** Get all parts whose names begin with the letter C.

```
SELECT P#, PNAME, COLOR, WEIGHT, CITY
FROM    P
WHERE   PNAME LIKE 'C%'
```

Result:

P#	PNAME	COLOR	WEIGHT	CITY
P5	Cam	Blue	12	Paris
P6	Cog	Red	19	London

In general, a LIKE predicate takes the form

```
column LIKE constant [ ESCAPE character ]
```

where "column" must designate a column of type string (CHAR, VARCHAR, GRAPHIC, or VARGRAPHIC), and "constant" must be of a compatible data type. For a given record, the predicate evaluates to *true* if the value within the designated column conforms to the pattern specified by "constant." Provided no escape clause is specified, characters within "constant" are interpreted as follows:

- The _ character (break or underscore) stands for *any single character.*
- The % character (percent) stands for *any sequence of n characters* (where *n* may be zero).
- All other characters simply stand for themselves.

In the example, therefore, the SELECT statement will retrieve records from table P for which the PNAME value begins with the letter C and has any sequence of zero or more characters following that C.

Here are some more examples of LIKE:

`ADDRESS LIKE '%Berkeley%'`	—will evaluate to *true* if ADDRESS contains the string 'Berkeley' anywhere inside it
`S# LIKE 'S__'`	—will evaluate to *true* if S# is exactly 3 characters long and the 1st is an S
`PNAME LIKE '%c___'`	—will evaluate to *true* if PNAME is 4 characters long or more and the last but three is a c
`STRING LIKE '\_%'` `ESCAPE '\'`	—will evaluate to *true* if STRING begins with an underscore character (see below)

In this last example, the blackslash character "\" has been specified as the escape character, which means that the special interpretation given to the characters "_" and "%" can be disabled if desired by preceding such characters with a blackslash character.

NOT LIKE is also available for example:

`CITY NOT LIKE '%E%'`	—will evaluate to *true* if CITY does not contain an E

6.2.10 *Retrieval Involving NULL.*   Suppose for the sake of the example
that supplier S5 has a status of null, rather than 30. Get supplier numbers
for suppliers with status greater than 25.

```
SELECT S#
FROM    S
WHERE   STATUS > 25
```

Result: `S#`
        `--`
        `S3`

Supplier S5 does not qualify. As explained in Chapter 4, whenever one
of the operands of a comparison is null, then, regardless of the comparison
operator involved, the result of the comparison is *never* considered to be
true—even if the other operand is also null. In other words, if STATUS
happens to be null, then none of the following comparisons evaluates to
*true:**

```
STATUS > 25
STATUS <= 25
STATUS = 25
STATUS ~= 25
STATUS = NULL        [This is illegal syntax. See below.]
STATUS ~= NULL       [So is this.]
STATUS > NULL        [So is this.]
STATUS <= NULL       [So is this.]
```

Thus, if we issue the query

```
SELECT S#
FROM    S
WHERE   STATUS <= 25
```

and compare the result with that of the previous query, supplier S5 will not
appear in either of them. The result is:

```
S#
--
S1
S2
S4
```

A special predicate of the form

```
column IS [ NOT ] NULL
```

---

*As explained in Chapter 4, they all evaluate to the *unknown* truth value. The SE-
LECT statement retrieves records for which the WHERE predicate evaluates to
true, not to *false* and not to *unknown.*

is provided for testing for the presence [or absence] of null values. For example:

```
SELECT  S#
FROM    S
WHERE   STATUS IS NULL
```

Result: S#
       --
       S5

The syntax "STATUS = NULL" is illegal, because *nothing*—not even null itself—is considered to be equal to null (in the context of a WHERE or HAVING clause).

We note in conclusion that it is not possible to SELECT NULL; that is, the symbol NULL is not allowed in a SELECT clause. For example, the following is ***ILLEGAL***:

```
SELECT  P#, 'Weight =', NULL
FROM    P
WHERE   WEIGHT IS NULL
```

6.3 JOIN QUERIES

The ability to "join" two or more tables is one of the most powerful features of relational systems. In fact, it is the availability of the join operation, almost more than anything else, that distinguishes relational from nonrelational systems (see Appendix B). So what is a join? Loosely speaking, it is *a query in which data is retrieved from more than one table*. Here is a simple example.

6.3.1 Simple Equijoin.   Get all combinations of supplier and part information such that the supplier and part in question are located in the same city (i.e., are "colocated," to coin an ugly but convenient term).

```
SELECT  S.*, P.*
FROM    S, P
WHERE   S.CITY = P.CITY
```

Notice that the field references in the WHERE clause here *must* be qualified by the names of the containing tables (for otherwise they would be ambiguous). Result:

S#	SNAME	STATUS	S.CITY	P#	PNAME	COLOR	WEIGHT	P.CITY
S1	Smith	20	London	P1	Nut	Red	12	London
S1	Smith	20	London	P4	Screw	Red	14	London
S1	Smith	20	London	P6	Cog	Red	19	London
S2	Jones	10	Paris	P2	Bolt	Green	17	Paris
S2	Jones	10	Paris	P5	Cam	Blue	12	Paris

S#	SNAME	STATUS	S.CITY	P#	PNAME	COLOR	WEIGHT	P.CITY
S3	Blake	30	Paris	P2	Bolt	Green	17	Paris
S3	Blake	30	Paris	P5	Cam	Blue	12	Paris
S4	Clark	20	London	P1	Nut	Red	12	London
S4	Clark	20	London	P4	Screw	Red	14	London
S4	Clark	20	London	P6	Cog	Red	19	London

We have shown the two CITY columns in this result explicitly as S.CITY and P.CITY, to avoid ambiguity.

Explanation: It is clear from the English language statement of the problem that the required data comes from two tables, namely S and P. In the SQL formulation of the query, therefore, we first name both those tables in the FROM clause, and we then express the connexion between them (i.e., the fact that the CITY values must be equal) in the WHERE clause. To understand how this works, imagine yourself looking at two rows, one row from each of the two tables—say the two rows shown here:

S#	SNAME	STATUS	CITY		P#	PNAME	COLOR	WEIGHT	CITY
S1	Smith	20	London		P1	Nut	Red		12	London

|_____ identical _____|

From these two rows you can see that supplier S1 and part P1 are indeed "colocated." These two rows will generate the result row

S#	SNAME	STATUS	S.CITY	P#	PNAME	COLOR	WEIGHT	P.CITY
S1	Smith	20	London	P1	Nut	Red	12	London

because they satisfy the predicate in the WHERE clause (S.CITY = P.CITY). Similarly for all other pairs of rows having matching CITY values. Notice that supplier S5 (located in Athens) does not appear in the result, because there are no parts stored in Athens; likewise, part P3 (stored in Rome) also does not appear in the result, because there are no suppliers located in Rome.

The result of this query is said to be a *join* of tables S and P over matching CITY values. The term "join" is also used to refer to the operation of constructing such a result. The condition S.CITY = P.CITY is said to be a *join condition* or *join predicate.*

A number of further points arise in connexion with this example, some major, some minor.

■ There is no requirement that the fields in a join predicate be identically named, though they very often will be.

■ There is no requirement that the comparison operator in a join predicate be equality, though it very often will be. Examples of where it is not are given below (Example 6.3.2 and latter part of Example 6.3.6). If it is equality, then the join is called an *equijoin*.

- The WHERE clause in a join-SELECT can include other conditions in addition to the join predicate itself. Example 6.3.3 below illustrates this possibility.

- It is of course possible to SELECT just specified fields from a join, instead of necessarily having to SELECT all of them. Examples 6.3.4– 6.3.6 below illustrate this possibility.

- The expression

```
SELECT  S.*, P.*
FROM    S, P
   . . . . .
```

can be further abbreviated to simply

```
SELECT  *
FROM    S, P
   . . . . .
```

Alternatively, of course, it can be expanded to

```
SELECT  S#, SNAME, STATUS, S.CITY,
        P#, PNAME, COLOR, WEIGHT, P.CITY
FROM    S, P
   . . . . .
```

In this formulation, S.CITY and P.CITY in the SELECT clause *must* be referred to by their qualified names, as shown, because the unqualified name CITY would be ambiguous.

- The equijoin by definition must produce a result containing two identical columns. If one of those two columns is eliminated, what is left is called the *natural* join. To construct the natural join of S and P over cities in SQL, we could write:

```
SELECT  S#, SNAME, STATUS, S.CITY,
        P#, PNAME, COLOR, WEIGHT
FROM    S, P
WHERE   S.CITY = P.CITY
```

Natural join is probably the single most useful form of join—so much so, that we often use the unqualified term "join" to refer to this case specifically.

- It is also possible to form a join of three, four, . . . , or any number of tables (up to a maximum of 16 in SQL/DS). Example 6.3.5 below shows a join involving three tables.

- The following is an alternative (and helpful) way to think about how joins may conceptually be constructed. First, form the *Cartesian prod-*

uct of the tables listed in the FROM clause. The Cartesian product of a set of *n* tables is the table consisting of all possible rows *r*, such that *r* is the concatenation of a row from the first table, a row from the second table, . . . , and a row from the *n*th table. For example, the Cartesian product of table S and table P (in that order) is the following table (let us call it CP):

CP	S#	SNAME	STATUS	S.CITY	P#	PNAME	COLOR	WEIGHT	P.CITY
	S1	Smith	20	London	P1	Nut	Red	12	London
	S1	Smith	20	London	P2	Bolt	Green	17	Paris
	S1	Smith	20	London	P3	Screw	Blue	17	Rome
	S1	Smith	20	London	P4	Screw	Red	14	London
	S1	Smith	20	London	P5	Cam	Blue	12	Paris
	S1	Smith	20	London	P6	Cog	Red	19	London
	S2	Jones	10	Paris	P1	Nut	Red	12	London
	.	.	.	.	.	.	.	.	.
	.	.	.	.	.	.	.	.	.
	.	.	.	.	.	.	.	.	.
	S5	Adams	30	Athens	P6	Cog	Red	19	London

The complete table contains 5*6 = 30 rows.

Now eliminate from this Cartesian product all those rows that do not satisfy the join predicate. What is left is the required join. In the case at hand, we eliminate from CP all those rows in which S.CITY is not equal to P.CITY; and what is left is exactly the join shown earlier.

By the way, it is perfectly possible (though perhaps unusual) to formulate a SQL query whose result is a Cartesian product. For example:

```
SELECT  S.*, P.*
FROM    S, P
```

Result: Table CP as shown above.

6.3.2 *Greater-Than Join.*

Get all combinations of supplier and part information such that the supplier city follows the part city in alphabetical order.

```
SELECT  S.*, P.*
FROM    S, P
WHERE   S.CITY > P.CITY
```

Result:

S#	SNAME	STATUS	S.CITY	P#	PNAME	COLOR	WEIGHT	P.CITY
S2	Jones	10	Paris	P1	Nut	Red	12	London
S2	Jones	10	Paris	P4	Screw	Red	14	London
S2	Jones	10	Paris	P6	Cog	Red	19	London
S3	Blake	30	Paris	P1	Nut	Red	12	London
S3	Blake	30	Paris	P4	Screw	Red	14	London
S3	Blake	30	Paris	P6	Cog	Red	19	London

6.3.3   *Join Query with an Additional Condition.*   Get all combinations of supplier information and part information where the supplier and part concerned are colocated, but omitting suppliers with status 20.

```
SELECT  S.*, P.*
FROM    S, P
WHERE   S.CITY = P.CITY
AND     S.STATUS ~= 20
```

Result:

S#	SNAME	STATUS	S.CITY	P#	PNAME	COLOR	WEIGHT	P.CITY
S2	Jones	10	Paris	P2	Bolt	Green	17	Paris
S2	Jones	10	Paris	P5	Cam	Blue	12	Paris
S3	Blake	30	Paris	P2	Bolt	Green	17	Paris
S3	Blake	30	Paris	P5	Cam	Blue	12	Paris

6.3.4   *Retrieving Specified Fields from a Join.*   Get all supplier-number/ part-number combinations such that the supplier and part in question are colocated.

```
SELECT  S.S#, P.P#
FROM    S, P
WHERE   S.CITY = P.CITY
```

Result:

S#	P#
S1	P1
S1	P4
S1	P6
S2	P2
S2	P5
S3	P2
S3	P5
S4	P1
S4	P4
S4	P6

6.3.5   *Join of Three Tables.*   Get all pairs of city names such that a supplier located in the first city supplies a part stored in the second city. For example, supplier S1 supplies part P1; supplier S1 is located in London, and part P1 is stored in London; so (London,London) is a pair of cities in the result.

```
SELECT  DISTINCT S.CITY, P.CITY
FROM    S, SP, P
WHERE   S.S# = SP.S#
AND     SP.P# = P.P#
```

Result:

S.CITY	P.CITY
London	London
London	Paris
London	Rome
Paris	London
Paris	Paris

As an exercise, the reader should decide which particular supplier/part combinations give rise to which particular result rows in this example.

6.3.6 *Joining a Table with Itself.*   Get all pairs of supplier numbers such that the two suppliers concerned are colocated.

```
SELECT  FIRST.S#, SECOND.S#
FROM    S FIRST, S SECOND
WHERE   FIRST.CITY = SECOND.CITY
```

This query involves a join of table S with itself (over matching cities), as we now explain. Suppose for a moment that we had two separate copies of table S, the "first" copy and the "second" copy. Then the logic of the query is as follows: We need to be able to examine all possible pairs of supplier rows, one from the first copy of S and one from the second, and to retrieve the two supplier numbers from such a pair of rows when the city values are equal. We therefore need to be able to reference two supplier rows at the same time. In order to distinguish between the two references, we introduce two *range variables* FIRST and SECOND, each of which "ranges over" table S. At any particular time, FIRST represents some row from the "first" copy of table S, and SECOND represents some row from the "second" copy.* The result of the query is found by examining all possible pairs of FIRST/SECOND values and checking the WHERE predicate in every case:

```
S#   S#
--   --
S1   S1
S1   S4
S2   S2
S2   S3
S3   S2
S3   S3
S4   S1
S4   S4
S5   S5
```

We can tidy up this result by extending the WHERE clause as follows:

```
SELECT  FIRST.S#, SECOND.S#
FROM    S FIRST, S SECOND
WHERE   FIRST.CITY = SECOND.CITY
AND     FIRST.S# < SECOND.S#
```

The effect of the condition FIRST.S# < SECOND.S# is twofold: (a) It eliminates pairs of supplier numbers of the form (x,x); (b) it guarantees that the pairs (x,y) and (y,x) will not both appear.

---

*Of course, SQL/DS does not really construct two physical copies of the table. Our explanation is purely conceptual in nature. Note also that the IBM manuals use the (grotesquely!) misleading term "join variable" (among others) in place of the more orthodox, and more accurate, term "range variable."

Result:

```
S#   S#
--   --
S1   S4
S2   S3
```

This is the first example we have seen in which the explicit use of range variables has been necessary. However, it is never wrong to introduce range variables, even when they are not absolutely required, and sometimes they can help to make the statement clearer. (They can also save writing, if table names are on the lengthy side.) In general, a range variable is a variable that ranges over some specified table—i.e., a variable whose only permitted values are the rows of that table. In other words, if range variable R ranges over table T, then, at any given time, R represents some row or record r of T. For example, the query "Get supplier number and status for suppliers in Paris" (the example from the beginning of Section 6.2) could be expressed as follows:

```
SELECT  SX.S#, SX.STATUS
FROM    S SX
WHERE   SX.CITY = 'Paris'
```

The range variable here is SX, and it ranges over table S. The SELECT statement can be paraphrased:

"For each possible value of the range variable SX, retrieve the S# and STATUS components of that value, if and only if the CITY component has the value Paris."

As a matter of fact, SQL *always* requires queries to be formulated in terms of range variables. If no such variables are specified explicitly, then SQL assumes the existence of *implicit* variables with the same name(s) as the corresponding table(s). For example, the query

```
SELECT  *
FROM    S
```

is treated by SQL as if it had been expressed as follows:

```
SELECT  S.*
FROM    S S
```

This latter formulation at least arguably makes it a little clearer that the symbol "S" in the expression "S.*" really means *range variable* S, not *table* S.

6.4 SUMMARY

We have now come to the end of the first of our two chapters on the SELECT statement. We have illustrated:

- The SELECT clause itself, including the use of general scalar expressions and "SELECT *"
- The use of DISTINCT to eliminate duplicates, including the use of DISTINCT with a join
- The FROM clause (with one or more tables), including the use of range variables
- The use of ORDER BY to order the result
- The WHERE clause, including:
  - simple comparisons
  - Boolean operators AND, OR, NOT
  - special operators [NOT] BETWEEN, [NOT] IN, [NOT] LIKE
  - special comparison "field IS [NOT] NULL"
  - join predicates

In the next chapter we will consider some more complex features of the SELECT statement—to be specific, the subquery feature, the existential quantifier, the use of aggregate functions, and the UNION operator.

EXERCISES

All of the following exercises are based on the suppliers-parts-projects database (see the exercises in Chapter 5). In each one, you are asked to write a SELECT statement for the indicated query. For convenience we repeat the structure of the database below:

```
S    ( S#, SNAME, STATUS, CITY )
P    ( P#, PNAME, COLOR, WEIGHT, CITY )
J    ( J#, JNAME, CITY )
SPJ  ( S#, P#, J#, QTY )
```

Simple Queries

6.1 Get full details of all projects.

6.2 Get full details of all projects in London.

6.3 Get supplier numbers for suppliers who supply project J1, in supplier number order.

6.4 Get all shipments where the quantity is in the range 300 to 750 inclusive.

6.5 Get a list of all part-color/part-city combinations, with duplicate color/city pairs eliminated.

6.6 Get all shipments where the quantity is nonnull.

6.7 Get project numbers and cities where the city has an "o" as the second letter of its name.

Joins

6.8 Get all supplier-number/part-number/project-number triples such that the indicated supplier, part, and project are all colocated.

6.9 Get all supplier-number/part-number/project-number triples such that the indicated supplier, part, and project are not colocated.

6.10 Get all supplier-number/part-number/project-number triples such that no two of the indicated supplier, part, and project are located in the same city.

6.11 Get part numbers for parts supplied by a supplier in London.

6.12 Get part numbers for parts supplied by a supplier in London to a project in London.

6.13 Get all pairs of city names such that a supplier in the first city supplies a project in the second city.

6.14 Get part numbers for parts supplied to any project by a supplier in the same city as that project.

6.15 Get project numbers for projects supplied by at least one supplier not in the same city.

6.16 Get all pairs of part numbers such that some supplier supplies both the indicated parts.

ANSWERS TO SELECTED EXERCISES

The following answers are not necessarily the only ones possible.

6.1
```
SELECT J#, JNAME, CITY
FROM   J
```

Or:
```
SELECT *
FROM   J
```

6.2
```
SELECT J#, JNAME, CITY
FROM   J
WHERE  CITY = 'London'
```

Or:
```
SELECT *
FROM   J
WHERE  CITY = 'London'
```

6.3 ```
SELECT DISTINCT S#
FROM   SPJ
WHERE   J# = 'J1'
ORDER   BY S#
```

**6.4** ```
SELECT  S#, P#, J#, QTY
FROM    SPJ
WHERE   QTY >= 300
AND     QTY <= 750
```

Or: ```
SELECT S#, P#, J#, QTY
FROM   SPJ
WHERE   QTY BETWEEN 300 AND 750
```

**6.5** ```
SELECT  DISTINCT COLOR, CITY
FROM    P
```

6.6 ```
SELECT S#, P#, J#, QTY
FROM   SPJ
WHERE   QTY IS NOT NULL
```

The foregoing is the "official" answer. However, the following will also work:

```
SELECT  S#, P#, J#, QTY
FROM    SPJ
WHERE   QTY = QTY
```

6.7 ```
SELECT J#, CITY
FROM   J
WHERE   CITY LIKE '_o%'
```

Or: ```
SELECT J#, CITY
FROM   J
WHERE   SUBSTR (CITY, 2, 1) = 'o'
```

**6.8** ```
SELECT  S#, P#, J#
FROM    S, P, J
WHERE   S.CITY = P.CITY
AND     P.CITY = J.CITY
```

6.9 ```
SELECT S#, P#, J#
FROM   S, P, J
WHERE   NOT
        (S.CITY = P.CITY AND P.CITY = J.CITY)
```

Or: ```
SELECT  S#, P#, J#
FROM    S, P, J
WHERE   S.CITY ~= P.CITY
OR      P.CITY ~= J.CITY
```

6.10 ```
SELECT S#, P#, J#
FROM   S, P, J
WHERE   S.CITY ~= P.CITY
AND   P.CITY ~= J.CITY
AND   J.CITY ~= S.CITY
```
```

6.11 SELECT DISTINCT P#
    FROM   SPJ, S
    WHERE SPJ.S# = S.S#
    AND   CITY = 'London'

6.12 SELECT DISTINCT P#
    FROM   SPJ, S, J
    WHERE SPJ.S# = S.S#
    AND   SPJ.J# = J.J#
    AND   S.CITY = 'London'
    AND   J.CITY = 'London'

6.13 SELECT DISTINCT S.CITY, J.CITY
    FROM   S, SPJ, J
    WHERE S.S# = SPJ.S#
    AND   SPJ.J# = J.J#

6.14 SELECT DISTINCT P#
    FROM   SPJ, S, J
    WHERE SPJ.S# = S.S#
    AND   SPJ.J# = J.J#
    AND   S.CITY = J.CITY

6.15 SELECT DISTINCT J.J#
    FROM   SPJ, S, J
    WHERE SPJ.S# = S.S#
    AND   SPJ.J# = J.J#
    AND   S.CITY ¬= J.CITY

6.16 SELECT SPJX.P#, SPJY.P#
    FROM   SPJ SPJX, SPJ SPJY
    WHERE SPJX.S# = SPJY.S#
    AND   SPJX.P# > SPJY.P#

7

♦

Data Manipulation II:
Retrieval Operations
(Continued)

7.1 INTRODUCTION

In this chapter we complete our treatment of the SQL SELECT statement.
The plan of the chapter is as follows:

- Section 7.2 introduces the concept of *subqueries* or *nested SELECTs*.
  As a matter of historical interest, we remark that it was the fact that
  one SELECT could be nested inside another that was the original justification for the "Structured" in the name "Structured Query Language"; however, later additions to the language have made nested
  SELECTs per se very much less important than they used to be.

- Section 7.3 is concerned with the *existential quantifier* EXISTS, a feature that (in this writer's opinion) ranks with join as one of the most
  important and fundamental features of the entire SQL language—
  though not perhaps the most easy to use.

- Section 7.4 discusses the *aggregate functions* COUNT, SUM, AVG, etc.; in particular, it describes the use of the GROUP BY and HAVING clauses in connexion with those functions.*

- Section 7.5 discusses the UNION operator.

- Finally, in an attempt to tie together a number of the ideas introduced in this and the previous chapter, Section 7.6 presents an example of a very complex SELECT and shows in principle how that SELECT might be processed by SQL/DS.

As you can see, the chapter is rather long, and you may wish to omit some of the more complicated portions on a first reading. However, you should probably read at least the first part of each section on your first pass through. One of the reasons for the length of the chapter is that SQL is a highly redundant language, in the sense that it frequently provides several different ways of formulating the same query. Since we are trying to be reasonably comprehensive in our coverage of that language, the chapter necessarily contains a certain amount of redundancy also.

One final introductory remark (which may not be very intelligible until you have read the body of the chapter): Despite our general objective of comprehensiveness, we deliberately do not include any detailed description of the ANY and ALL versions of the comparison operators (>ANY, =ALL, etc.). The reader who requires such a detailed description is referred to the IBM manuals. Our reasons for excluding those operators from this book are that they are entirely superfluous—there is no query that can be formulated with them that cannot equally well (in fact, better) be formulated using EXISTS—and furthermore they are confusing and (in this writer's opinion) dangerously error-prone. For example, the (valid) SELECT statement

```
SELECT  S.S#
FROM    S
WHERE   S.CITY ~=ANY ( SELECT P.CITY
                       FROM    P      )
```

does *not* select supplier numbers for suppliers whose city is "not equal to any" part city. The equivalent EXISTS formulation makes the correct interpretation clear:

```
SELECT  S.S#
FROM    S
WHERE   EXISTS ( SELECT P.CITY
                 FROM    P
                 WHERE   P.CITY ~= S.CITY )
```

---

*The official SQL/DS term for "aggregate function" is "column function."

("select supplier numbers for suppliers such that there exists some part city that is different from the supplier city"). The natural intuitive interpretation of ~ =ANY as "not equal to any" is both incorrect and very misleading. Analogous criticisms apply to all of the ANY and ALL operators.

   Note: For reasons of compatibility with the SQL standard, SOME was added to Version 2 of SQL/DS as an alternative spelling for ANY. Needless to say, however, the foregoing criticisms apply to the SOME versions of the operators also.

7.2 SUBQUERIES

In this section we discuss *subqueries* or *nested SELECTs*. Loosely speaking, a subquery is a SELECT–FROM–WHERE expression that is nested inside another such expression.* Subqueries are typically used to represent the set of values to be searched via an IN predicate, as the following example illustrates.

7.2.1 Simple Subquery.   Get supplier names for suppliers who supply part P2.

```
SELECT SNAME
FROM   S
WHERE  S# IN
     ( SELECT S#
       FROM   SP
       WHERE  P# = 'P2' )
```

Result: SNAME

       Smith
       Jones
       Blake
       Clark

   Explanation: The system evaluates the overall query (conceptually, at any rate) by evaluating the nested subquery first. That subquery returns the set of supplier *numbers* for suppliers who supply part P2, namely the set (S1,S2,S3,S4). The original query is thus equivalent to the following simpler query:

```
SELECT SNAME
FROM   S
WHERE  S# IN
     ( 'S1', 'S2', 'S3', 'S4' )
```

Hence the result is as shown earlier.

---

*A subquery may also include GROUP BY and HAVING clauses. ORDER BY and UNION are illegal, however.

The implicit name qualification in this example merits some additional discussion. Observe in particular that the "S#" to the left of the IN is implicitly qualified by "S", whereas the "S#" in the subquery is implicitly qualified by "SP". The general rule is as follows: An unqualified field name is assumed to be qualified by a table name (or range variable name— see Examples 7.2.3–7.2.5 below) that appears in the (unique) FROM clause that is most immediately part of the same query or subquery. In the case of the S# to the left of the IN, that clause is "FROM S"; in the case of the S# in the subquery, it is the clause "FROM SP". By way of clarification, we repeat the original query with all assumed qualifications shown explicitly:

```
SELECT  S.SNAME
FROM    S
WHERE   S.S# IN
      ( SELECT  SP.S#
        FROM    SP
        WHERE   SP.P# = 'P2' )
```

It is always possible to override the implicit assumptions with explicit qualifications (see Examples 7.2.3–7.2.5 below). In fact, many people feel that explicit qualification should *always* be used, even when it is strictly unnecessary, simply as a matter of good discipline. A good rule of thumb is: When in doubt, qualify.

There is one more (important) point to make before we move on to our next subquery example: The original problem—"Get supplier names for suppliers who supply part P2"—can equally well be expressed as a *join* query, as follows:

```
SELECT  S.SNAME
FROM    S, SP
WHERE   S.S# = SP.S#
AND     SP.P# = 'P2'
```

Explanation: The join of S and SP over supplier numbers consists of a table of 12 rows (one for each row in SP), in which each row consists of the corresponding row from SP extended with SNAME, STATUS, and CITY values for the supplier identified by the S# value in that row. Of these twelve rows, four are for part P2; the final result is thus obtained by extracting the SNAME values from those four rows.

The two formulations of the original query—one using a subquery, one using a join—are equally correct. It is purely a matter of taste as to which formulation a given user might prefer. At least, this statement is true in principle; unfortunately, there is no guarantee that the two formulations will *perform* equally well. In fact, the IBM manuals seem to indicate that the subquery formulation will never perform better than the join formulation and may very well perform worse, and hence that subqueries should generally be avoided. This fact is somewhat ironic, given that subqueries were the original justification for the SQL language in the first place.

7.2.2 Subquery with Multiple Levels of Nesting.   Get supplier names for suppliers who supply at least one red part.

```
SELECT  SNAME
FROM    S
WHERE   S# IN
      ( SELECT S#
        FROM    SP
        WHERE   P# IN
              ( SELECT P#
                FROM    P
                WHERE   COLOR = 'Red' ) )
```

Result: SNAME
```
-----
Smith
Jones
Clark
```

Explanation: The innermost subquery evaluates to the set (P1,P4,P6). The next outermost subquery evaluates in turn to the set (S1,S2,S4). Last, the outermost SELECT evaluates to the final result shown. In general, subqueries can be nested to any depth.

To make sure you understand this example, try the following exercises:

(a) Rewrite the query with all name qualifications shown explicitly.

(b) Write an equivalent join formulation of the same query.

7.2.3 Correlated Subquery.   Get supplier names for suppliers who supply part P2 (same as Example 7.2.1).

We show another solution to this problem in order to illustrate another point.

```
SELECT  SNAME
FROM    S
WHERE   'P2' IN
      ( SELECT P#
        FROM    SP
        WHERE   S# = S.S# )
```

Explanation: In the last line here, the unqualified reference to S# is implicitly qualified by SP; the other reference is *explicitly* qualified by S. This example differs from the preceding ones in that the inner subquery cannot be evaluated once and for all before the outer query is evaluated, because that inner subquery depends on a *variable,* namely S.S#, whose value changes as the system examines different rows of table S. Conceptually, therefore, evaluation proceeds as follows:

(a) The system examines the first row of table S; let us assume this is the row for S1. The variable S.S# thus currently has the value S1, so the system evaluates the inner subquery

```
( SELECT  P#
  FROM    SP
  WHERE   S# = 'S1' )
```

to obtain the set (P1,P2,P3,P4,P5,P6). Now it can complete its processing for S1; it will select the SNAME value for S1, namely Smith, if and only if P2 is in this set (which of course it is).

(b) Next the system moves on to repeat this kind of processing for the next supplier, and so on, until all rows of table S have been dealt with.

A subquery such as the one in this example is said to be a *correlated* subquery. A correlated subquery is one whose value depends upon some variable that receives its value in some outer query; such a subquery therefore has to be evaluated repeatedly (once for each value of the variable in question), instead of once and for all. We show another example of a correlated subquery below (Example 7.2.5); several further examples are given in Sections 7.3 and 7.4.

Some users like to use explicit range variables in conjunction with correlated subqueries, in order to make the correlation clearer (see Example 6.3.6 in Chapter 6 if you need to refresh your memory concerning range variables). For example:

```
SELECT  SX.SNAME
FROM    S SX
WHERE   'P2' IN
        ( SELECT  P#
          FROM    SP
          WHERE   S# = SX.S# )
```

The range variable in this example is SX, introduced in the FROM clause and then used as an explicit qualifier in the WHERE clause in the subquery (and in the outer SELECT clause). The operation of the overall statement can now be more clearly (and more accurately) explained as follows:

▪ SX is a variable that ranges over the records of table S (i.e., a variable that, at any given time, represents some record of table S).

▪ For each possible value of SX in turn, do the following:
  ▪ evaluate the subquery to obtain a set, p say, of part numbers;
  ▪ add the current value of SX.SNAME to the result set, if and only if P2 is in the set p.

In the previous version of this query, the symbol "S" was really performing two different functions: It stood for the suppliers base table itself (of course), and also for a variable that ranged over the records of that base table. As already stated, many users find it clearer to use two different symbols to distinguish between the two different functions.

It is never wrong to introduce a range variable, and sometimes it is essential (see Example 7.2.5 below).

7.2.4 Subquery and Outer Query Referring to Same Table.
Get supplier numbers for suppliers who supply at least one part supplied by supplier S2.

```
SELECT DISTINCT S#
FROM    SP
WHERE   P# IN
      ( SELECT P#
        FROM    SP
        WHERE   S# = 'S2' )
```

Result:
```
s#
--
S1
S2
S3
S4
```

Notice here that references to SP in the subquery do not mean the same thing as references to SP in the outer query. The two SP's are really *different variables*. Explicit range variables can be used to make this fact explicit:

```
SELECT DISTINCT SPX.S#
FROM    SP SPX
WHERE   SPX.P# IN
      ( SELECT SPY.P#
        FROM    SP SPY
        WHERE   SPY.S# = 'S2' )
```

Equivalent join query:

```
SELECT DISTINCT SPX.S#
FROM    SP SPX, SP SPY
WHERE   SPX.P# = SPY.P#
AND     SPY.S# = 'S2'
```

Notice that at least one explicit range variable *must* be introduced in this latter formulation.

7.2.5 Correlated Subquery and Outer Query Referring to Same Table.
Get part numbers for all parts supplied by more than one supplier. (Another solution to this problem is given later as Example 7.4.9.)

```
SELECT DISTINCT SPX.P#
FROM    SP SPX
WHERE   SPX.P# IN
      ( SELECT SPY.P#
        FROM    SP SPY
        WHERE   SPY.S# ~= SPX.S# )
```

Result:
```
P#
--
P1
P2
P4
P5
```

The operation of this query can be explained as follows: "For each row in turn, say SPX, of table SP, extract the P# value, if and only if that P# value appears in some row, say SPY, of table SP whose S# value is *not* equal to the S# value in row SPX." Note again that at least one explicit range variable *must* be used in this query.

7.2.6 Subquery with Comparison Operator Other Than IN.

Get supplier numbers for suppliers who are located in the same city as supplier S1.

```
SELECT S#
FROM    S
WHERE   CITY =
      ( SELECT CITY
        FROM    S
        WHERE   S# = 'S1' )
```

Result:
```
S#
--
S1
S4
```

Sometimes the user may know that a given subquery should return exactly one value, as in this example. In such a case a simple scalar comparison operator (such as $=$, $>$, etc.) can be used in place of the more usual IN. However, an error will occur if the subquery in fact returns more than one value and IN has not been used. An error will *not* occur if the subquery returns no values at all; instead, the comparison is treated exactly as if the subquery had returned a null. In other words, if x is a variable, then the comparison

```
x  simple-comparison-operator ( subquery )    ,
```

where "subquery" returns an empty set, evaluates, not to *true* or *false,* but to the *unknown* truth value. See Chapter 6, Example 6.2.10, and Chapter 4 for more discussion of the unknown truth value.

Note, incidentally, that the comparison in the foregoing example must be written as shown, with the subquery following the comparison operator. In other words, the following is illegal:

```
SELECT  S#
FROM    S
WHERE   (SELECT  CITY
         FROM    S
         WHERE   S# = 'S1') = CITY
```

Note also that, although subqueries in general can include GROUP BY and HAVING clauses (see Section 7.4), those clauses are not permitted when the subquery appears in conjunction with a simple scalar comparison operator such as $=$, $<$, etc.

7.3   THE EXISTENTIAL QUANTIFIER

7.3.1   *Query Using EXISTS.*   Get supplier names for suppliers who supply part P2 (same as Examples 7.2.1 and 7.2.3).

```
SELECT  SNAME
FROM    S
WHERE   EXISTS
      ( SELECT  *
        FROM    SP
        WHERE   S# = S.S#
        AND     P# = 'P2' )
```

Explanation: EXISTS here represents the *existential quantifier,* a notion borrowed from formal logic. Let the symbol "*x*" designate some arbitrary variable. In logic, then, the *existentially quantified predicate*

```
EXISTS x ( predicate-involving-x )
```

evaluates to *true* if and only if "predicate-involving-x" is *true* for some value of the variable x. For example, suppose the variable x stands for any integer in the range 1 to 10 (i.e., x ranges over the set of integers from 1 to 10). Then the predicate

```
EXISTS x ( x < 5 )
```

evaluates to *true*. By contrast, the predicate

```
EXISTS x ( x < 0 )
```

evaluates to *false*.

In SQL, an existentially quantified predicate is represented by an expression of the form "EXISTS (SELECT * FROM . . .)". Such an expression evaluates to *true* if and only if the result of evaluating the subquery represented by the "SELECT * FROM . . . " is not empty—in other words, if and only if there exists a record in the FROM table of the subquery satisfying the WHERE condition of that subquery. (In practice, that subquery will always be of the correlated variety.)

To see how this works out in the example at hand, consider each SNAME value in turn and see whether it causes the existence test to evaluate to *true*. Suppose the first SNAME value is Smith, so that the corresponding S# value is S1. Is the set of SP records having S# equal to S1 and P# equal to P2 empty? If the answer is no, then there exists an SP record with S# equal to S1 and P# equal to P2, and so Smith should be one of the values retrieved. Similarly for each of the other SNAME values.

Although this first example merely shows another way of formulating a query for a problem that we already know how to handle in SQL (using either join or IN), in general EXISTS is one of the most important features of the entire SQL language. In fact, any query that can be expressed using IN can alternatively be formulated using EXISTS; however, the converse is not true (see Example 7.3.3 below for an illustration).

7.3.2   *Query Using NOT EXISTS.*   Get supplier names for suppliers who do not supply part P2 (inverse of Example 7.3.1).

```
SELECT  SNAME
FROM    S
WHERE   NOT EXISTS
      ( SELECT  *
        FROM    SP
        WHERE   S# = S.S#
        AND     P# = 'P2' )
```

Result: SNAME

         Adams

The query may be paraphrased: "Select supplier names for suppliers such that there does not exist a shipment relating them to part P2." Notice how easy it is to convert the solution to the previous problem (Example 7.3.1) into this solution.

Incidentally, the parenthesized subquery in an EXISTS expression does not necessarily have to involve the "SELECT *" form of SELECT; it may, for example, be of the form "SELECT field . . . ". In practice, however, it almost always will be of the "SELECT * " form, as our examples have already suggested.

7.3.3   *Query Using NOT EXISTS.*   Get supplier names for suppliers who supply all parts.

There are two quantifiers commonly encountered in logic, EXISTS and

FORALL. FORALL is the *universal* quantifier. In logic, the *universally quantified predicate*

```
FORALL x ( predicate-involving-x )
```

evaluates to *true* if and only if "predicate-involving-*x*" is *true* for all values of the variable *x*. For example, if (again) the variable *x* stands for any integer in the range 1 to 10, then the predicate

```
FORALL x ( x < 100 )
```

evaluates to *true,* whereas the predicate

```
FORALL x ( x < 5 )
```

evaluates to *false.*

FORALL is fundamentally what is needed to express the query at hand; what we would like to say is something like "Select supplier names where, FORALL parts, there EXISTS an SP record saying that the supplier supplies the part." Unfortunately, SQL does not directly support FORALL. However, any predicate involving FORALL can always be converted into an equivalent predicate involving EXISTS instead, by virtue of the following identity:

```
FORALL x ( p ) ≡ NOT ( EXISTS x ( NOT ( p ) ) )
```

Here *p* is any predicate involving the variable *x*. For example, suppose once again that *x* stands for any integer in the range 1 to 10. Then the predicate

```
FORALL x ( x < 100 )
```

(which of course evaluates to *true*) is equivalent to the predicate

```
NOT ( EXISTS x ( NOT ( x < 100 ) ) )
```

("there does not exist an *x* such that it is not the case that *x* is less than 100"—i.e., "there is no *x* such that *x* is greater than or equal to 100"). Likewise, the predicate

```
FORALL x ( x < 5 )
```

(which is *false*) is equivalent to the predicate

```
NOT ( EXISTS x ( NOT ( x < 5 ) ) )
```

("there does not exist an *x* such that it is not the case that *x* is less than 5"—i.e., "there is no *x* such that *x* is greater than or equal to 5").

As another example, suppose the variables x and y represent real numbers. Then the predicate

```
FORALL x ( EXISTS y ( y > x ) )
```

(which is *true*) is equivalent to

```
NOT ( EXISTS x ( NOT ( EXISTS y ( y > x ) ) ) )
```

("there is no real number x such that there is no real number y such that y is greater than x").*

Turning now to the problem at hand, we can convert the expression "Supplier names where, FORALL parts, there EXISTS an SP record saying that the supplier supplies the part" into the equivalent expression "Supplier names where NOT EXISTS a part such that NOT EXISTS an SP record saying that the supplier supplies the part." Hence the SQL formulation is:

```
SELECT SNAME
FROM    S
WHERE   NOT EXISTS
      ( SELECT *
        FROM    P
        WHERE   NOT EXISTS
              ( SELECT *
                FROM    SP
                WHERE   S# = S.S#
                AND     P# = P.P# ) )
```

```
Result: SNAME
        -----
        Smith
```

The query may be paraphrased: "Select supplier names for suppliers such that there does not exist a part that they do not supply." In general, the easiest way to tackle complicated queries such as this one is probably to write them in a "pseudoSQL" form with FORALL quantifiers first, and then convert them, more or less mechanically, into real SQL involving NOT EXISTS instead.

7.3.4 Query Using NOT EXISTS.   Get supplier names for suppliers who supply at least all those parts supplied by supplier S2.

One way to tackle this (complex) problem is to break it down into a set

---

*Incidentally, this example illustrates the important point that if the predicate involves both FORALL and EXISTS, then the order of quantifiers matters. The expression FORALL x (EXISTS y ($y > x$)) is *true*. However, the expression EXISTS y (FORALL x ($y > x$)) ("there is a real number y such that, for all real numbers x, y is greater than x"—i.e., "there exists a number greater than all other numbers"), which is obtained from the first expression by simply inverting the order of the quantifiers, is *false*.

of simpler problems and deal with them one at a time. Thus we can first
discover the set of part numbers for parts supplied by supplier S2:

```
SELECT  P#
FROM    SP
WHERE   S# = 'S2'
```

Result: P#
        --
        P1
        P2

Using CREATE TABLE and INSERT (to be discussed in Chapter 8),
it is possible to save this result in a table in the database, say table TEMP.
Then we can go on to discover the set of supplier names for suppliers who
supply all parts listed in TEMP (very much as in Example 7.3.3):

```
SELECT  SNAME
FROM    S
WHERE   NOT EXISTS
        ( SELECT *
        FROM    TEMP
        WHERE   NOT EXISTS
                ( SELECT *
                FROM    SP
                WHERE   SP.S# = S.S#
                AND     SP.P# = TEMP.P# ) )
```

Result: S#
        --
        S1
        S2

Table TEMP can now be dropped.

It is often a good idea to handle complex queries in this step-at-a-time
manner, for ease of understanding. However, it is also possible to express
the entire query as a single SELECT, eliminating the need for TEMP entirely:

```
SELECT  SNAME
FROM    S
WHERE   NOT EXISTS
        ( SELECT *
        FROM    SP SPY
        WHERE   S# = 'S2'
        AND     NOT EXISTS
                ( SELECT *
                FROM    SP SPZ
                WHERE   SPZ.S# = S.S#
                AND     SPZ.P# = SPY.P# ) )
```

7.3.5   *Query Using Implication.*   Get supplier names for suppliers who
supply at least all those parts supplied by supplier S2 (same as previous
example).

We use this example again to illustrate another very useful concept, that of *logical implication*. The original problem can be rephrased as follows: "Get supplier names for suppliers (S*x*, say) such that, FORALL parts P*y*, IF supplier S2 supplies part P*y*, THEN supplier S*x* supplies part P*y*." The expression

```
IF p THEN q
```

(where *p* and *q* are predicates) is a *logical implication predicate.* It is defined to be equivalent to the predicate

```
NOT ( p )   OR   q
```

In other words, the implication "IF *p* THEN *q*" (also read as "*p* IMPLIES *q*") is *false* if and only if *q* is *false* and *p* is *true,* as the truth table below indicates:

```
p  |  q  |  IF p THEN q
---+-----+--------------
T  |  T  |      T
T  |  F  |      F
F  |  T  |      T
F  |  F  |      T
```

Note: The value of "IF *p* THEN *q*" if *p* or *q* is *unknown* is left as an exercise for the reader.

Many problems are very naturally expressed in English in terms of logical implication (see the exercises at the end of this chapter for several examples). SQL does not support implication directly; but the foregoing definition shows how any predicate involving implication can be converted into another that does not. For example, let *p* be the predicate "Supplier S2 supplies part P*y*," and let *q* be the predicate "Supplier S*x* supplies part P*y*." Then the predicate

```
IF p THEN q
```

is equivalent to the predicate

```
NOT ( supplier S2 supplies part Py )
OR  ( supplier Sx supplies part Py )
```

or, in SQL terms,

```
NOT EXISTS
   ( SELECT *
     FROM    SP SPY
     WHERE   SPY.S# = 'S2' )
OR  EXISTS
   ( SELECT *
     FROM    SP SPZ
     WHERE   SPZ.S# = Sx
     AND     SPZ.P# = SPY.P# )
```

Hence the predicate

```
FORALL Py ( IF p THEN q )    ,
```

which is equivalent to

```
NOT EXISTS Py ( NOT ( IF p THEN q ) )   ,
```

that is, to

```
NOT EXISTS Py ( NOT ( NOT ( p )  OR  q ) )   ,
```

becomes

```
NOT EXISTS Py ( p  AND  NOT  ( q ) )   ,
```

or, in SQL terms,

```
NOT EXISTS
  ( SELECT *
    FROM    SP SPY
    WHERE   SPY.S# = 'S2'
    AND     NOT EXISTS
          ( SELECT *
            FROM    SP SPZ
            WHERE   SPZ.S# = Sx
            AND     SPZ.P# = SPY.P# ) )
```

Hence the overall query becomes

```
SELECT SNAME
FROM    S
WHERE   NOT EXISTS
      ( SELECT *
        FROM    SP SPY
        WHERE   SPY.S# = 'S2'
        AND     NOT EXISTS
              ( SELECT *
                FROM    SP SPZ
                WHERE   SPZ.S# = S.S#
                AND     SPZ.P# = SPY.P# ) )
```

which is as shown before, under Example 7.3.4. Thus the notion of implication provides the basis for a systematic approach to a certain class of (rather complicated) queries and their conversion into an equivalent SQL form. Exercises 7.12–7.18 at the end of the chapter provide practice in that approach.

7.4 AGGREGATE FUNCTIONS

Although quite powerful in many ways, the SELECT statement as so far described is still inadequate for many practical problems. For example, even a query as simple as "How many suppliers are there?" cannot be expressed using only the constructs introduced up till now. SQL therefore provides a number of special *aggregate* (or *column*) *functions* to enhance its basic retrieval power. The aggregate functions currently available are COUNT, SUM, AVG, MAX, and MIN.* Apart from the special case of "COUNT(*)" (see below), each of these functions operates on the collection of scalar values in one column of some table—possibly (in fact, probably) a *derived* table, i.e., a table constructed in some way from the given base tables—and produces a single scalar value, defined as follows, as its result:

COUNT—number of values in the column

SUM   —sum of the values in the column

AVG   —average of the values in the column

MAX   —largest value in the column

MIN   —smallest value in the column

For SUM and AVG, the argument must be numeric. In general, the argument may optionally be preceded by the keyword DISTINCT, to indicate that redundant duplicate values are to be eliminated before the function is applied.† For MAX and MIN, however, DISTINCT is irrelevant and should be omitted.

Aggregate functions are unfortunately subject to numerous rules and restrictions, most of them apparently arbitrary:

1. For COUNT, DISTINCT *must* be specified; the special function COUNT(*)—DISTINCT not allowed—is provided to count all rows in a table without any duplicate elimination.

2. If DISTINCT is specified, the argument must be specified as a simple column name such as WEIGHT; if DISTINCT is not specified, the argument may consist of a general scalar expression such as WEIGHT * 454. However, that scalar expression cannot in turn involve any aggregate functions.

3. If and only if DISTINCT is not specified, the function reference can itself be an operand in a scalar expression; e.g., AVG (WEIGHT) * 2 is legal, but AVG (DISTINCT WEIGHT) * 2 is not.

4. Within any given (sub)query, DISTINCT can appear at most once at a given level of nesting (i.e., excluding any subqueries that may appear

---

*EXISTS is also considered as an aggregate function, but it differs from the functions discussed in the present section in that it returns a truth value (*true* or *false*), not a value of one of the recognized SQL/DS data types—i.e., it is not a *computational* function.

†The alternative to DISTINCT is ALL. ALL is assumed if nothing is specified.

nested within the given (sub)query). For example, the following is illegal:

```
SELECT SUM ( DISTINCT QTY ), AVG ( DISTINCT QTY )
FROM    SP
  . . . . .
```

and so is this:

```
SELECT DISTINCT ...
FROM    ...
GROUP  BY ...
HAVING SUM ( DISTINCT ... ) ...
```

However, the following is legal:

```
SELECT DISTINCT ...
FROM    ...
WHERE   ... IN
      ( SELECT DISTINCT ...
        . . . . .    )
```

5. Any nulls in the argument column are always eliminated before the function is applied, regardless of whether DISTINCT is specified, except for the case of COUNT(*), where nulls are handled just like non-null values.

6. If the argument happens to be an empty set, COUNT returns a value of zero; the other functions all return null.

Now for some specific examples of the use of aggregate functions.

7.4.1 *Aggregate Function in the SELECT Clause.* Get the total number of suppliers.

```
SELECT COUNT(*)
FROM    S
```

Result: ─
   5

7.4.2 *Aggregate Function in the SELECT Clause, with DISTINCT.* Get the total number of suppliers currently supplying parts.

```
SELECT COUNT (DISTINCT S#)
FROM    SP
```

Result: ─
   4

7.4.3 *Aggregate Function in the SELECT Clause, with a Predicate.* Get the number of shipments for part P2.

```
SELECT  COUNT(*)
FROM    SP
WHERE   P# = 'P2'
```

Result: _
       4

7.4.4   *Aggregate Function in the SELECT Clause, with a Predicate.*   Get the total quantity of part P2 supplied.

```
SELECT  SUM (QTY)
FROM    SP
WHERE   P# = 'P2'
```

Result: ____
       1000

Note: Unless a GROUP BY or HAVING clause appears (see later), a SELECT clause that includes any aggregate function references must consist *entirely* of such references. Thus, for example, the following is illegal:

```
SELECT  P#, SUM (QTY)
FROM    SP
WHERE   P# = 'P2'
```

7.4.5   *Aggregate Function in a Subquery.*   Get supplier numbers for sup-pliers with status value less than the current maximum status value in the S table.

```
SELECT  S#
FROM    S
WHERE   STATUS <
        ( SELECT MAX (STATUS)
          FROM   S )
```

Result: S#
       --
       S1
       S2
       S4

7.4.6   *Aggregate Function in Correlated Subquery.*   Get supplier number, status, and city for all suppliers whose status is greater than or equal to the average for their particular city.

```
SELECT  S#, STATUS, CITY
FROM    S SX
WHERE   STATUS >=
        ( SELECT AVG (STATUS)
          FROM   S SY
          WHERE  SY.CITY = SX.CITY )
```

```
Result: S#    STATUS   CITY
        --    ------   ------
        S1        20   London
        S3        30   Paris
        S4        20   London
        S5        30   Athens
```

It is not possible to include the average status for each city in this result (why not?).

7.4.7 Use of GROUP BY.   Example 7.4.6 showed how it is possible to compute the total quantity supplied for some specific part. Suppose, by contrast, that it is desired to compute the total quantity supplied for *each* part: i.e., for each part supplied, get the part number and the total shipment quantity for that part.

```
SELECT  P#, SUM (QTY)
FROM    SP
GROUP   BY P#
```

```
Result: P#
        --    ----
        P1     600
        P2    1000
        P3     400
        P4     500
        P5     500
        P6     100
```

Explanation: The GROUP BY operator conceptually rearranges the table represented by the FROM clause into partitions or *groups,* such that within any one group all rows have the same value for the GROUP BY field. In the example, table SP is grouped so that one group contains all the rows for part P1, another contains all the rows for part P2, and so on.* The SELECT clause is then applied to each group of the partitioned table (rather than to each row of the original table). Each expression in the SELECT clause must be *single-valued per group:* e.g., it can be the GROUP BY field itself, or a constant, or an aggregate function such as SUM that operates on all values of a given field within a group and reduces those values to a single value.

Note that GROUP BY does not imply ORDER BY; to guarantee that the result in the foregoing example appears in P# order, the clause ORDER BY P# must be specified as well (after the GROUP BY clause).

A table can be grouped by any combination of its fields. See Section 7.6 for an illustration of grouping over more than one field.

---

*Of course, this does not mean that the table is physically rearranged in the data-base. Our explanation is purely conceptual in nature.

7.4.8   *Use of WHERE with GROUP BY.*   For each part supplied, get the part number and the total and maximum quantity supplied of that part, excluding shipments from supplier S1.

```
SELECT  P#, SUM (QTY), MAX (QTY)
FROM    SP
WHERE   S# ~= 'S1'
GROUP   BY P#
```

Result:
```
P#
--   ---   ---
P1   300   300
P2   800   400
P4   300   300
P5   400   400
```

Rows that do not satisfy the WHERE clause are eliminated before any grouping is done.

7.4.9   *Use of HAVING.*   Get part numbers for all parts supplied by more than one supplier (same as Example 7.2.5).

```
SELECT  P#
FROM    SP
GROUP   BY P#
HAVING  COUNT(*) > 1
```

Result:
```
P#
--
P1
P2
P4
P5
```

   HAVING is to groups what WHERE is to rows (if HAVING is specified, GROUP BY should have been specified also.* In other words, HAVING is used to eliminate groups just as WHERE is used to eliminate rows. Expressions in a HAVING clause must be single-valued per group.

   We have already shown (in Example 7.2.5) that this query can be formulated without GROUP BY (and without HAVING), using a correlated subquery. However, the formulation of Example 7.2.5 is really based on a somewhat different perception of the logic involved in answering the question. It is also possible to formulate a query using essentially the *same* logic

---

*Actually it is possible—though very unusual—to omit the GROUP BY, in which case the entire table is treated as a single group.

as in the GROUP-BY/HAVING version, but without making explicit use of GROUP BY and HAVING at all:

```
SELECT DISTINCT P#
FROM    SP SPX
WHERE   1 <
        ( SELECT COUNT(*)
          FROM    SP SPY
          WHERE   SPY.P# = SPX.P# )
```

The following version (using table P in place of SPX) may perhaps be clearer:

```
SELECT P#
FROM    P
WHERE   1 <
        ( SELECT COUNT (S#)
          FROM    SP
          WHERE   P# = P.P# )
```

Yet another formulation uses EXISTS, as follows:

```
SELECT P#
FROM    P
WHERE   EXISTS
        ( SELECT *
          FROM    SP SPX
          WHERE   SPX.P# = P.P#
          AND     EXISTS
                  ( SELECT *
                    FROM    SP SPY
                    WHERE   SPY.P# = P.P#
                    AND     SPY.S# ~= SPX.S# ) )
```

All of these alternative versions are in some respects preferable to the GROUP-BY/HAVING version, in that they are at least logically cleaner, and they specifically do not require those additional language constructs. It is certainly not clear from the original English statement of the problem— "Get part numbers for all parts supplied by more than one supplier"—that grouping per se is what is needed to answer the question (and indeed it is not needed). Nor is it immediately obvious that a HAVING condition is required rather than a WHERE condition. The GROUP-BY/HAVING version begins to look more like a procedural prescription for *solving* the problem, instead of just a straightforward logical statement of what the problem *is*. On the other hand, there is no denying that the GROUP-BY/HAVING version is the most succinct. Then again, there are some problems of this same general nature for which GROUP BY and HAVING are simply inadequate, so that one of the alternative approaches *must* be used; see Exercise 7.24 for an example of such a problem. And note too that GROUP BY suffers from the severe restriction that it works only to one level; it is not possible to break a table into groups, then to break each of those groups into lower-level groups, and so on, and then to apply some aggregate function, say SUM or AVG, at each level of grouping.*

7.5 UNION

The union of two sets is the set of all elements belonging to either or both of the original sets. Since a relation is a set (a set of rows), it is possible to construct the union of two relations; the result will be a set consisting of all rows appearing in either or both of the original relations. However, if that result is itself to be another relation and not just a heterogeneous mixture of rows, the two original relations must be *union-compatible;* that is, the rows in the two relations must be "the same shape" (loosely speaking). As far as SQL/DS is concerned, two tables are union-compatible, and the UNION operator can be applied to them, only if:

(a) They have the same number of columns, *m* say;

(b) For all *i* (*i* = 1,2, . . . ,*m*), the *i*th column of the first table and the *i*th column of the second table have *exactly* the same data type. In particular:

  - If the data type is DECIMAL(*p*,*q*), then *p* must be the same for both columns and *q* must be the same for both columns.
  - If the data type is CHAR(*n*), VARCHAR(*n*), GRAPHIC(*n*), or VAR-GRAPHIC(*n*), then *n* must be the same for both columns.
  - If NOT NULL applies to either column, then it must apply to both.

7.5.1 Query Involving UNION.   Get part numbers for parts that either weigh more than 16 pounds or are supplied by supplier S2 (or both).

```
SELECT  P#
FROM    P
WHERE   WEIGHT > 16

UNION

SELECT  P#
FROM    SP
WHERE   S# = 'S2'
```

   Result: __
              P1
              P2
              P3
              P6

---

*This effect ("groups within groups," etc.) can be achieved through QMF, however. See Chapter 19.

Several points arise from this simple example.

- Redundant duplicates are always eliminated from the result of a UNION unless the UNION operator explicitly includes the ALL quali- fier (see below). Thus, in the example, part P2 is selected by both of the two constituent SELECTs, but it appears only once in the final result. By contrast, the statement

```
SELECT P#
FROM   P
WHERE  WEIGHT > 16

UNION  ALL

SELECT P#
FROM   SP
WHERE  S# = 'S2'
```

will return part numbers P1, P2, P2 (again), P3, and P6.

- The primary reason for including UNION ALL in the language is that there are many situations in which a union is required and the user *knows* that there will not be any duplicates in the result. In such a case, any attempt by the system to eliminate duplicates will simply impose an undersirable (and unnecessary) performance penalty. Examples illus- trating this point appear below.*

- Any number of SELECTs can be UNIONed together. We might extend the original example (version with ALL omitted) to include part num- bers for red parts by appending the following:

```
UNION

SELECT P#
FROM   P
WHERE  COLOR = 'Red'
```

Note: The same effect could also be achieved by adding the clause

```
OR     COLOR = 'Red'
```

to the first of the original SELECTs.

- Parentheses can be used if desired to force a particular order of evalua- tion if multiple UNIONs are involved. Note that, for example, the expressions x UNION ALL (y UNION z) and (x UNION ALL y)

---

*The ALL option was added in SQL/DS Version 2 Release 2. Note that with UNION (in contrast to the SELECT clause and the aggregate functions) there is no explicit DISTINCT option as an alternative to ALL. Note too that if there were such an alternative the default would have to be DISTINCT, not ALL, for compati- bility with earlier releases.

UNION *z* are not equivalent (in general). Parentheses are unnecessary, however, if either all of the UNIONs specify ALL or none of them does.

▪ Any ORDER BY clause in the query must appear as part of the final SELECT only, and must identify ordering columns by their ordinal position (i.e., by number), not by name.

▪ The ability to include constants in a SELECT clause is frequently useful in connexion with UNION. For example, to indicate which of the two WHERE conditions each individual part in the result happens to satisfy:

```
SELECT P#, 'weight > 16 lb'
FROM   P
WHERE  WEIGHT > 16

UNION  ALL

SELECT P#, 'supplied by S2'
FROM   SP
WHERE  S# = 'S2'

ORDER  BY 2, 1
```

```
Result: __  --------------
        P1  supplied by S2
        P2  supplied by S2
        P2  weight > 16 lb
        P3  weight > 16 lb
        P6  weight > 16 lb
```

We have specified UNION ALL in this version of the problem because it is obvious now that there will be no duplicates to eliminate. (Of course, it would be nice if the optimizer could deduce this fact for itself.)

▪ The reader may be wondering whether SQL also supports any analogs of the INTERSECTION and DIFFERENCE operators (since union, intersection, and difference are commonly treated together in discussions of set theory). The intersection of two sets is the set of all elements belonging to both of the original sets; the difference of two sets is the set of all elements belonging to the first of the original sets and not to the second. SQL does not support these two operators directly, but each of them can be simulated by means of the EXISTS function. For details, the reader is referred to Appendix B.

7.6 CONCLUSION

We have now covered all of the features of the SQL SELECT statement that we intend to illustrate in this book. To conclude the chapter, we present a very contrived example that shows how many (by no means all) of those features can be used together in a single query. We also give a conceptual algorithm for the evaluation of SQL queries in general.

7.6.1 *A Comprehensive Example.*

For all red and blue parts such that the total quantity supplied is greater than 350 (excluding from the total all shipments for which the quantity is less than or equal to 200), get the part number, the weight in grams, the color, and the maximum quantity supplied of that part; and order the result by descending part number within ascending values of that maximum quantity.

```
SELECT P.P#, 'Weight in grams =', P.WEIGHT * 454, P.COLOR,
            'Max shipped quantity =', MAX (SP.QTY)
FROM    P, SP
WHERE   P.P# = SP.P#
AND     P.COLOR IN ('Red','Blue')
AND     SP.QTY > 200
GROUP   BY P.P#, P.WEIGHT, P.COLOR
HAVING  SUM (SP.QTY) > 350
ORDER   BY 6, P.P# DESC
```

Result:

```
P#                             COLOR
--  ------------------  ----  -----  ---------------------  ---
P1  Weight in grams =   5448  Red    Max shipped quantity =  300
P5  Weight in grams =   5448  Blue   Max shipped quantity =  400
P3  Weight in grams =   7718  Blue   Max shipped quantity =  400
```

Explanation: The clauses of a SELECT statement are executed in the order suggested by that in which they must be written*—with the exception of the SELECT clause itself, which is applied between the HAVING clause (if any) and the ORDER BY clause (if any). In the example, therefore, we can imagine the result being constructed as follows.

1. *FROM.* The FROM clause is evaluated to yield a new table that is the Cartesian product of tables P and SP.

2. *WHERE.* The result of Step 1 is reduced by the elimination of all rows

---

*Please note that (once again) our explanation is purely conceptual in nature. SQL/DS does *not* actually execute queries in the manner described (which would be intolerably inefficient in practice). Instead, it chooses some other more efficient method—a method that is, however, guaranteed to produce the same final result as the conceptual method described. Indeed, choosing such a "more efficient method" is precisely one of the functions of the SQL/DS optimizer (see Chapter 2).

Note also that if the query involves any UNIONs, the individual SELECT–FROM–WHERE (etc.) blocks representing the UNION operands are evaluated first in accordance with the conceptual method described (excluding the ORDER BY if any), the results are then UNIONed together, and finally the ORDER BY is applied.

that do not satisfy the WHERE clause. In the example, rows not satisfying the predicate

```
P.P# = SP.P# AND P.COLOR IN ('Red','Blue') AND SP.QTY > 200
```

are eliminated.

3. *GROUP BY.* The result of Step 2 is grouped by values of the field(s)
   named in the GROUP BY clause. In the example, those fields are P.P#,
   P.WEIGHT, and P.COLOR. *Note:* Logically, P.P# alone would be sufficient as the grouping field, since P.WEIGHT and P.COLOR are themselves single-valued per part number. However, SQL/DS is not aware
   of this latter fact, and will raise an error condition if P.WEIGHT and
   P.COLOR are omitted from the GROUP BY clause, because they *are*
   included in the SELECT clause.

4. *HAVING.* Groups not satisfying the condition

```
SUM (SP.QTY) > 350
```

   are eliminated from the result of Step 3.

5. *SELECT.* Each group in the result of Step 4 generates a single result
   row, as follows. First, the part number, weight, color, and maximum
   quantity are extracted from the group. Second, the weight is converted
   to grams. Third, the two character string constants "Weight in grams
   =" and "Max shipped quantity =" are inserted at the appropriate
   points in the row.

6. *ORDER BY.* The result of Step 5 is ordered in accordance with the
   specifications of the ORDER BY clause to yield the final result.

It is of course true that the query shown above is quite complex—but
think how much work it is doing. A conventional program to do the same
job in a language such as COBOL could easily be nine pages long instead
of just nine lines as above, and the work involved in getting that program
operational would be significantly greater than that needed to construct the
SQL version shown. In practice, of course, most queries will be much simpler than this one anyway.

EXERCISES

As in the previous chapter, all of the following exercises are based on the suppliers-
parts-projects database (see the exercises in Chapter 5). In each one, you are asked
to write a SELECT statement for the indicated query (except for numbers 7.15–18
and 7.26, q.v.). For convenience we repeat the structure of the database below:

```
S     ( S#, SNAME, STATUS, CITY )
P     ( P#, PNAME, COLOR, WEIGHT, CITY )
J     ( J#, JNAME, CITY )
SPJ   ( S#, P#, J#, QTY )
```

Within each section, the exercises are arranged in approximate order of increasing difficulty. You should try at least some of the easy ones in each group. Numbers 7.12–18 are quite difficult.

Subqueries

7.1 Get project names for projects supplied by supplier S1.

7.2 Get colors of parts supplied by supplier S1.

7.3 Get part numbers for parts supplied to any project in London.

7.4 Get project numbers for projects using at least one part available from supplier S1.

7.5 Get supplier numbers for suppliers supplying at least one part supplied by at least one supplier who supplies at least one red part.

7.6 Get supplier numbers for suppliers with a status lower than that of supplier S1.

7.7 Get supplier numbers for suppliers supplying some project with part P1 in a quantity greater than the average shipment quantity of part P1 for that project. (*Note:* This exercise requires the AVG function.)

EXISTS

7.8 Repeat Exercise 7.3 to use EXISTS in your solution.

7.9 Repeat Exercise 7.4 to use EXISTS in your solution.

7.10 Get project numbers for projects not supplied with any red part by any London supplier.

7.11 Get project numbers for projects supplied entirely by supplier S1.

7.12 Get part numbers for parts supplied to all projects in London.

7.13 Get supplier numbers for suppliers who supply the same part to all projects.

7.14 Get project numbers for projects supplied with at least all parts available from supplier S1.

For the next four exercises (7.15–18), convert the SQL SELECT statement shown back into an English equivalent.

7.15
```
SELECT DISTINCT J#
FROM    SPJ SPJX
WHERE   NOT EXISTS
      ( SELECT *
        FROM    SPJ SPJY
        WHERE   SPJY.J# = SPJX.J#
        AND     NOT EXISTS
```

```
                    ( SELECT *
                      FROM    SPJ SPJZ
                      WHERE   SPJZ.P# = SPJY.P#
                      AND     SPJZ.S# = 'S1' ) )


7.16 SELECT DISTINCT J#
     FROM    SPJ SPJX
     WHERE   NOT EXISTS
             ( SELECT *
               FROM    SPJ SPJY
               WHERE   EXISTS
                       ( SELECT *
                         FROM    SPJ SPJA
                         WHERE   SPJA.S# = 'S1'
                         AND     SPJA.P# = SPJY.P# )
               AND     NOT EXISTS
                       ( SELECT *
                         FROM    SPJ SPJB
                         WHERE   SPJB.S# = 'S1'
                         AND     SPJB.P# = SPJY.P#
                         AND     SPJB.J# = SPJX.J# ) )


7.17 SELECT DISTINCT J#
     FROM    SPJ SPJX
     WHERE   NOT EXISTS
             ( SELECT *
               FROM    SPJ SPJY
               WHERE   EXISTS
                       ( SELECT *
                         FROM    SPJ SPJA
                         WHERE   SPJA.P# = SPJY.P#
                         AND     SPJA.J# = SPJX.J# )
               AND     NOT EXISTS
                       ( SELECT *
                         FROM    SPJ SPJB
                         WHERE   SPJB.S# = 'S1'
                         AND     SPJB.P# = SPJY.P#
                         AND     SPJB.J# = SPJX.J# ) )


7.18 SELECT DISTINCT J#
     FROM    SPJ SPJX
     WHERE   NOT EXISTS
             ( SELECT *
               FROM    SPJ SPJY
               WHERE   EXISTS
                       ( SELECT *
                         FROM    SPJ SPJA
                         WHERE   SPJA.S# = SPJY.S#
                         AND     SPJA.P# IN
                                 ( SELECT P#
                                   FROM    P
                                   WHERE   COLOR = 'Red' )
                         AND     NOT EXISTS
                                 ( SELECT *
                                   FROM    SPJ SPJB
                                   WHERE   SPJB.S# = SPJY.S#
                                   AND     SPJB.J# = SPJX.J# ) ) )
```

Aggregate Functions

7.19 Get the total number of projects supplied by supplier S1.

7.20 Get the total quantity of part P1 supplied by supplier S1.

7.21 For each part being supplied to a project, get the part number, the project number, and the corresponding total quantity.

7.22 Get project numbers for projects whose city is first in the alphabetic list of such cities.

7.23 Get project numbers for projects supplied with part P1 in an average quantity greater than the greatest quantity in which any part is supplied to project J1.

7.24 Get supplier numbers for suppliers supplying every project with part P1 in a quantity greater than the average quantity in which part P1 is supplied to that project.

Union

7.25 Construct an ordered list of all cities in which at least one supplier, part, or project is located.

7.26 Show the result of the following SELECT:

```
SELECT  P.COLOR
FROM    P
UNION
SELECT  P.COLOR
FROM    P
```

ANSWERS TO SELECTED EXERCISES

The following answers are not necessarily the only ones possible.

7.1
```
SELECT  JNAME
FROM    J
WHERE   J# IN
        ( SELECT  J#
          FROM    SPJ
          WHERE   S# = 'S1' )
```

7.2
```
SELECT  DISTINCT COLOR
FROM    P
WHERE   P# IN
        ( SELECT  P#
          FROM    SPJ
          WHERE   S# = 'S1' )
```

7.3
```
SELECT  DISTINCT P#
FROM    SPJ
WHERE   J# IN
        ( SELECT  J#
          FROM    J
          WHERE   CITY = 'London' )
```

```
7.4   SELECT  DISTINCT  J#
      FROM    SPJ
      WHERE   P#  IN
            ( SELECT  P#
              FROM    SPJ
              WHERE   S#  =  'S1'  )


7.5   SELECT  DISTINCT  S#
      FROM    SPJ
      WHERE   P#  IN
            ( SELECT  P#
              FROM    SPJ
              WHERE   S#  IN
                    ( SELECT  S#
                      FROM    SPJ
                      WHERE   P#  IN
                            ( SELECT  P#
                              FROM    P
                              WHERE   COLOR  =  'Red'  )  )  )


7.6   SELECT  S#
      FROM    S
      WHERE   STATUS  <
            ( SELECT  STATUS
              FROM    S
              WHERE   S#  =  'S1'  )


7.7   SELECT  DISTINCT  S#
      FROM    SPJ  SPJX
      WHERE   P#  =  'P1'
      AND     QTY  >
            ( SELECT  AVG(QTY)
              FROM    SPJ  SPJY
              WHERE   P#  =  'P1'
              AND     SPJY.J#  =  SPJX.J#  )


7.8   SELECT  DISTINCT  P#
      FROM    SPJ
      WHERE   EXISTS
            ( SELECT  *
              FROM    J
              WHERE   J#  =  SPJ.J#
              AND     CITY  =  'London'  )


7.9   SELECT  DISTINCT  SPJX.J#
      FROM    SPJ  SPJX
      WHERE   EXISTS
            ( SELECT  *
              FROM    SPJ  SPJY
              WHERE   SPJY.P#  =  SPJX.P#
              AND     SPJY.S#  =  'S1'  )


7.10  SELECT  J#
      FROM    J
      WHERE   NOT  EXISTS
            ( SELECT  *
              FROM    SPJ
```

```
          WHERE   J# = J.J#
          AND     P# IN
                  ( SELECT P#
                    FROM    P
                    WHERE   COLOR = 'Red' )
          AND     S# IN
                  ( SELECT S#
                    FROM    S
                    WHERE   CITY = 'London' ) )
```

7.11
```
      SELECT  DISTINCT J#
      FROM    SPJ SPJX
      WHERE   NOT EXISTS
              ( SELECT *
                FROM    SPJ SPJY
                WHERE   SPJY.J# = SPJX.J#
                AND     SPJY.S# ~= 'S1' )
```

7.12
```
      SELECT  DISTINCT P#
      FROM    SPJ SPJX
      WHERE   NOT EXISTS
              ( SELECT *
                FROM    J
                WHERE   CITY = 'London'
                AND     NOT EXISTS
                        ( SELECT *
                          FROM    SPJ SPJY
                          WHERE   SPJY.P# = SPJX.P#
                          AND     SPJY.J# = J.J# ) )
```

7.13
```
      SELECT  DISTINCT S#
      FROM    SPJ SPJX
      WHERE   EXISTS
              ( SELECT P#
                FROM    SPJ SPJY
                WHERE   NOT EXISTS
                        ( SELECT J#
                          FROM    J
                          WHERE   NOT EXISTS
                                  ( SELECT *
                                    FROM    SPJ SPJZ
                                    WHERE   SPJZ.S# = SPJX.S#
                                    AND     SPJZ.P# = SPJY.P#
                                    AND     SPJZ.J# = J.J# ) ) )
```

This rather complex SELECT statement may be paraphrased: "Get all suppliers (SPJX.S#) such that there exists a part (SPJY.P#) such that there does not exist any project (J.J#) such that the supplier does not supply the part to the project"—in other words, suppliers such that there exists some part that they supply to all projects. Note the use of "SELECT P# FROM . . ." and "SELECT J# FROM . . ." in two of the EXISTS references; "SELECT * " would not be incorrect, but "SELECT P#" (for instance) seems a fraction closer to the intuitive formulation—there must exist a *part* (identified by a part number), not just a row in the shipments table.

```
7.14 SELECT DISTINCT J#
     FROM    SPJ SPJX
     WHERE   NOT EXISTS
           ( SELECT P#
             FROM    SPJ SPJY
             WHERE   SPJY.S# = 'S1'
             AND     NOT EXISTS
                   ( SELECT *
                     FROM    SPJ SPJZ
                     WHERE   SPJZ.P# = SPJY.P#
                     AND     SPJZ.J# = SPJX.J# ) )
```

7.15 Get project numbers for projects that use only parts that are available from supplier S1.

7.16 Get project numbers for projects that are supplied by supplier S1 with some of every part that supplier S1 supplies.

7.17 Get project numbers for projects such that at least some of every part they use is supplied to them by supplier S1.

7.18 Get project numbers for projects that are supplied by every supplier who supplies some red part.

```
7.19 SELECT COUNT (DISTINCT J#)
     FROM    SPJ
     WHERE   S# = 'S1'
```

```
7.20 SELECT SUM (QTY)
     FROM    SPJ
     WHERE   P# = 'P1'
     AND     S# = 'S1'
```

```
7.21 SELECT P#, J#, SUM(QTY)
     FROM    SPJ
     GROUP   BY P#, J#
```

```
7.22 SELECT J#
     FROM    J
     WHERE   CITY =
           ( SELECT MIN(CITY)
             FROM    J )
```

```
7.23 SELECT J#
     FROM    SPJ
     WHERE   P# = 'P1'
     GROUP   BY J#
     HAVING AVG(QTY) >
           ( SELECT MAX(QTY)
             FROM    SPJ
             WHERE   J# = 'J1' )
```

```
7.24 SELECT DISTINCT S#
     FROM    SPJ SPJX
     WHERE   NOT EXISTS
           ( SELECT *
             FROM    J
```

```
        WHERE   NOT EXISTS
                ( SELECT *
                  FROM    SPJ SPJY
                  WHERE   SPJY.S# = SPJX.S#
                  AND     SPJY.P# = 'P1'
                  AND     SPJY.J# = J.J#
                  AND     SPJY.QTY >
                        ( SELECT AVG (QTY)
                          FROM    SPJ SPJZ
                          WHERE   SPJZ.J# = J.J#
                          AND     SPJZ.P# = 'P1' ) ) )
```

7.25
```
SELECT CITY FROM S
UNION
SELECT CITY FROM P
UNION
SELECT CITY FROM J
ORDER  BY 1
```

7.26
```
-----
Red
Green
Blue
```

8

♦

Data Manipulation III: Update Operations

8.1 INTRODUCTION

In the last two chapters we considered the SQL retrieval statement (SELECT) in considerable detail. Now we turn our attention to the update statements INSERT, UPDATE, and DELETE. *Note:* The term "update" unfortunately has two distinct meanings in SQL; it is used generically to refer to all three operations as a class, and also specifically to refer to the UPDATE operation per se. We will distinguish between the two meanings in this book by always using lower case when the generic meaning is intended and upper case when the specific meaning is intended.

Like the SELECT statement, the three update statements operate on both base tables and views. However, for reasons that are beyond the scope of this chapter, *not all views are updatable.* If the user attempts to perform an update operation on a nonupdatable view, SQL/DS will simply reject the operation, with some appropriate message to the user. For the purposes of the present chapter, therefore, let us assume that all tables to be updated are base tables, and defer the question of views (and of updating views, in particular) to Chapter 10.

The next three sections discuss the three update operations in detail. The syntax of those operations follows the same general pattern as that already shown for the SELECT operation; for convenience, an outline of that general syntax for the operation in question is given at the beginning of the relevant section.

8.2 INSERT

The INSERT statement has the general form

```
INSERT
INTO    table [ ( field [, field ] ... ) ]
VALUES ( constant [, constant ] ... )
```

or

```
INSERT
INTO    table [ ( field [, field ] ... ) ]
subquery
```

In the first format, a row is INSERTed into "table" having the specified values for the specified fields; the ith constant in the list of constants corresponds to the ith field in the list of fields. In the second format, "subquery" is evaluated and a copy of the result (multiple rows, in general) is INSERTed into "table"; the ith column of that result corresponds to the ith field in the list of fields. In both cases, omitting the list of fields is equivalent to specifying a list of all fields in the table (see Example 8.2.2 below).

8.2.1 Single-Record INSERT. Add part P7 (city Athens, weight 24, name and color at present unknown) to table P.

```
INSERT
INTO    P ( P#, CITY, WEIGHT )
VALUES ( 'P7', 'Athens', 24 )
```

A new part record is created with the specified part number, city, and weight, and with the name and color fields set to null. (Of course, these last two fields must not have been defined as NOT NULL in the CREATE TABLE statement for table P, or the INSERT will fail and the database will remain unchanged.) Note that the left-to-right order in which fields are named in the INSERT statement does not have to be the same as the left-to-right order in which they were specified in the CREATE (or ALTER) statement.

8.2.2 *Single-Record INSERT, with Field Names Omitted.* Add part P8 (a sprocket, color pink, weight 14, city Nice) to table P.

```
INSERT
INTO    P
VALUES ('P8', 'Sprocket', 'Pink', 14, 'Nice' )
```

Omitting the list of fields is equivalent to specifying a list of all fields in the table, in the left-to-right order in which they were defined in the CREATE (or ALTER) statement. As with "SELECT *", this shorthand may be convenient for interactive SQL; however, it is potentially dangerous in embedded SQL (i.e., SQL within an application program), because the assumed list of fields may change if the access module is regenerated and the definition of the table has changed in the interim. In practice, we recommend always specifying the list of fields explicitly in an embedded SQL context.

8.2.3 *Single-Record INSERT.* Insert a new shipment with supplier number S20, part number P20, and quantity 1000.

```
INSERT
INTO    SP ( S#, P#, QTY )
VALUES ('S20', 'P20', 1000 )
```

Since by definition the three update operations change the state of the database, there is always the possibility that they may change it in some incorrect way and thereby violate the integrity of the data. The example illustrates this point: The database would clearly be incorrect if the INSERT were executed, because it would now include a shipment for a nonexistent supplier and a nonexistent part. In fact, the example illustrates a very specific kind of integrity violation, namely a *referential* integrity violation. Referential integrity is discussed in Chapter 12.

8.2.4 *Multiple-Record INSERT.* For each part supplied, get the part number and the total quantity supplied of that part (as in Example 7.4.7), and save the result in the database.

```
CREATE TABLE TEMP
        ( P#       CHAR(6) NOT NULL,
          TOTQTY   INTEGER,
        PRIMARY KEY ( P# ) )

INSERT
INTO    TEMP ( P#, TOTQTY )
        SELECT P#, SUM(QTY)
        FROM   SP
        GROUP  BY P#
```

The SELECT is executed, just like an ordinary SELECT, but the result, instead of being returned to the user, is copied into table TEMP. Now the user can do anything he or she pleases with that copy—query it further, print it, even update it; none of those operations will have any effect what-soever on the original data. Eventually, when it is no longer required, table TEMP can be dropped:

```
DROP TABLE TEMP
```

The foregoing example illustrates very nicely why the closure property of relational systems (discussed in Section 6.2) is so important: The overall procedure works precisely because the result of a SELECT is another table. It would *not* work if the result was something other than a table.

It is not necessary for the target table to be initially empty for a multiple-record INSERT, incidentally, though for the foregoing example it is. If it is not, the new records are simply added to those already present.

One important use for INSERT . . . SELECT is in the construction of what is called an *outer join*. As explained in Chapter 6, the ordinary join of two tables does not include a result row for any row in either of the two original tables that has no matching row in the other. For example, the ordinary join of tables S and P over cities does not include any result row for supplier S5 or for part P3, because no parts are stored in Athens and no suppliers are located in Rome (see Example 6.3.1). In a sense, therefore (a very imprecise sense), the ordinary join may be considered to *lose information* for such unmatched rows. Sometimes, however, it may be desirable to be able to preserve that information. Consider the following example.

8.2.5 Using INSERT . . . SELECT to Construct an Outer Join.   For each supplier, get the supplier number, name, status, and city, together with part numbers for all parts supplied by that supplier. If a given supplier supplies no parts at all, then show the information for that supplier in the result concatenated with a blank part number.

```
CREATE TABLE OJEX
       ( S#       CHAR(5)   NOT NULL,
         SNAME    CHAR(20)  NOT NULL,
         STATUS   SMALLINT  NOT NULL,
         CITY     CHAR(15)  NOT NULL,
         P#       CHAR(6)   NOT NULL,
       PRIMARY KEY ( S#, P# ) )

INSERT
INTO    OJEX
        SELECT S.*, SP.P#
        FROM   S, SP
        WHERE  S.S# = SP.S#

INSERT
INTO    OJEX
        SELECT S.*, 'bb'
        FROM   S
        WHERE  NOT EXISTS
               ( SELECT *
                 FROM    SP
                 WHERE   SP.S# = S.S# )
```

Now table OJEX looks like this:

S#	SNAME	STATUS	CITY	P#
S1	Smith	20	London	P1
S1	Smith	20	London	P2
S1	Smith	20	London	P3
S1	Smith	20	London	P4
S1	Smith	20	London	P5
S1	Smith	20	London	P6
S2	Jones	10	Paris	P1
S2	Jones	10	Paris	P2
S3	Blake	30	Paris	P2
S4	Clark	20	London	P2
S4	Clark	20	London	P4
S4	Clark	20	London	P5
S5	Adams	30	Athens	bb

(We are using bb to represent a string of blanks.)

Explanation: The first twelve result rows as shown correspond to the first of the two INSERT . . . SELECTs, and represent the ordinary natural join of S and SP over supplier numbers (except that the QTY column is not included). The final result row corresponds to the second of the two INSERT . . . SELECTs, and preserves information for supplier S5, who does not supply any parts. The overall result is the *outer* natural join of S and SP over S#—again, ignoring QTY. (The ordinary join, by contrast, is sometimes referred to as an *inner* join.)

Note that two separate INSERT . . . SELECTs are needed, because a subquery cannot contain a UNION.

One final comment on this example: Outer join is extremely important in practice, and it is a pity that systems do not provide direct support for it (this is a criticism of relational products in general, not just of SQL/DS). It should not be necessary to have to indulge in circumlocutions of the kind illustrated in the example.

8.3 UPDATE

The UPDATE statement has the general form

```
UPDATE table
SET     field = scalar-expression
     [, field = scalar-expression ] ...
[ WHERE  predicate ]
```

All records in "table" that satisfy "predicate" are UPDATEd in accordance with the assignments ("field = scalar-expression") in the SET clause. The "scalar-expression"'s are (at their most complex) simple scalar expressions involving fields of "table" and/or scalar functions and/or constants (no aggregate functions allowed). For each record to be UPDATEd (i.e., each record that satisfies "predicate," or all records if the WHERE clause is omitted), references in the ''scalar-expressions'' to fields within that record stand for the values of those fields before any of the assignments have been executed.

8.3.1   Single-Record UPDATE.   Change the color of part P2 to yellow, increase its weight by 5, and set its city to ''unknown'' (i.e., NULL; we assume for the sake of the example that field P.CITY is allowed to accept nulls).

```
UPDATE  P
SET     COLOR = 'Yellow',
        WEIGHT = WEIGHT + 5,
        CITY = NULL
WHERE   P# = 'P2'
```

8.3.2   Multiple-Record UPDATE.   Double the status of all suppliers in London.

```
UPDATE  S
SET     STATUS = 2 * STATUS
WHERE   CITY = 'London'
```

8.3.3   UPDATE with a Subquery.   Set the shipment quantity to zero for all suppliers in London.

```
UPDATE  SP
SET     QTY = 0
WHERE   'London' =
        ( SELECT CITY
          FROM   S
          WHERE  S.S# = SP.S# )
```

8.4   DELETE

The DELETE statement has the general form

```
  DELETE
  FROM    table
[ WHERE   predicate ]
```

All records in ''table'' that satisfy ''predicate'' are DELETEd.

8.4.1   Single-Record DELETE.   Delete supplier S5.

```
DELETE
FROM    S
WHERE   S# = 'S5'
```

8.4.2   Multiple-Record DELETE.   Delete all shipments with quantity greater than 300.

```
DELETE
FROM    SP
WHERE   QTY > 300
```

8.4.3 *Multiple-Record DELETE.*   Delete all shipments.

```
DELETE
FROM    SP
```

SP is still a known table ("DELETE all records" is not a DROP), but it is now empty.

8.4.4 *DELETE with a Subquery.*   Delete all shipments for suppliers in London.

```
DELETE
FROM    SP
WHERE   'London' =
        ( SELECT  CITY
          FROM    S
          WHERE   S.S# = SP.S# )
```

8.5 CONCLUSION

This brings us to the end of our detailed discussion of the four data manipulation statements of SQL, namely SELECT, INSERT, UPDATE, and DELETE. Most of the complexity of those statements (what complexity there is) resides in the SELECT statement; once you have a reasonable understanding of SELECT, the other statements are fairly straightforward, as you can see. In practice, of course, the SELECT statement is usually pretty straightforward as well.

Despite the foregoing, however, the update operations do suffer from one minor problem that is worth calling out explicitly, namely as follows. If the WHERE clause in UPDATE or DELETE includes a subquery, then the FROM clause in that subquery must not refer to the table that is the target of that UPDATE or DELETE. Likewise, in the subquery form of INSERT, the FROM clause in the subquery must not refer to the table that is the target of that INSERT. So, for example, to delete all suppliers whose status is lower than the average, the following will *not* work:

```
DELETE
FROM    S
WHERE   STATUS <
        ( SELECT  AVG (STATUS)
          FROM    S )
```

Instead, it is necessary to proceed one step at a time, as follows:

```
SELECT  AVG (STATUS)
FROM    S
```

Result: _____
         22

Hence:

```
DELETE
FROM    S
WHERE   STATUS < 22
```

The reasons for the foregoing restrictions are not inherent but are merely a consequence of the way the operators are implemented in SQL/DS.

In conclusion, we point out that the fact that there are only four data manipulation operations in SQL is one of the reasons for the ease of use of that language (less to learn, less to remember, etc.). And the fact that there *are* only four such operations is a consequence of the simplicity of the relational data structure. As we pointed out in Chapter 1, all data in a relational database is represented in exactly the same way, namely as values in column positions within rows of tables. Since there is only one way to represent anything, we need only one operator for each of the four basic functions (retrieve, change, insert, delete). By contrast, systems based on a more complex data structure fundamentally require $4n$ operations, where n is the number of ways that data can be represented in that system. In CODASYL-based systems, for example, where data can be represented either as records or as links between records, we typically find a STORE operation to create a record and a CONNECT operation to create a link; an ERASE operation to destroy a record and a DISCONNECT operation to destroy a link; a MODIFY operation to change a record and a RECONNECT operation to change a link; and so on. (Actually, CODASYL systems usually provide more than two ways of representing data, but records and links are the two most important.)

EXERCISES

As usual, all of the following exercises are based on the suppliers-parts-projects database:

```
S     ( S#, SNAME, STATUS, CITY )
P     ( P#, PNAME, COLOR, WEIGHT, CITY )
J     ( J#, JNAME, CITY )
SPJ   ( S#, P#, J#, QTY )
```

Write INSERT, DELETE, or UPDATE statements (as appropriate) for each of the following problems.

8.1 Change the color of all red parts to orange.

8.2 Delete all projects for which there are no shipments.

8.3 Increase the shipment quantity by 10 percent for all shipments by suppliers that supply a red part.

8.4 Insert a new supplier (S10) into table S. The name and city are White and New York, respectively; the status is not yet known.

8.5 Construct a table containing a list of part numbers for parts that are supplied either by a London supplier or to a London project.

8.6 Construct a table containing a list of project numbers for projects that are either located in London or are supplied by a London supplier.

8.7 Add 10 to the status of all suppliers whose status is currently less than that of supplier S4.

8.8 Construct the outer natural join of projects and shipments over project numbers.

8.9 Construct the outer natural join of parts and projects over cities.

8.10 Construct a table showing complete supplier, part, and project information (together with shipment quantity) for each shipment, together with "preserved" information for every supplier, part, and project that does not appear in the shipment table. (See Example 8.2.5 for the meaning of "preserved" in this context.)

ANSWERS TO SELECTED EXERCISES

As usual the following solutions are not necessarily unique. Also, note that several of those solutions involve the creation of a temporary result table. We have specified a primary key for each such table as a matter of good discipline; but it should be pointed out that the integrity checking implied by those primary keys will certainly lead to some performance overhead (see Chapter 12). As a consequence, an installation might decide that it is acceptable *not* to specify a primary key for such comparatively short-lived tables.

8.1
```
UPDATE  P
SET     COLOR = 'Orange'
WHERE   COLOR = 'Red'
```

8.2
```
DELETE
FROM    J
WHERE   J# NOT IN
      ( SELECT J#
        FROM   SPJ )
```

8.3
```
CREATE TABLE REDS
        ( S#  CHAR(5) NOT NULL,
        PRIMARY KEY ( S# ) )

INSERT INTO REDS ( S# )
        SELECT DISTINCT S#
        FROM   SPJ, P
        WHERE  SPJ.P# = P.P#
        AND    COLOR = 'Red'
```

```
UPDATE SPJ
SET    QTY = QTY * 1.1
WHERE  S# IN
     ( SELECT S#
       FROM   REDS )

DROP TABLE REDS
```

Note that the following single-statement "solution" is illegal (why?).

```
UPDATE SPJ
SET    QTY = QTY * 1.1
WHERE  S# IN
     ( SELECT DISTINCT S#
       FROM   SPJ, P
       WHERE  SPJ.P# = P.P#
       AND    P.COLOR = 'Red' )
```

8.4 INSERT
```
     INTO   S ( S#, SNAME, CITY )
     VALUES ( 'S10', 'White', 'New York' )
```

8.5 CREATE TABLE LP
```
        ( P# CHAR(6) NOT NULL,
        PRIMARY KEY ( P# ) )

     INSERT INTO LP ( P# )
          SELECT DISTINCT P#
          FROM   SPJ
          WHERE  S# IN
               ( SELECT S#
                 FROM   S
                 WHERE  CITY = 'London' )
          OR     J# IN
               ( SELECT J#
                 FROM   J
                 WHERE  CITY = 'London' )
```

8.6 CREATE TABLE LJ
```
        ( J#  CHAR(4) NOT NULL,
        PRIMARY KEY ( J# ) )

     INSERT INTO LJ ( J# )
          SELECT J#
          FROM   J
          WHERE  CITY = 'London'
          OR     J# IN
               ( SELECT DISTINCT J#
                 FROM   SPJ
                 WHERE  S# IN
                      ( SELECT S#
                        FROM   S
                        WHERE  CITY = 'London' ) )
```

Note: The following is illegal:

```
     INSERT INTO LJ ( J# )
          SELECT J#
          FROM   J
          WHERE  CITY = 'London'
```

```
          UNION
          SELECT  DISTINCT  J#
          FROM    SPJ
          WHERE   'London'  =
                  ( SELECT CITY
                    FROM    S
                    WHERE   S.S#  =  SPJ.S#  )
```

UNION is never allowed in a subquery (in any context).

8.7
```
SELECT  STATUS
FROM    S
WHERE   S#  =  'S4'
```

Result:
```
STATUS
------
    20
```

Hence:

```
UPDATE  S
SET     STATUS  =  STATUS  +  10
WHERE   STATUS  <  20
```

8.8
```
CREATE  TABLE  RES8
        ( J#        CHAR(4)   NOT NULL,
          JNAME     CHAR(10)  NOT NULL,
          CITY      CHAR(15)  NOT NULL,
          S#        CHAR(5)   NOT NULL,
          P#        CHAR(6)   NOT NULL,
          QTY       INTEGER,
        PRIMARY KEY ( S#, P#, J# ) )
```

```
INSERT
INTO    RES8
        SELECT  J.*,  SPJ.S#,  SPJ.P#,  SPJ.QTY
        FROM    J, SPJ
        WHERE   J.J#  =  SPJ.J#
```

```
INSERT
INTO    RES8
        SELECT  J.*,  'bb',  'bb',  0
        FROM    J
        WHERE   NOT EXISTS
                ( SELECT  *
                  FROM    SPJ
                  WHERE   SPJ.J#  =  J.J#  )
```

8.9
```
CREATE  TABLE  RES9
        ( P#        CHAR(6)   NOT NULL,
          PNAME     CHAR(20)  NOT NULL,
          COLOR     CHAR(6)   NOT NULL,
          WEIGHT    SMALLINT  NOT NULL,
```

```
                CITY     CHAR(15) NOT NULL,
                J#       CHAR(4)  NOT NULL,
                JNAME    CHAR(10) NOT NULL,
             PRIMARY KEY ( P#, J# ) )

      INSERT
      INTO    RES9
                SELECT P.*, J#, JNAME
                FROM   P, J
                WHERE  P.CITY = J.CITY

      INSERT
      INTO    RES9
                SELECT P.*, 'bb', 'bb'
                FROM   P
                WHERE  NOT EXISTS
                     ( SELECT *
                       FROM   J
                       WHERE  J.CITY = P.CITY )

      INSERT
      INTO    RES9
                SELECT 'bb', 'bb', 'bb', 0, J.CITY, J.J#, J.JNAME
                FROM   J
                WHERE  NOT EXISTS
                     ( SELECT *
                       FROM   P
                       WHERE  P.CITY = J.CITY )


8.10  CREATE TABLE RES10
             ( S# ..., SNAME ..., STATUS ..., SCITY ...,
               P# ..., PNAME ..., COLOR ..., WEIGHT ..., PCITY ...,
               J# ..., JNAME ..., JCITY ..., QTY ...,
             PRIMARY KEY ( S#, P#, J# ) )

      INSERT
      INTO    RES10
                SELECT S.*, P.*, J.*, SPJ.QTY
                FROM   S, P, J, SPJ
                WHERE  S.S# = SPJ.S#
                AND    P.P# = SPJ.P#
                AND    J.J# = SPJ.J#

      INSERT
      INTO    RES10
                SELECT S.*,'bb','bb','bb', 0,'bb','bb','bb','bb', 0
                FROM   S
                WHERE  NOT EXISTS
                     ( SELECT *
                       FROM   SPJ
                       WHERE  SPJ.S# = S.S# )

      INSERT
      INTO    RES10
                SELECT 'bb','bb', 0,'bb', P.*,'bb','bb','bb', 0
                FROM   P
                WHERE  NOT EXISTS
                     ( SELECT *
                       FROM   SPJ
                       WHERE  P.P# = SPJ.P# )
```

```
INSERT
INTO    RES10
        SELECT 'bb','bb', 0,'bb','bb','bb','bb', 0,'bb', J.*, 0
        FROM    J
        WHERE   NOT EXISTS
              ( SELECT *
                FROM    SPJ
                WHERE   SPJ.J# = J.J# )
```

The Catalog

9.1 INTRODUCTION

We have mentioned the catalog several times in this book already. Basically, the catalog is the repository for a collection of information (*descriptors*) concerning various objects that are of interest to SQL/DS itself. Examples of such objects are base tables, views, indexes, access modules, access privileges, and so on. Catalog information is essential if the system is to be able to do its job properly. For example, the optimizer uses catalog information about indexes (as well as other information) to choose an access strategy, as explained in Chapter 2. Likewise, the authorization subsystem (see Chapter 11) uses catalog information about access privileges to grant or deny specific user requests.

A significant advantage of a relational system like SQL/DS is that *the catalog in such a system itself consists of relations* (or tables—*system* tables, so called to distinguish them from ordinary user tables). As a result, users can interrogate the catalog using the standard facilities of their normal query language (SQL, in the case of SQL/DS)—a very nice feature of such systems.

In SQL/DS specifically, the catalog consists of some 16 or so system tables.* It is not our purpose here to give an exhaustive description of those tables; rather, we wish merely to give a basic—and deliberately somewhat simplified—introduction to their structure and content, and to give some idea as to how the information contained in those tables can be helpful to the user as well as to the system. The only catalog tables we mention at this point are the following:

- SYSCATALOG

  This catalog table contains a row for every table (base table or view) in the entire database. For each such table, it gives the table name (TNAME), the user ID of the user that created the table (CREATOR), the number of columns in the table (NCOLS), and many other items of information.

- SYSCOLUMNS

  This catalog table contains a row for every column of every table in the entire database. For each such column, it gives the column name (CNAME), the name of the table of which that column is a part (TNAME), the data type of the column (COLTYPE), and many other things besides.

- SYSINDEXES

  This catalog table contains a row for every index in the database. For each such index, it gives the index name (INAME), the name of the indexed table (TNAME), the user ID of the user that created the index (ICREATOR), and so on.

For example, the catalog structure for the suppliers-and-parts database might be as indicated in Fig. 9.1 (in outline; of course, almost all the details have been omitted).

One final note on terminology: The SQL/DS manuals actually refer to each catalog table as a separate catalog, and thus talk about, e.g., the SYSCATALOG catalog, the SYSCOLUMNS catalog, etc. We prefer to use

---

*The catalog is *not* the same across different SQL implementations, because the catalog for a particular system necessarily contains a great deal of information that is specific to that system. In particular, the SQL/DS and DB2 catalogs are different.

```
SYSCATALOG   TNAME     CREATOR   NCOLS      ...
             ------    -------   -----   - - - -
             S         CJDATE       4      ...
             P         CJDATE       5      ...
             SP        CJDATE       3      ...

SYSCOLUMNS   CNAME     TNAME     COLTYPE        ...
             ------    ------    --------   - - - -
             S#        S         CHAR         ...
             SNAME     S         CHAR         ...
             STATUS    S         SMALLINT     ...
             CITY      S         CHAR         ...
             P#        P         CHAR         ...
             PNAME     P         CHAR         ...
             COLOR     P         CHAR         ...
             WEIGHT    P         SMALLINT     ...
             CITY      P         CHAR         ...
             S#        SP        CHAR         ...
             P#        SP        CHAR         ...
             QTY       SP        INTEGER      ...

SYSINDEXES   INAME     TNAME     ICREATOR       ...
             -----     ------    --------   - - - -
             XS        S         CJDATE       ...
             XP        P         CJDATE       ...
             XSP       SP        CJDATE       ...
             XSC       S         CJDATE       ...
```

Fig. 9.1 Catalog structure for the suppliers-and-parts database (outline)

the term "catalog" to refer to the entire collection of such tables, for reasons of consistency with other products (including in particular DB2).

9.2   QUERYING THE CATALOG

As indicated in Section 9.1, a nice feature of the catalog in a relational system like SQL/DS is that it can be queried by means of ordinary SQL retrieval operations (SELECT statements), just as ordinary tables can. For example, to find out what tables contain an S# column:

```
SELECT  TNAME
FROM    SYSTEM.SYSCOLUMNS
WHERE   CNAME = 'S#'
```

Result: TNAME

         S
         SP

The "creator" for the catalog tables is considered to be SYSTEM. Thus, to refer to a catalog table such as SYSCOLUMNS, you will need to use SYSTEM as a prefix for the table name (as in the FROM clause in this example); otherwise, SQL/DS will assume that you are referring to a table of your own (i.e., the default prefix is your own user ID, as explained in Chapter 5).

Another example: What columns does table S have?

```
SELECT  CNAME
FROM    SYSTEM.SYSCOLUMNS
WHERE   TNAME = 'S'
```

Result:
```
CNAME
------
S#
SNAME
STATUS
CITY
```

And one more example: How many tables has user CJDATE created?

```
SELECT  COUNT(*)
FROM    SYSTEM.SYSCATALOG
WHERE   CREATOR = 'CJDATE'
```

A user who is not familiar with the structure of the database can use queries such as these to discover that structure. For example, a user who wishes to query the suppliers-and-parts database (say), but does not have any detailed knowledge as to exactly what tables exist in that database and exactly what columns they contain, can use catalog queries to obtain that knowledge first before going on to formulate the data queries per se. In a traditional (nonrelational) system, those initial queries would typically have to be directed to the system *dictionary* instead of to the database. Indeed, the SQL/DS catalog can be regarded as a rudimentary dictionary (rudimentary, in that it contains only information that is directly needed by SQL/DS, whereas a full-scale dictionary typically contains much additional information, such as report definitions, graph definitions, terminal descriptions, etc.). The important difference—and a significant ease-of-use benefit for SQL/DS—is that in SQL/DS the catalog and the database are queried through *the same interface,* namely SQL; in traditional systems, by contrast, the dictionary and the database have always been distinct and have been accessed through different interfaces. It is interesting to speculate as to whether the SQL/DS catalog will ever be extended to provide a full-fledged dictionary function.

Note: After the foregoing was first written, IBM announced an auxiliary product for SQL/DS (and DB2) called the Data Base Relational Application Directory (DBRAD). We mentioned this product briefly in Section 3.2. DBRAD is still not a full dictionary product, but it might be considered a step in the right direction. It includes a set of database tables, the *application directory* (logically an extension of the system catalog), which can be used to contain information regarding application programs, application data objects, etc., together with their interrelationships (which programs use which data objects? which objects are contained within which other objects? and so on). It also provides a set of standard dialogs for producing reports from the application directory and/or from the system catalog. DBRAD is intended to help in the development and maintenance of COBOL, PL/I, and CSP applications (see Chapter 21). It can also be used to assist with data and system administration. See Chapter 24 for more information.

9.3 UPDATING THE CATALOG

We have seen how the catalog can be queried by means of the SQL SELECT statement. However, the catalog *cannot* be updated using the SQL INSERT, UPDATE, and DELETE statements, and SQL/DS will reject any attempt to do so.* The reason is, of course, that allowing such operations would potentially be very dangerous: It would be far too easy to destroy information (inadvertently or otherwise) in the catalog so that SQL/DS would no longer be able to function correctly. Suppose, for example, that the following were allowed:

```
DELETE
FROM     SYSTEM.SYSCOLUMNS
WHERE    TNAME = 'S'
AND      CNAME = 'S#'
```

Its effect would be to remove the row

```
( S#, S, CHAR, ... )
```

from the SYSCOLUMNS table. *As far as SQL/DS is concerned, the S# column in the S table would now no longer exist*—i.e., SQL/DS would no longer have any knowledge of that column. Thus, attempts to access data on the basis of values of that column—e.g.,

```
SELECT CITY
FROM    S
WHERE   S# = 'S4'
```

—would fail (the system would produce some error message, such as "undefined column"). Perhaps worse, attempts to update supplier records could go disastrously wrong—for example, inserting a new record might

---

*Unless the user concerned has "DBA authority" (see Chapter 11). Under exceptional circumstances, a user with DBA authority may indeed need to update (or ALTER) a catalog table, and SQL/DS does in fact permit such an operation. But this is a *very* special case, and we ignore it for the remainder of this chapter.

conceivably cause the supplier number to be taken as the supplier name, the supplier name as the status, and so on.

For reasons such as these, INSERT, UPDATE, and DELETE operations are (as already stated) not permitted against tables in the catalog. Instead, it is the *data definition* statements (CREATE TABLE, CREATE INDEX, etc.) that perform such updates. For example, the CREATE TABLE statement for table S causes (a) an entry to be made for S in the SYSCATALOG table and (b) a set of four entries, one for each of the four columns of the S table, to be made in the SYSCOLUMNS table. (It also causes a number of other things to happen too, which are however of no concern to us here.) Thus CREATE is in some ways the analog of INSERT for the catalog. Likewise, DROP is the analog of DELETE, and ALTER is the analog of UPDATE.

Aside: The catalog also includes entries for the catalog tables themselves, of course. However, those entries are not created by explicit CREATE TABLE operations. Instead, they are created automatically by SQL/DS itself as part of the system installation procedure. In effect, they are "hard-wired" into the system.

Although (as we have just seen) the regular SQL updating statements cannot be used to update the catalog, there are two SQL statements, namely COMMENT and LABEL, that do perform a kind of limited catalog updating function. We discuss each in turn.

COMMENT

The catalog tables SYSCATALOG and SYSCOLUMNS each include a column—not shown in Fig. 9.1—called REMARKS, which can be used (in any particular row) to contain a text string that describes the object identified by the rest of that row. The COMMENT statement is used to enter such descriptions into the REMARKS column in these two tables. The following examples illustrate the two basic formats of that statement.

```
COMMENT ON TABLE S IS
        'Each row represents one supplier'
```

The specified string is stored in the REMARKS field in the row for table S in the SYSCATALOG table, replacing any value previously stored at that position. The table being COMMENTed on can be either a base table or a view.

```
COMMENT ON COLUMN P.CITY IS
        'Location of (unique) warehouse storing this part'
```

The specified string is stored in the REMARKS field in the row for column P.CITY in the SYSCOLUMNS table, replacing any value previously stored at that position. The column being COMMENTed on can be a column of either a base table or a view.

Comments can be retrieved via the regular SQL SELECT statement.

LABEL

The catalog tables SYSCATALOG and SYSCOLUMNS each also include a column (again not shown in Fig. 9.1), called TLABEL and CLABEL respectively, which can be used in any particular row to contain a text string that is to be used in reports involving the object identified by the rest of that row. The LABEL statement is used to enter such strings into those columns. The following examples illustrate the two basic formats of that statement.

```
LABEL ON TABLE S IS 'Supplier'

LABEL ON COLUMN P.CITY IS 'Warehouse location'
```

One reason for introducing such labels is that they can be longer than regular SQL/DS names (maximum 30 characters instead of 18). Labels, like comments, can be applied to both base tables and views (or to columns thereof). They can be retrieved via the regular SQL SELECT statement (also via DESCRIBE—see Chapter 15).

9.4 SYNONYMS

It is convenient to close this chapter with a brief discussion of *synonyms,* although the topic does not really have much to do with the catalog as such (except inasmuch as synonyms are recorded in the catalog, like most other objects). Briefly, a synonym is an alternative name for a table (base table or view). In particular, you can define a synonym for a table that was created by some other user and for which you would otherwise have to use a fully qualified name. For example, suppose user ALPHA issues the statement:

```
CREATE TABLE SAMPLE ...
```

User BETA can refer to this table as ALPHA.SAMPLE—for instance,

```
SELECT *
FROM   ALPHA.SAMPLE
```

Alternatively, user BETA can issue:

```
CREATE SYNONYM ZTEST FOR ALPHA.SAMPLE
```

and can now refer to the table as simply ZTEST—for instance,

```
SELECT *
FROM    ZTEST
```

The name ZTEST is completely private and local to user BETA. Another
user GAMMA can also have a private and local name ZTEST, distinct from
user BETA's.

Another example:

```
CREATE SYNONYM TABLES FOR SYSTEM.SYSCATALOG
```

There is also a DROP SYNONYM statement—syntax:

```
DROP SYNONYM synonym
```

For example:

```
DROP SYNONYM TABLES
```

In SQL/DS, dropping a table (base table or view) does *not* cause synonyms
on that table to be dropped automatically.

EXERCISES

9.1 Sketch the details of the catalog for the suppliers-parts-projects database.

Now write SELECT statements for the following queries (numbers 9.2–9.8).

9.2 Which tables include a CITY column?

9.3 How many columns are there in the shipments table?

9.4 List the names of all catalog tables.

9.5 List the names of all users that have created a table with a CITY column, together with the names of the tables concerned.

9.6 List the names of all users that have created at least one table, together with
the number of tables created in each case.

9.7 List the names of all tables that have at least one index.

9.8 List the names of all tables that have more than one index.

9.9 Write statements to do the following:
(a) Create an appropriate comment on the SPJ table.
(b) Change that comment to "Ignore previous comment".
(c) Create an appropriate comment on the P# column of the SPJ table.
(d) Create an appropriate comment on the XS index.
(e) Create an appropriate label for the P# column of the SPJ table.
(f) Create an appropriate synonym for the SYSCOLUMNS table.
(g) Drop that synonym.

ANSWERS TO SELECTED EXERCISES

As usual the following solutions are not necessarily unique.

9.2
```
SELECT  TNAME
FROM    SYSTEM.SYSCOLUMNS
WHERE   CNAME = 'CITY'
```

9.3
```
SELECT  NCOLS
FROM    SYSTEM.SYSCATALOG
WHERE   TNAME = 'SPJ'
```

9.4
```
SELECT  TNAME
FROM    SYSTEM.SYSCATALOG
WHERE   CREATOR = 'SYSTEM'
```

9.5
```
SELECT  CREATOR, TNAME
FROM    SYSTEM.SYSCATALOG
WHERE   TNAME IN
      ( SELECT  TNAME
        FROM    SYSTEM.SYSCOLUMNS
        WHERE   CNAME = 'CITY' )
```

9.6
```
SELECT  CREATOR, COUNT(*)
FROM    SYSTEM.SYSCATALOG
GROUP   BY CREATOR
```

9.7
```
SELECT  TNAME
FROM    SYSTEM.SYSINDEXES
```

9.8
```
SELECT  TNAME
FROM    SYSTEM.SYSINDEXES
GROUP   BY TNAME
HAVING  COUNT (INAME) > 1
```

9.9

(a) `COMMENT ON TABLE SPJ IS 'Appropriate comment'`

(b) `COMMENT ON TABLE SPJ IS 'Ignore previous comment'`

(c) `COMMENT ON COLUMN SPJ.P# IS 'Appropriate comment'`

(d) Trick question! It is not possible to COMMENT ON an index.

(e) `LABEL ON COLUMN SPJ.P# IS 'Part shipped'`

(f) `CREATE SYNONYM COLS FOR SYSTEM.SYSCOLUMNS`

(g) `DROP SYNONYM COLS`

Views

10.1 INTRODUCTION

Recall from Chapter 1 that a view is a *virtual table*—that is, a table that does not exist in its own right but looks to the user as if it did. (By contrast, a base table is a *real* table, in the sense that, for each row of such a table, there really is some stored counterpart of that row in physical storage. See Chapter 16). Views are not supported by their own, physically separate, distinguishable stored data. Instead, their *definition* in terms of other tables is stored in the catalog (actually in a catalog table called SYSVIEWS). Here is an example:

```
CREATE VIEW GOOD_SUPPLIERS
    AS SELECT S#, STATUS, CITY
       FROM   S
       WHERE  STATUS > 15
```

155

When this CREATE VIEW is executed, the subquery following the AS (which is in fact the definition of the view) is *not* executed; instead, it is simply saved in the catalog, under the specified view name (GOOD_SUPPLIERS). To the user, however, it is now as if there really were a table in the database called GOOD_SUPPLIERS, with rows and columns as shown in the unshaded portions (only) of Fig. 10.1 below.

GOOD_SUPPLIERS is in effect a "window" into the real table S. Furthermore, that window is *dynamic:* Changes to S will be automatically and instantaneously visible through that window (provided, of course, that those changes lie within the unshaded portion of S); likewise, changes to GOOD_SUPPLIERS will automatically and instantaneously be applied to the real table S (see Section 10.4, later), and hence of course be visible through the window.

Now, depending on the user's level of sophistication (and perhaps also on the application concerned), the user may or may not realize that GOOD_SUPPLIERS really is a view; some users may be aware of that fact (and of the fact that there is a real table S underneath), others may genuinely believe that GOOD_SUPPLIERS is a "real" table in its own right. Either way, it makes little difference: The point is, users can operate on GOOD_SUPPLIERS just as if it were a real table (with certain exceptions, to be discussed later). For instance, here is an example of a retrieval operation (SELECT statement) against GOOD_SUPPLIERS:

```
SELECT *
FROM    GOOD_SUPPLIERS
WHERE   CITY ~= 'London'
```

As you can see, this SELECT certainly looks just like a normal SELECT on a conventional base table. The system (actually a subcomponent of the RDS) handles such an operation by converting it into an equivalent operation on the underlying base table (or base tables, plural—see Section 10.2). In the example, the equivalent operation is

```
SELECT S#, STATUS, CITY
FROM    S
WHERE   CITY ~= 'London'
AND     STATUS > 15
```

GOOD_SUPPLIERS	S#	SNAME	STATUS	CITY
	--	-----	------	------
	S1	Smith	20	London
	S2	Jones	10	Paris
	S3	Blake	30	Paris
	S4	Clark	20	London
	S5	Adams	30	Athens

Fig. 10.1 GOOD_SUPPLIERS as a view of base table S (unshaded portions)

This new statement can now be compiled and executed in the usual way. The conversion is done by (in effect) *merging* the SELECT issued by the user with the SELECT that was saved in the catalog when the view was defined. From the catalog, the system knows that "FROM GOOD_SUPPLIERS" really means "FROM S"; it also knows that any selection from GOOD_SUPPLIERS must be further qualified by the WHERE condition "STATUS > 15"; and it also knows that "SELECT *" (from GOOD SUPPLIERS) really means "SELECT S#, STATUS, CITY" (from S). Hence it is able to translate the original SELECT on the virtual table GOOD SUPPLIERS into an equivalent SELECT on the real table S—equivalent, in the sense that the effect of executing that SELECT on the real table S is as if there really were a base table called GOOD_SUPPLIERS, and the original SELECT were executed on that.

Update operations are treated in a similar manner. For example, the operation

```
UPDATE  GOOD_SUPPLIERS
SET     STATUS = STATUS + 10
WHERE   CITY = 'Paris'
```

will be converted into

```
UPDATE S
SET     STATUS = STATUS + 10
WHERE   CITY = 'Paris'
AND     STATUS > 15
```

INSERT and DELETE operations are handled analogously.

10.2 VIEW DEFINITION

The general syntax of CREATE VIEW is

```
CREATE VIEW view [ ( column [, column ] ... ) ]
     AS subquery
```

As usual, the subquery cannot include either UNION or ORDER BY;* apart from these restrictions, however, any SELECT that can appear as a standalone statement can also appear in a CREATE VIEW statement. Here are some examples.

1.  ```
    CREATE VIEW REDPARTS ( P#, PNAME, WT, CITY )
         AS SELECT P#, PNAME, WEIGHT, CITY
            FROM    P
            WHERE   COLOR = 'Red'
    ```

---

*UNION and ORDER BY can be used in retrieval operations involving the view, of course.
    ```

The effect of this statement is to create a new view called *xyz*.REDPARTS, where *xyz* is the user ID for the user issuing the CREATE VIEW statement. User *xyz* can refer to the view as simply REDPARTS; other users can refer to it as *xyz*.REDPARTS (alternatively, of course, they can introduce a synonym for it, as discussed in Chapter 9). The view has four columns, called P#, PNAME, WT, and CITY, corresponding respectively to the four columns P#, PNAME, WEIGHT, and CITY of the underlying base table P#. If column names are not specified explicitly in the CREATE VIEW, then the view inherits column names from the source of the view in the obvious way (in the example, the inherited names would be P#, PNAME, WEIGHT, and CITY). Column names *must* be specified explicitly (for all columns of the view) if

(a) any column of the view is derived from a function, an operational expression, or a constant (and so has no name that can be inherited), or if

(b) two or more columns of the view would otherwise have the same name.

See the next two examples for illustrations of each of these two cases.

2.  ```
    CREATE VIEW PQ ( P#, TOTQTY )
         AS SELECT P#, SUM (QTY)
            FROM   SP
            GROUP  BY P#
    ```

In this example, there is no name that can be inherited for the second column, since that column is derived from a function; hence column names *must* be specified explicitly, as shown. Notice that this view is not just a simple row-and-column subset of the underlying base table (unlike the views REDPARTS and GOOD_SUPPLIERS shown earlier). It might be regarded instead as a kind of statistical summary or compression of that underlying table.

3.  ```
    CREATE VIEW CITY_PAIRS ( SCITY, PCITY )
         AS SELECT S.CITY, P.CITY
            FROM   S, SP, P
            WHERE  S.S# = SP.S#
            AND    SP.P# = P.P#
    ```

The meaning of this particular view is that a pair of city names (x,y) will appear in the view if a supplier located in city x supplies a part stored in city y. For example, supplier S1 supplies part P1; supplier S1 is located in London and part P1 is stored in London; and so the pair (London,London) appears in the view. Notice that the definition of this view involves a join, so that this is an example of a view that is derived from multiple underlying tables. (*Note:* We could have included the specification DISTINCT in the definition of this view if we had wished. Compare Example 6.3.5 in Chapter 6.)

4.  ```
    CREATE VIEW LONDON_REDPARTS
         AS SELECT P#, WT
            FROM    REDPARTS
            WHERE   CITY = 'London'
    ```

Since the definition of a view can be any valid subquery, and since a subquery can select data from views as well as from base tables, it is perfectly possible to define a view in terms of other views, as in this example.

The syntax of DROP VIEW is

```
DROP VIEW view
```

The specified view is dropped (i.e., its definition is removed from the catalog). Any views defined in terms of that view are automatically dropped too. Here is an example:

```
DROP VIEW REDPARTS
```

If a base table is dropped, all views defined on that base table (or on views of that base table, etc.) are automatically dropped too.

There is no ALTER VIEW statement. Altering a base table (via ALTER TABLE) has no effect on any existing views.

10.3 RETRIEVAL OPERATIONS

We have already explained in outline (in Section 10.1) how retrieval operations on a view are converted into equivalent operations on the underlying base table(s). Usually that conversion process is quite straightforward and works perfectly well, without any surprises for the user. Occasionally, however, such surprises can occur. In particular, problems can arise if the user tries to treat a view field as a conventional field and that view field is derived from something other than a simple field of the underlying base table—for example, if it is derived from a function. Consider the following example.

View definition:

```
CREATE VIEW PQ ( P#, TOTQTY )
     AS SELECT P#, SUM (QTY)
        FROM    SP
        GROUP   BY P#
```

(this is the "statistical summary" view, Example 2 from Section 10.2).

Attempted query:

```
SELECT *
FROM    PQ
WHERE   TOTQTY > 500
```

If we apply the simple merging process described in Section 10.1 to combine this query with the view definition stored in the catalog, we obtain something like the following:
```

```
SELECT  P#, SUM (QTY)
FROM    SP
WHERE   SUM (QTY) > 500
GROUP   BY P#
```

And this is not a valid SELECT statement. Predicates in a WHERE clause are not allowed to refer to aggregate functions such as SUM. What the original query should be converted to is something more along the following lines:

```
SELECT  P#, SUM (QTY)
FROM    SP
GROUP   BY P#
HAVING  SUM (QTY) > 500
```

However, SQL/DS is not capable of performing such a conversion.

Here is another example of a situation in which the conversion does not work (again using the statistical summary view PQ). The attempted query is:

```
SELECT  AVG (TOTQTY)
FROM    PQ
```

"Converted" form:

```
SELECT  AVG ( SUM (QTY) )
FROM    SP
GROUP   BY P#
```

Again this is illegal. SQL does not allow aggregate functions to be nested in this fashion.

The general principle that these two examples* violate is: The converted form of the original query must always be a legal SQL SELECT statement.

10.4   UPDATE OPERATIONS

We have already stated (in Chapter 8) that *not all views are updatable.* We are now in a position to be able to amplify that statement. *Note:* Before going any further, we should stress the point that SQL/DS—like most other systems at the time of writing—does not in fact handle the updating of views in a very systematic manner. In what follows, therefore, we first consider the question of view updating from a somewhat theoretical standpoint, then go on to discuss the more directly practical question of how SQL/DS actually behaves. The whole subject of view updating in general is

---

*And others like them; there is unfortunately no claim that this section is exhaustive in any sense (surprises can occur in many other circumstances also). SQL really does not do a very good job on views.

discussed in much more detail (but rather formally) in the book *Relational Database: Selected Writings,* by C. J. Date (Addison-Wesley, 1986).

First, consider the two views GOOD_SUPPLIERS and CITY_PAIRS defined earlier in this chapter. For convenience, we repeat their definitions below:

```
CREATE VIEW GOOD_SUPPLIERS              CREATE VIEW CITY_PAIRS
                                            ( SCITY, PCITY )
    AS SELECT S#, STATUS, CITY          AS SELECT S.CITY, P.CITY
       FROM   S                            FROM   S, SP, P
       WHERE  STATUS > 15                  WHERE  S.S# = SP.S#
                                           AND    SP.P# = P.P#
```

Of these two views, GOOD_SUPPLIERS is logically updatable, while CITY_PAIRS is logically not. It is instructive to examine why this is so. In the case of GOOD_SUPPLIERS:

(a) We can INSERT a new row into the view—say the row (S6,40,Rome)— by actually inserting the corresponding row (S6,NULL,40,Rome) into the underlying base table. *Note:* We assume for the sake of the example that field SNAME is not defined to be NOT NULL.

(b) We can DELETE an existing row from the view—say the row (S1,20,London)—by actually deleting the corresponding row (S1,Smith,20,London) from the underlying base table.

(c) We can UPDATE an existing field in the view—say to change the city for supplier S1 from London to Rome—by actually making that same change in the corresponding field in the underlying base table.

We will refer to a view such as GOOD_SUPPLIERS, which is derived from a single base table by simply eliminating certain rows and certain columns of that table, *while preserving that table's primary key,* as a *key-preserving-subset* view. (Remember from Chapter 1 that the primary key is basically just a unique identifier.) Such views are inherently updatable, as the foregoing discussion shows by example.

Now consider the view CITY_PAIRS (which is certainly not a key-preserving-subset view). As explained earlier, one of the rows in that view is the row (London,London). Suppose it were possible to DELETE that row. What would such a DELETE signify?—i.e., what updates (DELETEs or otherwise) on the underlying data would such a DELETE correspond to? The only possible answer has to be "We don't know"; there is simply no way (in general) that we can go down to the underlying base tables and make an appropriate set of updates there. In fact, such an "appropriate set of updates" does not even exist; there is no set of updates (in general) that could be applied to the underlying data that would have *precisely* the effect of removing the row (London,London) from the view while leaving everything else in the view unchanged. In other words, *the original DELETE is an inherently unsupportable operation.* Similar arguments can be made to show that INSERT and UPDATE operations are also inherently not supportable on this view.

Thus we see that some views are inherently updatable, whereas others are inherently not. *Note the word "inherently" here.* It is not just a question of some systems being able to support certain updates while others cannot. *No* system can consistently support updates on a view such as CITY_PAIRS unaided (by "unaided" we mean "without help from some human user"). As a consequence of this fact, it is possible to classify views as indicated in the following Venn diagram (Fig. 10.2).

Note carefully from the diagram that although key-preserving-subset

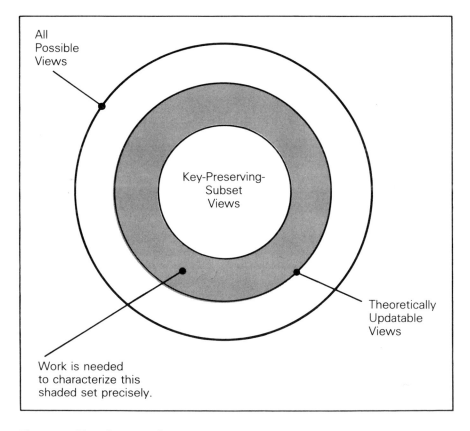

Fig. 10.2 Classification of views

views (such as GOOD_SUPPLIERS) are always theoretically updatable, *not all theoretically updatable views are key-preserving-subset views.* In other words, there are some views that *are* theoretically updatable that are *not* key-preserving-subset views. The trouble is, although we know that such views exist, we do not know precisely which ones they are; it is still (in part) a research problem to pin down precisely what it is that characterizes such views.

Now, although it is true that SQL/DS does support the concept of a primary key, it is unfortunately the case that that support was added only recently—it was not included in the first few releases. As a result, SQL/DS's view-updating mechanism does not operate in terms of key-preserving-subset views. Instead, it operates in terms of what we will call *row-and-column-subset* views. A row-and-column-subset view is a view that is derived from a single base table by simply eliminating certain rows and certain columns of that table. A row-and-column-subset view may or may not be a key-preserving-subset view. (More precisely, all key-preserving-subset views are row-and-column-subset views, but the converse is not true.) For the purposes of this book, therefore, the important point is the following:

In SQL/DS, only row-and-column-subset views can be updated.

(Actually even this statement is still not 100 percent accurate. We will make it more precise in a moment.) SQL/DS is not alone in this regard, by the way; very few products currently support update operations on views that are not row-and-column-subsets, and *no* product currently supports update operations on all views that are theoretically updatable.

The fact that not all views are updatable is frequently expressed as "You cannot update a join." That statement is *not* an accurate characterization of the situation, nor indeed of the problem: There are some views that are not joins that are not updatable, and there are some views that are joins that are (theoretically) updatable—although not updatable in SQL/DS. But it is true that joins represent the "interesting case," in the sense that it would be very convenient to be able to update a view whose definition involved a join. Now, it may well be the case that such views will indeed be updatable in some future release; but we are concerned here only with what SQL/DS will currently allow. Let us now make it clear exactly what that is. In SQL/DS, a view that is to accept updates must be derived from a single base table. Moreover:

(a) If a field of the view is derived from an expression involving a scalar operator or a scalar function or a constant, then INSERT operations are not allowed, and UPDATE operations are not allowed on that field. However, DELETE operations are allowed.

(b) If a field of the view is derived from an aggregate function, then the view is not updatable.

(c) If the definition of the view involves GROUP BY or HAVING, then the view is not updatable.

(d) If the definition of the view involves DISTINCT, then the view is not updatable.

(e) If the definition of the view includes a nested subquery and the FROM clause in that subquery refers to the base table on which the view is defined, then the view is not updatable.

(f) If the FROM clause in the view definition involves multiple (explicit or implicit) range variables, then the view is not updatable.

In addition, of course, a view defined over a nonupdatable view is itself not updatable.

Let us examine the reasonableness of these restrictions. We consider each of the cases (a)–(f) in turn. For each case, we begin by considering an example of a view that illustrates the restriction.

Case (a): View field derived from an expression involving a scalar operator
(or a scalar function or a constant)

```
CREATE VIEW P_IN_GRAMS ( P#, GMWT )
     AS SELECT P#, WEIGHT * 454
        FROM    P
```

Assuming that table P is as given in Fig. 1.2 (Chapter 1), the set of rows visible through this view is as follows:

```
P_IN_GRAMS    P#    GMWT
              --    ----
              P1    5448
              P2    7718
              P3    7718
              P4    6356
              P5    5448
              P6    8626
```

It should be clear that P_IN_GRAMS cannot support INSERT operations, nor UPDATE operations on the field GMWT. (Each of those operations would require the system to be able to convert a gram weight back into pounds, without any instructions as to how to perform such a conversion.) On the other hand, DELETE operations can be supported (e.g., deleting the row for part P1 from the view can be handled by deleting the row for part P1 from the underlying base table), and so can UPDATE operations on field P# (such UPDATEs simply require a corresponding UPDATE on field P# of that base table). Similar considerations apply to a view that includes a field that is derived from a scalar function or a constant.

Case (b): View field derived from an aggregate function

```
CREATE VIEW TQ ( TOTQTY )
       AS SELECT SUM (QTY)
              FROM    SP
```

Sample value:

```
TQ    TOTQTY
      ------
        3100
```

It should be obvious that none of INSERT, UPDATE, DELETE makes any sense on this view.

Case (c): View defined with GROUP BY (and/or HAVING)

```
CREATE VIEW PQ ( P#, TOTQTY )
       AS SELECT P#, SUM (QTY)
              FROM    SP
              GROUP  BY P#
```

Sample values:

```
PQ   P#    TOTQTY
     --    ------
     P1       600
     P2      1000
     P3       400
     P4       500
     P5       500
     P6       100
```

It is obvious that view PQ cannot support INSERT operations, nor UPDATE operations against field TOTQTY. DELETE operations, and UPDATE operations against field P#, theoretically *could* be defined to DELETE or UPDATE all corresponding rows in table SP—for example, the operation

```
DELETE
FROM    PQ
WHERE   P# = 'P1'
```

could be defined to translate into

```
DELETE
FROM    SP
WHERE   P# = 'P1'
```

—but such operations could equally well be expressed directly in terms of table SP anyway. And it is at least arguable that a user who is issuing such operations should have to know exactly which real records are affected by those operations.

Case (d): View defined with DISTINCT

```
CREATE VIEW CC
     AS SELECT DISTINCT COLOR, CITY
        FROM   P
```

Sample values (with corresponding part number(s) shown):

```
CC    COLOR  CITY
      -----  ------
      Red    London    (from P1,P4,P6)
      Green  Paris     (from P2)
      Blue   Rome      (from P3)
      Blue   Paris     (from P5)
```

Again, it should be clear that view CC cannot support INSERT operations (INSERTs on the underlying table P require the user to specify a P# value, because part numbers are defined to be NOT NULL). As in case (c), DELETE and UPDATE operations *could* theoretically be defined (to DELETE or UPDATE all corresponding rows in P), but the remarks on this possibility under case (c) apply again here, with perhaps even more force.

Here is another example of case (d):

```
CREATE VIEW PC
     AS SELECT DISTINCT P#, COLOR
        FROM   P
```

Sample values:

```
PC    P#    COLOR
      --    -----
      P1    Red
      P2    Green
      P3    Blue
      P4    Red
      P5    Blue
      P6    Red
```

This is an example of a view that is obviously updatable in theory—all possible INSERT, UPDATE, and DELETE operations against the view are clearly well-defined. In fact, the view is really a row-and-column-subset view (actually, it is a key-preserving-subset view); but *SQL/DS is not aware of that fact*. To put it another way, SQL/DS is not aware of the fact that the DISTINCT specification is actually superfluous here; instead, it simply assumes that the presence of DISTINCT means that any given row of the view *might* be derived from multiple rows of the base table, as in the previous example, and so does not consider the view to be updatable.

Case (e): View involving subquery over same table

```
CREATE VIEW S_UNDER_AVG
    AS SELECT S#, SNAME, STATUS, CITY
       FROM   S
       WHERE  STATUS <
              ( SELECT AVG (STATUS)
                FROM   S )
```

UPDATE and DELETE operations against S_UNDER_AVG are illegal because they would violate the restriction on such operations mentioned at the end of Chapter 8 (Section 8.5). INSERT operations are illegal also for essentially similar reasons.

Case (f): View involving multiple (explicit or implicit) range variables

```
CREATE VIEW CITY_PAIRS ( SCITY, PCITY )
          AS SELECT S.CITY, P.CITY
             FROM   S, P
             WHERE  S.S# = SP.S#
             AND    SP.P# = P.P#
```

This view is not updatable, for reasons that have already been adequately discussed at the beginning of this section. However, consider this next example:

```
CREATE VIEW P2_SUPPLIERS
        AS SELECT S.*
           FROM   S, SP
           WHERE  S.S# = SP.S#
           AND    SP.P# = 'P2'
```

This view is also not updatable in SQL/DS, even though (once again) it is in fact a key-preserving-subset view; once again, SQL/DS is not capable of recognizing that fact. What makes this example interesting is that in this case a semantically equivalent view can be defined that *is* updatable, viz.:

```
CREATE VIEW P2_SUPPLIERS
        AS SELECT S.*
           FROM   S
           WHERE  S# IN
                  ( SELECT S#
                    FROM   SP
                    WHERE  P# = 'P2' )
```

This version does not violate the "multiple tables in the FROM clause" rule.

Finally, we return to the GOOD_SUPPLIERS view once again, in order to discuss a number of remaining issues. The definition of that view (to repeat) is:

```
CREATE VIEW GOOD_SUPPLIERS
   AS SELECT S#, STATUS, CITY
      FROM   S
      WHERE  STATUS > 15
```

This view is a row-and-column-subset view and is therefore updatable. But note the following:

(a) First, to repeat a point made earlier in this section, a successful INSERT against GOOD_SUPPLIERS will have to generate a null for the missing field SNAME. Of course, field SNAME must not have been defined with the specification NOT NULL if the INSERT is to succeed.

(b) With the data values given in Fig. 1.2, supplier S2 will not be visible through the GOOD_SUPPLIERS view. But that does not mean that the user can INSERT a record into that view with supplier number value S2, or UPDATE one of the other records so that its supplier number value becomes S2. Such an operation must be rejected, just as if it had been applied directly to table S.

(c) Last, consider the following UPDATE:

```
UPDATE GOOD_SUPPLIERS
SET    STATUS = 0
WHERE  S# = 'S1'
```

The effect of this UPDATE will be to remove supplier S1 from the view, since the S1 record will no longer satisfy the view-defining predicate. Likewise, the INSERT operation

```
INSERT
INTO   GOOD_SUPPLIERS ( S#, STATUS, CITY )
VALUES ( 'S8', 7, 'Stockholm' )
```

will create a new supplier record, but that record will instantly vanish from the view, because (again) the record does not satisfy the view-defining predicate. Avoiding situations like these is the user's responsibility.

10.5 LOGICAL DATA INDEPENDENCE

We have not yet really explained what views are for. One of the things they are for is the provision of what is called *logical data independence*. The notion of *physical* data independence was introduced in Chapter 2: A system like SQL/DS is said to provide physical data independence because users and user programs are independent of the physical structure of the stored database. A system provides *logical* data independence if users and user programs are also independent of the *logical* structure of the database. There are two aspects to such independence, namely *growth* and *restructuring*.

Growth

As the database grows to incorporate new kinds of information, so the definition of the database must also grow accordingly. (*Note:* We discuss the question of growth in the database here only for completeness; it is important, but it has nothing to do with views as such.) There are two possible types of growth that can occur:

1. The expansion of an existing base table to include a new field (corresponding to the addition of new information concerning some existing type of object—for example, the addition of a COST field to the parts base table);

2. The inclusion of a new base table (corresponding to the addition of a new type of object—for example, the addition of a projects table to the suppliers-and-parts database).

Neither of these two kinds of change should have any effect on existing users at all (unless those users have been using "SELECT *" or INSERT with the list of field names omitted; as mentioned earlier in this book, the meanings of such statements may change if they happen to be "reprepped" and the definition of the table concerned has changed in the interim).

Restructuring

Occasionally it may become necessary to restructure the database in such a way that, although the overall information content remains the same, the placement of information within that database changes—i.e., the allocation of fields to tables is altered in some way. Before proceeding further, we make the point that such restructuring is generally undesirable; however, it is sometimes unavoidable. For example, it may be necessary to split a table "vertically," so that commonly required columns can be stored on a faster device and less frequently required columns on a slower device. Let us consider this case in some detail. Suppose for the sake of the example that it becomes necessary (for some reason—the precise reason is not important here) to replace base table S by the following two base tables:

```
SX   ( S#, SNAME, CITY )
SY   ( S#, STATUS )
```

Aside: This replacement operation is not entirely trivial, by the way. One way it might be handled is by means of the following sequence of SQL operations:

```
CREATE TABLE SX
      ( S#         CHAR(5)   NOT NULL,
        SNAME      CHAR(20)  NOT NULL,
        CITY       CHAR(15)  NOT NULL,
      PRIMARY KEY ( S# ) )

CREATE TABLE SY
      ( S#         CHAR(5)   NOT NULL,
        STATUS     SMALLINT,
      PRIMARY KEY ( S# ) )

INSERT INTO SX ( S#, SNAME, CITY )
        SELECT S#, SNAME, CITY
        FROM   S

INSERT INTO SY ( S#, STATUS )
        SELECT S#, STATUS
        FROM   S

DROP TABLE S
```

To return to the main topic of discussion: The crucial point to observe in the example is that *the old table S is the* (*natural*) *join of the two new tables SX and SY* (over supplier numbers). For example, in table S we had the row (S1,Smith,20,London); in SX we now have the row (S1,Smith,London) and in SY the row (S1,20); join them together and we get the row (S1,Smith,20,London), as before. So we create a *view* that is exactly that join, and we name it S:

```
CREATE VIEW S ( S#, SNAME, STATUS, CITY )
    AS SELECT SX.S#, SX.SNAME, SY.STATUS, SX.CITY
       FROM   SX, SY
       WHERE  SX.S# = SY.S#
```

Any program that previously referred to base table S will now refer to view S instead. SELECT operations will continue to work exactly as before (though they will require additional analysis at prep time and will incur additional overhead at run time). However, update operations will no longer work, because (as explained in Section 10.4) SQL/DS will not allow updates against a view that is defined as a join. In other words, a user performing update operations is not immune to this type of change, but instead must make some manual alterations to the update statements concerned (and then "reprep" them).

Thus we have shown that SQL/DS does *not* provide complete protection against changes in the logical structure of the database (which is why such changes are not a good idea in the first place). But things may not be as bad as they seem, even if manual program alterations are necessary. First, it is easy to discover which programs have to be altered in the light of any such changes; that information can be obtained from the catalog. Second, it is easy to find the statements that need to be changed in those programs; quite apart from anything else, they all start with the prefix EXEC SQL.

Third (and most significant), SQL is a very high-level language. The number of statements that have to be changed is therefore usually small, and the meaning of those statements is usually readily apparent; as a result, the necessary changes are usually easy to make. It is *not* like having to change statements in a comparatively low-level language such as COBOL (or the database language of a nonrelational system), where the meaning of a given statement is likely to be highly dependent on the dynamic flow of control through the program to the statement in question. So, even though it is true that manual corrections must be made, the amount of work involved may not be all that great in practice.

To return to the SX-SY example for a moment: Actually, the view S (defined as the join of SX and SY) is a good example of a join view that *is* theoretically updatable. If we assume that there is a one-to-one correspondence between SX and SY at all times (so that any supplier appearing in SX also appears in SY, and vice versa), then the effect of all possible update operations on view S is clearly defined in terms of SX and SY. (Exercise: Do you agree with this statement?) Thus the example illustrates, not only why the ability to update join views would be a useful system feature, but also a case where such updating appears to be a feasible proposition.

10.6 ADVANTAGES OF VIEWS

We conclude this chapter with a brief summary of the advantages of views.

- They provide a certain amount of logical data independence in the face of restructuring in the database, as explained in the previous section.

- They allow the same data to be seen by different users in different ways (possibly even at the same time).

  This consideration is obviously important when there are many different categories of user all interacting with a single integrated database.

- The user's perception is simplified.

  It is obvious that the view mechanism allows users to focus on just the data that is of concern to them and to ignore the rest. What is perhaps not so obvious is that, for retrieval at least, that mechanism can also considerably simplify users' data manipulation operations. In particular, because the user can be provided with a view in which all underlying tables are joined together, the need for explicit operations to step from table to table can be greatly reduced. As an example, consider the view CITY_PAIRS, and contrast (a) the SELECT needed to find cities storing parts that are available from London, using that view, with (b) the SELECT needed to obtain the same result directly from the underlying base tables. In effect, the complex selection process has been moved out of the realm of data manipulation and into that of data definition (in fact, the distinction between the two realms is far from clearcut in relational languages like SQL).

- Automatic security is provided for hidden data.

  "Hidden data" refers to data not visible through some given view. Such data is clearly secure from access through that particular view. Thus, forcing users to access the database via views is a simple but effective mechanism for authorization control. We will discuss this aspect of views in greater detail in the next chapter.

EXERCISES

10.1 Define relation SP of the suppliers-and-parts database as a view of relation SPJ of the suppliers-parts-projects database.

10.2 Create a view from the suppliers-parts-projects database consisting of all projects (project number and city fields only) that are supplied by supplier S1 or use part P1.

10.3 Is your solution to Exercise 10.2 an updatable view? If not, give an updatable version.

10.4 Create a view consisting of supplier numbers and part numbers for suppliers and parts that are not "colocated."

10.5 Create a view consisting of supplier records for suppliers that are located in London (only).

10.6 Given the view definition:

```
CREATE VIEW SUMMARY ( S#, P#, MAXQ, MINQ, AVGQ )
     AS SELECT S#, P#, MAX (QTY), MIN (QTY), AVG (QTY)
        FROM   SPJ
        GROUP  BY S#, P#
        HAVING SUM (QTY) > 50
```

state which of the following operations are legal and, for those that are, give the translated equivalents:

```
(a)  SELECT *
     FROM   SUMMARY
```

```
(b)  SELECT *
     FROM   SUMMARY
     ORDER  BY MAXQ
```

```
(c)  SELECT *
     FROM   SUMMARY
     WHERE  S# ~= 'S1'
```

(d) SELECT *
     FROM   SUMMARY
     WHERE   MAXQ > 250

(e) SELECT MAXQ - MINQ, S#, P#
     FROM   SUMMARY
     WHERE   S# = 'S1'
     AND   P# = 'P1'

(f) SELECT S#
     FROM   SUMMARY
     GROUP   BY S#

(g) SELECT S#, MAXQ
     FROM   SUMMARY
     GROUP   BY S#, MAXQ

(h) SELECT S.S#, SUMMARY.AVGQ
     FROM   S, SUMMARY
     WHERE   S.S# = SUMMARY.S#

(i) UPDATE SUMMARY
     SET   S# = 'S2'
     WHERE   S# = 'S1'

(j) UPDATE SUMMARY
     SET   MAXQ = 1000
     WHERE   S# = 'S1'

(k) DELETE
     FROM   SUMMARY
     WHERE   S# = 'S1'

10.7 State the rules concerning the updatability of views in SQL/DS.

10.8 Suppose the database is restructured in such a way that tables *A* and *B* are replaced by their natural join *C*. To what extent can the view mechanism conceal that restructuring from existing users?

10.9 Create a view consisting of names of all cities that appear either in the suppliers table or in the parts table.

ANSWERS TO SELECTED EXERCISES

10.1 The problem here is: How should the field SP.QTY be defined? The sensible answer seems to be that, for a given (S#,P#) pair, SP.QTY should be the *sum* of all SPJ.QTY values, taken over all J#'s for that (S#,P#) pair:

```
CREATE VIEW SP ( S#, P#, QTY )
    AS SELECT S#, P#, SUM (QTY)
       FROM    SPJ
       GROUP   BY S#, P#
```

10.2 CREATE VIEW JC (J#, CITY)
     AS SELECT DISTINCT J.J#, J.CITY
        FROM   J, SPJ
        WHERE   J.J# = SPJ.J#
        AND   (SPJ.S# = 'S1' OR
               SPJ.P# = 'P1')

10.3 The view defined in the answer to Exercise 10.2 above is not updatable, because it names multiple tables in the FROM clause. Here is an updatable equivalent:

```
CREATE VIEW JC ( J#, CITY )
    AS SELECT J.J#, J.CITY
       FROM    J
       WHERE   J.J# IN
               ( SELECT J#
                 FROM    SPJ
                 WHERE   S# = 'S1' )
          OR   J.J# IN
               ( SELECT J#
                 FROM    SPJ
                 WHERE   P# = 'P1' )
```

10.4 CREATE VIEW NON_COLOCATED
     AS SELECT S#, P#
        FROM   S, P
        WHERE   S.CITY ~= P.CITY

10.5 CREATE VIEW LONDON_SUPPLIERS
     AS SELECT S#, SNAME, STATUS
        FROM   S
        WHERE   CITY = 'London'

We have omitted the CITY column from the view, since we know its value must be London for every row visible through the view. Note, however, that this omission means that any record INSERTed through the view will instantly vanish from the view, since its CITY field will be set to null (we assume for the sake of the example that NOT NULL does not apply to that field).

10.6 Only (a), (c), and (e) are legal. Note in particular that (h) is not legal: A view in SQL/DS whose definition includes a GROUP BY cannot be joined to another table. We give the translated equivalent for (e) only:

```
SELECT MAX (QTY) - MIN (QTY), S#, P#
FROM    SPJ
WHERE   S# = 'S1'
AND     P# = 'P1'
GROUP   BY S#, P#
HAVING SUM (QTY) > 50
```

10.9 Cannot be done; SQL does not permit UNION to appear in a view definition (for no particularly good reason).

Security and Authorization

11.1 INTRODUCTION

The term "security" is used in database contexts to mean the protection of the data in the database against unauthorized disclosure, alteration, or destruction. SQL/DS, like most other relational systems, goes far beyond most nonrelational systems in the degree of security it provides. The unit of data that can be individually protected ranges all the way from an entire table to a specific data value at a specific row-and-column position within such a table. A given user can have different access privileges on different objects (e.g., SELECT privilege only on one table, SELECT and UPDATE privileges on another, and so on). Also, of course, different users can have different privileges on the same object; e.g., user *A* could have SELECT privilege (only) on a given table, while another user *B* could simultaneously have both SELECT and UPDATE privileges on that same table.

There are two more or less independent features of the system that are involved in the provision of security in SQL/DS:

1. The view mechanism, which (as mentioned at the end of the previous chapter) can be used to hide sensitive data from unauthorized users, and

2. The authorization subsystem, which allows users having specific privileges selectively and dynamically to grant those privileges to other users, and subsequently to revoke those privileges if desired.

We examine the view mechanism in Section 11.3 and the authorization subsystem (specifically, the GRANT and REVOKE statements) in Section 11.4.

Of course, all decisions as to which specific privileges should be granted to which specific users are policy decisions, not technical ones. As such, they are clearly outside the jurisdiction of SQL/DS per se. All that SQL/DS can do is *enforce* those decisions once they are made. In order that SQL/DS should be able to perform this function properly:

(a) The results of those decisions must be made known to the system (this is done by means of the GRANT and REVOKE statements) and must be remembered by the system (this is done by saving them in the catalog, in the form of *authorization constraints*).

(b) There must be a means of checking a given access request against the applicable authorization constraints. (By "access request" here we mean the combination of requested operation plus target object plus requesting user.) Most such checking is done at the time the original request is compiled. However, if a check fails at compile time, it will be repeated when the request concerned is executed (the necessary authorization may have been granted since the program was originally compiled). If the check fails again at execution time, of course, the request will be rejected.

(c) In order that it may be able to decide which constraints are applicable to a given request, the system must be able to recognize the source of that request—that is, it must be able to recognize which particular user a particular request is coming from. Before getting into a discussion of the view mechanism and the authorization subsystem as such, then, we must first say something about user identification.

11.2 USER IDENTIFICATION

Users are known to SQL/DS by their "user ID." If you are a legitimate user of the system, some responsible person in your organization (probably the database administrator—see Section 11.4, later) will have assigned a user ID for your particular use. It is your responsibility to identify yourself by supplying that ID when you sign on to the system. Details of exactly how you perform this identification process depend to some extent on the environment in which you are operating. For example, in ISQL under VSE, you can supply your ID (and a password) at the time ISQL is invoked. ISQL then plugs those values in as parameters to an embedded SQL CONNECT statement (see below) and executes that statement on your behalf. The net effect is to "connect" you to SQL/DS.

The syntax of CONNECT is as follows:

```
CONNECT user IDENTIFIED BY password [ TO database ]
```

Here "user" is a user ID and "password" is that user's password. SQL/DS checks that the password is valid before establishing the requested connexion and allowing the user to proceed. (User IDs and corresponding passwords are kept in the SQL/DS catalog.) *Note:* The optional "TO database" clause (VM only) allows the user to connect to another database (on another SQL/DS system). See the discussion of database switching in Chapter 3.

As our ISQL example above suggests, the CONNECT statement is intended primarily for use within application programs (i.e., in embedded SQL). In such a case, "user" and "password" would typically be specified by means of program variables. However, the statement can be used interactively also. For more information, see the IBM manuals.

Details of the sign-on procedure (and hence of precisely how the user ID is specified and validated) in the various SQL/DS environments are beyond the scope of this text. From this point on, we will simply assume (as SQL/DS must assume) that any user request that purports to come from user *xyz* (say) does in fact come from user *xyz*.

11.3   VIEWS AND SECURITY

To illustrate the use of views for security purposes, we present a series of examples, based once again (for the most part) on the suppliers-and-parts database. *Note:* The creator of a view must have at least the SELECT privilege on all the tables referenced in the view definition. See the discussion of access privileges in the next section.

1. For a user permitted access to complete supplier records, but only for suppliers located in Paris:

```
CREATE VIEW PARIS_SUPPLIERS
     AS SELECT S#, SNAME, STATUS, CITY
        FROM   S
        WHERE  CITY = 'Paris'
```

Users of this view see a "horizontal subset"—or (better) a row subset or *value-dependent* subset—of base table S.

2. For a user permitted access to all supplier records, but not to supplier ratings (STATUS values):

```
CREATE VIEW S#_NAME_CITY
     AS SELECT S#, SNAME, CITY
        FROM   S
```

Users of this view see a "vertical subset"—or (better) a column subset or *value-independent* subset—of base table S.

3. For a user permitted access to supplier records for suppliers in Paris (only), but not to supplier ratings:

```
CREATE VIEW PARIS_S#_NAME_CITY
     AS SELECT S#, SNAME, CITY
        FROM   S
        WHERE  CITY = 'Paris'
```

Users of this view see a row-and-column subset of base table S.

4. For a user permitted access to catalog rows (i.e., SYSCATALOG entries) for tables created by that user only:*

```
CREATE VIEW MY_TABLES
     AS SELECT *
        FROM   SYSTEM.SYSCATALOG
        WHERE  CREATOR = USER
```

USER is a "special register"—i.e., a zero-argument scalar function—whose value is a user ID (see Chapter 4). It can appear wherever a character string constant can appear. The user ID in question is the user ID for the user issuing the *manipulative* statement that causes the USER reference to be evaluated. In the case at hand, for instance, it does not represent the ID of the user who creates the view, but rather the ID of the user who *uses* the view. For example, if user Joe issues the statement

```
SELECT *
FROM   MY_TABLES
```

then SQL/DS will effectively convert that statement into

```
SELECT *
FROM   SYSTEM.SYSCATALOG
WHERE  CREATOR = 'JOE'
```

---

*For the sake of the example, we ignore the fact that in practice the entire SQL/DS catalog (with the sole exception of password information) is freely visible to everyone.

Like the view in the first example above, this view represents a "horizontal subset" of the underlying base table. In the present example, however, different users see different subsets (in fact, no two users' subsets overlap). Such subsets are sometimes described as *context-dependent,* because their precise value depends on the context in which they are used.

5. For a user permitted access to average shipment quantities per supplier, but not to any individual quantities:

```
CREATE VIEW AVQ ( S#, AVGQTY )
   AS SELECT S#, AVG(QTY)
      FROM   SP
      GROUP  BY S#
```

Users of this view see a *statistical summary* of the underlying base table SP.

As the foregoing examples illustrate, the view mechanism of SQL/DS provides a very important measure of security "for free" ("for free" because the view mechanism is included in the system for other purposes anyway, as explained in Chapter 10). What is more, many authorization checks—even value-dependent checks—can be applied at compile time instead of at execution time, a significant performance benefit. However, the view-based approach to security does suffer from some slight awkwardness on occasion—in particular, if some user needs different privileges over different subsets of the same table at the same time. Consider the following example. Suppose a given user is allowed to SELECT ratings (i.e., status values) for all suppliers but is allowed to UPDATE them only for suppliers in Paris. Then two views will be needed:

```
CREATE VIEW ALL_RATINGS          CREATE VIEW PARIS_RATING_
   AS SELECT S#, STATUS             AS SELECT S#, STATUS
      FROM   S                         FROM   S
                                       WHERE  CITY = 'Paris'
```

SELECT operations can be directed at ALL_RATINGS, but UPDATE operations must be directed at PARIS_RATINGS instead. This fact can lead to rather obscure programming. Consider, for example, the structure of a program that scans and prints all supplier ratings and also updates some of them (those for suppliers in Paris) as it goes.

Another drawback has to do with the fact that (as explained in Chapter 10), when a record is INSERTed or UPDATEd through a view, SQL/DS does not require that the new or updated record satisfy the view-defining predicate. Thus, for example, view PARIS_SUPPLIERS above can prevent the user from seeing suppliers who are not in Paris, but it cannot prevent the user from inserting such a supplier or from moving an existing Paris supplier to some other city. Of course, any such operation will cause the new or updated record to vanish from the view, but it will still appear in the underlying base table.

11.4 GRANT AND REVOKE

The view mechanism discussed in Section 11.3 allows the database to be conceptually divided up into (possibly overlapping) subsets in various ways so that sensitive information can be hidden from unauthorized users. However, it does not allow for the specification of the operations that *authorized* users may execute against those subsets. That function is performed by the SQL statements GRANT and REVOKE, which we now discuss.

First, in order to be able to perform any operation at all on any object at all, the user must hold the appropriate *privilege* (or authority) for the operation and object in question; otherwise, the operation will be rejected with an appropriate error message or exception code. For example, to execute the statement

```
SELECT *
FROM   S
```

successfully, the user must hold the SELECT privilege on table S.

The privileges recognized by SQL/DS include several different table privileges (SELECT, INSERT, etc., also REFERENCES—see Chapter 12) and a miscellaneous set of other privileges (CONNECT, RESOURCE, RUN, and DBA). Briefly (and simplifying slightly):

(a) Table privileges are needed in order to perform operations on tables (both base tables and views);

(b) The CONNECT privilege is needed in order to connect to the database in the first place;

(c) The RESOURCE privilege is needed in order to create a base table;*

(d) The RUN privilege is needed in order to invoke an access module;

(e) The DBA ("database administrator") privilege is the highest privilege of all. A user holding the DBA privilege can perform any operation in the entire system, providing it is legal. (An example of an operation that would not be "legal" in this sense would be an attempt to drop one of the catalog tables. Even a user with DBA authority cannot do that.)

---

*More precisely, the RESOURCE privilege is needed to create a base table *in a public DBspace,* also to "acquire" a private DBspace. No special privilege is needed to create a base table in your own private DBspace. DBspaces (public and private) are discussed in Chapter 16.

We now present a description (slightly simplified) of how the overall SQL/DS security mechanism works. When a given database is first installed on the system, a single specially privileged user must be designated as the (first or only) DBA for that database. (The database administrator is identified to SQL/DS by a user ID, of course, just like everyone else.) That user, who is automatically given the DBA privilege, will be responsible for overall control of the database throughout its lifetime. Initially, then, there is one user who can do everything—in particular, he or she can grant privileges to other users—and nobody else can do anything at all.*

Next, a user who creates an object—say a base table—is automatically given full privileges on that object, including in particular the privilege of granting such privileges to another user. Of course, "full privileges" here does not include privileges that do not make sense. For example, if user U has the SELECT privilege (only) on base table T, and if U creates some view V that is based on T, then U certainly does not receive any update privileges on V. Likewise, if U creates a view V that is a join of tables $T1$ and $T2$, then U does not receive any update privileges on V, regardless of whether U holds such privileges on $T1$ and $T2$, because SQL/DS does not permit *any* update operations against a join view.

GRANT

Granting privileges is done by means of the GRANT statement. The general format of that statement is:

```
GRANT privileges [ ON object ] TO users
```

where "privileges" is a list of one or more privileges, separated by commas, or the phrase ALL PRIVILEGES (meaning all *table* privileges†); "users" is either a list of one or more user IDs, separated by commas, or the keyword PUBLIC (meaning all users); and "object" is the name of an object of the

---

*Of course, this paragraph should not be construed to mean that there really is a single person who remains *the* database administrator for all time (even if, e.g., that person leaves the company). Rather, there is a single *user ID* that is considered by the system to identify the person in charge. Anyone who can connect to the system under that ID (and can supply the necessary password) will be treated as that person so long as he or she remains signed on. The password *can* of course be changed from time to time, and probably should be.

†It follows that ALL PRIVILEGES can never be used in a GRANT on a view, because not all table privileges apply to views (see later). *Note:* The keyword PRIVILEGES in ALL PRIVILEGES is just noise and can be omitted.

appropriate type (e.g., a table, in the case of table privileges). The ON clause applies only to table and RUN privileges. Here are some examples:

Table privileges:

```
GRANT SELECT ON S TO CHARLEY

GRANT SELECT, UPDATE (STATUS,CITY) ON S TO JUDY, JACK, JOHN

GRANT ALL PRIVILEGES ON S TO TED, SHARON

GRANT SELECT ON P TO PUBLIC
```

Other privileges:

```
GRANT CONNECT TO ALEX

GRANT RESOURCE TO LINDA, JILL

GRANT RUN ON AM335 TO JUDY, JACQUES, MARYANN

GRANT DBA TO PHIL
```

It is not our purpose here to give an exhaustive treatment of all the privileges that SQL/DS recognizes. We will, however, give a complete treatment of table privileges, since those are probably the ones of widest interest. The privileges that apply to tables (both base tables and views) are as follows (excluding REFERENCES, which is discussed in Chapter 12):

```
SELECT
UPDATE        (can be column-specific)
DELETE
INSERT
```

The remaining two apply to base tables only:

```
ALTER         (privilege to execute ALTER on the table)
INDEX         (privilege to execute CREATE INDEX on the table)
```

To *create* a base table, as already mentioned, requires RESOURCE authority. To create a view requires SELECT authority on every table referenced in the definition of that view, as mentioned in Section 11.3. Note that SELECT authority, unlike UPDATE authority, is not column-specific. The reason for this fact is that the effect of a column-specific SELECT authority can always be obtained by granting (non-column-specific) SELECT authority on a *view* consisting of just the relevant columns.

Note that there is no specific "DROP" privilege. Instead, a table (base table or view) can be dropped only by the user who created it (or by a user holding DBA authority).

REVOKE

If user *U1* grants some privilege to some other user *U2*, user *U1* can subsequently *revoke* that privilege from user *U2*. Revoking privileges is done by means of the REVOKE statement, whose general format is very similar to that of the GRANT statement:

```
REVOKE privileges [ ON object ] FROM users
```

Revoking a given privilege from a given user causes all access modules dependent on that privilege to be flagged as invalid, and hence causes an automatic "reprep" on the next invocation of each such module. The process is essentially analogous to what happens when an object such as an index is dropped.

Here are some examples of the REVOKE statement:

```
REVOKE SELECT ON S FROM CHARLEY
```

```
REVOKE UPDATE ON S FROM JOHN
```

```
REVOKE RESOURCE FROM NANCY, JACK
```

```
REVOKE DBA FROM SAM
```

It is not possible to be column-specific when revoking an UPDATE privilege.

The GRANT Option

If user *U1* has the authority to grant a privilege *P* to another user *U2*, then user *U1* also has the authority to grant that privilege *P* to user *U2* "with the GRANT option" (by specifying WITH GRANT OPTION in the GRANT statement). Passing the GRANT option along from *U1* to *U2* in this way means that *U2* in turn now has the authority to grant the privilege *P* to some third user *U3*. And therefore, of course, *U2* also has the authority to pass the GRANT option for *P* along to *U3* as well, etc., etc. For example:

User *U1:*

```
GRANT SELECT ON S TO U2 WITH GRANT OPTION
```

User *U2:*

```
GRANT SELECT ON S TO U3 WITH GRANT OPTION
```

User *U3:*

```
GRANT SELECT ON S TO U4 WITH GRANT OPTION
```

And so on. If user *U1* now issues

```
REVOKE SELECT ON S FROM U2
```

then the revocation will *cascade* (that is, *U2*'s GRANT to *U3* and *U3*'s GRANT to *U4* will also be revoked automatically). Note, however, that it does *not* follow that *U2* and *U3* and *U4* no longer have SELECT authority on table S—they may additionally have obtained that authority from some other user *U5*. When *U1* REVOKEs, it is only authorities that are derived from *U1* that are in fact canceled. For example, consider the following sequence of events:

User *U1* at time *t1:*

```
GRANT SELECT ON S TO U2 WITH GRANT OPTION
```

User *U5* at time *t2:*

```
GRANT SELECT ON S TO U2 WITH GRANT OPTION
```

User *U2* at time *t3:*

```
GRANT SELECT ON S TO U3
```

User *U1* at time *t4:*

```
REVOKE SELECT ON S FROM U2
```

(*t1* < *t2* < *t3* < *t4*). User *U1*'s REVOKE at time *t4* will not in fact remove the SELECT privilege on table S from user *U2*, because user *U2* has also received that privilege from *U5* at time *t2*. Furthermore, since user *U2*'s GRANT to user *U3* was at time *t3* and *t3* > *t2*, it is possible that that GRANT was of the privilege that was received from user *U5* rather than from *U1*, so user *U3* does not lose the privilege either. And if the REVOKE at time *t4* is from user *U5* instead of user *U1*, users *U2* and *U3* would *still* keep the privilege; *U2* keeps the privilege received from *U1*, and *U2*'s GRANT *could* have been of the privilege received from *U1* instead of *U5*, and so *U3* again does not lose the privilege either. However, suppose the sequence of events had been as follows:

User *U1* at time *t1:*

```
GRANT SELECT ON S TO U2 WITH GRANT OPTION
```

User *U2* at time *t2:*

```
GRANT SELECT ON S TO U3 WITH GRANT OPTION
```

User *U5* at time *t3:*

```
GRANT SELECT ON S TO U2 WITH GRANT OPTION
```

User *U1* at time *t4:*

```
REVOKE SELECT ON S FROM U2
```

User *U1*'s REVOKE at time *t4* will not remove the SELECT privilege on table S from user *U2*, because user *U2* has also received that privilege from *U5* at time *t3*. In contrast with the previous example, however, it *will* remove the privilege from user *U3* at this time, because user *U2*'s GRANT at time *t2 must* have been of the privilege received from user *U1*.

It is not possible to revoke the GRANT option without at the same time revoking the privilege to which that option applies.

11.5 CONCLUSION

We conclude this chapter with the following observation: There is no point in a DBMS providing an extensive set of security controls if it is possible to bypass those controls. In particular, SQL/DS's security mechanism would be almost useless if (for example) it were possible to access SQL/DS data from a conventional program via conventional I/O operations. (Remember from Chapter 1 that SQL/DS data is stored in operating system files or data sets.*) For this reason, SQL/DS works in harmony with all the other software components in its environment—VM, CMS, VSE, VSAM, RACF (Resource Access Control Facility), etc.—to guarantee that the total system is secure. In addition, the security facilities of CICS can be used to provide all of the standard CICS controls—for example, to restrict the set of terminals from which specific applications or commands can be invoked.

EXERCISES

Exercises 11.1 and 11.2 refer to a base table called STATS, defined as follows:

```
CREATE TABLE STATS
      ( USERID        CHAR(8)    NOT NULL,
        SEX           CHAR(1),
        DEPENDENTS    DECIMAL(2),
        OCCUPATION    CHAR(20),
        SALARY        DECIMAL(7),
        TAX           DECIMAL(7),
        AUDITS        DECIMAL(2),
     PRIMARY KEY ( USERID ) )
```

11.1 Write SQL statements to give:

    (a) User Ford SELECT privileges over the entire table.
    (b) User Smith INSERT and DELETE privileges over the entire table.
    (c) Each user SELECT privileges over that user's own record (only).

---

*As a matter of fact, the internal structure of those files is significantly different from the structure that the operating system expects anyway, because all space management within them is done by SQL/DS, not by the operating system (see Chapter 16). In VSE, for example, SQL/DS data is stored in VSAM data sets, but those data sets cannot be processed through normal VSAM record I/O operations (though they may be accessible via VSAM control interval mode operations).

(d) User Nash SELECT privileges over the entire table and UPDATE privileges over the SALARY and TAX fields (only).

(e) User Todd SELECT privileges over the USERID, SALARY, and TAX fields (only).

(f) User Ward SELECT privileges as for Todd and UPDATE privileges over the SALARY and TAX fields (only).

(g) User Pope full privileges (SELECT, UPDATE, INSERT, DELETE) over records for preachers (only).

(h) User Jones SELECT privileges as for Todd and UPDATE privileges over the TAX and AUDITS fields (only).

(i) User King SELECT privileges for maximum and minimum salaries per occupation class, but no other privileges.

(j) User Clark DROP privileges on the table.

11.2 For each of parts (a) through (j) under Exercise 11.1, write SQL statements to remove the indicated privilege(s) from the user concerned.

11.3 Let p represent some privilege; let $U1, U2, \ldots, U8$ be a set of authorization IDs; and let $U1$ and $U5$ initially be the only holders of p. Further, assume that $U1$ and $U5$ hold the GRANT option for p. Consider the following sequence of events (note that all GRANTs include the specification WITH GRANT OPTION):

User U1 at time *t1:*	`GRANT p TO U2 WITH GRANT OPTION`
User U1 at time *t2:*	`GRANT p TO U3 WITH GRANT OPTION`
User U1 at time *t3:*	`GRANT p TO U4 WITH GRANT OPTION`
User U2 at time *t4:*	`GRANT p TO U6 WITH GRANT OPTION`
User U5 at time *t5:*	`GRANT p TO U2 WITH GRANT OPTION`
User U5 at time *t6:*	`GRANT p TO U3 WITH GRANT OPTION`
User U5 at time *t7:*	`GRANT p TO U6 WITH GRANT OPTION`
User U4 at time *t8:*	`GRANT p TO U7 WITH GRANT OPTION`
User U1 at time *t9:*	`REVOKE p FROM U2`
User U1 at time *t10:*	`REVOKE p FROM U4`
User U3 at time *t11:*	`GRANT p TO U1 WITH GRANT OPTION`
User U1 at time *t12:*	`REVOKE p FROM U3`
User U3 at time *t13:*	`GRANT p TO U7 WITH GRANT OPTION`
User U5 at time *t14:*	`REVOKE p FROM U6`
User U1 at time *t15:*	`GRANT p TO U5 WITH GRANT OPTION`
User U5 at time *t16:*	`GRANT p TO U8 WITH GRANT OPTION`
User U8 at time *t17:*	`GRANT p TO U5 WITH GRANT OPTION`
User U1 at time *t18:*	`GRANT p TO U8 WITH GRANT OPTION`
User U5 at time *t19:*	`REVOKE p FROM U8`
User U1 at time *t20:*	`GRANT p TO U3 WITH GRANT OPTION`

At the end of this sequence, who still holds p?

ANSWERS TO SELECTED EXERCISES

11.1 (a) `GRANT SELECT ON STATS TO FORD`

(b) `GRANT INSERT, DELETE ON STATS TO SMITH`

(c) CREATE VIEW MY_REC
        AS SELECT *
            FROM   STATS
            WHERE   USERID = USER

    GRANT SELECT ON MY_REC TO PUBLIC

(d) GRANT SELECT, UPDATE (SALARY, TAX)
            ON STATS TO NASH

(e) CREATE VIEW UST
        AS SELECT USERID, SALARY, TAX
            FROM   STATS

    GRANT SELECT ON UST TO TODD

(f) CREATE VIEW UST
        AS SELECT USERID, SALARY, TAX
            FROM   STATS

    GRANT SELECT, UPDATE (SALARY, TAX)
            ON UST TO WARD

(g) CREATE VIEW PREACHERS
        AS SELECT *
            FROM   STATS
            WHERE   OCCUPATION = 'Preacher'

    GRANT SELECT, INSERT, UPDATE, DELETE ON PREACHERS TO POPE

    Note that the following GRANT would be incorrect (why?):

    GRANT ALL PRIVILEGES ON PREACHERS TO POPE

(h) CREATE VIEW UST
        AS SELECT USERID, SALARY, TAX
            FROM   STATS

    CREATE VIEW UTA
        AS SELECT USERID, TAX, AUDITS
            FROM   STATS

    GRANT SELECT ON UST TO JONES

    GRANT UPDATE (TAX, AUDITS) ON UTA TO JONES

(i) CREATE VIEW SALBOUNDS (OCCUPATION, MAXSAL, MINSAL)
        AS SELECT OCCUPATION, MAX (SALARY), MIN (SALARY)
            FROM   STATS
            GROUP   BY OCCUPATION

    GRANT SELECT ON SALBOUNDS TO KING

(j) GRANT DBA TO CLARK

Dropping a table is not an explicitly grantable privilege. A table can be dropped only by its creator or by someone holding the DBA privilege.

11.2 (a) REVOKE SELECT ON STATS FROM FORD

(b) REVOKE INSERT, DELETE ON STATS FROM SMITH

(c) REVOKE SELECT ON MY_REC FROM PUBLIC

Or perhaps simply:

DROP VIEW MY_REC

For (d) through (j) below we generally ignore the possibility of simply dropping the view (if applicable).

(d) REVOKE SELECT, UPDATE ON STATS FROM NASH

(e) REVOKE SELECT ON UST FROM TODD

(f) REVOKE SELECT, UPDATE ON UST FROM WARD

(g) REVOKE ALL PRIVILEGES ON PREACHERS FROM POPE

Note that this REVOKE ALL *is* legal, even though the corresponding GRANT ALL was not. "ALL" in REVOKE ALL does not literally mean all table privileges (as it does in GRANT ALL), but rather all table privileges that the user issuing the REVOKE has granted.

(h) REVOKE SELECT ON UST FROM JONES

REVOKE UPDATE ON UTA FROM JONES

(i) REVOKE SELECT ON SALBOUNDS FROM KING

(j) REVOKE DBA FROM CLARK

11.3 All users except *U4* and *U6* (i.e., users *U1, U2, U3, U5, U7, U8*) still hold *p*.

♦

Integrity

12.1 INTRODUCTION

The term "integrity" is used in database contexts to refer to the accuracy, validity, or correctness of the data in the database. Maintaining integrity is of paramount importance, for obvious reasons; and it is desirable, again for obvious reasons, that the task of maintaining integrity be handled by the system rather than by the user (to the maximum extent possible). In order that it may carry out this task, the system needs to be aware of any *integrity constraints* or *rules* that apply to the data; it then needs to monitor update operations to ensure that they do not violate any of those constraints or rules. As a trivial example,* the suppliers-and-parts database might be

---

*Trivial it may be, but it cannot readily be handled in the current version of SQL/DS.

subject to the rule that supplier numbers must conform to a certain pattern, consisting of an "S" followed by up to four decimal digits. INSERT and UPDATE operations should therefore be monitored to ensure that they do not introduce a supplier number that fails to conform to this pattern.

The general idea, then, is that integrity constraints should be specified as part of the database definition; they will then be stored in the system catalog, and used by the system to control updates to the database. Now, any given database is likely to be subject to a very large number of constraints. For example, the following might all be constraints that apply to the suppliers-and-parts database:

- Supplier numbers must be of the form S*nnnn* (where *nnnn* stands for up to four decimal digits);
- Part numbers must be of the form P*nnnnn* (where *nnnnn* stands for up to five decimal digits);
- Supplier status values must be in the range 1–100;
- Supplier and part cities must be drawn from a certain list;
- Part colors must be drawn from a certain list;
- Part weights must be greater than zero;
- Shipment quantities must be a multiple of 100;
- All red parts must be stored in London;
- If the supplier city is London, then the status must be 20;

and so on. However, most such constraints are *specific*, in the sense that they apply to one specific database. All of the examples above are specific in this sense. The relational model, by contrast, includes two *general* integrity rules—general, in the sense that they apply, not just to some specific database such as suppliers-and-parts, but rather to *every* database (or, at least, every database that claims to conform to the model). These two general rules have to do, respectively, with *primary keys* and with what are called *foreign keys*. They are discussed in detail in Sections 12.2 and 12.3, respectively. It is perhaps worth mentioning in passing that SQL/DS does a reasonably good job on the two general integrity rules (as of Version 2 Release 2, when primary and foreign key support was introduced); unfortunately, however, it is still rather weak on database-specific rules.

Following the discussions in Sections 12.2 and 12.3, Sections 12.4–12.6 go on to examine certain specific aspects of the SQL/DS support for these concepts in more depth. Specifically, Section 12.4 treats the question of referential cycles, Section 12.5 discusses some implementation restrictions, and Section 12.6 covers a number of miscellaneous integrity topics.

12.2 PRIMARY KEYS

We have referred informally to the term "primary key" several times already in this book. Informally, the primary key of a table is just a unique identifier for that table. For example, the primary keys for tables S, P, and SP of the suppliers-and-parts database are S.S#, P.P#, and SP.(S#,P#), respectively. Note that, as the last of these examples indicates, the primary key is allowed to be *composite*; in fact, it is possible, though perhaps unusual, to have a table where the only unique identifier (i.e., the primary key) is the combination of *all* the columns in the table—i.e., the table is "all key." An example would be the table that results from eliminating the QTY column from table SP.

It is also possible, though again unusual, for a table to have *more than one* unique identifier. As an example, let us suppose that every supplier always has a unique supplier number *and* a unique supplier name. (This happens to be the case with our sample data values—Fig. 1.2—but here we are supposing that it is true *for all time*; it is not just chance, i.e., it is not just a question of the values that happen to appear in the table at some specific instant.) In such a case we would say that the table has multiple *candidate* keys; we would then choose one of those candidate keys to be the *primary* key, and the remainder would then be said to be *alternate* keys.

Let us now make these ideas a little more precise.

Definition

Column CK (possibly composite) of table T is a *candidate key* for T if and only if it satisfies the following two time-independent properties:

1. *Uniqueness*: At any given time, no two rows of T have the same value for CK.

2. *Minimality*: If CK is composite, then no component of CK can be eliminated without destroying the uniqueness property.

Note that the relational model *requires* every table to have at least one candidate key, and hence *requires* every table to have a primary key, as we shall see in a moment. *Note*: These requirements are equivalent to the requirement that, at any given time, no two rows in the table are identical. SQL/DS unfortunately does not have such a requirement; we shall return to this point in a moment also.

Next, from the set of candidate keys for a given table, exactly one is designated as *the primary key* for that table; the remainder, if any, are called *alternate keys*. An alternate key is thus a candidate key that is not the primary key. It is important to understand that, in practice, it is the *primary* key that is the really significant one; candidate and alternate keys are merely concepts that necessarily arise during the process of defining the more important concept "primary key."

(*Note*: The rationale by which the primary key is chosen, in cases where there are several candidate keys, is outside the scope of the relational model per se. In practice the choice is usually straightforward.)

So why are primary keys important? One very important answer to this question is that primary key support is prerequisite to foreign key support, as we shall see in Section 12.3. A more fundamental answer is that primary keys provide the basic *record-level addressing mechanism* in a relational system. That is, the only system-guaranteed way of pinpointing some specific record (or row) is *by its primary key value*. For example, the SQL request

```
SELECT  *
FROM    P
WHERE   P# = 'P3'
```

is guaranteed to retrieve (at most) one record. (By contrast, the request

```
SELECT  *
FROM    P
WHERE   CITY = 'Paris'
```

will retrieve an unpredictable number of records, in general.) It follows that *primary keys are just as fundamental to the successful operation of a relational system as main memory addresses are to the successful operation of the underlying machine*. Tables that do not have a primary key—i.e., tables that permit duplicate rows—are bound to display strange and anomalous behavior in certain circumstances (details beyond the scope of this book). This is why we *strongly* recommend that users always conform to the primary key discipline. As indicated above, SQL/DS does in fact permit tables to exist that have no primary key, but we *strongly* recommend that users never exercise this option.

One further preliminary remark before we get into the details of SQL/DS per se: Although it is true that *all* relational tables do in fact possess a primary key, in practice it is *base* tables to which the concept is most directly applicable and for which it is most important. SQL/DS does permit—but unfortunately does not require—the definition of primary keys for base tables.

Primary Key Definition in SQL/DS

Primary keys can be defined when the base table is created via CREATE TABLE, or added to an existing base table via ALTER TABLE. CREATE

TABLE is the normal case; ALTER TABLE is intended mainly to assist in migrating tables from an earlier SQL/DS release that did not support primary keys. Note that every column participating in a primary key must be declared to be NOT NULL.

Here again is the syntax of CREATE TABLE (repeated from Chapter 5, but ignoring the "IN dbspace" specification):

```
CREATE TABLE base-table
  ( column-definition [, column-definition ] ...
  [, primary-key-definition ]
  [, foreign-key-definition [, foreign-key-definition ] ... ] )
```

where "primary-key-definition" is as follows:*

```
PRIMARY KEY ( column [, column ] ... )
```

(for the syntax of "foreign-key-definition," see Section 12.3). Here is an example:

```
CREATE TABLE SP
      ( S#       CHAR(5)   NOT NULL,
        P#       CHAR(6)   NOT NULL,
        QTY      INTEGER,
      PRIMARY KEY ( S#, P# ) ... )
```

(The "...") represents some missing foreign key definitions. Again, see Section 12.3.)

Creating a table with a primary key definition causes SQL/DS to create a UNIQUE index on the column or columns that make up that primary key (in exactly their specified left-to-right order, if multiple columns are involved). SQL/DS will then use that index to reject any attempt to violate the primary key uniqueness constraint. *Note*: The index will be the clustering index for the table. See Chapter 16 for a discussion of clustering indexes.

Here is the syntax for adding a primary key definition to an existing base table:

```
ALTER TABLE base-table ADD primary-key-definition
```

The table must not already possess a defined primary key. Assuming the operation is successful, an appropriate UNIQUE index will again be created automatically. (This time, however, it will probably not be a clustering in-

---

*As explained subsequently, SQL/DS automatically creates a UNIQUE index on the primary key. The PRIMARY KEY clause therefore optionally includes certain additional specifications by which the user can control certain aspects of that index—e.g., the sort order (ASC or DESC) for each column (as in CREATE INDEX). We ignore those aspects here.

dex, unless the table in question has no other indexes. Again, see Chapter 16.) *Note:* An attempt to add a primary key definition will fail if the table currently violates the necessary uniqueness constraint.

It is also possible to remove the primary key definition from an existing base table:

```
ALTER TABLE base-table DROP PRIMARY KEY
```

Any foreign key definitions (see Section 12.3) that previously referred to the now dropped primary key will automatically be dropped. (The user must hold the ALTER privilege on the tables containing those foreign keys.) The index that previously enforced uniqueness of the now dropped primary key will also be dropped automatically.

Entity Integrity

We conclude this section with a note on the first of the two general integrity rules of the relational model, namely the *entity* integrity rule, which is as follows:

- No component of the primary key of a base table is allowed to accept nulls.

The justification for this rule is basically that primary key values in base tables serve to identify entities in the real world—for example, supplier number values in table S serve to identify suppliers—and it simply does not make sense to record information in the database about an entity whose identity is unknown. For further discussion, see Appendix B.

Note carefully that, in the case of composite primary keys, the entity integrity rule says that every individual value of the primary key must be *wholly* (not just partially) nonnull. In the case of the shipments table, for example, with composite primary key SP.(S#,P#), S# and P# must *both* have "nulls not allowed"; neither S# nor P# is allowed to accept nulls.

SQL/DS supports the entity integrity rule, because it requires an explicit declaration of NOT NULL for all primary key components and hence enforces the "nulls not allowed" constraint.

12.3 FOREIGN KEYS

Consider the following (attempted) INSERT operation on the usual suppliers-and-parts database (Fig. 1.2):

```
INSERT
INTO    SP ( S#, P#, QTY )
VALUES ( 'S20', 'P20', 1000 )
```

It should be clear that, if this INSERT were to be accepted, there would be a loss of integrity, because the database would now include a shipment for a nonexistent supplier and a nonexistent part. In fact, the example illustrates a very specific kind of loss of integrity, namely a loss of *referential* integrity. In this section we examine the question of referential integrity in some detail. As the example suggests, the basic idea is quite simple:

- It is clear in the case of suppliers-and-parts that every value appearing in column SP.S# at any given time ought simultaneously to appear in column S.S# (the primary key of the S table)—for otherwise the database would include a shipment for a nonexistent supplier. Likewise, every value appearing in column SP.P# at any given time ought simultaneously to appear in column P.P# (the primary key of the P table), for otherwise the database would include a shipment for a nonexistent part.

- Columns such as SP.S# and SP.P# are examples of what are called *foreign keys*. We can define this concept (loosely) as follows: A foreign key is a column (possibly composite) in one table whose values are required to match values of the primary key in some other table (or possibly in the same table—see later).

  Note, incidentally, that the converse is *not* a requirement—that is, the primary key corresponding to some given foreign key might contain a value that currently does not appear as a value of that foreign key. In the case of the sample data for suppliers-and-parts in Fig. 1.2, for instance, the supplier number S5 appears in table S but not in table SP (supplier S5 does not currently supply any parts).

- A foreign key value represents a *reference* to the record containing the matching primary key value (the *target record*). The problem of ensuring that the database does not contain any invalid foreign key values is therefore known as the *referential integrity* problem. The constraint that values of a given foreign key must match values of the corresponding primary key is known as a *referential constraint*. We refer to the table that contains the foreign key as the *referencing* table and the table that contains the corresponding primary key as the *target* or *referenced* table. We can represent the situation diagrammatically as follows:

$$S \leftarrow SP \rightarrow P$$

(each arrow means that there is a foreign key in the table from which the arrow emerges that refers to the primary key of the table to which the arrow points).

  Two asides: First, SQL/DS documentation (perversely) shows the arrows going the other way (i.e., from the target table to the referencing table). Our convention accords better with intuition and is consistent with relational literature. Second, SQL/DS uses the terms "parent table" and "dependent table" instead of "target table" and "referencing table," respectively. We prefer our own terms, for reasons too numerous to be stated here.

We now proceed to make these ideas a little more precise. We begin with a formal definition of the term "foreign key"—a definition, however, that is deliberately a trifle more restrictive than that adopted in SQL/DS. We will return to this point in a moment.

Definition

Column FK (possibly composite) of base table T2 is a *foreign key* if and only if it satisfies the following two time-independent properties:

1. Each value of FK is either wholly null or wholly nonnull. (By "wholly null or wholly nonnull," we mean that, if FK is composite, then each value of FK either has all components null or all components nonnull, not a mixture of the two.)

2. There exists a base table T1 (the target table) with primary key PK such that each nonnull value of FK is identical to the value of PK in some row of T1.

Note: The relational model allows tables T1 and T2 to be one and the same; i.e., it allows a table to contain a foreign key that refers to the primary key of that same table. An example might be the table

```
EMP   ( EMP#, ..., SALARY, ..., MGR_EMP#, ... )   ,
```

in which column MGR_EMP# represents the employee number of the manager of the employee identified by EMP#. Such a table is known as a *self-referencing* table. However, SQL/DS does not currently support self-referencing tables; we therefore ignore them for the rest of this chapter.

Note that foreign keys, unlike primary keys, must sometimes have "nulls allowed." (We remark, however, that nulls in a foreign key column are likely to be of the "property does not apply" variety, rather than the "value unknown" variety.) For example, suppose that in a given company it is legal for some employee to be currently assigned to no department at all. For such an employee, the department number column (which is a foreign key) would have to contain a null in the record representing that employee in the database.

Note: As mentioned earlier, our definition of foreign key is slightly more restrictive than the definition actually used in SQL/DS. The fact is, there is a certain amount of disagreement in the open literature as to the most satisfactory definition of the term. For example, some authorities (and some systems, including SQL/DS, as we shall see) do not require composite foreign key values to be wholly null or wholly nonnull, but instead allow some components to be null and others nonnull simultaneously. Likewise, some authorities allow there to be multiple target tables instead of just one. The foreign key definition given above is offered in the belief that:

(a) It is the most satisfactory in most commonly-occurring practical situations; and

(b) It is upwards-compatible with a weaker definition (such as one that permits partially null composite foreign keys), should such a weakening ever prove desirable.

Let us consider some of the implications of the foreign key concept. To fix our ideas, let us concentrate on the suppliers table S and the shipments table SP, where we have a referential constraint from SP.S# in the SP table to S.S# in the S table (for simplicity, let us ignore the parts table P). It should be clear that there are basically four potential situations in which the referential constraint might be violated, namely as follows:

- *Case 1*: An INSERT (or PUT) on the SP table might introduce a shipment for which there is no matching supplier. For example:

```
INSERT
INTO    SP ( S#, P#, QTY )
VALUES ( 'S20', ... )
```

- *Case 2*: An UPDATE on column SP.S# of the SP table might introduce a shipment supplier number for which there is no matching supplier. For example:

```
UPDATE SP
SET     S# = 'S20'
WHERE   ...
```

- *Case 3*: A DELETE on the S table might remove a supplier for which there exists a matching shipment. For example:

```
DELETE
FROM    S
WHERE   S# = 'S1'
```

- *Case 4*: An UPDATE on column S.S# of the S table might remove a supplier number for which there exists a matching shipment. For example:

```
UPDATE S
SET     S# = 'S20'
WHERE   S# = 'S1'
```

In order to enforce the referential constraint, therefore, the system must somehow deal with all four of these cases. Let us now turn to the question of foreign key support in SQL/DS specifically; in particular, let us see how SQL/DS deals with each of the four potential problems just outlined. We begin by explaining how foreign keys are defined in the first place.

Foreign Key Definition in SQL/DS

Like primary keys, foreign keys can be defined when the base table is created (via CREATE TABLE) or added to an existing base table (via ALTER TABLE). CREATE TABLE is the more usual case; however, ALTER TABLE is needed if there is a constraint cycle (see Section 12.4) or if the table is being migrated from an earlier SQL/DS release. *Note*: There is no requirement that there be an index on a foreign key, but indexes are usually a good idea for performance reasons. For example, it is very common to perform a primary-key-to-foreign-key join, and an index on the foreign key may very well improve the performance of such a join. Foreign key indexes can also improve the performance of referential integrity enforcement.

The syntax of a foreign key definition is as follows:

```
FOREIGN KEY [ foreign-key ] ( column [, column ] ... )
        REFERENCES base-table [ ON DELETE effect ]
```

where "effect" is RESTRICT or CASCADE or SET NULL. If the ON DELETE clause is omitted, ON DELETE RESTRICT is assumed. Here is an example:

```
CREATE TABLE SP
      ( S#        CHAR(5)   NOT NULL,
        P#        CHAR(6)   NOT NULL,
        QTY       INTEGER,
      PRIMARY KEY ( S#, P# ) ,
      FOREIGN KEY SFK ( S# ) REFERENCES S
                             ON DELETE CASCADE ,
      FOREIGN KEY PFK ( P# ) REFERENCES P
                             ON DELETE RESTRICT )
```

Explanation:

1. Let T2 be the table containing the foreign key, and let T1 be the target table (i.e., the table named in the REFERENCES specification), thus:

$$T2 \rightarrow T1$$

Table T1 must have a defined primary key.

2. The optional "foreign-key" is a name (a "constraint name"), unique within the containing table, that will be used by SQL/DS in diagnostic messages relating to this foreign key (the name is also used in ALTER . . .

DROP statements—see later in this section). We have introduced the names SFK and PFK in our example. If the user does not supply a name, SQL/DS will assign one anyway; it is probably a good idea in practice for the user to supply a name. *Note*: The foreign key name is *not* considered as a column name and cannot be used in data manipulation statements such as SELECT.

3. The foreign key and the target primary key must contain the same number of columns, n say, and the ith column of the foreign key and the ith column of the target primary key must have the same data type (i here is in the range 1 to n and refers to the left-to-right order in which the columns are listed in the containing foreign or primary key definition). Note, therefore, that a foreign key will be composite if and only if the primary key it matches is composite also.

4. The ON DELETE clause defines the *delete rule* for the target table with respect to this foreign key—that is, it defines what happens if an attempt is made to delete a record from the target table (i.e., a target record). As explained above, the possible specifications are RESTRICT, CASCADE, and SET NULL (and RESTRICT is assumed if nothing is specified). The meanings are as follows:

- RESTRICT: The delete is "restricted" to the case where there are no matching records in the referencing table (it is rejected if any such records exist).
- CASCADE: The delete "cascades" to delete all matching records in the referencing table also.
  - Note that, in general, table T2 might in turn be referenced by a foreign key in some other table T3. If the delete rule for T2's reference to T1 is CASCADE, however, SQL/DS will not permit any such table T3 to exist—i.e., it will not permit a table such as T2 to be a target table.
- SET NULL: In this case, the foreign key must have "nulls allowed." The target record is deleted and the foreign key is set to null in all matching records in the referencing table.
  - If the foreign key is composite, then SQL/DS actually requires only that *at least one component* of the foreign key have nulls allowed, and SET NULL sets such components (only) to null in matching records and leaves other components unchanged. (A composite foreign key value that is partly null is ALWAYS regarded as satisfying the referential constraint in SQL/DS, *regardless of the values of the nonnull components*—a state of affairs that can lead to great complexity. For this reason among others, we recommend that composite foreign keys either have nulls al-

lowed for all components or nulls not allowed for all components, not a mixture of the two.)

With the SP definition shown above, therefore, an attempt to delete a specific supplier record will cascade to delete all shipments for that supplier also; an attempt to delete a specific part record will succeed only if there are no shipments for that part.

5. There is no "ON UPDATE" clause to define an "update rule" for (the primary key of) the target table with respect to this foreign key. Instead, any attempt to update the primary key in a record of the target table is restricted to the case where there are no matching records in the referencing table (it is rejected if any such records exist). In effect, the only update rule supported is RESTRICT, and that rule can be stated only implicitly, not explicitly.

6. In order to define a foreign key (via either CREATE TABLE or ALTER TABLE—see below) that refers to some target table T1, the user must possess the REFERENCES privilege on table T1. Note, however, that a user who deletes a record in table T1 and thereby deletes or updates one or more records in some other table T2 (thanks to a CASCADE or SET NULL delete rule) does *not* require any particular privilege—not even the SELECT privilege—on table T2.

Let us now see how these rules enable SQL/DS to deal with the four potential problem cases identified earlier. Once again we use the suppliers-and-parts example to fix our ideas.

- *Case 1*: An INSERT (or PUT) on the SP table might introduce a shipment for which there is no matching supplier.

    This situation is prevented by virtue of the fact that SP.S# is a foreign key in table SP matching the primary key S.S# of table S. Such an INSERT or PUT will simply be rejected. Of course, an INSERT or PUT that introduces a shipment for a supplier that does already exist in table S (and a part that does already exist in table P) will be accepted.

- *Case 2*: An UPDATE on column SP.S# of the SP table might introduce a shipment supplier number for which there is no matching supplier.

    This situation is also prevented by virtue of the fact that SP.S# is a foreign key in table SP matching the primary key S.S# of table S. Such an UPDATE will simply be rejected. Of course, an UPDATE that introduces an SP.S# value that does already exist in table S (and does not introduce an SP.P# value that does not already exist in table P) will be accepted.

- *Case 3*: A DELETE on the S table might remove a supplier for which there exists a matching shipment.

  This situation is handled by the delete rule (CASCADE in the sample definition shown earlier). In general, RESTRICT would mean that the delete will be accepted only if there *are* no such matching shipments; CASCADE would mean that any such matching shipments will be removed anyway; and SET NULL (not possible in the case of suppliers-and-parts, because SP.S# does not have "nulls allowed") would mean that any such matching shipments will not be removed but will be updated so that they are no longer "matching."

- *Case 4*: An UPDATE on column S.S# of the S table might remove a supplier number for which there exists a matching shipment.

  This situation is handled by the (implicit) update rule RESTRICT, which means that the update will be accepted only if no such matching shipments exist.

We now briefly discuss the use of ALTER TABLE to add and remove foreign key definitions. The syntax for adding such a definition is as follows:

```
ALTER TABLE base-table ADD foreign-key-definition
```

If "base-table" is nonempty (as it might be if it is a table that is being migrated from an earlier release of SQL/DS), the ALTER TABLE will fail if the table already contains a foreign key value for which no corresponding record exists in the target table.

The syntax for removing a foreign key definition is:

```
ALTER TABLE base-table DROP foreign-key
```

Here "foreign-key" is the foreign key *name* assigned when the foreign key was defined. The user must hold the REFERENCES privilege on the table previously referenced by the foreign key (i.e., the target table).

One final point regarding data definition: If a base table is dropped, any foreign key definitions referring to that table are dropped automatically (the user does *not* need to hold the ALTER privilege on those referencing tables). The delete rules (CASCADE, etc.) for those foreign keys are *not* invoked; thus, e.g., dropping table S does not cause all records in table SP to be deleted.

Referential Integrity

For completeness, we close this section with a note on the second of the two general integrity rules of the relational model, namely the referential integrity rule. The referential integrity rule simply states that the database must not contain any unmatched foreign key values (i.e., nonnull foreign key values for which there does not exist a matching value of the corresponding primary key). SQL/DS obviously enforces this rule, as the discussions above demonstrate.

12.4 REFERENTIAL CYCLES

Section 12.3 explained the basic foreign key concept and described the relevant SQL/DS data definition statements. An understanding of the material of that section is probably sufficient to deal with most of the situations that are likely to arise in practice. However, there are a number of additional detailed points that need to be made in any reasonably comprehensive treatment of the subject. The points in question (a slightly mixed bag) are discussed in this section and in Sections 12.5–12.6, later. The present section deals with referential cycles.

First we need to introduce the concept of a "referential path" (not an official SQL/DS term). Let tables Tn, $T(n-1)$, . . ., $T2$, $T1$ be such that there is a referential constraint from table Tn to table $T(n-1)$, a referential constraint from table $T(n-1)$ to table $T(n-2)$, . . ., and a referential constraint from table $T2$ to table $T1$:

$$Tn \rightarrow T(n-1) \rightarrow T(n-2) \rightarrow \ldots \rightarrow T2 \rightarrow T1$$

Then the chain of arrows from Tn to $T1$ represents a referential path from Tn to $T1$. We can define this concept (recursively) as follows: There is a *referential path from table Tn to table T1* if and only if (a) table Tn references table $T1$ directly or (b) table Tn references some table $T(n-1)$ such that there is a referential path from table $T(n-1)$ to table $T1$.

Now we can define the term *referential cycle* (or constraint cycle). Briefly, we say that a referential cycle exists if there is a referential path from some table T to itself. One special case, the self-referencing table, has already been mentioned in Section 12.3; a self-referencing table constitutes a cycle involving just a single table. (As explained in Section 12.3, however, SQL/DS does not support self-referencing tables.) More generally, a cycle might involve any number of tables: If there is a referential constraint from table Tn to table $T(n-1)$, a referential constraint from table $T(n-1)$ to table $T(n-2)$, . . ., a referential constraint from table $T2$ to table $T1$, and a referential constraint from table $T1$ to table Tn, then we have a cycle involving n tables (i.e., a cycle of length n):

$$Tn \rightarrow T(n-1) \rightarrow T(n-2) \rightarrow \ldots \rightarrow T2 \rightarrow T1 \rightarrow Tn$$

SQL/DS does support cycles of length n (for n greater than one). Here is an example of a cycle of length two:

```
EMP  ( EMP#,  ..., SALARY,  ..., DEPT#  ... )

DEPT ( DEPT#,  ..., MGR_EMP#,  ..., BUDGET  ... )
```

In table EMP, EMP# is the primary key and DEPT# is a foreign key referring to DEPT; in table DEPT, DEPT# is the primary key and
MGR_EMP# (employee number for the department manager) is a foreign
key referring to EMP.

In order to specify the referential constraints that form a cycle, it is
necessary to use ALTER TABLE for at least one of those specifications,
because a FOREIGN KEY clause cannot refer to a table that does not yet
exist. The general pattern is thus:

```
CREATE TABLE T1 ( ... PRIMARY KEY ... )

CREATE TABLE T2 ( ... PRIMARY KEY ... ,
     FOREIGN KEY ... REFERENCES T1 ... )
.........................

CREATE TABLE Tn ( ... PRIMARY KEY ... ,
     FOREIGN KEY ... REFERENCES T(n-1) ... )

ALTER TABLE T1 ADD FOREIGN KEY ... REFERENCES Tn ...
```

By way of example, we give the data definition (in outline) for the
EMP/DEPT cycle introduced above:

```
CREATE TABLE EMP
     ( EMP#      NOT NULL ,
       ...       ,
       SALARY    ,
       ...       ,
       DEPT#     ,
       ...       ,
       PRIMARY KEY ( EMP# ) )

CREATE TABLE DEPT
     ( DEPT#     NOT NULL ,
       ...       ,
       MGR_EMP#  ,
       ...       ,
       BUDGET    ,
       ...       ,
       PRIMARY KEY ( DEPT# ) ,
       FOREIGN KEY MFK ( MGR_EMP# ) REFERENCES EMP )

ALTER TABLE EMP ADD FOREIGN KEY DFK ( DEPT# ) REFERENCES DEPT
```

In general, it is likely in a cycle that at least one of the foreign keys will
have nulls allowed. In the cycle shown above, for example, at least one of
the two foreign keys EMP.DEPT# and DEPT.MGR_EMP# will probably
have nulls allowed; for otherwise it would be impossible to INSERT the
first record (either an EMP record or a DEPT record) into the database—
unless the tables are loaded with referential constraints deactivated. See Section 12.6 for a discussion of constraint deactivation.

12.5 IMPLEMENTATION RESTRICTIONS

The current release of SQL/DS suffers from certain implementation restrictions, which we summarize in the present section. *Note*: It might be possible to relax some of these restrictions at some future time. The basic problem in most cases is that (for performance reasons) SQL/DS applies the primary and foreign key integrity checks to each individual record *as it updates that record*, whereas in some cases it ought really to defer the checking to the end of the overall statement. (In fact, in some cases it ought to defer the checking to "COMMIT time," i.e., to the end of the *transaction*. See Chapter 14 for a discussion of transactions and COMMIT time.) *Note*: As mentioned at the end of the previous section, SQL/DS does provide the ability to "deactivate" the checking for a period of time, but this facility still does not completely solve the problem.

■ As a trivial example, suppose we had a table T with two records, with primary key values 1 and 2, respectively. Consider the request "double every primary key value in T." The correct result is that the records should now have primary key values 2 and 4, respectively. However, SQL/DS will reject the request entirely, on the grounds that if it updated the record with primary key value 1 first (to yield 2) it would run into a primary key uniqueness violation.

As a consequence of such record-at-a-time integrity checking, *different record-level processing sequences can yield different results* (in general); in other words, the result of a given set-level SQL operation might be unpredictable. Most of the restrictions explained below (both in the present subsection and the next) represent attempts to outlaw situations in which such unpredictability might otherwise occur.

The restrictions are as follows:

1. Any UPDATE statement that assigns a value to a primary key must be "single-record" (i.e., there must be at most one record at execution time that satisfies the predicate in the WHERE clause). Thus, for example, the following UPDATE is valid:

```
UPDATE  S
SET     S# = 'S10'
WHERE   S# = 'S5'
```

whereas the following may or may not be valid, depending on the values in the database:

```
UPDATE  S
SET     S# = 'S10'
WHERE   CITY = 'Athens'
```

2. No UPDATE CURRENT statement is allowed to update a primary key value. (See Chapter 13 for an explanation of UPDATE CURRENT.)

3. If

  (a) the user issues a DELETE on table T1, and

  (b) there is a referential constraint from table T2 and table T1, and

  (c) the WHERE clause in the DELETE statement includes a subquery,

then the FROM clause in that subquery must not refer to table T2 unless the delete rule from T2 to T1 is RESTRICT. For example, if the referential constraint from shipments (table SP) to suppliers (table S) has a delete rule of CASCADE, then the following (an attempt to delete all suppliers who supply some part in a quantity greater than 100) is illegal:

```
DELETE
FROM    S
WHERE   100 <
      ( SELECT QTY
        FROM    SP
        WHERE   SP.S# = S.S# )
```

Instead, the user should first compile a list of relevant supplier numbers, and then delete all suppliers whose number is given in that list as a separate operation.

4. If table Tn is connected to table T1 via two or more distinct referential paths, then every foreign key in table Tn that is involved in any of those paths must have the same delete rule, and furthermore that rule must not be SET NULL. For an illustration of this restriction, see Exercise 12.6 at the end of the chapter.

  For completeness, we repeat two implementation restrictions that have already been discussed in Sections 12.3 and 12.4.

5. Cycles of length one (i.e., self-referencing tables) are not supported.

6. If table T2 references table T1 and the delete rule is CASCADE, then table T2 cannot itself have any other tables that reference it (i.e., table T2 cannot be a target table). Note the implication that a referential cycle cannot involve a delete rule of CASCADE anywhere in the cycle.

12.6 MISCELLANEOUS TOPICS

We conclude this chapter with a brief discussion of a few miscellaneous integrity topics.

Constraint Deactivation

In some situations, it is desirable to be able to prevent the system from performing certain integrity checks until some specified future time. One such situation was touched on at the end of Section 12.4: In a referential cycle, it might be impossible ever to insert the first record if the system insisted on performing all integrity checks immediately (i.e., at the time of performing the relevant update). SQL/DS therefore provides a means for deactivating, and later reactivating, certain integrity constraints; further-more, such deactivation and subsequent reactivation can be applied on an individual constraint-by-constraint basis.

Before we can amplify these ideas, we need to introduce a few more new terms and concepts:

- *Active vs. inactive constraints*

  For the purposes of this subsection, the term "constraint" means either a primary key uniqueness constraint or a foreign key referential con-straint. At any given time, each such constraint is either *active* or *inac-tive*. *Note*: The equivalent IBM terms are activated and deactivated, respectively. We feel our own terms are more appropriate for describing constraint *states*; we reserve "activate" and "deactivate" for the oper-ations of switching a constraint from one state to another.

  The initial state of a constraint is always active. If a constraint is inactive, update operations are not subject to the checking normally implied by that constraint; also, in the case of a referential constraint, DELETEs on target records do not cause any CASCADE or SET NULL operations to be performed.

- *Generally accessible vs. accessible-only-to-owner tables*

  At any given time, a given table T is either *generally accessible* (meaning "accessible to all suitably authorized users") or *accessible-only-to-owner* (meaning "accessible to the user who created table T and to users with DBA authority, but not to anyone else"; we will use the term "owner" to refer generically to any user who has access to an accessible-only-to-owner table). A table is generally accessible only if all constraints in which it is involved are active; it is accessible-only-to-owner if any of those constraints are inactive. (When we say that a given table T is "involved in" a constraint C, we mean that C is the primary key uniqueness constraint for T or that C is a referential con-straint in which T is either the target or the referencing table.) Thus, *deactivating any constraint always places at least one table T into the accessible-only-to-owner state* (unless T was in that state already anyway); similarly, reactivating the last inactive constraint in which some table T is involved places T back into the generally accessible state.

Note: Again our terms are different from IBM's: IBM refers to the two states "generally accessible" and "accessible-only-to-owner" as active and inactive, respectively, but we prefer our terms as more descriptive (albeit a trifle clumsy) and more sharply distinguished from the terms used for constraint states.

The rationale behind the foregoing is as follows: If a table is involved in some inactive constraint, then *some* user—namely, the owner—must be able to access that table, for otherwise it would be totally useless. On the other hand, since the table might contain some invalid data, *most* users should not be allowed to access it at all—not even for retrieval. An attempt by such a user to access such a table in any way will fail with a "data not available" condition.

Note that an accessible-only-to-owner table might still be involved in some active constraints, and updates (by the owner) on that table will still be subject to the usual checking for those constraints.

Now we can explain how constraints can be deactivated and (re)activated. The following statement will deactivate a primary key uniqueness constraint:

```
ALTER TABLE base-table DEACTIVATE PRIMARY KEY
```

ALTER . . . DEACTIVATE PRIMARY KEY causes the primary key index on "base-table" to be dropped. The primary key uniqueness constraint becomes inactive. (Note, however, that the primary key NOT NULL constraint remains in force.) An implicit "ALTER . . . DEACTIVATE FOREIGN KEY" is performed for all referential constraints that refer to this primary key (see below). The primary key uniqueness constraint remains inactive until it is explicitly activated again, as follows:

```
ALTER TABLE base-table ACTIVATE PRIMARY KEY
```

This statement attempts to create a new primary key index on "base-table." All existing rows in the table are checked for uniqueness of primary key values (if the check fails, of course, the index creation fails and the constraint remains inactive). Assuming the ACTIVATE succeeds, an implicit "ALTER . . . ACTIVATE FOREIGN KEY" is performed for all referential constraints that were implicitly deactivated by the previous DEACTIVATE PRIMARY KEY. (Note, however, that those constraints will still remain inactive if, e.g., they have been subject to an explicit DEACTIVATE in their own right or if they are violated by existing data values.)

We turn now to referential constraints. The following statement will deactivate a referential constraint:

```
ALTER TABLE base-table DEACTIVATE FOREIGN KEY foreign-key
```

Here "foreign-key" is the name assigned when the foreign key was created (see Section 12.3). The referential constraint from that foreign key to its corresponding target primary key becomes inactive.

A deactivated referential constraint can be reactivated as follows:

```
ALTER TABLE base-table ACTIVATE FOREIGN KEY foreign-key
```

The referential constraint corresponding to "foreign-key" is checked for all existing rows in "base-table" (if the check fails, of course, the constraint remains inactive).

Composite Keys

As explained earlier in the chapter, the relational model does permit primary and foreign keys to be composite. However, there are good reasons, most of them beyond the scope of this book, to be very sparing in the use of composite keys. In fact, every time a composite key arises during the database design process, it is a good idea to ask yourself very carefully whether it might not be better to introduce a new, simple (noncomposite) column to act as the key instead. In the case of shipments, for example, it might be worth introducing a new SHIP# column ("shipment number") as the primary key. (The composite column SP.(S,#P#) would then be an alternate key.) For further discussion of this point, the reader is referred to the book *Relational Database: Selected Writings*, by C. J. Date (Addison-Wesley, 1986).

Even if you do decide to use composite keys, we recommend that you still treat them for the most part as *indivisible entity identifiers* (except perhaps for retrieval purposes); in other words, treat them as if they were simple, even though they are in fact composite. In order to adhere to this guideline:

1. Do not allow key values to be partly null.

2. Do not allow keys to overlap.

This is not the place to examine these recommendations in depth; they are discussed in more detail in a paper (still in preparation at the time of writing) devoted to foreign keys and related matters, by C. J. Date (see Appendix H).

Other Integrity Constraints

As explained in Section 12.1, every database will be subject to numerous additional integrity constraints, over and above the basic primary and foreign key constraints described in Sections 12.2–12.5. We close this chapter with a complete list (not a very long list!) of additional integrity features supported by SQL/DS.

- Data type checking

  SQL/DS will ensure that every value introduced into a given column is of the appropriate data type. For example, it will reject an attempt to introduce the string 'XYZ' into a column defined as DECIMAL(3).

- NOT NULL

  See Chapter 4. Of course, it is not only primary key columns that need to be specified NOT NULL, in general.

- UNIQUE indexes

  See Chapter 5. Of course, it is not only primary keys that need to be unique, in general.

EXERCISES

12.1 Define the terms primary key and foreign key.

12.2 State the entity integrity rule and the referential integrity rule.

12.3 Write a suitable set of data definition statements to specify the necessary primary and foreign key integrity constraints for the suppliers-parts-projects database (Fig. 5.1).

12.4 How would your answer to Exercise 12.3 be different if the database was being migrated from an earlier release of SQL/DS that did not support primary and foreign keys?

12.5 Using the sample suppliers-parts-projects data values from Fig. 5.1, say what the effect of each of the following operations is:
    (a) UPDATE project J7, setting CITY to New York
    (b) UPDATE part P5, setting P# to P4
    (c) UPDATE supplier S5, setting S# to S8
    (d) DELETE supplier S3, if the relevant delete rule is CASCADE
    (e) DELETE part P2, if the relevant delete rule is RESTRICT
    (f) DELETE project J4, if the relevant delete rule is SET NULL
    (g) UPDATE shipment S1-P1-J1, setting S# to S2
    (h) UPDATE shipment S5-P5-J5, setting J# to J7
    (i) UPDATE shipment S5-P5-J5, setting J# to J8
    (j) INSERT shipment S5-P6-J7

    (k) INSERT shipment S4-P7-J6
    (l) INSERT shipment S1-P2-null

12.6 (Based on an example in "An Introduction to the Unified Database Language," in *Relational Database: Selected Writings,* by C. J. Date, Addison-Wesley, 1986.) An education database contains information about an in-house company training scheme. For each training course, the database contains details of all prerequisite courses for that course and all offerings for that course; and for each offering it contains details of all teachers and all students for that offering. The database also contains information about employees. The relevant tables are as follows:

```
COURSE    ( COURSE#, TITLE )
PREREQ    ( SUP_COURSE#, SUB_COURSE# )
OFFERING  ( COURSE#, OFF#, OFFDATE, LOCATION )
TEACHER   ( COURSE#, OFF#, EMP# )
STUDENT   ( COURSE#, OFF#, EMP#, GRADE )
EMPLOYEE  ( EMP#, ENAME, JOB )
```

The meaning of the PREREQ table is that the superior course, represented by SUP_COURSE#, has the subordinate course, represented by SUB_COURSE#, as an immediate prerequisite; the other tables are intended to be self-explanatory. Write a suitable set of SQL data definitions for this database.

12.7 Invent a database of your own that involves a cycle of referential constraints. Invent some sample data for that database. Write an appropriate set of data definitions, with suitable PRIMARY KEY and FOREIGN KEY clauses. Consider the effects of some sample INSERTs, DELETEs, and (primary and foreign key) UPDATEs on your sample data.

12.8 Suppose it is required to change the supplier number of supplier Sx to Sy (where Sx and Sy are given).
    (a) First, the following UPDATE will not work. Why not?

```
UPDATE S
SET     S# = Sy
WHERE   S# = Sx
```

    (b) Second, the following sequence of UPDATEs also will not work. Again, why not?

```
UPDATE SP
SET     S# = Sy
WHERE   S# = Sx

UPDATE S
SET     S# = Sy
WHERE   S# = Sx
```

       (Nor does it make any difference if the two UPDATEs are interchanged, of course.)
    (c) The problem might be solved (in a somewhat heavy-handed manner) by making use of the SQL/DS "constraint deactivation" facility. Show an appropriate solution.

(d) More likely, however, it will prove desirable to write a program to handle the problem. You are therefore recommended to return to this exercise and to write such a program after reading Chapter 13 on embedded SQL.

ANSWERS TO SELECTED EXERCISES

We remind the reader that it is usually a good idea to have an index on a foreign key. However, such indexes are not included in the answers below (except in those cases where the foreign key is in fact the leading portion of the primary key of the containing table, where the primary key index generated by SQL/DS automatically provides the desired function).

12.3
```
CREATE TABLE S
        ( S#       CHAR(5)   NOT NULL ,
          SNAME    CHAR(20)  NOT NULL ,
          STATUS   SMALLINT  NOT NULL ,
          CITY     CHAR(15)  NOT NULL ,
          PRIMARY KEY ( S# ) )

CREATE TABLE P
        ( P#       CHAR(6)   NOT NULL ,
          PNAME    CHAR(20)  NOT NULL ,
          COLOR    CHAR(6)   NOT NULL ,
          WEIGHT   SMALLINT  NOT NULL ,
          CITY     CHAR(15)  NOT NULL ,
          PRIMARY KEY ( P# ) )

CREATE TABLE J
        ( J#       CHAR(4)   NOT NULL ,
          JNAME    CHAR(10)  NOT NULL ,
          CITY     CHAR(15)  NOT NULL ,
          PRIMARY KEY ( J# ) )

CREATE TABLE SPJ
        ( S#       CHAR(5)   NOT NULL ,
          P#       CHAR(6)   NOT NULL ,
          J#       CHAR(4)   NOT NULL ,
          QTY      INTEGER ,
          PRIMARY KEY ( S#, P#, J# ) ,
          FOREIGN KEY SFK ( S# ) REFERENCES S
                                 ON DELETE CASCADE ,
          FOREIGN KEY PFK ( P# ) REFERENCES P
                                 ON DELETE CASCADE ,
          FOREIGN KEY JFK ( J# ) REFERENCES J
                                 ON DELETE CASCADE )
```

12.4 Remove the PRIMARY KEY and FOREIGN KEY clauses from the CREATE TABLE statements and replace them by the following:

```
ALTER TABLE S    ADD PRIMARY KEY ( S# )
ALTER TABLE P    ADD PRIMARY KEY ( P# )
ALTER TABLE J    ADD PRIMARY KEY ( J# )
ALTER TABLE SPJ  ADD PRIMARY KEY ( S#, P#, J# )

ALTER TABLE SPJ ADD FOREIGN KEY SFK ( S# ) REFERENCES S
                                           ON DELETE CASCADE
ALTER TABLE SPJ ADD FOREIGN KEY PFK ( P# ) REFERENCES P
                                           ON DELETE CASCADE
```

```
ALTER TABLE SPJ ADD FOREIGN KEY JFK ( J# ) REFERENCES J
                                       ON DELETE CASCADE
```

12.5 (a) Accepted

(b) Rejected (violates primary key constraint on P and implicit "update rule" RESTRICT on P.P#)

(c) Rejected (violates implicit "update rule" RESTRICT on S.S#)

(d) Accepted (supplier S3 and all shipments for supplier S3 deleted)

(e) Rejected (violates delete rule RESTRICT on P)

(f) Impossible (delete rule cannot be SET NULL, because SPJ.J# must be NOT NULL—it is part of the primary key of SPJ)

(g) Accepted

(h) Rejected (violates primary key constraint on SPJ)

(i) Rejected (violates foreign key constraint on SPJ.J#)

(j) Accepted

(k) Rejected (violates foreign key constraint on SPJ.P#)

(l) Rejected (violates entity integrity on SPJ)

12.6
```
CREATE TABLE COURSE
     ( COURSE# ... NOT NULL ,
       TITLE   ... NOT NULL ,
     PRIMARY KEY ( COURSE# ) )

CREATE TABLE PREREQ
     ( SUP_COURSE# ... NOT NULL ,
       SUB_COURSE# ... NOT NULL ,
     PRIMARY KEY ( SUB_COURSE#, SUP_COURSE# ) ,
     FOREIGN KEY SUP ( SUP_COURSE# ) REFERENCES COURSE
                                 ON DELETE RESTRICT ,
     FOREIGN KEY SUB ( SUB_COURSE# ) REFERENCES COURSE
                                 ON DELETE RESTRICT )

CREATE TABLE OFFERING
     ( COURSE#  ... NOT NULL ,
       OFF#     ... NOT NULL ,
       OFFDATE  ... NOT NULL ,
       LOCATION ... NOT NULL ,
     PRIMARY KEY ( COURSE#, OFF# ) ,
     FOREIGN KEY OFK ( COURSE# ) REFERENCES COURSE
                            ON DELETE RESTRICT )

CREATE TABLE EMPLOYEE
     ( EMP#   ... NOT NULL ,
       ENAME  ... NOT NULL ,
       JOB    ... NOT NULL ,
     PRIMARY KEY ( EMP# ) )

CREATE TABLE TEACHER
     ( COURSE# ... NOT NULL ,
       OFF#    ... NOT NULL ,
       EMP#    ... NOT NULL ,
     PRIMARY KEY ( COURSE#, OFF#, EMP# )
     FOREIGN KEY TC ( COURSE#, OFF# ) REFERENCES OFFERING
                                  ON DELETE CASCADE ,
     FOREIGN KEY TE ( EMP# )          REFERENCES EMPLOYEE
                                  ON DELETE CASCADE )
```

```
CREATE TABLE STUDENT
        ( COURSE#  ... NOT NULL ,
          OFF#     ... NOT NULL ,
          EMP#     ... NOT NULL ,
          GRADE    ... NOT NULL ,
          PRIMARY KEY ( COURSE#, OFF#, EMP# )
          FOREIGN KEY SC ( COURSE#, OFF# ) REFERENCES OFFERING
                                           ON DELETE CASCADE ,
          FOREIGN KEY SE ( EMP# )          REFERENCES EMPLOYEE
                                           ON DELETE CASCADE )
```

Note: Columns TEACHER.COURSE# and STUDENT.COURSE# could also be regarded as foreign keys, both of them referring to COURSE. However, if the referential constraints from TEACHER to OFFERING, STUDENT to OFFERING, and OFFERING to COURSE are all properly maintained, the referential constraints from TEACHER to COURSE and STUDENT to COURSE will be maintained automatically. Note, however, that if those latter constraints are declared, then the delete rules *must* be stated as CASCADE, to be consistent with the existing declarations (see Section 12.5).

12.7 A simple example of a structure that involves a cycle might be a banking system, in which each account has one owner (a bank customer), each bank customer has one personal banker (a bank officer), and each personal banker has one account giving information about that personal banker's customers.

12.8 (a) The attempt to UPDATE the supplier record for supplier Sx will not work (in general) because of the implicit RESTRICT rule on updating primary keys; supplier Sx might currently have some matching shipments.

(b) The attempt to UPDATE the shipment records for supplier Sx first will not work for two reasons: First, it would violate the foreign key constraint; second, SQL/DS does not currently permit multiple-record UPDATEs on primary keys (note that SP.S# is a component of the primary key of SP, as well as being a foreign key).

(c)
```
ALTER TABLE S DEACTIVATE PRIMARY KEY
ALTER TABLE SP DEACTIVATE PRIMARY KEY

UPDATE S
SET     S# = Sy
WHERE   S# = Sx

UPDATE SP
SET     S# = Sy
WHERE   S# = Sx

ALTER TABLE SP ACTIVATE PRIMARY KEY
ALTER TABLE S ACTIVATE PRIMARY KEY
```

(d) Here is a possible program to perform the update:

```
UPDS#: PROC OPTIONS (MAIN) ;          /* change S# "Sx" to "Sy" */
           DCL SX              CHAR(5) ;
           DCL SY              CHAR(5) ;
           DCL SNAME           CHAR(20) ;
```

```
      DCL STATUS            FIXED BINARY(15) ;
      DCL CITY              CHAR(15) ;
      DCL P#                CHAR(6) ;
      DCL MORE_SHIPMENTS BIT(1) ;

      EXEC SQL INCLUDE SQLCA ;

      EXEC SQL DECLARE Y CURSOR FOR
              SELECT S.SNAME, S.STATUS, S.CITY
              FROM    S
              WHERE   S.S# = :SX
              FOR UPDATE OF SNAME ;

      EXEC SQL DECLARE Z CURSOR FOR
              SELECT SP.P#
              FROM    SP
              WHERE   SP.S# = :SX ;

      EXEC SQL WHENEVER NOT FOUND CONTINUE ;
      EXEC SQL WHENEVER SQLERROR CONTINUE ;
      EXEC SQL WHENEVER SQLWARNING CONTINUE ;

      ON CONDITION ( DBEXCEPTION )
      BEGIN ;
         PUT SKIP LIST ( SQLCA ) ;
         EXEC SQL ROLLBACK WORK ;
         GO TO QUIT ;
      END ;
GET LIST ( SX, SY ) ;
EXEC SQL OPEN Y ;
IF SQLCODE ~= 0
THEN SIGNAL CONDITION ( DBEXCEPTION ) ;

/* fetch column values for supplier Sx */
EXEC SQL FETCH Y INTO :SNAME. :STATUS, :CITY ;
IF SQLCODE ~= 0
THEN SIGNAL CONDITION ( DBEXCEPTION ) ;

/* make sure supplier Sx stays X-locked -- see Chap. 14 --  */
/* thus preventing concurrent creation of new shipments for */
/* supplier Sx and concurrent UPDATE/DELETE on supplier Sx  */
EXEC SQL UPDATE S
         SET    SNAME = :SNAME        /* effectively a no-op */
         WHERE  CURRENT OF Y ;
IF SQLCODE ~= 0
THEN SIGNAL CONDITION ( DBEXCEPTION ) ;

/* insert new supplier Sy record */
EXEC SQL INSERT
         INTO   S ( S#, SNAME, STATUS, CITY )
         VALUES ( :SY, :SNAME, :STATUS, :CITY ) ;
IF SQLCODE ~= 0
THEN SIGNAL CONDITION ( DBEXCEPTION ) ;

/* prepare to loop through shipments for Sx */
EXEC SQL OPEN Z ;
IF SQLCODE ~= 0
THEN SIGNAL CONDITION ( DBEXCEPTION ) ;
MORE_SHIPMENTS = '1'B ;

/* loop through shipments for Sx */
DO WHILE ( MORE_SHIPMENTS ) ;
```

```
          EXEC SQL FETCH Z INTO :P# ;
          SELECT ;                    /* a PL/I SELECT, not a SQL SELECT */
             WHEN ( SQLCODE = 100 )
                MORE_SHIPMENTS = '0'B ;
             WHEN ( SQLCODE ~= 100 & SQLCODE ~= 0 )
                SIGNAL CONDITION ( DBEXCEPTION ) ;
             WHEN ( SQLCODE = 0 )
                DO ;
                    /* update current shipment -- */
                    /* but not via cursor Z  !!!  */
                    EXEC SQL UPDATE SP
                               SET    S# = :SY
                               WHERE  S# = :SX
                               AND    P# = :P# ;
                    IF SQLCODE ~= 0
                    THEN SIGNAL CONDITION ( DBEXCEPTION ) ;
                END ;
          END ;    /* PL/I SELECT */
       END ;    /* DO WHILE */
       EXEC SQL CLOSE Z ;
       /* delete supplier Sx */
       EXEC SQL DELETE
               FROM    S
               WHERE   CURRENT OF Y ;
       IF SQLCODE ~= 0
       THEN SIGNAL CONDITION ( DBEXCEPTION ) ;
       EXEC SQL CLOSE Y ;
       EXEC SQL COMMIT WORK ;
QUIT:
       RETURN ;
END ;    /* UPDS# */
```

The foregoing code assumes that any attempt to introduce a new shipment for supplier Sx (via an INSERT or UPDATE on table SP) will request at least a shared lock on the supplier record for Sx (see Chapter 14). We remark that this example provides additional evidence in support of the claim in Section 12.6 that it is often a good idea to avoid composite keys. If table SP had a noncomposite primary key SHIP#, the entire loop over shipments could be replaced by the single statement.

```
    UPDATE SP
    SET     S# = Sy
    WHERE   S# = Sx
```

Of course, if SQL/DS supported a CASCADE update rule (as it should), the entire program could be replaced by the single UPDATE statement shown in part (a) of the exercise:

```
    UPDATE S
    SET     S# = Sy
    WHERE   S# = Sx
```

♦

Application Programming I: Embedded SQL

13.1 INTRODUCTION

In Chapter 1 we explained that SQL was used in SQL/DS both as an inter-active query language and as a database programming language. Up to this point, however, we have more or less ignored the programming aspects of SQL and have tacitly assumed (where it made any difference) that the lan-guage was being used interactively. Now we turn our attention to those programming aspects specifically. In the present chapter we discuss the principal ideas behind "embedded SQL" (as it is usually called); in the next chapter we examine the concept of transaction processing; and in Chapter 15 we present an introduction (only) to a somewhat more complex subject, namely "dynamic SQL." But first things first.

The fundamental principle underlying embedded SQL, which we refer to as *the dual-mode principle,* is that *any SQL statement that can be used at the terminal can also be used in an application program.* Of course, as pointed out in Chapter 1, there are various differences of detail between a given interactive SQL statement and its corresponding embedded form, and SELECT statements in particular require significantly extended treatment in the programming environment (see Section 13.4); but the principle is nevertheless broadly true. (Its converse is not, incidentally; that is, there are a number of SQL statements that are programming statements only and cannot be used interactively, as we shall see.)

Note clearly that the dual-mode principle applies to the entire SQL language, not just to the data manipulation operations. It is true that the data manipulation operations are far and away the ones most frequently used in a programming context, but there is nothing wrong in embedding (for example) CREATE TABLE statements in a program, if it makes sense to do so for the application at hand.

The programming languages currently supported by SQL/DS—the so-called "host languages"—are PL/I, COBOL, FORTRAN, APL, BASIC, Prolog, the REXX procedure language, and System/370 Assembler Language. In Section 13.2 we consider the mechanics of embedding SQL in these languages. Then in Sections 13.3 and 13.4 we present the major ideas behind the embedding of SQL data manipulation statements specifically. Finally, in Section 13.5, we present a comprehensive programming example.

Note: For reasons of brevity and definiteness, all of our examples (etc.) are given in terms of PL/I. But of course the ideas are fairly general and translate into the other host languages with only comparatively minor differences. At least, this statement is true for the other compiled languages (COBOL, FORTRAN, Assembler Language); the interpreted languages (APL, BASIC, Prolog, REXX) do not follow the same pattern but instead make use of the facilities discussed in Chapter 15. The reader is referred to the IBM manuals for details of the differences among the different host languages.

13.2 PRELIMINARIES

Before we can get into the embedded SQL statements per se, it is necessary to cover a number of preliminary details. Most of those details are illustrated by the program fragment shown in Fig. 13.1.

Points arising:

1. Embedded SQL statements are prefixed by EXEC SQL (so that they can easily be distinguished from statements of the host language), and are terminated by a special termination symbol (a semicolon for PL/I).

2. An *executable* SQL statement (from now on we will usually drop the "embedded") can appear wherever an executable host statement can ap-

```
      EXEC SQL BEGIN DECLARE SECTION ;
               DCL GIVENS#  CHAR(5) ;
               DCL RANK     FIXED BIN(15) ;
               DCL CITY     CHAR(15) ;
      EXEC SQL END DECLARE SECTION ;

               DCL ALPHA    ... ;
               DCL BETA     ... ;

      EXEC SQL INCLUDE SQLCA ;

                . . . . . . . . . . .

               IF ALPHA > BETA THEN
GETSTC:
      EXEC SQL SELECT STATUS, CITY
               INTO   :RANK, :CITY
               FROM   S
               WHERE  S# = :GIVENS# ;
                . . . . . . . . . .

               PUT SKIP LIST ( RANK, CITY ) ;
```

Fig. 13.1 Fragment of a PL/I program with embedded SQL

pear. Note the qualifier "executable" here: Unlike interactive SQL, embedded SQL includes some statements that are purely declarative, not executable. For example, BEGIN and END DECLARE SECTION (see the figure) are not executable statements.

3. SQL statements can include references to host variables; such references are prefixed with a colon to distinguish them from SQL field names. Host variables can appear in SQL data manipulation statements wherever a constant is permitted. They are also used to designate a target for retrieval. In other words, they can appear in the following positions (loosely speaking):

- INTO clause in SELECT or FETCH (target for retrieved value)
- SELECT clause (value to be retrieved)
- WHERE or HAVING clause (value to be compared)
- SET clause in UPDATE (source for updated value)
- VALUES clause in INSERT (source for inserted value)
- element of a scalar expression in SELECT, WHERE, HAVING, or SET (not VALUES), where that expression in turn evaluates to the value to be retrieved, compared, or used as the source for update

They can also appear in CONNECT (see Chapter 11) and in certain embedded-only statements (details to follow). They cannot appear in any other SQL contexts.

4. All host variables that will be referenced in SQL statements must be defined within an "embedded SQL declare section," which is delimited by the BEGIN and END DECLARE SECTION statements (see the figure). Arrays and structures are not permitted. A host variable must not appear within an embedded SQL statement before it is defined. Host variables and database fields can have the same name.

5. After any SQL statement has been executed, feedback information is returned to the program in an area called the SQL Communication Area (SQLCA). In particular, a numeric status indicator is returned in a field of the SQLCA called SQLCODE. A SQLCODE value of zero means that the statement executed successfully; a positive value means that the statement did execute, but constitutes a warning that some exceptional condition occurred (for example, a value of +100 indicates that no data was found to satisfy the request); and a negative value means that an error occurred and the statement did not complete successfully. In principle, therefore, every SQL statement in the program should be followed by a test on SQLCODE (and appropriate action taken if the value is not what was expected), but we do not show any such tests in Fig. 13.1. (In practice such explicit testing of SQLCODE values may *not* be necessary, as we show in Section 13.5.)

The SQL Communication Area is included in the program by means of the embedded SQL statement INCLUDE SQLCA. *Note:* The EXEC SQL INCLUDE statement can also be used to include program source text from a library data set.

6. Host variables must have a data type compatible with the SQL data type of fields they are to be compared with or assigned to or from. Data type compatibility is defined in Chapter 4 (Section 4.5). If significant digits or characters are lost on assignment (either to or from the database) because the receiving field is too small, an error indication is returned to the program.

So much for the preliminaries. In the rest of this chapter we concentrate on the SQL data manipulation operations SELECT, UPDATE, DELETE, and INSERT specifically. As already indicated, most of those operations can be handled in a fairly straightforward fashion (i.e., with only minor changes to their syntax). SELECT statements require special treatment, however. The problem is that executing a SELECT statement causes a *table* to be retrieved—a table that, in general, contains multiple records—and languages such as PL/I, COBOL, etc. are simply not well equipped to handle more than one record at a time. It is therefore necessary to provide some kind of bridge between the set-at-a-time level of SQL and the record-at-a-time level of the host; and *cursors* provide such a bridge. A cursor is a new kind of SQL object, one that applies to embedded SQL only (because of course interactive SQL has no need of it). It consists essentially of a kind of *pointer* that can be used to run through a set of records, pointing to each of the records in the set in turn and thus providing addressability to those records one at a time. However, we defer detailed discussion of cursors to Section 13.4, and consider first (in Section 13.3) those statements that have no need of them.

13.3 OPERATIONS NOT INVOLVING CURSORS

The data manipulation statements that do not need cursors are as follows:

- "Singleton SELECT"
- UPDATE (except the CURRENT form—see Section 13.4)
- DELETE (again, except the CURRENT form—Section 13.4)
- INSERT

We give examples of each of these statements in turn.

13.3.1 Singleton SELECT. Get status and city for the supplier whose supplier number is given by the host variable GIVENS#.

```
EXEC SQL SELECT STATUS, CITY
         INTO   :RANK, :CITY
         FROM   S
         WHERE  S# = :GIVENS# ;
```

We use the term "singleton SELECT" to mean a SELECT statement for which the retrieved table contains at most one row. In the example, if there exists exactly one record in table S satisfying the WHERE condition, then the STATUS and CITY values from that record will be delivered to the host variables RANK and CITY as requested, and SQLCODE will be set to zero. If no S record satisfies the WHERE condition, SQLCODE will be set to +100; and if more than one does, the program is in error, and SQLCODE will be set to a negative value. In these last two cases, the host variables RANK and CITY will remain unchanged.

The foregoing example raises another point. What if the SELECT statement does indeed select exactly one record, but the STATUS value in that record happens to be null? (Remember that STATUS was not defined to be NOT NULL, so nulls are possible.) With the SELECT statement as shown above, an error will occur (SQLCODE will be set to a negative value). If there is a chance that the source of a retrieval operation might be null, the user should include an *indicator variable* in the INTO clause in addition to the normal target variable, as illustrated in the following example.

```
EXEC SQL SELECT STATUS, CITY
         INTO    :RANK:RANKIND, :CITY
         FROM    S
         WHERE   S# = :GIVENS# ;
   IF RANKIND = -1 THEN /* STATUS was null */ ... ;
```

If the field to be retrieved is null and an indicator variable has been specified, then that indicator variable will be set to the value −1* and the ordinary target variable will remain unchanged. Indicator variables are specified as shown—i.e., immediately following the corresponding ordinary target variable and separated from that target variable by a colon (optionally preceded by the explicit keyword INDICATOR). They should be declared as 15-bit signed binary integers.

Note: Indicator variables should not be used in a WHERE or HAVING clause. For example, the following will *not* work:

```
RANKIND = -1 ;
EXEC SQL SELECT CITY
         INTO    :CITY
         FROM    S
         WHERE   STATUS = :RANK:RANKIND ;
```

The correct way to select cities where the status is null is:

```
EXEC SQL SELECT CITY
         INTO    :CITY
         FROM    S
         WHERE   STATUS IS NULL ;
```

13.3.2   *UPDATE.* Increase the status of all London suppliers by the amount given by the host variable RAISE.

```
EXEC SQL UPDATE S
         SET     STATUS = STATUS + :RAISE
         WHERE   CITY = 'London' ;
```

If no S records satisfy the WHERE condition, SQLCODE will be set to +100. Indicator variables can be used on the right-hand side of an assignment in the SET clause; for example, the sequence

```
RANKIND = -1 ;
EXEC SQL UPDATE S
         SET     STATUS = :RANK:RANKIND
         WHERE   CITY = 'London' ;
```

will set the status for all London suppliers to null. So also of course will the statement

---

*It will be set to −2 if the null is not directly derived from a database field but is instead generated by SQL/DS. SQL/DS will generate a null if an error (e.g., division by zero or a data type conversion error) occurs in computing the value of some expression to be retrieved.

```
EXEC SQL UPDATE S
         SET     STATUS = NULL
         WHERE   CITY = 'London' ;
```

13.3.3   DELETE.   Delete all shipments for suppliers whose city is given by the host variable CITY.

```
EXEC SQL DELETE
         FROM    SP
         WHERE   :CITY =
               ( SELECT CITY
                 FROM   S
                 WHERE  S.S# = SP.S# ) ;
```

Again SQLCODE will be set to + 100 if no records satisfy the WHERE condition.

13.3.4   INSERT.   Insert a new part (part number, name, and weight given by host variables PNO, PNAME, PWT, respectively; color and city unknown) into table P.

```
EXEC SQL INSERT
         INTO    P ( P#, PNAME, WEIGHT )
         VALUES ( :PNO, :PNAME, :PWT ) ;
```

(We assume for the sake of the example that nulls are allowed for fields P.COLOR and P.CITY.) Once again indicator variables are legal; for example, if PCOLOR and PCITY are two further host variables, and if COLORIND and CITYIND are corresponding indicator variables, then the sequence

```
COLORIND = -1 ;
CITYIND  = -1 ;
EXEC SQL INSERT
         INTO    P ( P#, PNAME, COLOR, WEIGHT, CITY )
         VALUES ( :PNO, :PNAME, :PCOLOR:COLORIND,
                  :PWT,    :PCITY:CITYIND ) ;
```

has the same effect as the INSERT shown above.

For simplicity, we will ignore indicator variables and the possibility of nulls in most of what follows (both in this chapter and in the next two chapters).

13.4   OPERATIONS INVOLVING CURSORS

Now we turn to the case of a SELECT that selects a whole set of records, not necessarily just one. As explained in Section 13.2, what is needed here is a mechanism for accessing the records in the set one by one; and *cursors* provide such a mechanism. The process is illustrated in outline in the example of Fig. 13.2, which is intended to retrieve supplier details (S#, SNAME, and STATUS) for all suppliers in the city given by the host variable Y.

```
EXEC SQL DECLARE X CURSOR FOR        /* define cursor X    */
         SELECT S#, SNAME, STATUS
         FROM   S
         WHERE  CITY = :Y ;

EXEC SQL OPEN X ;                     /* execute the query  */
         DO for all S records accessible via X ;
            EXEC SQL FETCH X INTO :S#, :SNAME, :STATUS ;
                                      /* fetch next supplier */
            .........
         END ;
EXEC SQL CLOSE X ;                    /* deactivate cursor X */
```

Fig. 13.2 Retrieving multiple records

Explanation:

1. The DECLARE X CURSOR . . . statement defines a cursor called X, with an associated query as specified by the SELECT that forms part of that DECLARE. The SELECT is not executed at this point; DECLARE CURSOR is a purely declarative statement.

2. The SELECT *is* (effectively) executed when the cursor is opened, in the procedural part of the program.

3. The FETCH . . . INTO . . . statement is then used to retrieve records of the result table one at a time. The INTO clause in that statement must specify a list of *n* host variables, where *n* is the number of expressions in the SELECT clause in the cursor declaration. (Note that the SELECT in the cursor declaration does not have an INTO clause of its own.) Each time the FETCH is executed, the current value of the *i*th expression in the SELECT clause in the cursor declaration is assigned to the *i*th variable in the INTO clause ($i = 1$ to *n*). In the example, therefore, the supplier number is assigned to the host variable S#, the supplier name to the host variable SNAME, and the status to the host variable STATUS. (For simplicity we have given each host variable the same name as the corresponding database field.)

4. Since there will be multiple records in the result table (in general), the FETCH will normally appear within a loop (DO . . . END in PL/I); the loop will be repeated so long as there are more records still to come in that result table. An attempt to FETCH the next record when no records remain will set SQLCODE to $+100$. That condition can then be used to cause exit from the loop on the next attempt at iteration.

5. On exit from the loop cursor X is closed (deactivated) via an appropriate CLOSE statement.

Now let us consider cursors and cursor operations in more detail. First, a cursor is declared by means of a DECLARE CURSOR statement, which takes the general form

```
EXEC SQL DECLARE cursor CURSOR
         FOR union-expression
         [ FOR UPDATE OF field(s) | ORDER BY field(s) ] ;
```

where "union-expression" is defined as follows—

```
union-term  |  union-expression UNION [ ALL ] union-term
```

—and "union-term" in turn is either a SELECT–FROM–WHERE–GROUP BY–HAVING expression or a union-expression in parentheses. *Note:* This is the general form of a cursor declaration. In practice, most such declarations do not involve UNION at all (see, e.g., Fig. 13.2).

As already stated, the DECLARE CURSOR statement is declarative, not executable; it declares a cursor with the specified name and having the specified subquery (or set of UNIONed subqueries) permanently associated with it. Notice that those subqueries can include (and typically will include) host variable references. If the cursor will be used in UPDATE CURRENT statements (see later in this section), then the declaration must include a FOR UPDATE clause, specifying all fields that will be updated via this cursor; if not, and if DELETE CURRENT statements will also not be used (again, see later in this section), then it may optionally include an ORDER BY clause (possibly with ASC/DESC specifications), as in a conventional SELECT statement. That ORDER BY clause will control the order in which result rows are retrieved via FETCH. Note, therefore, that it is not possible to retrieve a set of records via a cursor in some specified order *and* UPDATE (or DELETE) some of those records via that same cursor at the same time. See Exercise 13.4 at the end of this chapter.

A program can include any number of DECLARE CURSOR statements, each of which must (of course) be for a different cursor.

Three executable statements are provided specifically for operating on cursors: OPEN, FETCH, and CLOSE.

1. The statement

```
EXEC SQL OPEN cursor ;
```

opens or *activates* the specified cursor (which must not currently be open). In effect, the union-expression associated with that cursor is executed (using the current values for any host variables referenced within that expression); a set of records is thus identified and becomes the *active set* for the cursor. The cursor also identifies a *position* within that set, namely the position just before the first record in the set. (Active sets are always considered to have an ordering, so that the concept of position has meaning. The ordering is either that defined by ORDER BY, if specified, or a system-determined ordering otherwise.)

2. The statement

```
EXEC SQL FETCH cursor INTO target [, target ] ... ;
```

where each "target" is of the form

```
: host-variable [ [ INDICATOR ] : host-variable ]
```

(as in singleton SELECT), and where the identified cursor must be open, advances that cursor to the next record in the active set and then assigns values from that record to host variables as explained earlier. If there is no next record when FETCH is executed, then SQLCODE is set to +100 and no data is retrieved.

Note, incidentally, that FETCH (i.e., "fetch next") is the *only* cursor movement operation. It is not possible to move a cursor (e.g.) "forward three positions" or "backward two positions" or "directly to the ith record," etc.

3. The statement

```
EXEC SQL CLOSE cursor ;
```

closes or *deactivates* the specified cursor (which must currently be open). The cursor now has no corresponding active set. However, it can now be opened again, in which case it will acquire another active set—probably not exactly the same set as before, especially if the values of host variables referenced in the cursor declaration have changed in the meantime. Note that changing the values of those host variables while the cursor is open has no effect on the active set.

Two further statements can include references to cursors. These are the CURRENT forms of UPDATE and DELETE. If a cursor, X say, is currently positioned on a particular record in the database, then it is possible to UPDATE or DELETE the "current of X," i.e., the record on which X is positioned. Syntax:

```
EXEC SQL UPDATE table
        SET    field = scalar-expression
            [, field = scalar-expression ] ...
        WHERE  CURRENT OF cursor ;


EXEC SQL DELETE
        FROM   table
        WHERE  CURRENT OF cursor ;
```

For example:

```
EXEC SQL UPDATE S
         SET    STATUS = STATUS + :RAISE
         WHERE  CURRENT OF X ;
```

UPDATE CURRENT and DELETE CURRENT are not permitted if the SELECT statement in the cursor declaration involves UNION (with or without ALL) or ORDER BY, or if that SELECT statement would define a nonupdatable view if it were part of a CREATE VIEW statement (see Section 10.4 in Chapter 10). In the case of UPDATE CURRENT, as explained earlier, the cursor declaration must include a FOR UPDATE clause identifying all the fields that appear as targets of a SET clause in an UPDATE CURRENT statement for that cursor.

The PUT statement

We close this section with a brief note on the use of cursors for storing new records into the database (instead of for retrieving records from the database, the more common use). Here is an example:

```
EXEC SQL DECLARE XYZ CURSOR
         FOR INSERT INTO S ( S#, SNAME, STATUS, CITY )
                       VALUES (:S#,:SNAME,:STATUS,:CITY ) ;

EXEC SQL OPEN XYZ ;
DO until no more S records to be stored ;
   move values for next S record
         into host variables S#, SNAME, STATUS, CITY ;
   EXEC SQL PUT XYZ ;
END ;
EXEC SQL CLOSE XYZ ;
```

From a logical standpoint, the effect of executing this set of statements is basically the same as the following:

```
DO until no more S records to be stored ;
   move values for next S record
         into host variables S#, SNAME, STATUS, CITY ;
   EXEC SQL INSERT INTO S ( S#, SNAME, STATUS, CITY )
                       VALUES (:S#,:SNAME,:STATUS,:CITY ) ;
END ;
```

However, the version using the cursor and PUT may potentially be more efficient. If (and only if) the preprocessor BLOCK option is specified (see the IBM manuals for details), SQL/DS will batch the records up into blocks and will only actually insert them into the table when the block is full (or when the cursor is closed).

13.5 A COMPREHENSIVE EXAMPLE

We conclude this chapter with a somewhat contrived, but nevertheless comprehensive, example (Fig. 13.3) to illustrate a number of additional points. The program accepts four input values: a part number (GIVENP#), a city

```
SQLEX: PROC OPTIONS (MAIN) ;

        EXEC SQL BEGIN DECLARE SECTION ;

        /* program input */

        DCL GIVENP#         CHAR(6) ;
        DCL GIVENCIT        CHAR(15) ;
        DCL GIVENINC        FIXED BINARY(15) ;
        DCL GIVENLVL        FIXED BINARY(15) ;

        /* targets for "fetch next supplier" */

        DCL S#              CHAR(5) ;
        DCL SNAME           CHAR(20) ;
        DCL STATUS          FIXED BINARY(15) ;
        DCL CITY            CHAR(15) ;

        EXEC SQL END DECLARE SECTION ;

        /* housekeeping variables */

        DCL DISP            CHAR(7) ;
        DCL MORE_SUPPLIERS BIT(1) ;

        /* SQL Communication Area and exception declarations */

        EXEC SQL INCLUDE SQLCA ;
        EXEC SQL WHENEVER NOT FOUND CONTINUE ;
        EXEC SQL WHENEVER SQLERROR CONTINUE ;
        EXEC SQL WHENEVER SQLWARNING CONTINUE ;

        /* cursor definition */

        EXEC SQL DECLARE Z CURSOR FOR
                SELECT S#, SNAME, STATUS, CITY
                FROM    S
                WHERE   EXISTS
                    ( SELECT *
                      FROM    SP
                      WHERE   SP.S# = S.S#
                      AND     SP.P# = :GIVENP# )
                FOR UPDATE OF STATUS ;

        /* database exception handler */

        ON CONDITION ( DBEXCEPTION )
        BEGIN ;
           PUT SKIP LIST ( SQLCA ) ;
           EXEC SQL ROLLBACK WORK ;
           GO TO QUIT ;
        END ;
```

Fig. 13.3 A comprehensive example (part 1 of 2)

name (GIVENCIT), a status increment (GIVENINC), and a status level
(GIVENLVL). The program scans all suppliers of the part identified by
GIVENP#. For each such supplier, if the supplier city is GIVENCIT, then
the status is increased by GIVENINC; otherwise, if the status is less than
GIVENLVL, the supplier is deleted. In all cases supplier information is
listed on the printer, with an indication of how that particular supplier was
handled by the program.

```
/* main program logic */

GET LIST ( GIVENP#, GIVENCIT, GIVENINC, GIVENLVL ) ;
EXEC SQL OPEN Z ;
IF SQLCODE ~= 0
THEN SIGNAL CONDITION ( DBEXCEPTION ) ;
MORE_SUPPLIERS = '1'B ;
DO WHILE ( MORE_SUPPLIERS ) ;
    EXEC SQL FETCH Z INTO :S#, :SNAME, :STATUS, :CITY ;
    SELECT ;                 /* a PL/I SELECT, not a SQL SELECT */
    WHEN ( SQLCODE = 100 )
        MORE_SUPPLIERS = '0'B ;
    WHEN ( SQLCODE ~= 100 & SQLCODE ~= 0 )
        SIGNAL CONDITION ( DBEXCEPTION ) ;
    WHEN ( SQLCODE = 0 )
        DO ;
            DISP = 'bbbbbb' ;
            IF CITY = GIVENCIT
            THEN
                DO ;
                    EXEC SQL UPDATE S
                             SET    STATUS = STATUS + :GIVENINC
                             WHERE  CURRENT OF Z ;
                    IF SQLCODE ~= 0
                    THEN SIGNAL CONDITION ( DBEXCEPTION ) ;
                    DISP = 'UPDATED' ;
                END ;
            ELSE
                IF STATUS < GIVENLVL
                THEN
                    DO ;
                        EXEC SQL DELETE
                                 FROM   S
                                 WHERE  CURRENT OF Z ;
                        IF SQLCODE ~= 0
                        THEN SIGNAL CONDITION ( DBEXCEPTION ) ;
                        DISP = 'DELETED' ;
                    END ;
            PUT SKIP LIST ( S#, SNAME, STATUS, CITY, DISP ) ;
        END ;    /* WHEN ( SQLCODE = 0 ) ... */
    END ;   /* PL/I SELECT */
END ;   /* DO WHILE */
EXEC SQL CLOSE Z ;
EXEC SQL COMMIT WORK ;
QUIT:
    RETURN ;
END ;   /* SQLEX */
```

Fig. 13.3 A comprehensive example (part 2 of 2)

Points arising:

1. First, we have ignored throughout the possibility that some item to be retrieved might be null. This simplification was introduced purely to reduce the size of the example.

2. As explained in Section 13.2, every SQL statement should in principle be followed by a test of the returned SQLCODE value. The WHENEVER statement is provided to simplify this process. The WHENEVER statement has the syntax:

```
EXEC SQL WHENEVER condition action ;
```

where "condition" is one of the following:

```
NOT FOUND
SQLWARNING
SQLERROR
```

and "action" is a GO TO statement, STOP, or CONTINUE. WHENEVER is not an executable statement; rather, it is a directive to the SQL preprocessor. "WHENEVER condition GO TO label" causes the preprocessor to insert an "IF condition GO TO label" statement after each executable SQL statement it encounters; "WHENEVER condition STOP" causes it to insert "IF condition STOP" statements instead; and "WHENEVER condition CONTINUE" causes the preprocessor not to insert any statements at all (the implication being that the programmer will insert appropriate statements by hand). STOP is not permitted for NOT FOUND. The three "conditions" are defined as follows:

```
NOT FOUND     means    SQLCODE = 100
SQLWARNING    means    SQLWARN0 is 'W'
SQLERROR      means    SQLCODE < 0
```

Note: SQLWARN0 is another field in the SQLCA. It is set to W if certain (usually nondisastrous) exceptions occur—for example, if a string value from the database has to be truncated during FETCH because the target host variable is too small. For details, see the IBM manuals. We have ignored SQLWARN0 entirely in the code of Fig. 13.3.

Each WHENEVER statement the preprocessor encounters on its sequential scan through the program text (for a particular condition) overrides the previous one it found (for that condition). At the start of the program text there is an implicit WHENEVER statement for each of the three possible conditions, specifying CONTINUE in each case.

In the sample program, all exception-testing is done explicitly, for tutorial reasons. If any exception occurs, control is passed to a procedure that prints diagnostic information (the SQL Communication Area, in the example), issues a ROLLBACK WORK (see paragraph 3. below), and then branches to the final RETURN.

3. When a program updates the database in any way, that update should initially be regarded as *tentative only* — tentative in the sense that, if something subsequently goes wrong, *the update may be undone* (either by the program itself or by the system). For example, if the program encounters an unexpected error, say an overflow condition, and terminates abnormally, then the system will automatically undo all such tentative updates on the program's behalf. Updates remain tentative until one of two things happens:

(a) A COMMIT WORK statement is executed, which makes all tentative updates firm ("committed"); or

(b) A ROLLBACK WORK statement is executed, which undoes all tentative updates.

Once committed, an update is guaranteed never to be undone (this is the definition of "committed").

In the example, the program issues COMMIT WORK when it reaches its normal termination, but issues ROLLBACK WORK if any SQL exception is encountered. Actually, that explicit COMMIT WORK is not strictly necessary; the system will automatically issue a COMMIT WORK on the program's behalf for any program that reaches normal termination. It will also automatically issue a ROLLBACK WORK on the program's behalf for any program that does not reach normal termination; in the example, however, an explicit ROLLBACK WORK *is* necessary, because the program is designed to reach its normal termination even if a SQL exception occurs. *Note*: Despite the foregoing, it is advisable as a general rule always to include explicit COMMIT and ROLLBACK WORK statements at appropriate points, even when they are logically unnecessary. See the IBM manuals for further discussion of this point.

The COMMIT and ROLLBACK WORK operations are discussed in more detail in the next chapter.

EXERCISES

13.1 Using the suppliers-parts-projects database, write a program with embedded SQL statements to list all supplier records, in supplier number order. Each supplier record should be immediately followed in the listing by all project records for projects supplied by that supplier, in project number order.

13.2 Why do you think the FOR UPDATE clause is required?

13.3 Revise your solution to Exercise 13.1 to do the following in addition:
   (a) Increase the status by 50 percent for any supplier who supplies more than
       two projects;
   (b) Delete any supplier who does not supply any projects at all.

13.4 Write a program to read and print all part records in part number order, deleting every tenth one as you go.

13.5 (Harder.) Given the tables

```
CREATE TABLE PARTS
      ( P#  ... NOT NULL,
        DESCRIPTION ... ,
      PRIMARY KEY ( P# ) )

CREATE TABLE PART_STRUCTURE
      ( MAJOR_P# ... NOT NULL,
        MINOR_P# ... NOT NULL,
        QTY      ... ,
      PRIMARY KEY ( MAJOR_P#, MINOR_P# ) ,
      FOREIGN KEY MAJOR ( MAJOR_P# ) REFERENCES PARTS ... ,
      FOREIGN KEY MINOR ( MINOR_P# ) REFERENCES PARTS ... )
```

where PART_STRUCTURE shows which parts (MAJOR_P#) contain which other
parts (MINOR_P#) as first-level components, write a SQL program to list all component parts of a given part, to all levels (the "parts explosion" problem). *Note:*
The following sample values may help you visualize this problem:

MAJOR_P#	MINOR_P#	QTY
P1	P2	2
P1	P4	4
P5	P3	1
P3	P6	3
P6	P1	9
P5	P6	8
P2	P4	3

13.6 Return to Exercise 12.8 in Chapter 12 if you have not already answered it.

ANSWERS TO SELECTED EXERCISES

13.1 There are basically two ways to write such a program. The first involves two
cursors, CS and CJ say, defined along the following lines:

```
EXEC SQL DECLARE CS CURSOR FOR
         SELECT S#, SNAME, STATUS, CITY
         FROM   S
         ORDER  BY S# ;

EXEC SQL DECLARE CJ CURSOR FOR
         SELECT J#, JNAME, CITY
         FROM   J
         WHERE  J# IN
              ( SELECT J#
                FROM   SPJ
                WHERE  S# = :CS_S# )
         ORDER BY J# ;
```

When cursor CJ is opened, host variable CS_S# will contain a supplier number value, fetched via cursor CS. The procedural logic is essentially as follows:

```
EXEC SQL OPEN CS ;
DO for all S records accessible via CS ;
    EXEC SQL FETCH CS INTO :CS_S#, :CS_SN, :CS_ST, :CS_SC ;
    print CS_S#, CS_SN, CS_ST, CS_SC ;
    EXEC SQL OPEN CJ ;
    DO for all J records accessible via CJ ;
        EXEC SQL FETCH CJ INTO :CJ_J#, :CJ_JN, :CJ_JC ;
        print CJ_J#, CJ_JN, CJ_JC ;
    END ;
    EXEC SQL CLOSE CJ ;
END ;
EXEC SQL CLOSE CS ;
```

The trouble with this solution is that it does not exploit the set-level processing capabilities of SQL to the full. In effect, the programmer is hand-coding a join. The second approach uses a single cursor, and so does take advantage of SQL's set-level nature; unfortunately, however, the join required is an *outer* join, so the program must first construct that outer join, as follows. (This second solution may therefore be less efficient than the first, because it effectively requires the same data to be scanned multiple times. Direct SQL support for an outer join operator, which is desirable anyway for usability reasons, might alleviate this problem.)

```
EXEC SQL CREATE TABLE TEMP
            ( S#       ...,
              SNAME    ...,
              STATUS   ...,
              SCITY    ...,
              J#       ...,
              JNAME    ...,
              JCITY    ... ) ;

EXEC SQL INSERT INTO TEMP
            SELECT S#, SNAME, STATUS, S.CITY, J#, JNAME, J.CITY
            FROM   S, SPJ, J
            WHERE  S.S# = SPJ.S# AND SPJ.J# = J.J# ;

EXEC SQL INSERT INTO TEMP
            SELECT S#, SNAME, STATUS, CITY, 'bb', 'bb', 'bb'
            FROM   S
            WHERE  NOT EXISTS
                 ( SELECT * FROM SPJ WHERE SPJ.S# = S.S# ) ;
```

Now:

```
EXEC SQL DECLARE CSJ CURSOR FOR
            SELECT S#, SNAME, STATUS, SCITY, J#, JNAME, JCITY
            FROM   TEMP
            ORDER  BY S#, J# ;

EXEC SQL OPEN CSJ ;
DO for all TEMP records accessible via CSJ ;
    EXEC SQL FETCH CSJ INTO :CS_S#, :CS_SN, :CS_ST, :CS_SC,
                           :CJ_J#, :CJ_JN, :CJ_JC ;
```

```
       IF CS_S# different from previous iteration
       THEN print CS_S#, CS_SN, CS_ST, CS_SC ;
       print CJ_J#, CJ_JN, CJ_JC ;
    END ;
    EXEC SQL CLOSE CSJ ;

    EXEC SQL DROP TABLE TEMP ;
```

13.2 Suppose the program includes a DECLARE CURSOR statement of the form

```
    EXEC SQL DECLARE C CURSOR FOR
             SELECT ...
             FROM    T
             ...... ;
```

The optimizer is responsible for choosing an access path corresponding to the cursor C. Suppose it chooses an index based on field F of table T. The set of records accessible via C when C is activated will then be ordered according to values of F. If the program were allowed to UPDATE a value of F via the cursor C—i.e., via an UPDATE statement of the form

```
    EXEC SQL UPDATE T
             SET    F = ...
             WHERE   CURRENT OF C ;
```

—then the updated record would probably have to be "moved" (logically speaking), because it would now belong in a different position with respect to the ordering of the active set. In other words, cursor C would effectively jump to a new position, with unpredictable results. To avoid such a situation, the user must warn the optimizer of any fields to be updated, so that access paths based on those fields will *not* be chosen.

13.3 The second of our two solutions to Exercise 13.1 operates on a copy of the real data. For this problem, therefore, we are forced to use the first approach. Also, cursor CS in that first solution does not permit updates, because its declaration involves an ORDER BY. Apart from these considerations, the solution is basically straightforward. The relevant embedded statements are

```
    EXEC SQL UPDATE S
             SET    STATUS = STATUS * 1.5
             WHERE  S# = :CS_S# ;

    EXEC SQL DELETE
             FROM   S
             WHERE  S# = :CS_S# ;
```

13.4 Outline procedure:

```
    EXEC SQL DECLARE CP CURSOR FOR
             SELECT P#, PNAME, COLOR, WEIGHT, CITY
             FROM   P
             ORDER  BY P# ;

    count = 0 ;
    EXEC SQL OPEN CP ;
    DO for all P records accessible via CP ;
        EXEC SQL FETCH CP INTO :P#, :PNAME, :COLOR, :WEIGHT :CITY ;
```

```
      print P#, PNAME, COLOR, WEIGHT, CITY ;
      count = count + 1 ;
      IF count is a multiple of 10 THEN
      EXEC SQL DELETE FROM P WHERE P# = :P# ;
   END ;
   EXEC SQL CLOSE CP ;
```

Note that the "DELETE FROM P" cannot be of the DELETE CURRENT variety, because the declaration of cursor CP involves an ORDER BY clause.

13.5 This is a good example of a problem that SQL in its current form does not handle well. The basic difficulty is as follows: We need to "explode" the given part to *n* levels, where the value of *n* is unknown at the time of writing the program. If it were possible, the most straightforward way of performing such an *n*-level "explosion" would be by means of a recursive program, in which each recursive invocation creates a new cursor, as follows (pseudocode):

```
      GET LIST ( GIVENP# ) ;
      CALL RECURSION ( GIVENP# ) ;
      RETURN ;

   RECURSION: PROC ( UPPER_P# ) RECURSIVE ;
      DCL UPPER_P# ... ;
      DCL LOWER_P# ... ;
      EXEC SQL DECLARE C "reopenable" CURSOR FOR
               SELECT MINOR_P#
               FROM   PART_STRUCTURE
               WHERE  MAJOR_P# = :UPPER_P# ;

      print UPPER_P# ;
      EXEC SQL OPEN C ;
      DO for all PART_STRUCTURE records accessible via C ;
         EXEC SQL FETCH C INTO :LOWER_P# ;
         CALL RECURSION ( LOWER_P# ) ;
      END ;
      EXEC SQL CLOSE C ;
   END ; /* of RECURSION */
```

We have assumed that the (fictitious) specification "reopenable" means that it is legal to issue "OPEN C" for a cursor C that is already open, and that the effect of such an OPEN is to create a new *instance* of the cursor for the specified query (using the current values of any host variables referenced in that query). We have further assumed that references to C in FETCH (etc.) are references to the "current" instance of C, and that CLOSE destroys that instance and reinstates the previous instance as "current." In other words, we have assumed that a reopenable cursor forms a *stack,* with OPEN and CLOSE serving as the "push" and "pop" operators for that stack.

Unfortunately, those assumptions are purely hypothetical today. There is no such thing as a reopenable cursor in SQL today (indeed, an attempt to issue "OPEN C" for a cursor C that is already open will fail). The foregoing code is illegal. But the example makes it clear that "reopenable cursors" would be a very desirable extension to current SQL.

Since the foregoing procedure does not work, we give a sketch of one possible (but very inefficient) procedure that does.

```
GET LIST ( GIVENP# ) ;
CALL RECURSION ( GIVENP# ) ;
RETURN ;

RECURSION: PROC ( UPPER_P# ) RECURSIVE ;
   DCL UPPER_P# ... ;
   DCL LOWER_P# ... INITIAL ( 'bbbbbb' ) ;
   EXEC SQL DECLARE C CURSOR FOR
            SELECT MINOR_P#
            FROM   PART_STRUCTURE
            WHERE  MAJOR_P# = :UPPER_P#
            AND    MINOR_P# > :LOWER_P#
            ORDER  BY MINOR_P# ;

   DO forever ;
      print UPPER_P# ;
      EXEC SQL OPEN C ;
      EXEC SQL FETCH C INTO :LOWER_P# ;
      IF not found THEN RETURN ;
      IF found THEN
      DO ;
         EXEC SQL CLOSE C ;
         CALL RECURSION ( LOWER_P# ) ;
      END ;
   END ;
END ; /* of RECURSION */
```

Note in this solution that the same cursor is used on every invocation of RECURSION. (By contrast, new instances of UPPER_P# and LOWER_P# are created dynamically each time RECURSION is invoked; those instances are destroyed at completion of that invocation.) Because of this fact, we have to use a trick—

```
... AND MINOR_P# > :LOWER_P# ORDER BY MINOR_P#
```

—so that, on each invocation of RECURSION, we ignore all immediate components (LOWER_P#s) of the current UPPER_P# that have already been processed.

Application Programming II: Transaction Processing

14.1 INTRODUCTION

The notion of transaction processing was touched on briefly at the end of the previous chapter. In this chapter, we explain in more detail what exactly a transaction is and what is meant by the term "transaction management." In particular, we discuss the problems of recovery and concurrency control that the transaction concept is intended to solve. Also, of course, we examine the relevant aspects of SQL/DS in some detail. Note, however, that much of the chapter is very general and could apply with little change to many other systems. The reader who is already familiar with the basic ideas of transaction processing may like to skip the background explanations and go directly to the SQL-specific material in Sections 14.3 and 14.5–14.7.

14.2 WHAT IS A TRANSACTION?

A transaction is a *logical unit of work*. (In fact, "logical unit of work" is the official SQL/DS term for the concept. But "transaction" is the term most often used in the open literature, and we choose to follow that usage here.) Consider the following example. Suppose for the sake of the example that table P, the parts table, includes an additional field TOTQTY representing the total shipment quantity for the part in question. In other words, the value of TOTQTY for any given part is equal to the sum of all SP.QTY values, taken over all SP records for that part. Now consider the following sequence of operations, the intent of which is to add a new shipment (55, P1, 1000) to the database:

```
        EXEC SQL WHENEVER SQLERROR GO TO UNDO ;
        EXEC SQL INSERT
                 INTO    SP ( S#, P#, QTY )
                 VALUES ('S5','P1',1000) ;
        EXEC SQL UPDATE P
                 SET     TOTQTY = TOTQTY + 1000
                 WHERE   P# = 'P1' ;
        EXEC SQL COMMIT WORK ;
                 GO TO FINISH ;
   UNDO :
        EXEC SQL ROLLBACK WORK ;
   FINISH :    RETURN ;
```

The INSERT adds the new shipment to the SP table, the UPDATE updates the TOTQTY field for part P1 appropriately.

The point of the example is that what is presumably intended to be a single, atomic operation—"Create a new shipment"—in fact involves *two* updates to the database. What is more, the database is not even consistent between those two updates; it temporarily violates the requirement that the value of TOTQTY for part P1 be equal to the sum of all SP.QTY values for part P1. Thus a logical unit of work (i.e., a transaction) is not necessarily just one SQL operation; rather, it is a *sequence* of several such operations, in general, that transforms a consistent state of the database into another consistent state, without necessarily preserving consistency at all intermediate points.

Now, it is clear that what must *not* be allowed to happen in the example is for one of the two updates to be executed and the other not (because then the database would be left in an inconsistent state). Ideally, of course, we would like a cast-iron guarantee that both updates will be executed. Unfortunately, it is impossible to provide any such guarantee: There is always a chance that things will go wrong, and go wrong moreover at the worst possible moment. For example, a system crash might occur between the two updates, or an I/O error might occur on the second of them, etc., etc. But a system that supports *transaction processing* does provide the next best thing to such a guarantee. Specifically, it guarantees that if the transaction executes some updates and then a failure occurs (for whatever reason) before the transaction reaches its normal termination, *then those updates will be undone.* Thus the transaction *either* executes in its entirety *or* is totally canceled (i.e., made as if it never executed at all). In this way a sequence of operations that is fundamentally not atomic can be made to look as if it really were atomic from an external point of view.

The system component that provides this atomicity (or semblance of atomicity) is known as the *transaction manager,* and the COMMIT and ROLLBACK WORK statements are the key to the way it operates:

- COMMIT WORK signals *successful* end-of-transaction: It tells the transaction manager that a logical unit of work has been successfully completed, the database is (or should be) in a consistent state again, and all of the updates made by that unit of work can now be "committed" or made permanent.

- ROLLBACK WORK, by contrast, signals *unsuccessful* end-of-transaction: It tells the transaction manager that something has gone wrong, the database might be in an inconsistent state, and all of the updates made by the logical unit of work so far must be "rolled back" or undone. ROLLBACK WORK thus causes a previous (and presumably correct) state of the database to be "recovered," which is why the overall problem under discussion in this section is usually referred to as the *recovery* problem.*

In the example, therefore, we issue a COMMIT WORK if we get through the two updates successfully, which will commit the changes in the database and make them permanent. If anything goes wrong, however—i.e., if either UPDATE returns a negative SQLCODE value—then we issue a ROLLBACK WORK instead, to undo any changes made so far.

Note: For the sake of the example, we show the COMMIT WORK and ROLLBACK WORK operations explicitly. However, as mentioned at the end of Chapter 13, under SQL/DS the system will automatically issue a COMMIT WORK for any program that reaches its normal termination, and will automatically issue a ROLLBACK WORK for any program that does not (regardless of the reason; in particular, if a program terminates abnormally because of a *system* failure, a ROLLBACK WORK will be is-

---

*We are assuming throughout this section that the data is in fact recoverable—in SQL/DS terms, that the data resides in a "recoverable DBspace." See Chapter 16 for further discussion of this point.

sued on its behalf when the system is restarted). In the example, therefore, we could have omitted the explicit COMMIT WORK, but not the explicit ROLLBACK WORK. (On the other hand, for reasons beyond the scope of this book, it is generally a good idea to make *all* COMMIT and ROLLBACK WORK operations explicit in SQL/DS wherever possible. This fact was also mentioned in Chapter 13.)

At this juncture the reader may be wondering how it is possible to undo an update. In fact, SQL/DS provides two distinct mechanisms by which updates can be undone, one based on *shadow pages* and the other (more conventional) based on *logging*. (The rationale for providing two mechanisms when one would be sufficient is beyond the scope of this text.) We explain the two (in outline) as follows.

- Shadow pages are used only for *individual transaction recovery* (i.e., only when an individual transaction has failed in isolation, not when the entire system has failed). When a record is updated in SQL/DS, that record is not actually changed in situ; instead, a new (i.e., updated) *copy* of the record—more accurately, a copy of the *page* containing the record (see Chapter 16)—is written to another location on the disk. The old copy is referred to as a *shadow*. Committing the transaction causes the shadow to be discarded and the updated copy to be treated as the current version. Rolling the transaction back, on the other hand, causes the updated copy to be discarded and the shadow reinstated as the current version, thus in effect "undoing" the original update.

- *System recovery* (i.e., recovery for all transactions that were running at the time of an overall system failure) is performed by means of the log. As mentioned in Chapter 2, SQL/DS includes a log in which details of all update operations—in particular, before and after values—are recorded. (In fact, the log entry for any given update is written to the log *before* that update is applied to the database. See the next section for an explanation of this point.) Thus, if a system failure occurs, then all uncommitted updates can be undone when the system is restarted by using the appropriate log entries to restore the updated records (more accurately, pages) to their previous values.

One final point: As explained in Chapter 1, the data manipulation statements of SQL are *set-level* and typically operate on multiple records at a time. What then if something goes wrong in the middle of such a statement? For example, is it possible that a multiple-record UPDATE could update some of its target records and then fail before updating the rest? The answer is no, it is not; SQL/DS guarantees that all SQL statements are individually atomic, at least so far as their effect on the database is concerned. If an error does occur in the middle of such a statement, then the database will remain totally unchanged.

14.3 COMMIT AND ROLLBACK WORK

From the previous section, it should be clear that COMMIT and ROLLBACK WORK are not really database operations at all, in the sense that SELECT, UPDATE, etc., are database operations. The COMMIT and ROLLBACK WORK statements are not instructions to the DBMS per se. Instead, they are instructions to the *transaction manager;* and the transaction manager may or may not be part of the DBMS—typically, in fact, the DBMS is subordinate to the transaction manager, in the sense that the DBMS is just one of possibly several "resource managers" that provide services to transactions running under that transaction manager. For example, in the case of SQL/DS in particular (at least under VSE and CICS), it is possible for a single transaction to interact simultaneously with two distinct resource managers, namely the SQL/DS DBMS and the DOS DL/I DBMS (not to mention the CICS resource manager itself).

Let us consider this case in a little more detail. Suppose the transaction updates both the DL/I database and the SQL/DS database. If the transaction completes successfully, then *all* of its updates, to both DL/I data and SQL/DS data, must be committed; conversely, if it fails, then *all* of its updates must be rolled back. What must not be possible is for the DL/I updates to be committed and the SQL/DS updates to be rolled back (or conversely); for then the transaction would no longer be atomic (all or nothing).

Thus, it obviously does not make sense for the transaction to issue, say, a COMMIT WORK to DL/I and a ROLLBACK WORK to SQL/DS. And even if it issued the same instruction to both, the system could still fail in between the two, with unfortunate results. Instead, therefore, the transaction issues a single *system-wide* COMMIT (or ROLLBACK) WORK to the transaction manager, and the transaction manager in turn guarantees that all resource managers will commit or will roll back the updates they are responsible for *in unison.* (What is more, it provides that guarantee even if the system fails in the middle of the process, thanks to a protocol known as *two-phase commit.* But the details of that protocol are beyond the scope of this book.) That is why the DBMS(s) is (are) subordinate to the transaction manager; COMMIT and ROLLBACK WORK must be global (system-wide) operations, and the transaction manager acts as the necessary central control point to ensure that this is so.*

---

*In the particular case under discussion (a transaction updating both DL/I data and SQL/DS data), the role of the transaction manager is played by CICS.

Before getting into details of COMMIT and ROLLBACK WORK per se, we first define the important notion of "synchronization point" (abbreviated synchpoint). A synchpoint represents a boundary point between two consecutive transactions; loosely speaking, it corresponds to the end of a logical unit of work, and thus to a point at which the database(s) is (are) in a state of consistency. Program initiation, COMMIT WORK, and ROLLBACK WORK each establish a synchpoint, and no other operation does. (Remember, however, that COMMIT and ROLLBACK WORK may sometimes be implicit.)

Note: We concentrate in what follows on the *application programming* environment. It is possible to enter COMMIT and ROLLBACK WORK statements interactively, but the practice is not recommended because (as will become clear later in this chapter) it might mean that locks will be held for an undesirably long time.

COMMIT WORK

A successful end-of-transaction is signaled and a synchpoint is established. All updates made by the program since the previous synchpoint are committed. All open cursors are closed. All locks are released.

ROLLBACK WORK

An unsuccessful end-of-transaction is signaled and a synchpoint is established. All updates made by the program since the previous synchpoint are undone. All open cursors are closed. All locks are released.

A number of points arise from the foregoing definitions that are worth spelling out explicitly.

1. First, note that *every* SQL operation in SQL/DS—with the sole exception of CONNECT—is executed within the context of some transaction. This includes data definition operations such as CREATE TABLE and data control operations such as GRANT. It also includes SQL operations that are entered interactively (e.g., through ISQL). The synchpoints for operations entered through ISQL are established in a manner to be explained in Chapter 17.

2. It follows from the definitions that transactions cannot be nested inside one another, because each COMMIT (or ROLLBACK) WORK terminates one transaction and starts another.

3. As a consequence of the previous point, we can see that a single program execution consists of a *sequence* of one or more transactions (frequently but not necessarily just one). If it is just one, it will often be possible to code the program without any explicit COMMIT or

ROLLBACK WORK statements at all, though (to repeat) this practice is not recommended.

Finally, it follows from all of the above that transactions are not only the unit of work but also the unit of *recovery*. For if a transaction successfully commits, then the transaction manager must guarantee that its updates will be permanently established in the database, even if the system crashes the very next moment. It is quite possible, for instance, that the system will crash after the COMMIT WORK has been honored but before the updates have been physically written to the database (they may still be waiting in the main storage buffer and so be lost at the time of the crash). Even if that happens, the system's restart procedure will still install those updates in the database; it is able to discover the values to be written by examining the relevant entries in the log. (It follows that the log must be physically written before commit processing can complete. This rule is known as the *Write-Ahead Log Protocol*.) Thus the restart procedure will recover any transactions that completed successfully but did not manage to get their updates physically written prior to the crash; hence, as stated earlier, the transaction can reasonably be defined as the unit of recovery.

14.4   THREE CONCURRENCY PROBLEMS

SQL/DS is a *shared system;* that is, it is a system that allows any number of transactions to access the same database at the same time. Any such system requires some kind of *concurrency control mechanism* to ensure that concurrent transactions do not interfere with each other's operation, and of course SQL/DS includes such a mechanism, namely *locking*. For the benefit of readers who may not be familiar with the problems that can occur in the absence of such a mechanism—in other words, with the problems that such a mechanism must be able to solve—this section is devoted to an outline explanation of those problems. We defer specific discussion of the SQL/DS facilities to Sections 14.5–14.7. Readers who are already familiar with the basic ideas of concurrency control may wish to turn straight to those sections.

There are essentially three ways in which things can go wrong—three ways, that is, in which a transaction, though correct in itself, can nevertheless produce the wrong answer because of interference on the part of some other transaction* (in the absence of suitable controls, of course). The three problems are:

---

*Note that the interfering transaction may also be correct in itself. It is the *interleaving* of operations from the two correct transactions that produces the overall incorrect result.

1. The *lost update* problem,

2. The *uncommitted dependency* problem, and

3. The *inconsistent analysis* problem.

We consider each in turn.

The Lost Update Problem

Consider the situation illustrated in Fig. 14.1. That figure is intended to be read as follows: Transaction *A* retrieves some record *R* at time *t1;* transaction *B* retrieves that same record *R* at time *t2;* transaction *A* updates the record (on the basis of the values seen at time *t1*) at time *t3;* and transaction *B* updates the same record (on the basis of the values seen at time *t2,* which are the same as those seen at time *t1*) at time *t4*. Transaction *A*'s update is lost at time *t4,* because transaction *B* overwrites it without even looking at it.

The Uncommitted Dependency Problem

The uncommitted dependency problem arises if one transaction is allowed to retrieve (or, worse, update) a record that has been updated by another transaction and has not yet been committed by that other transaction. For if it has not yet been committed, there is always a possibility that it never will be committed but will be rolled back instead—in which case the first transaction will have seen some data that now no longer exists (and in a sense "never" existed). Consider Figs. 14.2 and 14.3.

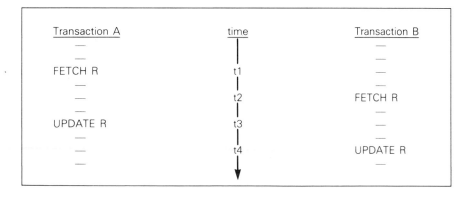

Fig. 14.1 Transaction *A* loses an update at time *t4*

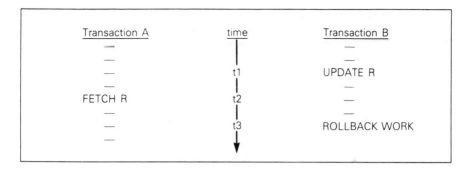

Fig. 14.2 Transaction *A* becomes dependent on an uncommitted change at time
t2

In the first example (Fig. 14.2), transaction *A* sees an uncommitted update (also called an uncommitted change) at time *t2*. That update is then undone at time *t3*. Transaction *A* is therefore operating on a false assumption—namely, the assumption that record *R* has the value seen at time *t2*, whereas in fact it has whatever value it had prior to time *t1*. As a result, transaction *A* may well produce incorrect output. Note, incidentally, that the rollback of transaction *B* may be due to no fault of *B*'s—it could, for example, be the result of a system crash. (And transaction *A* may already have terminated by that time, in which case the crash would not cause a rollback to be issued for *A* also.)

The second example (Fig. 14.3) is even worse. Not only does transaction *A* become dependent on an uncommitted change at time *t2*, but it actually loses an update at time *t3*—because the ROLLBACK WORK at time

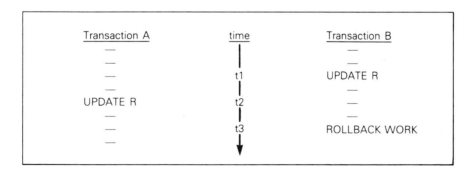

Fig. 14.3 Transaction *A* updates an uncommitted change at time *t2*, and loses that update at time *t3*

t3 causes record *R* to be restored to its value prior to time *t1*. This is another version of the lost update problem.

The Inconsistent Analysis Problem

Consider Fig 14.4, which shows two transactions *A* and *B* operating on account (ACC) records: Transaction *A* is summing account balances, transaction *B* is transferring an amount 10 from account 3 to account 1. The result produced by *A* (110) is obviously incorrect; if *A* were to go on to write that result back into the database, it would actually leave the database in an inconsistent state. We say that *A* has seen an inconsistent state of the

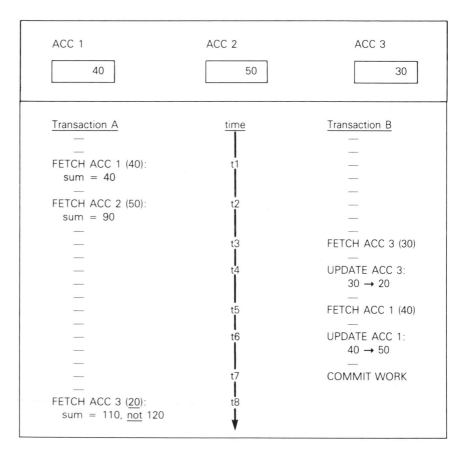

Fig. 14.4 Transaction *A* performs an inconsistent analysis

database and has therefore performed an inconsistent analysis. Note the difference between this example and the previous one: There is no question here of *A* being dependent on an uncommitted change, since *B* commits all its updates before *A* sees ACC 3.

14.5 HOW SQL/DS SOLVES THE THREE CONCURRENCY PROBLEMS

As mentioned at the beginning of the previous section, the SQL/DS concurrency control mechanism—like that of most other systems currently available—is based on a technique known as *locking*. The basic idea of locking is simple: When a transaction needs an assurance that some object that it is interested in—typically a database record—will not change in some unpredictable manner while its back is turned (as it were), it *acquires a lock* on that object. The effect of the lock is to lock other transactions out of the object, and thereby to prevent them from changing it. The first transaction is thus able to carry out its processing in the certain knowledge that the object in question will remain in a stable state for as long as that transaction wishes it to.

We now give a more detailed explanation of the way locking works in SQL/DS specifically. We start by making some simplifying assumptions:

1. We assume first that SQL/DS is operating in multiple-user mode. If instead it is operating in single-user mode, the question of concurrency control does not arise, and no locking is performed at all.

2. We assume for the most part that the only kind of object that is subject to the locking mechanism is the database record (i.e., a row of a base table). The question of locking other kinds of object is deferred to Section 14.6 (though perhaps we should point out right away that index entries are also subject to locking, just as database records are, and for exactly the same reasons).

3. We discuss only two kinds of lock, namely shared locks (S locks) and exclusive locks (X locks). Other types of lock exist in some systems (in fact, SQL/DS itself supports additional types, as we will see), but S and X are the most important ones for present purposes. *Note:* S and X locks are sometimes referred to as read and write locks, respectively.

4. We consider record-level operations only (FETCH, UPDATE CURRENT, etc.). For locking purposes, set-level operations (SELECT-FROM-WHERE, etc.) may be thought of just as shorthand for an appropriate series of record-level operations.

5. We assume that the data resides in public DBspaces (see Chapter 16).

Locking for data in private DBspaces is handled somewhat differently. A brief discussion of the private DBspace case appears in Section 14.6.

6. We assume that RR ("repeatable read") isolation level is in effect. See Section 14.6 for an explanation of this assumption, also for an explanation of the effects of relaxing it.

We now proceed with our detailed explanations.

1. First, if transaction *A* holds an exclusive (X) lock on record *R,* then a request from transaction *B* for a lock of either type on *R* will cause *B* to go into a wait state. *B* will wait until *A*'s lock is released.

2. Next, if transaction *A* holds a shared (S) lock on record *R,* then:
   (a) A request from transaction *B* for an X lock on *R* will cause *B* to go into a wait state (and *B* will wait until *A*'s lock is released);
   (b) A request from transaction *B* for an S lock on *R* will be granted (that is, *B* will now also hold an S lock on *R*).

These first two points can conveniently be summarized by means of a *compatibility matrix* (Fig. 14.5). The matrix is interpreted as follows: Consider some record *R;* suppose transaction *A* currently has a lock on *R* as indicated by the entries in the column headings (dash = no lock); and suppose some distinct transaction *B* issues a request for a lock on *R* as indicated by the entries down the left-hand side (for completeness we again include the "no lock" case). An N indicates a *conflict* (*B*'s request cannot be satisfied and *B* goes into a wait state), a Y indicates compatibility (*B*'s request is satisfied). The matrix is obviously symmetric.

To continue with our explanations:

3. Transaction requests for record locks are always implicit. When a transaction successfully FETCHes a record, it automatically acquires an S lock on that record. When a transaction successfully updates a record, it automatically acquires an X lock on that record (if it already holds an S lock on the record, as it will in a retrieve/update sequence, then the update "promotes" the S lock to X level).

4. All locks are held until the next synchpoint.*

Now we are in a position to see how SQL/DS solves the three problems described in the previous section. Again we consider them one at a time.

---

*X locks are always held until the next synchpoint. S locks are also held until that time, provided that (as we assume) RR isolation level is in effect. See Section 14.6 for further discussion.

	X	S	—
X	N	N	Y
S	N	Y	Y
—	Y	Y	Y

Fig. 14.5 Lock type compatibility matrix (X, S)

The Lost Update Problem

Fig. 14.6 is a modified version of Fig. 14.1, showing what would happen to the interleaved execution of that figure under the locking mechanism of SQL/DS. As you can see, transaction *A*'s UPDATE at time *t3* is not accepted, because it is an implicit request for an X lock on *R*, and such a request conflicts with the S lock already held by transaction *B;* so *A* goes into a wait state. For analogous reasons, *B* goes into a wait state at time

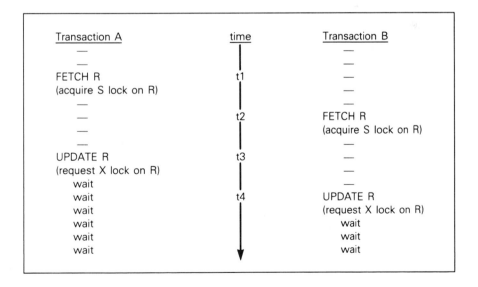

Fig. 14.6 No update is lost, but deadlock occurs at time *t4*

*t4.** Now both transactions are unable to proceed, so there is no question of any update being lost. SQL/DS thus solves the lost update problem by reducing it to another problem!—but at least it does solve the original problem. The new problem is called *deadlock.* To see how SQL/DS solves the deadlock problem, see Section 14.7. *Note:* In the interests of accuracy, however, it should be made clear that SQL/DS detects the deadlock as soon as it occurs and breaks it *immediately,* i.e., during the processing of the SQL statement that caused it. There will never be a situation in which two or more transactions are waiting for each other for an extended period of time, Fig. 14.6 notwithstanding.

The Uncommitted Dependency Problem

Figs. 14.7 and 14.8 are, respectively, modified versions of Figs. 14.2 and 14.3, showing what would happen to the interleaved executions of those figures under the locking mechanism of SQL/DS. As you can see, transaction *A*'s operation at time *t2* (FETCH in Fig. 14.7, UPDATE in Fig. 14.8) is not accepted in either case, because it is an implicit request for a lock on *R,* and such a request conflicts with the X lock already held by *B;* so *A* goes into a wait state. It remains in that wait state until *B* reaches a synch-

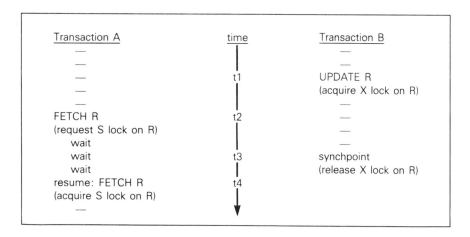

Fig. 14.7 Transaction *A* is prevented from seeing an uncommitted change at time *t2*

---

*B's wait is very brief, however. See the note at the end of the paragraph.

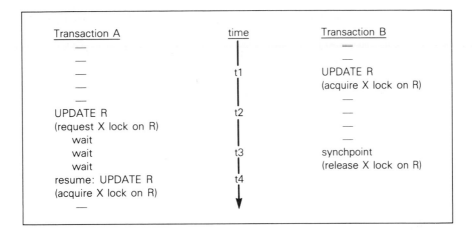

Transaction A	time	Transaction B
—		—
—		—
—	t1	UPDATE R
—		(acquire X lock on R)
—		—
UPDATE R	t2	—
(request X lock on R)		—
wait		—
wait	t3	synchpoint
wait		(release X lock on R)
resume: UPDATE R	t4	
(acquire X lock on R)		
—		

Fig. 14.8 Transaction *A* is prevented from updating an uncommitted change at
time *t2*

point (either commit or rollback), when *B*'s lock is released and *A* is able
to proceed; and at that point *A* sees a *committed* value (either the pre-*B*
value, if *B* terminates with a rollback, or the post-*B* value otherwise). Either
way, *A* is no longer dependent on an uncommitted update.

The Inconsistent Analysis Problem

Fig. 14.9 is a modified version of Fig. 14.4, showing what would happen to
the interleaved execution of that figure under the locking mechanism of
SQL/DS. As you can see, transaction *B*'s UPDATE at time *t6* is not accepted, because it is an implicit request for an X lock on ACC 1, and such
a request conflicts with the S lock already held by *A;* so *B* goes into a wait
state. Likewise, transaction *A*'s FETCH at time *t7* is also not accepted,
because it is an implicit request for an S lock on ACC 3, and such a request
conflicts with the X lock already held by *B;* so *A* goes into a wait state
(briefly) also. Thus, again, SQL/DS solves the original problem (the inconsistent analysis problem, in this case) by forcing a deadlock. As already
mentioned, deadlock is discussed in Section 14.7.

14.6 EXPLICIT LOCKING FACILITIES

*Note: We include this section here primarily for completeness. Some of the
material might not make much sense until the reader has studied Chapter
16.*

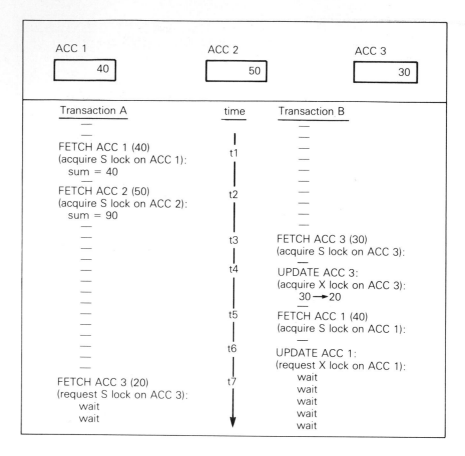

Fig. 14.9 Inconsistent analysis is prevented, but deadlock occurs at time *t7*

In addition to the implicit locking mechanism described in the previous section, SQL/DS provides certain explicit facilities which the user should at least be aware of (though the implicit facilities will be adequate in many situations). The explicit facilities—a somewhat mixed bag—consist of (1) the explicit SQL LOCK statement, (2) the ISOLATION preprocessor parameter, and (3) the LOCK parameter on ACQUIRE (or ALTER) DBSPACE.

The LOCK Statement

The SQL LOCK statement takes the form

```
LOCK type object IN mode MODE
```

where "type" is either TABLE (meaning a base table, not a view) or DBSPACE, "object" is the name of a base table or DBspace as appropriate, and "mode" is either SHARE or EXCLUSIVE. *Note:* DBspaces are logical address spaces on secondary storage; they are used to provide storage for base tables. A given DBspace can contain any number of base tables. For simplicity we concentrate here on LOCK TABLE, but most of the points apply with obvious detail-level changes to LOCK DBSPACE also.

Here is an example of LOCK TABLE:

```
LOCK TABLE SP IN EXCLUSIVE MODE
```

This LOCK TABLE acquires an X lock on the *entire SP base table* on behalf of the transaction issuing the statement. Of course, the transaction may have to wait for a while before it can acquire the lock, if some other transaction already holds a conflicting lock, either on the table itself or on some record within that table. Once the lock is acquired, no other transaction will be able to acquire any lock on the table or on any part of it—in other words, no other transaction will be able to access any part of the table in any way—until the original lock is released (i.e., until the transaction holding it reaches a synchpoint).

If SHARE is specified instead of EXCLUSIVE, then the transaction will of course acquire an S lock instead of an X lock. Again, of course, it may have to wait before it can acquire that lock. Once the lock is acquired, other transactions will not be able to acquire an X lock on the table or on any part of it until the original lock is released, but they *will* be able to acquire an S lock on the table or on some part of it before that time.

The purpose of the explicit LOCK statement is as follows. If a transaction accesses a large number of individual records and locks them one at a time as described in the previous section, then the locking overhead for that transaction may be quite high, in terms of both space and time (space for holding the locks in main storage and time for acquiring them). Consider, for example, a program that scans and prints some large percentage of the entire SP table. For such a program, it may well be better to acquire a single table-level lock as in the example above, and thus to dispense with the need for record-level locks (for that table) entirely. Of course, concurrency will suffer, but the performance of the individual transaction will improve, possibly to such an extent that overall system throughput will improve also.

Acquiring a table-level X lock will indeed (as just suggested) dispense with the need for record-level locks entirely for the table concerned. Acquiring a table-level S lock will dispense with the need for record-level S locks, but not for record-level X locks (again, for the table concerned); that is, if the program updates any record in the table, it will still need to acquire an

X lock on that particular record, in order to prevent concurrent transactions from seeing an uncommitted change.

Locks acquired by means of an explicit LOCK statement are released at the next synchpoint.

The ISOLATION Parameter

The ISOLATION preprocessor parameter specifies the *isolation level* for the access module being generated. There are two possible levels, RR ("repeatable read") and CS ("cursor stability"); however, there are *three* possible values for the ISOLATION parameter, namely RR, CS, and USER. USER means that the access module itself will choose RR or CS isolation level dynamically; for simplicity, we ignore this last possibility here (for details of this case, see the IBM manuals).

- Cursor stability means that if a transaction using the access module:

  (a) obtains addressability to some particular record by setting a cursor to point to it, and thus

  (b) acquires a lock on that record, and then

  (c) relinquishes its addressability to the record without updating it, and so

  (d) does not promote its existing lock to X level, then

  (e) that existing lock can be released without having to wait for the next synchpoint.

- Repeatable read means that record-level S locks are held until the next synchpoint, like X locks. Repeatable read is the default.

Isolation level CS may provide slightly more concurrency than isolation level RR, but from a theoretical standpoint, at least, it is generally not a good idea (that is why RR is the default). The problem with CS is that a transaction operating at that level may have a record changed "behind its back," as in Fig. 14.4, and so produce a wrong answer. In fact, if a transaction operates under isolation level CS, then it is *always* theoretically possible to define a second transaction that can run interleaved with the first in such a way as to produce an overall incorrect result. By contrast, a transaction that operates under isolation level RR can behave completely as if it were executing in a single-user system.*

---

*On the other hand, RR can lead to unacceptable overhead in some situations (especially as it applies to the entire access module, not to individual tables). In such cases it might be better to specify CS for the access module and then use explicit LOCK operations to achieve the effect of RR for specific tables (or DBspaces).

The explanations of Section 14.5 ("How SQL/DS Solves the Three Concurrency Problems") require some slight modification if isolation level CS is in effect, as follows:

- If a transaction obtains addressability to a record under CS, and if there is a possibility that the transaction may update that record (e.g., if the cursor was defined to be FOR UPDATE), then SQL/DS gives the transaction an update lock (U lock) instead of an S lock.

- U locks are compatible with S locks but not with other U locks (and of course not with X locks); that is, if transaction *A* holds a U lock on record *R,* then a request from transaction *B* for a U (or X) lock on *R* will cause *B* to go into a wait state. If transaction *A* now updates *R,* its U lock will be promoted to X level; otherwise the *U* lock will be released (like an S lock) when *A* relinquishes addressability to *R.*

The advantage of U locks (intuitively speaking) is that they may reduce the number of deadlocks. See Exercises 14.4 and 14.5 at the end of the chapter.

Note finally that although it is (normally) specified as a preprocessor parameter rather than as part of the program, the programmer does need to be aware of the isolation level, because the logic of the program may depend on it (i.e., it may affect the way the program has to be coded).

The LOCK Parameter

Our explanations of SQL/DS's locking mechanism in Section 14.5 were in terms of record (or row) locks. However, those explanations were purely *logical* in nature. Physically, SQL/DS can lock data in terms of *rows, pages,* or *DBspaces.* That is, when a given transaction logically locks some individual record, SQL/DS may physically lock just that record, or it may lock the page that contains that record, or it may lock the entire DBspace that contains that record. Which it does in any given situation depends on the LOCK parameter specified for the DBspace in question when that DBspace was ACQUIREd (or last ALTERed). For a given DBspace, the LOCK parameter can be specified as ROW, PAGE, or DBSPACE:*

- DBSPACE means that all locks acquired on data in the DBspace will be at the DBspace level. The advantage of DBspace locking (as explained under "The LOCK Statement" above) is that fewer locks are needed; the disadvantage is that there may be less concurrency also.

---

*We are tacitly assuming a public DBspace here. Locking for private DBspaces is always at the DBspace level. Furthermore, a request for a lock on a private DBspace never causes a wait; instead, if the lock is unavailable, a negative SQLCODE is returned. See Chapter 16 for more discussion of public and private DBspaces.

Our discussions in Section 14.5 tacitly assumed that DBspace locking was *not* in effect.

- PAGE (which is the default) means that locks acquired on data in the DBspace will be at the page level, whenever possible. Sometimes, however, SQL/DS may acquire page-level locks initially (for some given DBspace), but then trade all those locks in for a single DBspace-level lock, if the number of page-level locks reaches some installation-specified threshold (a process known as *lock escalation*).

- ROW means that locks will be acquired at the individual record level (except that again escalation may occur).

14.7 DEADLOCK

We have seen how locking can be used to solve the three basic problems of concurrency. Unfortunately, however, we have also seen that locking introduces problems of its own, principally the problem of deadlock. Section 14.5 gave two examples of deadlock. Fig. 14.10 shows a slightly more generalized version of the problem. *Note:* The LOCK operations shown in that figure are intended to represent any operations that acquire locks, not necessarily the explicit SQL LOCK statement specifically.

Deadlock is a situation in which two or more transactions are in a simultaneous wait state, each one waiting for one of the others to release a lock before it can proceed. Fig. 14.10 shows a deadlock involving two transactions, but deadlocks involving three, four, . . . transactions are also

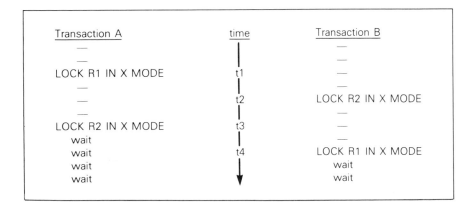

Fig. 14.10 An example of deadlock

possible, at least in theory. In practice however, deadlocks almost never involve more than two transactions.

If a deadlock occurs, SQL/DS will detect and break it immediately (i.e., during the processing of the SQL statement that caused it). Breaking a deadlock involves choosing one of the deadlocked transactions (actually the youngest) as the *victim* and rolling it back, thereby releasing its locks and allowing some other transaction to proceed. In general, therefore, *any operation that requests a lock*—which means *any executable SQL operation*—may be rejected with a negative SQLCODE indicating that the transaction has just been selected as the victim in a deadlock situation and has been rolled back. The problem of deadlock is thus a significant one so far as the application programmer is concerned, because application programs may need to include explicit code to deal with it if it arises. For example:

```
EXEC SQL ... ;
IF SQLCODE = value indicating "deadlock victim"
THEN DO ;
        reinitialize variables from initial input data ;
        GO TO beginning of program ;
     END ;
```

Here we are assuming that the program has saved its initial input data somewhere (not in the database!—why not?) in preparation for just such an eventuality.

14.8 SUMMARY

In this rather lengthy chapter we have discussed the question of transaction management, both in general terms and as it is addressed in SQL/DS specifically. A transaction is a logical unit of work—also a unit of recovery and (as can be seen from the last few sections) a unit of concurrency. Transaction management is the task of supervising the execution of transactions in such a way that each transaction can be considered as an all-or-nothing proposition, even given the possibility of arbitrary failures on the part of either individual transactions or the system itself, and given also the fact that multiple independent transactions may be executing concurrently and accessing the same data. In fact, the overall function of the system might well be defined as *the reliable execution of transactions.*

In SQL/DS specifically, transactions are delimited by *synchpoints,* which are established by program initiation, COMMIT WORK (successful termination), and ROLLBACK WORK (unsuccessful termination). SQL/DS guarantees the atomicity of transactions, as explained in Sections 14.2 and 14.3.

Concurrency control in SQL/DS is based on locking. Basically, every record a transaction accesses is locked; if the transaction goes on to update the record, then that lock will be promoted to exclusive level. Exclusive locks are held until the next synchpoint. This simple protocol solves the three basic problems of concurrency, but also introduces the possibility of deadlock; hence application programs must be prepared to deal with that eventuality. Deadlock is signaled by a negative SQLCODE value that may potentially be returned after any SQL operation that requests a lock.

EXERCISES

14.1 The following list represents the sequence of events in an interleaved execution of a set of transactions *T1, T2, . . ., T12,* all operating under isolation level RR. *A, B, . . ., H* are intended to be records, not cursors.

```
time t0 ..........
time t1 (T1)   :  FETCH  A
time t2 (T2)   :  FETCH  B
    -  (T1)    :  FETCH  C
    -  (T4)    :  FETCH  D
    -  (T5)    :  FETCH  A
    -  (T2)    :  FETCH  E
    -  (T2)    :  UPDATE  E
    -  (T3)    :  FETCH  F
    -  (T2)    :  FETCH  F
    -  (T5)    :  UPDATE  A
    -  (T1)    :  COMMIT
    -  (T6)    :  FETCH  A
    -  (T5)    :  ROLLBACK
    -  (T6)    :  FETCH  C
    -  (T6)    :  UPDATE  C
    -  (T7)    :  FETCH  G
    -  (T8)    :  FETCH  H
    -  (T9)    :  FETCH  G
    -  (T9)    :  UPDATE  G
    -  (T8)    :  FETCH  E
    -  (T7)    :  COMMIT
    -  (T9)    :  FETCH  H
    -  (T3)    :  FETCH  G
    -  (T10)   :  FETCH  A
    -  (T9)    :  UPDATE  H
    -  (T6)    :  COMMIT
    -  (T11)   :  FETCH  C
    -  (T12)   :  FETCH  D
    -  (T12)   :  FETCH  C
    -  (T2)    :  UPDATE  F
    -  (T11)   :  UPDATE  C
    -  (T12)   :  FETCH  A
    -  (T10)   :  UPDATE  A
    -  (T12)   :  UPDATE  D
    -  (T4)    :  FETCH  G
time tn ..........
```

What is the situation at time *tn*? Have any deadlocks occurred?

14.2 Consider the concurrency problems illustrated in Figs. 14.1–14.4 once again. What would happen in each case if all transactions were executing under isolation level CS instead of RR?

14.3 (Modified version of Exercise 13.4) Write a program to read and print all part records in part number order, deleting every tenth one as you go, and beginning a new transaction after every tenth record.

14.4 Draw a compatibility matrix showing the interactions among lock types X, U, and S.

14.5 The following list represents the sequence of events in an interleaved execution of a set of SQL/DS transactions *T1, T2, . . . , T12*, all operating under isolation level CS. As in Exercise 14.1, *A, B, . . . H* are records, not cursors. All FETCHes are intended to be "FOR UPDATE."

```
time t0 ..........
time t1 (T1)  :  FETCH A
time t2 (T2)  :  FETCH B
  -    (T1)  :  FETCH C
  -    (T4)  :  FETCH D
  -    (T5)  :  FETCH A
  -    (T2)  :  FETCH E
  -    (T2)  :  UPDATE E
  -    (T3)  :  FETCH F
  -    (T2)  :  FETCH F
  -    (T1)  :  COMMIT
  -    (T5)  :  UPDATE A
  -    (T6)  :  FETCH A
  -    (T5)  :  ROLLBACK
  -    (T6)  :  FETCH C
  -    (T6)  :  UPDATE C
  -    (T7)  :  FETCH G
  -    (T8)  :  FETCH H
  -    (T9)  :  FETCH G
  -    (T8)  :  FETCH E
  -    (T7)  :  COMMIT
  -    (T9)  :  UPDATE G
  -    (T9)  :  FETCH H
  -    (T3)  :  FETCH G
  -    (T10) :  FETCH A
  -    (T6)  :  COMMIT
  -    (T11) :  FETCH C
  -    (T12) :  FETCH D
  -    (T2)  :  UPDATE B
  -    (T10) :  UPDATE A
  -    (T4)  :  FETCH G
time tn ..........
```

What is the situation at time *tn*? Have any deadlocks occurred?

ANSWERS TO SELECTED EXERCISES

14.1 One deadlock has occurred, involving transactions *T2, T3, T9,* and *T8;* it was caused by *T2*'s request to UPDATE F, and was resolved by rolling back *T9*. The situation at time *tn* can be represented by means of a graph, the *Wait-For Graph* (see Fig. 14.11), in which the nodes represent transactions and a directed edge from note *Ti* to node *Tj* indicates that *Ti* is waiting for *Tj*. Edges are labeled with the name of the record and level of lock they are waiting for. Note that *T1, T6,* and *T7* have all completed successfully, *T5* and *T9* have completed unsuccessfully, and *T2,*

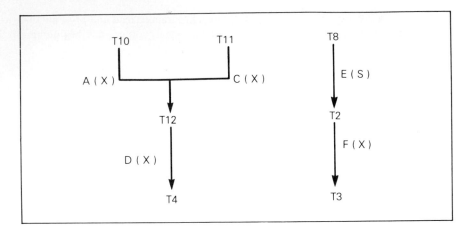

Fig. 14.11 The Wait-For Graph for Exercise 14.1

T3, T4, T8, T10, T11, and *T12* are still executing (though *T2, T8, T10,* and *T11* are all in the wait state).

14.2 Effects of isolation level CS:

- The lost update problem (Fig. 14.1): Same as RR.
- The uncommitted dependency problem (Figs. 14.2, 14.3): Same as RR.
- The inconsistent analysis problem (Fig. 14.4): Isolation level CS does not solve this problem; *A* must execute under RR in order to retain its locks until the next synchpoint, for otherwise it will still produce the wrong answer. (Alternatively, of course, *A* could use LOCK TABLE to lock the entire accounts table. This solution would work under both CS and RR isolation levels.)

14.3 This exercise is typical of a wide class of applications, and the following represents the typical approach to implementing such applications:

```
EXEC SQL DECLARE CP CURSOR FOR
         SELECT P#, PNAME, COLOR, WEIGHT, CITY
         FROM   P
         WHERE  P# > previous_P#
         ORDER  BY P# ;

previous_P# = 'bbbbbb' ;
eof = false ;
DO WHILE (eof = false) ;
   EXEC SQL OPEN CP ;
   DO count = 1 TO 10 ;
      EXEC SQL FETCH CP INTO :P#, ... ;
      IF SQLCODE = +100 THEN
         DO ;
            EXEC SQL CLOSE CP ;
            EXEC SQL COMMIT WORK ;
            eof = true ;
         END ;
```

```
      ELSE print P#, ... ;
   END ;
   EXEC SQL DELETE FROM P WHERE P# = :P# ;
   EXEC SQL CLOSE CP ;
   EXEC SQL COMMIT WORK ;
   previous_P# = P# ;
 END ;
```

Observe that we lose position within the parts table at the end of each transaction (even if we did not close cursor CP explicitly, the COMMIT WORK would close it automatically anyway). The foregoing code will therefore not be particularly efficient, because each new transaction requires a search on the parts table in order to reestablish position. The inefficiency is unavoidable, however. Matters may be improved somewhat if there happens to be an index on field P.P# (as in fact there will be, since P.P# is the primary key for table P) and the optimizer chooses that index as the access path for the table.

14.4 See Fig. 14.12.

14.5 One deadlock has occurred, involving transactions *T2, T3, T9,* and *T8*; it was caused by *T3*'s request to FETCH G, and was resolved by rolling back *T9*. Transactions *T1, T6,* and *T7* have all completed successfully, *T5* and *T9* have completed unsuccessfully, and *T2, T3, T4, T8, T10, T11,* and *T12* are still executing (though *T2, T4, T8,* and *T12* are all in the wait state). See Fig. 14.13 (overleaf).

	X	U	S	—
X	N	N	N	Y
U	N	N	Y	Y
S	N	Y	Y	Y
—	Y	Y	Y	Y

Fig. 14.12 Lock type compatibility matrix (X, U, S)

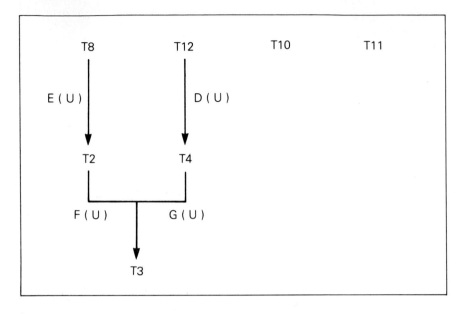

Fig. 14.13 The Wait-For Graph for Exercise 14.5.

15

♦

Application Programming III: Dynamic SQL

15.1 INTRODUCTION

"Dynamic SQL" consists of a set of embedded SQL facilities that are provided specifically to allow the construction of generalized, online (and possibly interactive) applications—where by "online application" we mean any program that is intended to support access to the database from an end-user at an online terminal. (The statements of dynamic SQL cannot themselves be entered interactively—they are available only in the embedded environment.) The topic of this chapter is therefore somewhat specialized; basically, the only people who need to know the material are people directly concerned with the writing of generalized applications. Other readers may wish to ignore the chapter altogether, at least on a first reading.

Consider what a typical online application has to do. In outline, the steps it must go through are as follows.

1. Accept a command from the terminal.

2. Analyze that command.

3. Issue appropriate SQL statements to the database.

4. Return a message and/or results to the terminal.

If the set of commands the program can accept is fairly small, as in the case of (perhaps) a program handling airline reservations, then the set of possible SQL statements to be issued may also be small and can be "hardwired" into the program. In this case, Steps 2 and 3 above will consist simply of logic to examine the input command and then branch to the part of the program that issues the predefined SQL statement(s). If, on the other hand, there can be great variability in the input—in other words, if the application is reasonably generalized—then it may not be practicable to predefine and "hardwire" SQL statements for every possible command. Instead, it will probably be necessary to construct the required SQL statements dynamically, and then prepare and execute those constructed statements dynamically. The facilities of dynamic SQL are provided to assist in this process.

Incidentally, the process just described is exactly what happens when SQL statements themselves are entered interactively—for example, through ISQL. ISQL itself is a generalized online application; it is ready to accept an extremely wide variety of input, namely any valid (or invalid!) SQL statement. It uses the facilities of dynamic SQL to construct suitable SQL statements corresponding to its input, to "prep" (compile) and execute those constructed statements, and to return messages and results back to the terminal.

If the statement to be dynamically bound and executed is a SELECT statement, special considerations apply. (As in ordinary embedded SQL, retrieval is more complicated and involves more work on the part of the user.) Section 15.2 therefore considers the other statements first, then Section 15.3 addresses the problem of SELECT statements specifically. Section 15.4 briefly describes an advanced feature known as extended dynamic SQL.

15.2 HANDLING STATEMENTS OTHER THAN SELECT

The two principal statements of dynamic SQL are PREPARE and EXECUTE. Their use is illustrated by the following (accurate but unrealistically simple) PL/I example.

```
     DCL SQLSOURCE CHAR(256) VARYING ;

     SQLSOURCE = 'DELETE FROM SP WHERE QTY < 100' ;
EXEC SQL PREPARE SQLOBJ FROM :SQLSOURCE ;
EXEC SQL EXECUTE SQLOBJ ;
```

Explanation:

1. The name SQLSOURCE identifies a PL/I varying length character string variable in which the program will construct the source form (i.e., character string representation) of some SQL statement—a DELETE statement, in our particular example.

2. The name SQLOBJ, by contrast, identifies a *SQL* variable, not a PL/I variable, that will be used (conceptually) to hold the object form—i.e., compiled representation—of the SQL statement whose source form is given in SQLSOURCE. (The names SQLSOURCE and SQLOBJ are arbitrary, of course.) The name SQLOBJ is said to be a *statement name.*

3. The assignment statement "SQLSOURCE = ... ;" assigns to SQLSOURCE the source form of a SQL DELETE statement. (As suggested in Section 15.1, the process of constructing such a source statement is likely to be somewhat more complicated in practice, involving the input and analysis of some command from the terminal.)

4. The PREPARE statement then takes that source statement and "preps" (compiles) it to produce an executable version, which it stores in SQLOBJ.

5. Finally, the EXECUTE statement executes that SQLOBJ version and thus (in the example) causes the actual DELETE to occur. Feedback information from the DELETE will be returned in the SQLCA as usual.

Note, incidentally, that since it denotes a SQL variable, not a PL/I variable, the statement name SQLOBJ does *not* have a colon prefix in the PREPARE and EXECUTE statements.

PREPARE

The syntax of the PREPARE statement is as follows.

```
EXEC SQL PREPARE statement FROM string ;
```

Here "string" is an expression of the host language (PL/I, in our example) that yields the character string representation of a SQL statement, and "statement" is the name of a SQL variable that will be used to contain the "prepped" version of that SQL statement. The statement to be PREPAREd must be one of the following (only):

```
UPDATE       (including CURRENT form)
DELETE       (including CURRENT form)
INSERT
SELECT       (excluding INTO form)

ACQUIRE      (excluding CREATE PROGRAM)
CREATE       (excluding DROP STATEMENT)
DROP
ALTER
COMMENT
LABEL

GRANT
REVOKE

LOCK
UPDATE STATISTICS
EXPLAIN
```

In other words, the following statements cannot be PREPAREd: BEGIN and END DECLARE SECTION, CLOSE, COMMIT WORK, CONNECT, CREATE PROGRAM, DECLARE CURSOR, DESCRIBE, DROP STATEMENT, EXECUTE, FETCH, INCLUDE, OPEN, PREPARE, PUT, ROLLBACK WORK, SELECT (INTO FORM) and WHENEVER. Also, the source form of a statement to be PREPAREd must not include either EXEC SQL or a statement terminator. Nor can it include any host variable references.

EXECUTE

The syntax of the EXECUTE statement is as follows.

```
EXEC SQL EXECUTE statement [ USING argument(s) ] ;
```

The PREPAREd SQL statement in the SQL variable identified by "statement" is executed. The USING clause is explained in the subsection "Arguments and Parameters" immediately following.

Arguments and Parameters

As already indicated, SQL statements that are to be PREPAREd cannot include any references to host variables. However, they can include *parameters,* denoted in the source form of the statement by question marks. Basically, parameters can appear wherever host variables can appear (with certain exceptions—details beyond the scope of this book). For example:

```
SQLSOURCE = 'DELETE
              FROM    SP
              WHERE   QTY  >  ?
              AND     QTY  <  ?' ;

EXEC SQL PREPARE SQLOBJ FROM :SQLSOURCE ;
```

Arguments to replace the parameters are specified when the statement is EXECUTEd, via the USING clause. For example:

```
EXEC SQL EXECUTE SQLOBJ USING :LOW, :HIGH ;
```

In the example, the statement actually executed is equivalent to the ordinary embedded SQL statement

```
EXEC SQL DELETE FROM SP WHERE QTY > :LOW AND QTY < :HIGH ;
```

In general, the USING clause in the EXECUTE statement takes the form

```
USING argument [, argument ] ...
```

where each "argument" in turn takes the form

```
: host-variable [ [ INDICATOR ] : host-variable ]
```

just like a target reference in an INTO clause. (The optional second host variable is a null indicator variable.) The ith argument in the list of arguments corresponds to the ith parameter (i.e., ith question mark) in the source form of the PREPAREd statement.

15.3 HANDLING SELECT STATEMENTS

As indicated earlier, the procedure outlined in Section 15.2 is adequate for the dynamic preparation and execution of all SQL operations (all SQL operations that may legally be PREPAREd, that is), except SELECT. The reason that SELECT is different is that it returns data to the program; all the other statements return feedback information (in the SQLCA) only.

A program using SELECT needs to know something about the data values to be retrieved, since it has to specify a set of target variables to receive those values. In other words, it needs to know at least how many values there will be in each result row, and also what the data types and lengths of those values will be. If the SELECT is generated dynamically, it will usually not be possible for the program to know this information in advance; therefore, it must obtain the information dynamically, using another dynamic SQL statement called DESCRIBE. In outline, the procedure such a program must go through is as follows.

1. It builds and prepares the SELECT statement *without* an INTO clause.
2. It uses DESCRIBE to interrogate the system about the results it can expect when the SELECT is executed. The description of those results is returned in an area called the SQL Descriptor Area (SQLDA).

3. Next, it allocates storage for a set of target variables to receive those results in accordance with what it has just learned from DESCRIBE, and places the addresses of those target variables back into the SQLDA.

4. Finally, it retrieves the result rows one at a time by means of a cursor, using the cursor statements OPEN, FETCH, and CLOSE. It can also use UPDATE CURRENT and DELETE CURRENT statements on those rows, if appropriate (however, those statements will probably have to be PREPAREd and EXECUTEd versions).

In order to make these ideas a little more concrete, we present a simple example to show what such a program might look like (in outline). The example is written in PL/I. Note that it *must* be written in a language like PL/I that provides explicit support for dynamic storage allocation. COBOL, for example, does not provide any such support; hence a generalized online application that is to perform data retrieval cannot be written in COBOL. (An online application that is to use only the facilities described in Section 15.2 can be written in COBOL if desired, however.)

```
            DCL SQLSOURCE CHAR(256) VARYING ;
EXEC SQL DECLARE X CURSOR FOR SQLOBJ ;

EXEC SQL INCLUDE SQLDA ;
/* Let the maximum number of expected values to be      */
/* retrieved be N.                                      */
            SQLSIZE = N ;
            ALLOCATE SQLDA ;

            SQLSOURCE = 'SELECT * FROM SP WHERE QTY > 100' ;
EXEC SQL PREPARE SQLOBJ FROM :SQLSOURCE ;

EXEC SQL DESCRIBE SQLOBJ INTO SQLDA ;

/* Now SQLDA contains the following information (among  */
/* other things):                                       */
/*  - actual number of values to be retrieved in SQLN   */
/*  - name (or label), data type, and length of ith     */
/*                          value in SQLVAR(i)           */

/* Using the information returned by DESCRIBE, the       */
/* program can now allocate a storage area for each      */
/* value to be retrieved, and place the address of the   */
/* ith such area in SQLVAR(i). Then:                     */

EXEC SQL OPEN X ;
            DO WHILE ( more-records-to-come ) ;
                EXEC SQL FETCH X
                    USING DESCRIPTOR SQLDA ;
                .....
            END ;
EXEC SQL CLOSE X ;
```

Explanation:

1. SQLSOURCE and SQLOBJ are basically as in Section 15.2; SQLSOURCE will contain the source form of a SQL statement (a SELECT

statement, of course, in this example), and SQLOBJ will contain the corresponding object form. X is a cursor for that SELECT; note that it is declared by a new form of the DECLARE CURSOR statement, as follows.

```
EXEC SQL DECLARE cursor CURSOR FOR statement ;
```

2. The declaration of the SQL Descriptor Area is brought into the program by the statement

```
EXEC SQL INCLUDE SQLDA ;
```

This statement generates a declaration for a PL/I BASED structure called SQLDA, also a declaration for a numeric variable called SQLSIZE. The program must set SQLSIZE to the value N, where N is an upper bound on the number of values to be retrieved per row by the SELECT statement, then allocate storage for SQLDA (the amount of storage allocated will be a function of the value of SQLSIZE).

3. Next, the desired SELECT statement is constructed in source form in SQLSOURCE, and is then PREPAREd to yield the corresponding object form in SQLOBJ. Then the program issues a DESCRIBE against SQLOBJ to obtain a description of the values expected per row from the SELECT. That description consists of two parts:

(a) The actual number of values to be retrieved (in a field of SQLDA called SQLN);

(b) The name or label,* the data type, and the length for each of those values (in an array of entries within SQLDA called SQLVAR).

Using this description, the program can now allocate storage for each of the values described. It then places the addresses of the storage areas it allocates back into the SQLDA—actually into the SQLVAR array.

4. Finally, the program uses OPEN, FETCH, and CLOSE statements on cursor X to retrieve the actual data. Note, however, that a new form of the FETCH statement is used; instead of an INTO clause, it has a USING DESCRIPTOR clause, and the structure named in that clause (usually SQLDA) in turn identifies the target variables for the values to be retrieved.

It is also possible to prepare a SELECT statement that includes parameters (identified by question marks). For example:

```
SQLSOURCE = 'SELECT  *
             FROM    SP
             WHERE   QTY > ?
             AND     QTY < ?' ;

EXEC SQL PREPARE SQLOBJ FROM :SQLSOURCE ;
```

---

*See the discussion of the LABEL statement in Chapter 9.

Arguments are specified in the corresponding OPEN statement. For example:

```
EXEC SQL OPEN X USING :LOW, :HIGH ;
```

(EXECUTE does not apply to SELECT. The function of EXECUTE is performed by OPEN when the statement to be executed is a SELECT.)

15.4 EXTENDED DYNAMIC SQL

The dynamic SQL facilities described in the previous two sections suffer from two major drawbacks, as follows:

1. All dynamically prepared statements are automatically dropped (destroyed) at the next synchpoint.

2. Such items as statement names and cursor names must be hard-coded into the program—they cannot be specified by means of host language (program) variables.

As a consequence, dynamic SQL as described so far in this chapter is not entirely satisfactory as a basis for constructing truly sophisticated generalized applications. An example of such an application would be a user-provided preprocessor that allows SQL statements to be embedded in a language not directly supported by SQL/DS, such as Pascal. Another example would be a compiler for a still higher-level interface built on top of the existing SQL interface. The IBM-provided preprocessors for PL/I, COBOL, etc., themselves constitute a third example.

The facilities described in the present section, by contrast, do allow statements to be dynamically prepared and then kept for as long as desired (actually until they are dropped explicitly). They also allow statement names, cursor names, etc., to be specified by means of host variables. They therefore provide the function missing from regular dynamic SQL. However, as the reader will surely appreciate, very few applications (and those typically rather complex ones) actually need to make use of such facilities in practice. Our discussion in this section is therefore very brief; our intent is merely to give some indication as to the range of facilities provided, without getting into too much detail.

The facilities together are referred to as *extended* dynamic SQL. They can be used only in Assembler Language programs. The facilities consist of two new statements (CREATE PROGRAM and DROP STATEMENT) and extended versions of the PREPARE, EXECUTE, DESCRIBE, DECLARE CURSOR, and OPEN/FETCH/PUT/CLOSE statements. The functions of these statements are as follows (in outline).

- CREATE PROGRAM

  Creates an empty access module (*not* a program!) and stores it in the database. The access module name can be specified (and typically would be specified) by means of a program variable.

- PREPARE (extended)

  Prepares a statement and adds it to an existing access module. The name of the access module can be specified by means of a program variable. SQL/DS returns a name for the prepared statement in another program variable.

- EXECUTE (extended)

  Executes a specified statement in a specified access module. Both the statement name and the access module name can be specified via program variables.

- DESCRIBE (extended)

  Describes (the result of) a specified SELECT statement in a specified access module. Both the statement name and the access module name can be specified via program variables.

- DECLARE CURSOR (extended)

  Declares a cursor for a specified SELECT or INSERT statement in a specified access module. The names of the cursor, statement, and access module can all be specified via program variables.

- OPEN/FETCH/PUT/CLOSE (extended)

  These statements are basically the same as the corresponding statements in regular dynamic SQL, except that the cursor name can be specified via a program variable in each case.

- DROP STATEMENT

  Drops a specified statement from a specified access module. The access module name can be specified via a program variable; the statement name *must* be so specified.

15.5 CONCLUSION

This brings us to the end of our discussion of the facilities of dynamic SQL, and indeed to the end of our three chapters on SQL application programming. Of those three chapters:

- Chapter 13 describes all major principles of the embedded SQL approach. The material of that chapter is thus relevant to all SQL programming, and should be of interest to anyone who is concerned in any way with application programming in SQL/DS.

- Chapter 14 is also concerned with principles that are relevant to all users—to be specific, it discusses the concepts of transaction management (concurrency and recovery), and it shows how those concepts are exposed in (the SQL/DS dialect of) the SQL language. However, the nature of SQL is such that users need to worry explicitly about such matters only very rarely; most of the time, SQL/DS's implicit mechanisms are entirely adequate.

- The present chapter, by contrast, has been concerned with a very specialized topic, namely that of how to write a generalized online application in SQL. Such an application requires the facilities of dynamic SQL—principally the PREPARE and EXECUTE statements, and (if it is a SELECT statement that is to be PREPAREd) also the DESCRIBE statement. *Note:* The other portions of the language are sometimes referred to as *static* SQL, to distinguish them from the dynamic facilities that we have been discussing in this chapter.

  It should be pointed out that it is of course possible to use the facilities of dynamic SQL whenever greater variability is required than is provided by the conventional static statements. In other words, it is not quite true to say that generalized online applications are the sole justification for dynamic SQL, though that statement is really not very wide of the mark. For example, the following statement:

```
EXEC SQL SELECT * FROM :TNV ;
```

(where TNV is not the name of a table but the name of a host variable whose *value* is the name of a table) is not a valid SELECT statement in conventional static SQL, but dynamic SQL can be used to achieve the desired effect.

To conclude the entire set of three chapters, we offer the following comment. The fact that SQL/DS uses essentially the same language (SQL) for both interactive and programmed access to the database has one very significant consequence: It means that the database portions of an application program can be tested and debugged interactively. Using the interactive interface, it is very easy for a programmer to create some test tables, load data into them, execute (interactive versions of) the programmed SQL statements against them, query the tables and/or the catalog to see the effect of those statements, and so on. In other words, the interactive interface provides a very convenient *programmer debugging facility*. Of course, it is attractive for other reasons too; for example, the data definition process is normally carried out through this interface, and so too is the process of granting and revoking authorization. Also, of course, the interface provides a rudimentary but serviceable ad hoc query facility.

16

♦

Storage Structure

16.1 INTRODUCTION

As explained in Chapter 5, data definition statements in SQL/DS can conveniently be divided into two classes, namely logical and physical—the logical statements having to do with objects that are genuinely of interest to users, such as base tables and views, and the physical statements having to do with objects that are more of interest to the database administrator (and of course the system itself). In this chapter we take a brief look at the latter class of objects. The data definition statements corresponding to those objects are a little complicated, however, involving (as they necessarily must) a great deal of low-level detail. In fact, most of those statements are not considered part of the SQL language at all, since they would not normally be used by the ordinary SQL user. For such reasons, we will not describe the statements in detail here; we content ourselves rather with a brief description of the objects themselves.

Fig. 16.1 is a schematic representation of the major storage objects and their interrelationships. The figure is meant to be interpreted as follows.

- SQL/DS can support multiple databases (but one SQL/DS system can access only one database at any given time).

- Any given database is divided up into a number of disjoint *DBspaces*— several user DBspaces and several system DBspaces, in general. Two system DBspaces are shown in the figure, one containing the catalog and the other access modules.

- A DBspace is a dynamically extendable collection of *pages*, where a page is a block of physical storage (it is the unit of I/O, i.e., the unit transferred between primary and secondary storage in a single I/O operation). All pages in SQL/DS are 4K (4096) bytes in size.

- Each user DBspace contains a set of stored tables, together with zero

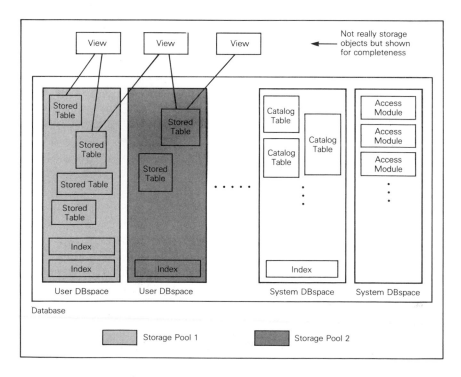

Fig. 16.1 The major storage objects of SQL/DS

or more indexes on those tables. (A stored table is the physical representation of a base table.) A given stored table and all of its associated
indexes must be wholly contained within a single DBspace.

■ As explained in Chapter 10, views are not stored objects at all. They
are included in the figure just to illustrate the point that a given view
can span multiple DBspaces—that is, it can include data from multiple
stored tables, and those stored tables do not necessarily all have to be
from the same DBspace.

■ Each DBspace has an associated *storage pool.* A storage pool is a collection of direct access files or data sets ("DBextents"). When a given
DBspace needs to be extended, SQL/DS acquires storage from the appropriate storage pool. As the figure indicates, different DBspaces can
have different storage pools. Note, therefore, that storage pools are in
a sense the most "physical" of all the various storage objects in SQL/
DS; databases, DBspaces, and even stored tables, are all still somewhat
"logical."

We now proceed to amplify the foregoing ideas.

16.2 DBSPACES

A DBspace can be thought of as a *logical address space* on secondary storage ("logical" because it is typically not just a set of physically adjacent
areas). Each DBspace holds a set of stored tables, together with their indexes (alternatively, it might hold a set of access modules; we ignore this
latter possibility in what follows). As the amount of data in those tables
and indexes grows, so storage will be acquired from the appropriate storage
pool and added to the DBspace to accommodate that growth. The theoretical maximum size of a DBspace is 32 billion bytes; however, the total database size cannot exceed 64 billion bytes,* and one DBspace cannot hold
more than 255 tables and indexes.

As just indicated, it is possible for a single DBspace to contain multiple
tables. The major advantage—not the only one—of storing multiple tables
in the same DBspace is the following: Stored records from different tables
can be clustered together in such a way as to improve access times to logically related records. For example, if tables S and SP were stored in the
same DBspace, then it would be possible (by loading the data in an appropriately interleaved manner) to store all the shipment records for supplier
S1 close to (i.e., on the same page as) the supplier record for S1, all the

*As a matter of interest, 64 billion bytes (in 4K pages) is approximately equivalent
to 128 volumes (i.e., 32 units) of IBM 3380D direct access storage.

shipment records for supplier S2 close to the supplier record for S2, and so on. Queries such as "Get details of supplier S1 and all corresponding shipments"—in particular, certain join queries—can then be handled efficiently, since the number of I/O operations will be reduced.

Note, however, that such cross-table clustering will not be maintained (in general) in the face of arbitrary updates; moreover, the optimizer has no understanding of such clustering. Also, sequential access to the data may well be slowed down, inasmuch as the system will now have to scan not only records of the table concerned, but also records of other tables that happen to be mixed in with the first table.

Acquiring DBspaces

Just as tables (and other objects) cannot be used until they have been created, so DBspaces cannot be used until they have been "acquired." Thus ACQUIRE can be thought of as the analog of CREATE for DBspaces (except that, unlike tables, DBspaces are limited to an installation-predefined upper limit on the number that can exist at the same time within the same database*). The syntax for ACQUIRE DBSPACE is:

```
ACQUIRE type DBSPACE NAMED dbspace [ other parameters ]
```

Here "type" is either PUBLIC or PRIVATE, "dbspace" is the name to be given to the newly acquired DBspace, and the optional "other parameters" have to do with such matters as the number of pages to be assigned to the DBspace, the storage pool from which the DBspace is to obtain its storage, the locking level for the DBspace (see Section 14.6), and so forth. (If any of the "other parameters" are omitted, SQL/DS automatically chooses a suitable default, of course.) Note that DBspaces do not actually occupy any space in the database (in effect, they do not really exist) until they are acquired. Even then, they only occupy as much space as they actually need at any given time—empty pages are never physically stored.

The basic difference between public and private DBspaces is as follows: Public DBspaces are intended for data that is to be used simultaneously by multiple concurrent users; private DBspaces are intended for data that is to be used only by one user at a time. Locking for a private DBspace is always at the level of the entire DBspace. Furthermore, a request for a lock on a private DBspace never causes a wait; if the lock is not available, a negative SQLCODE is returned to the user. DBA authority is required to acquire a public DBspace and RESOURCE authority is required to acquire a private DBspace. Also, the DBA can acquire a private DBspace on some other us-

---

*The DBA can subsequently increase this number if necessary, however.

er's behalf. A private DBspace is said to be owned by the user who acquired it (or by the user on whose behalf the DBA acquired it); public DBspaces can be regarded as being owned by the DBA.

Any given DBspace (public or private) is either *recoverable* or *nonrecoverable,* depending on whether the associated storage pool is recoverable or nonrecoverable (see Section 16.5). No logging is performed for a nonrecoverable DBspace.* Nonrecoverable DBspaces are thus more efficient in normal operation; however, they suffer from the obvious disadvantage that any undoing of updates after (e.g.) a system crash must be performed by the user in some manual fashion. Nonrecoverable DBspaces are intended for data that is primarily read-only (reference tables and the like), or for private or temporary data for which the benefits of full recoverability are not worth the usual system overhead. But recoverable DBspaces are probably the normal case.

Once the DBspace has been acquired, tables (and indexes) can be stored in it. The complete CREATE TABLE statement includes a parameter ("IN dbspace") that specifies the DBspace into which the new table is to go. However, it is always possible to omit that parameter (indeed, we have done exactly that in all examples in this book so far), in which case SQL/DS will choose a (recoverable) DBspace owned by the user issuing the CREATE TABLE and will place the table in that. It is an error if no such DBspace exists. As for indexes, CREATE INDEX always places the new index in the DBspace that contains the indexed table.

Certain properties of an acquired DBspace can be ALTERed via the ALTER DBSPACE statement (details beyond the scope of this text). An acquired DBspace remains available for use until it is the subject of an explicit DROP DBSPACE statement. Only the owner can ALTER or DROP a DBspace.

16.3 STORED TABLES

A stored table is the stored representation of a base table. It consists of a set of stored records, one for each data row in the base table in question. Each stored record will be wholly contained within a single page;† however,

---

*On the other hand, shadow paging *is* performed. Thus, individual transaction recovery can still be handled—i.e., updates can still be undone if an individual transaction failure occurs. However, system recovery (and media recovery—see Chapter 17) cannot be handled.

†Unless the record includes any long string fields, which have a special storage representation of their own. For details of this case, see the IBM manuals.

one stored table can be spread over multiple pages, and one page can contain stored records from multiple stored tables.

A stored record is *not* identical to the corresponding record of the base table. Instead, it consists simply of a byte string, made up as follows:

- A prefix, containing control information such as the internal system identifier for the stored table of which this stored record is a part; followed by

- Up to N stored fields, where N is the number of columns in the base table. There may be fewer than N stored fields if the stored record is varying length (i.e., if it includes any varying length fields) and one or more fields at the right-hand end are null. Nulls at the right-hand end of a varying length record are (usually) not physically stored.

Each stored field, in turn, consists of:

- A length prefix (if the field is varying length), giving the length of the actual data, including the null indicator prefix if there is one (see below);

- A null indicator prefix (if nulls are allowed), indicating whether the value in the data part of the field is to be (a) taken as a genuine data value or (b) ignored (i.e., interpreted as null);

- An encoded form of the actual data value. Stored data is encoded in such a manner that the System/370 "compare logical" instruction (CLC) will always yield the appropriate response when applied to two values of the same SQL data type. For example, INTEGER values are stored with their sign bit reversed. Thus all stored data fields are considered simply as byte strings by the DBSS; any interpretation of such a string as, e.g., an INTEGER value is performed above the DBSS interface. The advantage of such a scheme is that new data types can be introduced without any impact on the low-level components of the system. (As an exercise, the reader may like to try working out suitable encodings for the other SQL data types.)

All stored fields are byte-aligned. There are no gaps between fields. Varying length data occupies only as many bytes as are needed to store the actual value.

Internally, records are addressed by "record ID" or RID.* For exam-

---

*SQL/DS actually uses the term "tuple ID" (TID). As mentioned in Section 1.2, "tuple" is a formal relational term corresponding approximately to the notion of a record. We prefer RID to TID for consistency with DB2.

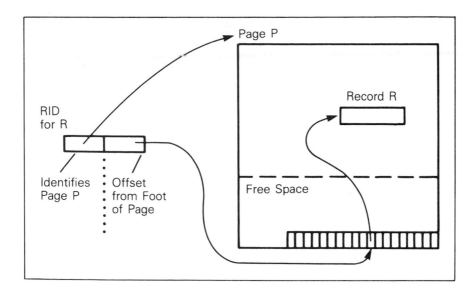

Fig. 16.2 Implementation of RIDs

ple, all pointers within indexes are RIDs. RIDs are unique within their containing DBspace. Fig. 16.2 shows how RIDs are implemented. The RID for a stored record *R* consists of two parts, namely the page number of the page *P* containing *R,* and a byte offset from the bottom of *P* identifying a slot that contains, in turn, the byte offset of *R* from the top of *P.* This scheme represents a good compromise between the speed of direct addressing and the flexibility of indirect addressing: Records can be rearranged within their containing page—e.g., to close up the gap when a record is deleted or to make room when a record is inserted—without having to change RIDs (only the local offsets at the foot of the page have to change); yet access to a record given the RID is fast, involving only a single page access.

Note: In rare cases it might involve two page accesses (but never more than two). This can happen if a varying length record is updated in such a way that it is now longer than it was before (i.e., the value in some varying length field has expanded), and there is not enough free space on the page to accommodate the increase. In such a situation, the updated record is placed on another ("overflow") page, and the original record is replaced by a pointer (another RID) to the new location. If the same thing happens again, so that the updated record has to be moved to still a third page, then the pointer in the original page is changed to point to this newest location.

16.4 INDEXES

Indexes in SQL/DS are based on a structure known as the *B-tree*. A B-tree is a multilevel, tree-structured index with the property that the tree is always balanced; that is, all leaf entries in the structure are equidistant from the root of the tree, and this property is maintained as new entries are inserted into the tree and existing entries are deleted. As a result, the index provides uniform and predictable performance for retrieval operations. Details of how this effect is achieved are beyond the scope of this book; however, Fig. 16.3 shows a simple example of what such an index might look like.

As you can see, the index consists of a root page, zero or more intermediate pages (at zero or more intermediate levels—there is one such intermediate level in the example), and a set of leaf pages. The leaf level contains an entry for each distinct value of the indexed field, giving the indexed field value and pointers (RIDs) to all records that contain that value for the indexed field; the leaf pages are chained together, so that they can be used for fast *sequential* access to the indexed data (in index sequence). Each level above the leaf level, in turn, contains an entry (highest field value plus pointer) for every page of entries in the level below; thus the root page and intermediate pages together provide fast *direct* access to the leaf pages, and hence fast direct access to the indexed data also.

A given stored table can have any number of associated indexes, and thus any number of logical orderings imposed on it. (It always has exactly one physical ordering, of course.) To perform an exhaustive search on a table according to a given index, the DBSS will access all records in the table in the sequence defined by that index; and since that sequence may be quite different from the table's physical sequence, a given data page may be accessed many times. (On the other hand, data pages not containing any records of the table will not be accessed at all.)

It follows that exhaustive search via an index could potentially be much slower than exhaustive search via physical sequence—*unless* the index concerned is a *clustering index:*

- In fact, if a table has any indexes at all, then exactly one—namely the first one created (usually the primary key index)—will be the clustering index for that table. A clustering index is an index that is used to control physical placement of the indexed records, such that the physical se-

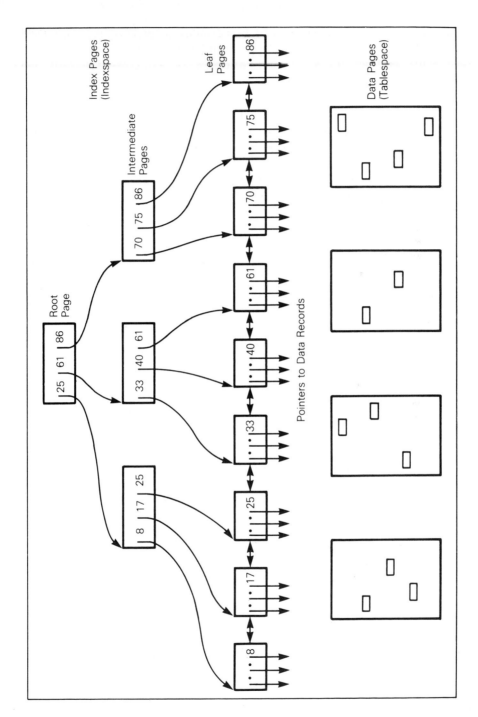

Fig. 16.3 Example of an index

283

quence of records in storage *is* the same as, or close to, the logical sequence of records as defined by the index. (Note that "clustering" here refers to clustering within a single table, not cross-table clustering as described in Section 16.2.)

- If table *T* has a clustering index *X,* then records should be initially loaded into *T* (via the DBS utility) in the order defined by *X;* they will be stored in the DBspace in order of arrival from left to right—i.e., in increasing address sequence—with periodic gaps to allow for future insertions. (Gap frequency is determined by a parameter on ACQUIRE DBSPACE.) Subsequent insertions to *T* will be stored in a gap if space exists and the record can be physically stored close to its logical position, otherwise at the right-hand end.

Clustering indexes are extremely important for optimization purposes: The optimizer will always try to choose an access path that is based on a clustering index, if one is available. As a practical matter, every table should have a clustering index unless it is extremely small, and maybe even then. Of course, if the installation follows our recommendation that every table have a primary key, then every table will have at least one index, and hence a fortiori every table will have a clustering index.

16.5 STORAGE POOLS

A storage pool is a collection of files or data sets ("DBextents"). Each DBspace has an associated storage pool (specified in ACQUIRE DBSPACE). When storage is needed for the DBspace, it is taken from the corresponding storage pool. Storage pools thus provide a means for the installation to control data separation and data affinity—for example, they can force two tables to be stored on different disk volumes—while at the same time they allow most of the details of physically allocating storage to be handled automatically by the system. Each storage pool is either *recoverable* or *nonrecoverable* (and DBspaces drawn from the pool are recoverable or nonrecoverable accordingly); see Section 16.2 for further discussion.

The DBextents in each storage pool consist of operating system files or data sets (many data sets per pool, in general). SQL/DS uses the facilities of the operating system for such things as direct access space management, data set cataloging, and physical transfer of pages into and out of main memory. However, space management within pages is handled by SQL/DS, not by the operating system, and the operating system's indexing mechanism is not used at all. Thus, as mentioned in Chapter 11, SQL/DS's

DBextents are not really conventional files at all; their internal format is not what the operating system expects, and it is not possible to access those files using conventional record-level I/O facilities (GETs and PUTs). For the same reason, it is not possible to use the facilities of SQL/DS (e.g., the SQL language) to access previously existing files.

♦

SQL/DS Tools

17.1 INTRODUCTION

The base SQL/DS product comes complete with the Interactive SQL facility (ISQL) and a set of utilities, the most important of which is the Data Base Services utility (DBS utility). These tools are critical to the day-to-day operation of the system. In this chapter we present a brief overview of the facilities offered by these tools. ISQL is discussed in Section 17.2, the DBS utility in Section 17.3, and other miscellaneous utility functions in Section 17.4.

17.2 ISQL

ISQL is the primary interactive interface to SQL/DS. It runs under CICS in VSE and under CMS in VM. It supports the following functions:

1. Interactive entry and execution of SQL statements,* including simple (line-at-a-time) text editing for such statements, control of the display screen, and simple formatting and report-writing

2. Interactive data entry

3. Creation and execution of stored SQL statements and routines

4. System monitoring

5. Administration and use of the DOS DL/I Extract facility

It also provides a set of "generic" commands (i.e., commands that are applicable to several different functions):

-   HELP, which provides access to an extensive set of online documentation

-   CANCEL, which permits a command (or transaction) in progress to be (abnormally) terminated

-   SET, which allows the user to set various session parameters, including AUTOCOMMIT (ON or OFF—see note below), ISOLATION (RR or CS—see Chapter 14), and numerous display parameters (e.g., the character to be used to represent null in display output—by default a question mark)

-   LIST, which displays the current settings of the parameters controlled by SET

Note: AUTOCOMMIT ON (default) means that each SQL statement entered is considered to be a separate transaction (ISQL is responsible for issuing the necessary COMMIT or ROLLBACK WORK in this case). AUTOCOMMIT OFF means that the user can enter a series of multiple SQL statements and no updates will be committed until an explicit COMMIT WORK is entered.

Interactive SQL Execution

Normally, each SQL statement is executed as soon as it is entered. However, ISQL provides a HOLD command, which allows a statement to be entered and held in the "command buffer" without being executed immediately. The CHANGE command allows simple text replacement to be performed on the contents of the command buffer. A held statement can subsequently be executed by means of the START command. Furthermore, the held

---

*The ISQL manual uses the term "SQL *commands.*" We stay with "SQL statements" for reasons of consistency.

statement can include "placeholders" (parameters), which will be replaced by arguments when the statement is STARTed. For example:
Held statement:

```
SELECT  *  -
FROM    S  -
WHERE   CITY = '&1'  -
AND     STATUS > &2
```

(Remember that each SQL statement line except the last requires a continuation character—by default a hyphen—in ISQL.)
Corresponding START command:

```
START ( London 15 )
```

The query as executed will retrieve records for suppliers in London with status greater than 15.

ISQL provides a set of scrolling and similar commands to control the display output from an executed SQL query: BACKWARD, FORWARD, LEFT, RIGHT, COLUMN, and TAB (most of which have the obvious meaning), also END (which indicates that the current output is finished with). It also provides FORMAT and PRINT commands, which support the production of simple reports from the output of a SQL query.

Data Entry

Data can be entered into a SQL/DS database via the usual SQL INSERT statement, of course. However, ISQL provides an alternative method that may be more convenient if multiple rows are to be entered, namely the INPUT command. "INPUT table" causes ISQL to display the field names for "table," together with their data types, in left-to-right order. Now the user can enter the data, one row at a time, by typing just the data values in that same left-to-right order (plus "enter" at the end of each row).

The SAVE command can be used to commit the data entered so far; SAVE commits all rows entered since INPUT (or since the last SAVE). Conversely, the BACKOUT command can be used to cancel all rows entered since INPUT (or since the last SAVE). The END command forces a SAVE and terminates the overall entry process. (*Note:* We are assuming here that AUTOCOMMIT is ON. SAVE and BACKOUT have no effect if AUTO-COMMIT is OFF.)

Stored Statements and Routines

The statement in the ISQL command buffer can be STOREd under a specified name, and subsequently RECALLed to the buffer and executed via START. Stored statements remain in existence until explicitly ERASEd. The

LIST command can be used to list stored statements; also, the RENAME command can be used to change their names.

Stored *routines* are an extension of the same idea. A stored routine consists of a set of SQL statements and/or ISQL commands, stored in a regular SQL/DS table with the special name ROUTINE. A simple example of such a table (containing just one routine, called CSQ) is shown in Fig. 17.1. *Note:* Each user can have his or her own ROUTINE table. The table should have a UNIQUE index on the field combination (NAME, SEQNO).

Entries are made in the table via the normal SQL (or ISQL) facilities— e.g., via the ISQL INPUT command. Likewise, the table is maintained via the normal SQL update operations. Routines can be shared among users via the normal SQL GRANT facilities (i.e., by granting the SELECT privilege on ROUTINE). Routines are executed by means of the ISQL RUN command—syntax:

```
RUN [ user . ] routine [ ( parameter [ parameter ] ... ) ]
```

For example:

```
RUN CJDATE.CSQ ( London 15 )
```

Of course, you do not need to specify "user" if you are running a routine of your own.

Two final points on routines:

1. A SELECT statement within a routine does not display its output at the terminal unless and until a DISPLAY command is executed. The purpose of this arrangement is to allow the DISPLAY to be preceded by a series of FORMAT commands to control the result layout, before that result is actually displayed to the user.

2. If a routine exists with the name PROFILE, that routine will be executed automatically when the user signs on to ISQL. Such a routine can be used to customize the session, e.g., by establishing appropriate values for the SET parameters (ISOLATION, AUTOCOMMIT, etc.), before the user starts normal ISQL operation.

```
ROUTINE  NAME   SEQNO  COMMAND                                    REMARKS
         ----   -----  ------------------------------------       --------
         CSQ       10  SELECT  S#, SNAME, STATUS, CITY  -
         CSQ       20  FROM    S                         -
         CSQ       30  WHERE   CITY = '&1'               -        note
         CSQ       40  AND     STATUS > &2                        params
         CSQ       50  DISPLAY
         CSQ       60  END
```

Fig. 17.1 Example of a routine table

System Monitoring

As mentioned in Chapter 2, certain ISQL commands permit the user to monitor system activity. See Chapter 2 for details.

DL/I Extract

The DL/I Extract facility of ISQL (VSE only) allows data to be copied from a DOS DL/I database into a SQL/DS database, where it may subsequently be accessed via normal SQL/DS facilities (in particular, via SQL statements). DL/I Extract provides an entire set of commands of its own (at least 20 of them). The details are beyond the scope of this book.

17.3 DATA BASE SERVICES UTILITY

The Data Base Services utility (DBS utility) is a general-purpose application that provides database support facilities for SQL/DS developers and administrators. It is primarily intended for transferring large volumes of data into and out of SQL/DS; in particular, it provides a set of data loading, unloading, and reloading facilities (and hence data reorganization facilities). It runs under ICCF and batch in VSE and under CMS (including CMS batch) in VM. *Note:* Many DBS facilities would most appropriately be performed in single-user mode (see Chapter 3).

DBS functions are requested by means of appropriate DBS commands, which are submitted in the form of a card image input file. The following commands are supported.

- DATALOAD: Loads data from a specified sequential file into one or more specified SQL/DS tables. The sequential file may consist of DATAUNLOAD command output (see below) or it may have been created by some other means. The tables need not be initially empty (DATALOAD thus provides a "data add" function as well as its usual "data load" function). Selective loading is also supported; i.e., it is possible to select just specified records and/or fields from the input file for loading into the specified table(s).

- DATAUNLOAD: Selectively unloads data from a specified table into a specified sequential file (in a user-defined format). The data to be unloaded is defined by means of a user-specified SQL SELECT statement. DATAUNLOAD can be used to export data from one SQL/DS database in a form suitable for subsequent import (via DATALOAD) to another.

- UNLOAD: Unloads the entire contents of a specified table (or DBspace) into a sequential file (in a system-defined format). The main purpose of UNLOAD is to produce input for a subsequent RELOAD operation (see below).

- RELOAD: Loads data into a specified table (or DBspace) from a sequential file created by the UNLOAD command. Optionally, RELOAD will create the necessary table(s) or delete existing data before performing the loading function. Together, UNLOAD and RELOAD constitute SQL/DS's data reorganization facility.

The DBS utility also supports the batch execution of SQL statements (all SQL statements are supported, with the exception of embedded-only statements such as cursor OPEN and CLOSE). Such statements are simply included in the utility command input file. This facility could provide a convenient means of performing data definition operations, for example; the file of definitional statements could be prepared offline and then submitted for execution as a batch job.

Finally, the DBS utility also provides a SET command (analogous to the SET command in ISQL), which allows the user to set various parameters that affect the DBS session. Many of the parameters in question are the same as those supported by ISQL, including AUTOCOMMIT and ISOLATION (see Section 17.2 for an explanation of these two). In addition, if a DATALOAD or RELOAD operation is to be performed during the DBS session, then the user can specify (via an additional parameter, "UPDATE STATISTICS") whether an appropriate UPDATE STATISTICS statement is to be executed following that DATALOAD or RELOAD. The UPDATE STATISTICS statement is described in the next section.

17.4   MISCELLANEOUS UTILITY FUNCTIONS

In this section, we briefly consider a few miscellaneous utility-type functions. The functions in question are the UPDATE STATISTICS, EXPLAIN, media recovery, and program preparation functions. *Note:* UPDATE STATISTICS and EXPLAIN are both officially regarded in SQL/DS as statements of the SQL language; in each case, however, the function performed is really more in the nature of a utility, which is why we include them in this section.

UPDATE STATISTICS

UPDATE STATISTICS computes certain statistics for a specified table or DBspace and writes them to the SQL/DS catalog, where they can be used by the system optimizer in its task of choosing access strategies. The syntax of UPDATE STATISTICS is:

```
UPDATE [ ALL ] STATISTICS FOR type object
```

Here "type" is TABLE (meaning *base* table) or DBSPACE, and "object" is the name of an object of the appropriate type. ALL means that statistics are to be computed for all columns of the table (or for all columns of all tables in the DBspace); omitting ALL means that statistics are to be computed for indexed columns only. (Even if ALL is specified, however, the statistics for nonindexed columns will only be estimates, not actual measured values.) For details of the specific statistics computed, the reader is referred to the IBM manuals.

Statistics should normally be updated whenever a table has been loaded, an index has been created, a table or DBspace has been reorganized, or generally whenever there has been a significant amount of update activity on some table. Performance-sensitive applications should then be "re-prepped" by, e.g., reissuing SQLPREP for them (see the subsection on "Program Preparation" below).

EXPLAIN

EXPLAIN gives the user information regarding the optimizer's choice of access strategy for a specified SQL statement. Such information can be useful for tuning existing applications, also for determining how projected applications will perform. The syntax of EXPLAIN (somewhat simplified) is as follows:

```
EXPLAIN type FOR statement
```

Here "type" is COST, PLAN, REFERENCE, STRUCTURE, or ALL (meaning the combination of all four previous possibilities), and "statement" is the SQL statement (SELECT, INSERT, UPDATE, or DELETE—in practice, usually SELECT) to be EXPLAINed. The various "types" have the following meanings:

- COST: Gives the estimated cost (a weighted sum of I/O cost and CPU cost) of executing the specified statement.
- PLAN: Gives information regarding indexes used, details of any sorts that will be needed, and (if the specified statement involves any joins) the order in which tables will be joined and the methods by which the individual joins will be performed.
- REFERENCE: Gives information as to how each column referenced in

the specified statement will be used (e.g., as a joining column) and, if the column is referenced in a search condition, an estimate of the number of rows that will satisfy that search condition.

- STRUCTURE: Gives an estimate of the number of rows returned for each (sub)query in the specified statement.

The output from EXPLAIN is placed into the appropriate one (or all four) of the following database tables: *xyz*.COST_TABLE, *xyz*.PLAN_TABLE, *xyz*.REFERENCE_TABLE, and *xyz*.STRUCTURE_ TABLE (*xyz* here is the authorization ID of the user issuing the EXPLAIN). The table(s) in question must already exist. Here is an example:

```
EXPLAIN PLAN FOR
       SELECT S.S#, P.P#
       FROM   S, P
       WHERE  S.CITY = P.CITY
```

When this EXPLAIN is executed, SQL/DS will place information regarding its implementation of the specified SELECT statement into the PLAN_TABLE of the user issuing the EXPLAIN. The user can then interrogate that table by means of ordinary SELECT statements in order to discover, for example, whether a particular index is being used or whether creating a new index might obviate the need for a sort.

A couple of further points:

- The EXPLAIN statement includes a "query number" option by which the user can give a unique numeric identifier to each statement being EXPLAINed. The query number is needed to distinguish between the results of distinct EXPLAINs.

- The EXPLAIN result does *not* include the source form of the statement being EXPLAINed. Instead, users are recommended to save that source form (together with the appropriate query number) in a table of their own, for purposes of subsequent reference.

For more details of EXPLAIN, see the IBM manuals.

Media Recovery

A *media failure* is a failure (such as a disk head crash) in which some portion of the database is physically destroyed. *Media recovery* is the process of recovering the database after such a failure has occurred. Media recovery involves restoring the database from a backup or archive copy, and then using log information—both current and archive log information, in general—to redo transactions completed since that database archive was created.

SQL/DS thus supports two kinds of archiving, database archiving and log archiving. A database archive is a copy of the database as of some particular time; similarly, a log archive is a copy of the log as of some particular time. *Note:* Creating either kind of archive has the effect of freeing space in the current log, because there is no longer any need to retain current log information regarding transactions that completed prior to the archive point.

In general, the installation can use either (a) database archiving only or (b) both database and log archiving. The differences are as follows:

(a) *Database archiving only:* On restart after a media failure, SQL/DS will restore the database from the latest database archive and then apply database changes from the current system log.

(b) *Database and log archiving:* On restart after a media failure, SQL/DS will restore the database from the latest database archive, apply database changes from subsequent log archives, and then apply database changes from the current system log. (Actually, it will archive the current log first and then apply the changes—see the discussion of log archiving below.)

The first option gives faster recovery times, but at the cost of having to archive the database more frequently. The second option gives slower recovery times, but has the advantage that if it is necessary to free space in the system log, then it is sufficient to archive the log only, not the database.

Having briefly outlined the archiving alternatives, we now describe the facilities available for creating archives. First, the database. The database can be archived:

1. Using the SQLEND ARCHIVE command, which shuts SQL/DS down and creates an archive as part of the shutdown process. This is the usual method.

2. Using the ARCHIVE command, which allows the operator to archive the database during normal SQL/DS operation.

3. Automatically by SQL/DS when it detects that the log is about to become full and database-only archiving is in effect.

4. Using offline operating system utilities such as the VSE VSAM backup facility or the VM VMBACKUP Management System. The system must be shut down using a SQLEND UARCHIVE command, and the archive then created. If a media failure occurs subsequently, the database can be restored from this archive offline; then SQL/DS can be requested on restart to apply log changes to the restored version.

The log can be archived:

1. Using the SQLEND LARCHIVE command, which shuts SQL/DS down and creates a log archive as part of the shutdown process. This is the usual method.

2. Using the LARCHIVE command, which allows the operator to archive the log during normal SQL/DS operation.

3. Automatically by SQL/DS when it detects that the log is about to become full and log archiving is in effect.

4. Automatically before archiving the database (SQLEND ARCHIVE, SQLEND UARCHIVE, or ARCHIVE command) if log archiving is in effect.

5. Automatically before restoring the database from a database archive if log archiving is in effect.

Program Preparation

As explained in Chapter 2, programs (more accurately, source modules) written in Assembler Language, COBOL, FORTRAN, or PL/I must be preprocessed ("prepped") before they can be compiled and link-edited. The prep process converts SQL statements embedded in the source module into an *access module* and stores that access module in the SQL/DS database; it also produces a modified form of the source module, in which the original SQL statements have been replaced by CALLs to SQL/DS (the SQL statements are also retained in the form of comments, however). That modified source module can now be compiled and link-edited in the usual way. Note, incidentally, that a single source program will consist of multiple source modules (in general) and will therefore typically generate multiple access modules.

The prep process can be performed in either single- or multiple-user mode. It is invoked via the SQLPREP EXEC in VM or via appropriate job control statements in VSE. The following parameters (among others) can be specified:

- The specific preprocessor to be invoked (ASM, COBOL, FORTRAN, or PLI)

- The name of the access module to be created

- The isolation level for the access module (RR, CS, or USER—see Chapter 14)

- Date and time string formats (see Appendix C)

- The database(s) against which the access module is to be prepped (see below for further discussion of the multiple database case)

A source module using database switching (refer back to Chapter 3 for a brief discussion of this possibility) must be prepped against every database it intends to use. The most convenient method of performing such a "multi-database prep" is to provide a list of all required databases to the SQLPREP EXEC (note that database switching is available only under VM, not under VSE; each database must be connected to its own SQL/DS system on its own virtual machine). The virtual machine on which the EXEC is invoked will establish communication with all other required virtual machines, and an appropriate access module will be created on each one.

Finally, the DBS utility (see Section 17.3) provides a facility by which an access module created on one SQL/DS system can be unloaded to an operating system file and subsequently reloaded (and reoptimized) from that file on a different SQL/DS system. This facility could be useful, for example, in moving an application from test status on a test machine to production status on a production machine.

◆

THE IBM
RELATIONAL
PRODUCTIVITY
FAMILY

18

◆

Related Products:
An Overview

18.1 INTRODUCTION

Up to this point in this book we have concentrated (for the most part) purely on the base SQL/DS product itself. Like most DBMSs, however, SQL/DS is accompanied by numerous auxiliary products—application development tools, database administration tools, end-user tools of various kinds, and so on. Such products are available both from IBM and from independent third-party vendors. In this part of the book we examine this area in some detail. The present chapter provides a general overview of the subject; Chapters 19–24 then go on to discuss certain specific products in depth. *Note:* All products mentioned run under both VSE and VM unless explicitly indicated otherwise.

It is obviously not possible in a book of this size to cover every product from every vendor in detail. We therefore limit detailed discussion to IBM's own products specifically (although we do at least mention some of the best-known competing products in passing, where appropriate). The IBM products are collectively known as *the IBM Relational Productivity Family*. At the heart of this family are four relational DBMSs:

- IBM DATABASE 2 (DB2) for the MVS environment
- Structured Query Language/Data System (SQL/DS) for the VM and VSE environments
- SQL/400 for the AS/400 environment
- Operating System/2 (OS/2) Extended Edition Database Manager for the OS/2 environment

DB2 is designed for both operational processing and end-user computing against large—possibly very large—centralized databases; SQL/DS and SQL/400 are intended for lower-volume operational processing and end-user computing against smaller, perhaps departmental, databases. The OS/2 Database Manager is intended (among other things) for end-user processing of private copies of data extracted from shared (e.g., SQL/DS) databases.

In addition to the base DBMSs, a variety of auxiliary products are available for each of the environments. Those auxiliary products can be broadly divided into the following categories:

- end-user tools
- application development tools
- copy management tools
- administration tools

The next four sections of this chapter (Sections 18.2–18.5) discuss each of these categories in turn and survey some of the available products in each category. Section 18.6 then offers a few comments on IBM's Systems Application Architecture (SAA) and future directions in this area.

One final preliminary remark before we delve into technical details: For obvious reasons, it is not really possible to include any Exercises or Answers sections in this part of the book. However, if the reader has access to any of the products described, then we strongly recommend at least trying out some of the examples discussed in the text. There is no substitute for genuine hands-on experience.

18.2 END-USER TOOLS

The simplicity and ease of use of relational systems such as SQL/DS make them particularly suitable for end-user computing: Users can get to the data directly and can develop simple applications on their own, instead of having to rely on the DP department to perform such functions for them. In other words, users are much more self-sufficient in a system like SQL/DS, and the load on the DP department is accordingly much reduced. Of course, this fact is one of the reasons why relational systems provide much more productivity than nonrelational systems.

The functions that end-users need to be able to perform (and hence the end-user tools that are needed to support those functions) can be classified as follows:

1. *Query:* The ability to retrieve (and update) data in the database and produce reports and graphs accordingly

2. *Decision support:* The ability to perform statistical analysis and business planning based on data in the database

3. *Application development:* The ability to build simple customized applications for operating on the database

IBM provides two major products to support these requirements, namely Query Management Facility (QMF) and Application System (AS):

▪ Query Management Facility (QMF)

   QMF is a query tool for both SQL/DS and DB2. It allows end-users to enter queries in either SQL or QBE ("Query-by-Example") and to produce a variety of reports and graphs from the results of those queries. In addition, it provides an application support interface that allows application programs to use QMF facilities also. QMF is discussed in Chapter 19. *Note:* The VM version of QMF provides the same functions for SQL/DS as the MVS version does for DB2. The VSE version is a different product and provides only a subset of the VM product functions.

▪ Application System (AS)

   AS provides facilities in all three of the areas mentioned above (query, decision support, application development), but IBM tends to emphasize its use for decision support. Like QMF, AS operates with both SQL/DS (VM only) and DB2; it also supports VSAM and sequential files. Queries can be entered in either SQL (for SQL/DS and DB2 only) or AS's own language. As with QMF, query results can be formatted into reports and graphs; the AS capabilities are more powerful than those of QMF but perhaps less user-friendly. AS decision support and business functions include project management, statistical analysis, financial planning, and text processing facilities. AS is discussed in Chapter 20.

Other IBM products in this area include Info Center/1, which provides similar capabilities to AS; The Information System (TIF), which is an end-user application development system; and Data Base Edit Facility (DBEDIT), which supports the development of simple data entry, retrieval, and maintenance applications. Each of these products supports both SQL/DS (VM only) and DB2. Major third-party products supporting SQL/DS include VMSQL/EDIT and VMSQL/REPORT from VM Software Inc. (VM only), FOCUS from Information Builders Inc., NOMAD2 from MUST Software International, and RAMIS from On-Line Software. These products compete primarily with AS. Other independent products include SAS, a statistics package from the SAS Institute, and Intellect, a natural language interface for both SQL/DS (VM only) and DB2 from Artificial Intelligence Corporation.

18.3   APPLICATION DEVELOPMENT TOOLS

As indicated in the previous section, end-user tools like AS and QMF can make significant contributions to productivity, because in many cases they can obviate the need to create application programs (in the traditional sense of that term) entirely. In most installations, however, there will still be some applications that are too complex to be dealt with by such tools and must therefore be handled by the DP department. Such applications can be created by means of either (a) a conventional programming language such as COBOL or PL/I, or (b) a suitable *application development tool.* The second of these alternatives, if feasible, is by far the preferred approach, for productivity reasons once again.

Aside: Before we go any further, a couple of editorial comments are necessary:

- First, by "application development tools" in this section we mean, primarily, tools that are intended for use by DP professionals rather than by end-users. Tools such as AS, by contrast, can be regarded as application development tools for the end-user.

- Second, application development tools are sometimes referred to as "fourth generation tools"—machine code, assembler language, and high-level languages representing the first three generations—and the interface to such tools is accordingly sometimes called a "fourth generation language" (4GL). However, we choose not to adopt the 4GL terminology in this book, since it does not seem to have any very precise definition.

IBM's principal application development tool is the Cross System Product (CSP). CSP is a complete application development system for MVS (TSO, CICS), VM, VSE, and PC applications. It provides a fully integrated environment for screen development, application coding, application testing and debugging, etc. CSP applications can process data stored in SQL/DS, DB2, and IMS databases, also in VSAM files. One advantage of CSP is that an application can be developed in one environment for execution in another; for example, an application could be developed and tested on SQL/DS under VM and then run on DB2 under MVS. CSP is discussed in Chapter 21.

We close this section with a brief note on one more IBM application development tool, the IBM Expert System Environment (ESE). ESE is an expert system shell that supports the development of expert system (knowledge-based) applications. It provides a SQL interface that allows such applications to access data stored in SQL/DS (VM only) and DB2.

18.4 COPY MANAGEMENT TOOLS

End-users often need to perform some kind of analysis or other processing on data stored in an operational database on a central machine or in a shared end-user database on a departmental machine. Sometimes this processing cannot be done directly on the machine or database where the data is stored, either because the system in question does not have the right tools or because the nature of the required processing is such that it would interfere unduly with overall system performance (e.g., it requires the data to be "frozen" at some specific point in time). The solution in such a situation is to perform a "data extract"—i.e., make a copy of the required data and transfer it to a system (possibly a PC) where the processing can be supported. Copy management is the process of managing such data extracts.

IBM has three products supporting copy management:

- Data Extract (DXT)

    DXT allows data to be extracted from both relational and nonrelational databases and files into SQL/DS and DB2.* It has two separate features, the *Relational Data Extract Feature* for extracting data from SQL/DS or DB2, and the *General Data Extract Feature* for extracting data from other sources (MVS only). DXT is covered in more detail in Chapter 22.

- Host Data Base View (HDBV)

    HDBV runs on an IBM PC that is connected via some communications link to a "host" machine running VM or MVS. It allows data to be

---

*In IBM jargon the verb "extract" can take an indirect object of the form "into target," thus: "Extract (some data) *into* (some target)."

copied to the PC from host files and databases. The host data required
is specified by the PC user by means of SQL, prompt panels, or stored
queries and procedures. The data is then retrieved via QMF, AS, Info
Center/1, or TIF, and copied down to the PC, where it can be accessed
via any of several familiar PC products, such as Lotus 1–2–3 or dBase
III. HDBV is discussed in Chapter 23. *Note:* Here and throughout this
part of the book we take the term "PC" to include both the original
IBM PC (or compatible machine) and the newer IBM Personal
System/2 (PS/2), unless explicitly stated otherwise.

- Enhanced Connectivity Facilities (ECF)

  Like HDBV, ECF permits VM and MVS host data to be copied to a
  PC. ECF consists of a Requester program on the PC and a Server program on the host; the two communicate using a set of protocols known
  as the Server-Requester Programming Interface (SRPI). The Requester
  passes SQL statements generated by the PC user to the host Server,
  which uses those statements to extract data from SQL/DS (VM only)
  or DB2. Predefined DXT extract requests can also be executed through
  ECF. The user can also invoke host commands and programs from
  the PC and can use host disks, files, and printers as though they were
  connected to the PC. ECF is also discussed in Chapter 23.

We conclude our brief discussion of copy management with a mention
of IXF (Integration Exchange Format). IXF is an IBM standard self-
defining file format. It is used as a basis for transferring data between programs, either user application programs or IBM program products or both.
IXF files can be created by QMF, AS, DXT, and ECF, and can be read by
QMF, AS, and ECF.

18.5 ADMINISTRATION TOOLS

The major SQL/DS administration tool supplied by IBM is the Data Base
Relational Application Directory (DBRAD). DBRAD supports a set of
database tables for defining application objects, user tables, programs, etc.,
together with the relationships between them. These tables form an
application-oriented extension to the SQL/DS (or DB2) catalog tables.
DBRAD includes a reporting mechanism that uses these two sets of tables
to produce (e.g.) where-used reports and impact reports about the effect of
changing an object. Import facilities exist to import application information from application program copy libraries, the catalog tables, and CSP
libraries (see Chapter 21). A model generator component can use the information stored in the DBRAD directory or the SQL/DS catalog to generate
application program data definitions and SQL data definition and manipulation statements.

18.6   THE IBM SYSTEMS APPLICATION ARCHITECTURE

As mentioned in the Preface to this book, IBM regards SQL/DS as a key member of its "Systems Application Architecture" (SAA) product set. SAA is intended to provide consistency across IBM's very diverse range of hardware and software offerings. It defines a set of common software interfaces, conventions, and protocols to be used by IBM's future program product offerings in the System/370 (TSO, CICS/MVS, IMS/DC, and VM/CMS), Application System/400 (OS/400), and PC (OS/2) environments. In this section we sketch the facilities of SAA very briefly, in order to provide some indication as to IBM's direction with regard to database management specifically.

SAA consists of four major components:

- *Common User Access* (interactive use of screens)
- *Common Programming Interface* (programming languages and services)
- *Common Communications Support* (communication protocols and services)
- *Common Applications* (application packages)

From a database standpoint, the most important piece of SAA is the Common Programming Interface. The Common Programming Interface, in turn, divides into components in two areas, namely languages and services. At the time of writing, the SAA languages are:

- C, COBOL, FORTRAN, RPG, PL/I
- A procedure language based on the REXX language
- Application generation statements based on CSP

The services components are:

- Database Interface (SQL)
- Dialog Interface based on the IBM PC EZ-VU product
- Presentation Interface similar to that in the IBM Graphical Data Display Manager product (GDDM)
- Query Interface based on (extensions to) QMF

Note in particular that SQL is defined as the common database interface (and of course SQL/DS is the provider of that interface for VM/CMS). IBM's overall database direction is thus clearly towards providing SQL-based relational DBMSs with QMF- and CSP-like tools in all SAA environments.

Query Management Facility

19.1 INTRODUCTION

As explained in Chapter 18, Query Management Facility (QMF) is an ad hoc query and report writing tool supporting end-user processing of data stored in either SQL/DS (under VM/CMS) or DB2 (under MVS/TSO). We focus in this book on the use of QMF with SQL/DS, but most of the material is equally applicable to its use with DB2. *Note:* A separate version of QMF for use with SQL/DS under VSE is also available, but that product supports only a subset of the functions discussed in this chapter.

A report in QMF is the displayed (or printed) output from a QMF query. QMF queries can be formulated in either of two languages, SQL or *QBE* ("Query-By-Example"). QBE is another relational language, comparable in some ways to SQL but more user-friendly in certain respects. However, it is clear that, so far as QMF is concerned at any rate, IBM regards

SQL as more important than QBE; we therefore do not discuss QBE in detail in this chapter, but instead defer such a discussion to an appendix (Appendix G). *Note:* The QBE language was previously supported by IBM as the interface to an "Installed User Program" (also called QBE) that ran on VM. However, QMF has nothing to do with that earlier product per se.

QMF reports are formatted in accordance with a set of report specifications called a *form*. When a given query is executed, the user has the option of specifying the corresponding form explicitly or of letting QMF create an appropriate *default* form. After viewing the report at the terminal, the user can revise the form and display the query output again in accordance with the revised version (without having to go back to the database to repeat the query). This cycle can be repeated as many times as necessary, until the user is satisfied. Thus a typical QMF session might go as follows (refer to Fig. 19.1):

1. The user constructs the query (any single SQL or QBE statement) in a QMF work area called QUERY.

2. The user issues RUN QUERY to execute the query in QUERY. The result is stored in another work area, called DATA (if it is too large to be kept entirely in main memory, it will be kept partly in an external "spill file").

3. QMF creates a default form for the result and displays the report accordingly. The form is kept in yet another work area, called FORM.

4. After inspecting the report, the user issues DISPLAY FORM to display the form in FORM, and proceeds to edit that form.

5. The user then issues DISPLAY REPORT to produce a revised report corresponding to the revised form. Note that it is not necessary to run the query again; the result has been kept in DATA, and DISPLAY REPORT uses the current FORM to format and display the current DATA.

6. Alternatively, the user can use DISPLAY CHART to display a chart or graph instead of a report (using the Interactive Chart Utility, ICU), or PRINT REPORT to obtain a hard copy.

7. Steps 4–6 are repeated as often as necessary.

Sections 19.2, 19.3, and 19.4 contain detailed discussions of query creation and execution, report formatting, and chart creation, respectively.

RUN QUERY, DISPLAY FORM, DISPLAY REPORT, DISPLAY CHART, etc., are examples of QMF *commands*. QMF allows a sequence of commands to be stored as a named *procedure*. QMF procedures permit the generation of "canned" production reports on a regular basis, possibly

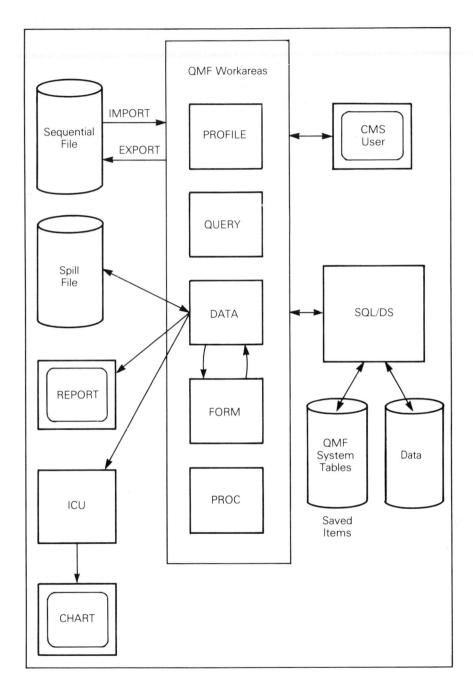

Fig. 19.1 QMF Structure

by users who have no knowledge of the details of QMF (or of SQL or QBE, come to that). QMF also provides a *Command Interface,* which allows an application program or CMS EXEC to invoke QMF commands. Section 19.5 contains an overview of the QMF commands and their use in procedures, and Section 19.6 briefly discusses the Command Interface. Then Section 19.7 discusses the QMF EXTRACT and ISPF commands and the QMF Document Interface. These facilities allow QMF to interface with certain other IBM products, namely DXT, ISPF/PDF, and document processors such as PROFS (Professional Office System) or DCF (Document Composition Facility).

Finally, a few additional preliminary remarks before we start our examination of QMF features and facilities in depth:

1. Although the emphasis in QMF is very naturally on data retrieval, the "query" the user enters can actually be *any SQL operation* (or any QBE operation)—it is not limited to retrieval but can include, for example, update operations such as INSERT and DELETE, data definition operations such as CREATE and DROP TABLE, and data control operations such as GRANT and REVOKE.

2. The emphasis in QMF is also on *interactive execution* (again very naturally). However, it is also possible to invoke QMF as a batch job ("QMF batch"), thanks to the builtin QMF application BATCH (see Section 19.6).

3. As usual we will base most of our examples on the familiar suppliers-and-parts database.

19.2 CREATING AND EXECUTING A QUERY

Creating a New Query

After logging on to CMS and invoking QMF, the user is presented with the QMF *home panel* (Fig. 19.2). Like most QMF panels, this panel offers the user three possible actions:

- Press PF key 1 to get help, or
- Type a QMF command on the command line, or
- Press a PF key to execute a preassigned QMF command.

To construct a new query, the user types DISPLAY QUERY (or presses PF key 6). QMF responds by displaying a panel for entering the query. The user can then type the query (in either SQL or QBE), using the QMF full-screen editor. A sample query is shown in Fig. 19.3. *Note:* As mentioned in Section 19.1, all examples in this chapter will be based on SQL; examples

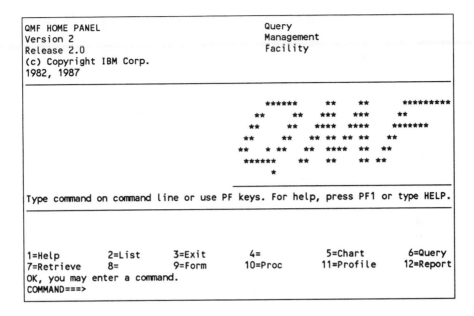

```
QMF HOME PANEL                        Query
Version 2                            Management
Release 2.0                          Facility
(c) Copyright IBM Corp.
1982, 1987


                        ******      **      **      *********
                   **        **   ***     ***       **
                   **        **   ****    ****      *******
                   **        **   ** ** ** **       **
                   **   * **      **   ****   **     **
                   ******     **      **      ** **

                             *

Type command on command line or use PF keys. For help, press PF1 or type HELP.



1=Help        2=List      3=Exit      4=          5=Chart      6=Query
7=Retrieve    8=          9=Form      10=Proc     11=Profile   12=Report
OK, you may enter a command.
COMMAND===>
```

Fig. 19.2 The QMF home panel

```
SQL QUERY                                                    LINE 1

SELECT     S.CITY, S.S#, SP.P#, SP.QTY
FROM       S, SP
WHERE      S.S# = SP.S#
ORDER BY   S.CITY, S.S#, SP.P#




*** END ***







1=Help        2=Run       3=End       4=Print     5=Chart      6=Draw
7=Backward    8=Forward   9=Form      10=Insert   11=Delete    12=Report
OK, cursor positioned.
COMMAND ===>                                        SCROLL ===> PAGE
```

Fig. 19.3 Sample QMF query (SQL)

of QBE can be found in Appendix G. Note that it is possible to switch dynamically between the two languages. The *default* language for any given user is defined in that user's "QMF profile," which is (typically) created by the *QMF administrator* but can be modified by the user at any time by means of appropriate QMF commands.

As already indicated, QMF queries can be created (and subsequently modified) using the builtin QMF full-screen editor. This editor provides simple commands for adding and deleting query lines, and is easy for a novice to learn and use. More experienced users who are familiar with more powerful editors (e.g., XEDIT or ISPF/PDF) can use one of those editors instead by issuing the QMF EDIT command. In this chapter, however, we restrict our attention for the most part to QMF's own editor.

QMF provides a DRAW command that can be used to assist in the process of constructing queries. DRAW "draws" a skeleton query on the screen for the table named in the DRAW command. For example, the command

```
DRAW S ( TYPE = SELECT )
```

will produce the following SELECT statement skeleton for the suppliers table (table S):

```
SELECT S#, SNAME, STATUS, CITY   -- S
FROM    S                        -- S
```

This skeleton query can now be edited to produce the query actually desired. *Note:* The "--S" at the right-hand side of each of the two lines of the skeleton query is a comment.

Once the query has been created, the user can execute it by issuing RUN QUERY (or by pressing PF key 2). The result is displayed at the user's terminal using the default form constructed automatically by QMF. That form can be displayed by issuing DISPLAY FORM (or by pressing PF key 9). Figs. 19.4 and 19.5 show the report and the default form, respectively, for the query of Fig. 19.3.

The user can now edit the form, if desired, and then display a revised report corresponding to that edited form by issuing DISPLAY REPORT or by pressing PF key 12. (A detailed discussion of form editing is deferred to Section 19.3.) These two steps can be repeated as many times as necessary, until the user is satisfied with the result; the final report can then be printed by issuing PRINT REPORT, or by pressing PF key 4. For example, the command

```
PRINT REPORT ( WIDTH=132 LENGTH=65 DATETIME=YES PAGENO=YES )
```

will print the current report (i.e., the current contents of DATA, formatted by the current FORM) on the printer specified in the user's QMF profile.

```
REPORT                                      LINE 1      POS 1    79

   CITY              S#    P#             QTY
   ----------------  ----- ------   --------------
   London            S1    P1             300
   London            S1    P2             200
   London            S1    P3             400
   London            S1    P4             200
   London            S1    P5             100
   London            S1    P6             100
   London            S4    P2             200
   London            S4    P4             300
   London            S4    P5             400
   Paris             S2    P1             300
   Paris             S2    P2             400
   Paris             S3    P2             200




1=Help       2=          3=End       4=Print     5=Chart      6=Query
7=Backward   8=Forward   9=Form      10=Left     11=Right     12=
OK, this is the REPORT from your RUN command.
COMMAND ===>                                        SCROLL ===> PAGE
```

Fig. 19.4 Report for the query of Fig. 19.3

```
FORM.MAIN

COLUMNS:              Total Width of Report Columns: 45
  NUM  COLUMN HEADING                          USAGE   INDENT  WIDTH  EDIT
  ---  -----------------------------------     -------  ------  -----  -----
   1   CITY                                               2      15     C
   2   S#                                                 2       5     C
   3   P#                                                 2       6     C
   4   QTY                                                2      11     L



PAGE:    HEADING ===>
         FOOTING ===>
FINAL:   TEXT ===>
BREAK1:  NEW PAGE FOR BREAK? ===> NO
         FOOTING ===>
BREAK2:  NEW PAGE FOR BREAK? ===> NO
         FOOTING ===>
OPTIONS :  OUTLINE? ===> YES        DEFAULT BREAK TEXT? ===> YES

1=Help     2=Check   3=End      4=Form.Columns 5=Form.Options 6=Query
7=Backward 8=Forward 9=Form.Page 10=Form.Final  11=Form.Break1 12=Report

COMMAND ===> OK, FORM is displayed.                 SCROLL ===> PAGE
```

Fig. 19.5 Default form for the query of Fig. 19.3

Pages will be 132 characters wide and 65 lines deep, will contain the current date and time, and will be numbered.

It is also possible to direct the hard copy report to a different printer by means of the PRINTER option on the PRINT command. For example, to print the report on the printer called DEPT1, the following command could be used:

```
PRINT REPORT ( PRINTER = DEPT1 )
```

Saving and Reexecuting a Query

At any given time, the QMF working area includes at most five current "QMF items": one query, one result (DATA), one form, one procedure, and one profile (refer to Fig. 19.1). Thus, e.g., executing a new query will cause the current contents of DATA to be overwritten. However, any current item can be saved for later use by means of an appropriate SAVE command. For instance, the command

```
SAVE QUERY AS CITYQUERY ( SHARE = YES )
```

will save the current query as CITYQUERY (and will also make it available for use by other users, thanks to the option SHARE = YES; if the SHARE option were omitted, only the user saving the query would subsequently be able to execute it).

Saved queries can subsequently be executed by means of the RUN QUERY command. For instance, the command

```
RUN CITYQUERY ( FORM = CITYFORM )
```

will execute the saved query CITYQUERY, formatting the result in accordance with a saved form named CITYFORM.

The command LIST QUERIES can be used to display a list of saved queries. Options exist to limit the output to just those queries saved by a particular user and/or having a particular generic name. For example, the command

```
LIST QUERIES ( OWNER = ALL  NAME = CITY% )
```

will list all saved queries having "CITY" as the first four characters of their name. The user can then enter various QMF commands on the screen alongside any given query in the list. For example, if the user types the command DISPLAY against the query name CITYQUERY, QMF will bring that query into the QUERY working area, thereby making it the current query again.

Variables (i.e., parameters) are permitted in saved queries. For example, if the query

```
SELECT  S#, SNAME
FROM    S
WHERE   CITY = &CITYNAME
```

is saved under the name CITYQUERY, it can be executed subsequently via the command

```
RUN CITYQUERY ( &CITYNAME = 'London' )
```

If the user forgets to supply a value for the &CITY variable, QMF will prompt for one.

Controlling Query Execution

QMF provides two mechanisms by which it is possible for the installation to exercise some control over its use (and hence over the use of certain system resources). The first consists of a simple cost estimate facility. During the execution of a query, QMF will display a status panel showing the estimated cost of that query in "timerons" (a fictitious unit of time). The user can then cancel the query if the cost seems too high.

The second, more sophisticated mechanism is the QMF *governor* facility, by which the QMF administrator can provide an Assembler Language exit routine to control, by individual user or user class, such matters as:

- the number of rows fetched from SQL/DS
- the time taken to execute a QMF command
- the QMF commands that can or cannot be used
- the time periods during which QMF can be used

The governor facility thus allows the installation to prevent users from entering queries, inadvertently or otherwise, that would use an excessive amount of some system resource or would interfere unduly with other activities in the system. A sample governor routine is provided with QMF that can be used to control the number of rows fetched and QMF command execution time.

19.3   CREATING A REPORT

After composing and executing a query, the user can produce a tailored report from the result by modifying the form, using a set of *form panels*. The starting point in this process is the default form produced by QMF when the query is first executed. That form can be displayed by issuing DISPLAY FORM (or by pressing PF key 9) after running the query; the effect is to display the form on a panel called FORM.MAIN (refer to Fig. 19.5).

FORM.MAIN supports a set of basic formatting functions; more extensive formatting can be performed using additional form panels. We will first discuss the use of FORM.MAIN and then move on to describe the other panels. As already indicated, the default form we will be using as a basis for discussion is the one shown in Fig. 19.5 (the default form for the sample query of Fig. 19.3).

Basic Formatting

To demonstrate basic formatting, we will make some updates to the default form of Fig. 19.5. The modified form is shown in Fig. 19.6, and the resulting report (displayed by issuing DISPLAY REPORT or by pressing PF key 12) is shown in Fig. 19.7. By comparing Fig. 19.6 with the original default form (Fig. 19.5), we can see the effect of each of the major components of FORM.MAIN.

- COLUMN HEADING

The column headings on the default form are the same as the column names in the table, unless column labels are being used (see the discussion of the

```
FORM.MAIN

COLUMNS:                Total Width of Report Columns: 40
 NUM  COLUMN HEADING                           USAGE    INDENT  WIDTH  EDIT
 ---  ------------------------------------     -------  ------  -----  -----
   1  City                                     BREAK1   3       8      C
   2  Supplier                                          3       8      C
   3  Part                                              3       4      C
   4  Quantity                                 SUM      3       8      L


PAGE:     HEADING ===> Shipments by Supplier City - Date: &DATE
          FOOTING ===> Page: &PAGE
FINAL:    TEXT ===> *** Grand Total
BREAK1:   NEW PAGE FOR BREAK? ===> NO
          FOOTING ===> * Total for &1
BREAK2:   NEW PAGE FOR BREAK? ===> NO
          FOOTING ===>
OPTIONS:  OUTLINE? ===> YES               DEFAULT BREAK TEXT? ===> YES

1=Help      2=Check     3=End       4=Form.Columns  5=Form.Options  6=Query
7=Backward  8=Forward   9=Form.Page  10=Form.Final   11=Form.Break1  12=Report

COMMAND ===> OK, cursor positioned.                        SCROLL ===> PAGE
```

Fig. 19.6 Modified form for the query of Fig. 19.3

```
Shipments by Supplier City - Date: 87/06/23

City       Supplier    Part    Quantity
--------   --------    ----    --------
London     S1          P1           300
           S1          P2           200
           S1          P3           400
           S1          P4           200
           S1          P5           100
           S1          P6           100
           S4          P2           200
           S4          P4           300
           S4          P5           400
                                --------
         * Total for London        2200

Paris      S2          P1           300
           S2          P2           400
           S3          P2           200
                                --------
         * Total for Paris           900
                                ========
         ***   Grand Total         3100
                                        Page:  1
```

Fig. 19.7 Tailored report using the form of Fig. 19.6

SQL LABEL statement in Section 9.3). Those headings can be changed to any name of up to 40 characters. An underscore starts a new line—i.e., it indicates that the rest of the heading (up to the next underscore) is to appear on the next line, centered beneath the portion on the previous line (up to nine lines are allowed in such a heading). In the example, the name CITY has been changed to City, and the names S#, P#, and QTY have been changed to the more meaningful names Supplier, Part, and Quantity, respectively.

■ USAGE

USAGE codes determine how data columns are to be processed in producing the report. If no USAGE code is specified for a given column, values in that column are simply displayed without any special processing. The meanings of the various USAGE codes are as follows.

- OMIT means that the column is to be omitted from the report.
- BREAK*n* (*n* = 1 to 6) specifies that a *control break* is to occur each time a value change occurs in the indicated column. The main purpose of specifying control breaks is to let QMF compute and display

subtotals (or similar partial results—see below) when the report is produced. In our example, a control break will occur each time the City value changes. Because USAGE for the Quantity column has been specified as SUM, QMF will sum the Quantity values at each control break. Note that a request for subtotals automatically causes QMF to compute a grand total also.

- In general, BREAK1 signifies the most significant (major) control break column, BREAK2 the next most significant, and so on. QMF will reorder the report columns (but not the form columns) left to right in the order of significance of the control breaks. *Note:* The original query must have included an appropriate ORDER BY specification for control breaks to make sense. See Fig. 19.3.

- BREAK*n*X is the same as BREAK*n,* except that the column is to be omitted from the report.

- The available "aggregate function" USAGE codes (with their meanings, where those meanings are not immediately obvious) are:
  — COUNT
  — FIRST
  — LAST
  — MAXIMUM
  — MINIMUM
  — SUM
  — CSUM (cumulative sum)
  — AVG
  — STDEV (standard deviation)
  — PCT (percentage of next subtotal)
  — CPCT (cumulative percentage of next subtotal)
  — TPCT (percentage of grand total)
  — TCPCT (cumulative percentage of grand total)

- The USAGE code GROUP causes one line of summary data to be displayed for each distinct value in the indicated column. (As with BREAK*n,* the data must be appropriately sorted for GROUP to make sense.) In our example, if we were to specify GROUP for the Supplier column (in addition to the BREAK1 and SUM codes already specified for the City and Quantity columns), the effect would be to group all rows for a particular supplier within a particular city together and to display a single line for that combination, giving the corresponding total quantity. The final result would thus look somewhat as follows (ignoring page headings and footings):

```
City         Supplier   Quantity
--------     --------   --------
London       S1            1300
             S4             900
                        --------
  * Total  for London     2200

Paris        S2             700
             S3             200
                        --------
  * Total  for Paris       900
                        ========
    *** Grand Total       3100
```

The Part column is automatically omitted from the report because no aggregate USAGE is specified for it.

- Finally, the USAGE code ACROSS can be used in conjunction with GROUP to produce a report in which each line of summary data for the GROUP column has an entry for each corresponding value of the ACROSS column. (As with BREAK*n* and GROUP, the data must be appropriately sorted for ACROSS to make sense.) For example, suppose we wanted to display quantity totals by city across all suppliers, as well as quantity totals for each individual supplier. By specifying ACROSS for Supplier and GROUP for City, the required result is produced:

```
            <-------------- Supplier --------------->
            <- S1 ->   <- S2 ->   <- S3 ->   <- S4 ->   <-TOTAL->
City        Quantity   Quantity   Quantity   Quantity   Quantity
--------    --------   --------   --------   --------   --------
London        1300          0          0        900       2200
Paris            0        700        200          0        900
            ========   ========   ========   ========   ========
              1300        700        200        900       3100
```

Note: The suppliers-and-parts database does not permit the same supplier to appear in more than one city. The foregoing report is thus unrealistically simple. Nevertheless, the example does serve to illustrate the basic idea of "across-summary" reporting.

- INDENT

INDENT specifies the number of blanks to appear between the indicated column and the one to its immediate left. All INDENT values in the example have been changed from 2 to 3.

- WIDTH

WIDTH specifies the width of the indicated column as it is to appear in the report (in terms of characters). In the example, the City, Supplier, Part, and

Quantity widths have been changed from 15 to 8, 5 to 8, 6 to 4, and 11 to 8, respectively.

- EDIT

EDIT codes determine how column values are to be formatted. Codes C and L mean character and decimal, respectively. Other options permit numbers to be displayed in scientific (floating point) style or in a variety of fixed point styles (e.g., with currency symbols inserted, leading zeros suppressed, etc.). It is also possible to supply installation-defined exit routines to perform customized column value formatting. The reader is referred to the QMF manuals for details of all these possibilities. No changes were made to the EDIT codes in our example.

- PAGE HEADING, PAGE FOOTING, FINAL

PAGE HEADING and FOOTING define one line of heading and footing text to be produced on each page of the report. FINAL defines one line of text to be displayed on the final summary line (if any) of the report. Our example uses the variable &DATE to display the current date (in the format YY/MM/DD) in the heading text, and &PAGE to display the current page number in the footing text. The variable &TIME can also be used to display the current time in the format HH:MM.

- BREAK1

Two options are possible here, each specifying what is to be done when a control break occurs in the BREAK1 column. The first specifies whether a new page is to be started; the second specifies the text to be displayed on the corresponding summary line. Such text can include references to variables of the form &*n*. If it does, QMF will substitute the current value of column *n* before displaying the summary line. In the example, the variable &1 refers to column 1 on the form, and the current value of City will be displayed each time a control break on City occurs. *Note:* Variables can also be used in heading and footing text.

- BREAK2

BREAK2 is the same as BREAK1, mutatis mutandis. *Note:* There are no BREAK3, BREAK4, etc. options on FORM.MAIN; for information on how to code the text for control breaks 3 through 6, see the subsection ''Advanced Formatting'' at the end of the present section.

- OPTIONS

FORM.MAIN includes two further options, OUTLINE and DEFAULT BREAK TEXT. The example specifies an OUTLINE option of YES, which causes values to be displayed in a control break column only when the value changes; NO causes a value to be displayed on every line. The DEFAULT BREAK TEXT option specifies what is to happen when control breaks are used and the user has not indicated any break footing text; YES causes a line of asterisks to be displayed, NO suppresses this default.

One final aspect of the form that should be mentioned is the line at the top showing "Total Width of Report Columns." This line gives the total report width, in characters. It cannot be changed directly, but is instead automatically updated by QMF every time a USAGE, INDENT, or WIDTH value is modified.

Advanced Formatting

The example discussed under "Basic Formatting" above gives some idea of how easy it is to use FORM.MAIN to produce a customized report. Sometimes, however, more sophisticated tailoring will be required. The form panels described in this subsection provide the necessary additional tailoring facilities. There are five additional panel types, namely FORM.COLUMNS, FORM.PAGE, FORM.FINAL, FORM.BREAK*n,* and FORM.OPTIONS, with functions as follows:

- FORM.COLUMNS: Contains the same column information as FORM.MAIN, except that more column entries can be displayed on a single screen.

- FORM.PAGE: Allows 100 lines of heading and 40 lines of footing text (compared with just one on FORM.MAIN). Other options control text alignment and position, and the number of blank lines before and after the heading and footing.

- FORM.FINAL: Allows 300 lines of final report text and offers similar formatting options to FORM.PAGE.

- FORM.BREAK*n:* There are six of these panels, one for each of the six control break levels. Up to 15 heading lines (40 for FORM.BREAK1) and 15 footing lines (50 for FORM.BREAK1) are allowed for each level; they are positioned using formatting options similar to those on FORM.PAGE. One further option controls whether column headings are to be repeated at each new control break.

- FORM.OPTIONS: Contains some fourteen different formatting options, controlling such matters as detail line spacing, line wrapping, final and break text width, the use of aggregate function names in column headings, automatic column reordering when using control breaks and grouping, page renumbering, column heading separators, and so forth.

These panels work in conjunction with FORM.MAIN to let the user construct more elaborate reports. Everything entered on FORM.MAIN is automatically reflected in a corresponding detailed form panel. Each of the detailed panels can be reached by selecting the appropriate PF key from FORM.MAIN (sec the PF keys in Fig. 19.5 or Fig. 19.6).

19.4   CREATING A CHART

Section 19.3 explained what is involved in creating a QMF report. However, a report is only one way of displaying a query result; a chart or graph is another. QMF uses the Interactive Chart Utility (ICU) of the IBM Graphic Data Display Manager (GDDM) to create and display charts. Although most aspects of such charts are controlled by QMF, users can specify and save certain chart format options of their own in the ICU.

The QMF command syntax to display a chart is

```
DISPLAY CHART ( ICUFORM = name )
```

The chart is formatted and displayed in accordance with the chart format identified by "name"—either one of the builtin chart formats provided by QMF or a user-defined chart format previously saved in the ICU. For example, to display a pie chart using a QMF-provided format called PIE, the user would enter

```
DISPLAY CHART ( ICUFORM = PIE )
```

Similarly, to display a chart saved in the ICU with the name MYPIE, the command

```
DISPLAY CHART ( ICUFORM = MYPIE )
```

would be used.

As already indicated, several ICU chart formats are provided by QMF to reduce the need for users to create and save their own chart formats. The builtin formats are BAR, PIE, LINE, TOWER, POLAR, HISTOGRAM, SURFACE, and SCATTER (these names are intended to be self-explanatory). By default, QMF formats data into a bar chart. This default format is stored under the name DSQCFORM in the ICU, and can be replaced by the user at any time.

To illustrate chart operation, we will use a modified version of the form in Fig. 19.6 (see Fig. 19.8), in which we have specified OMIT for the Supplier column and GROUP for the Part column. Executing the command

```
FORM.MAIN

COLUMNS:               Total Width of Report Columns: 40
 NUM  COLUMN HEADING                          USAGE    INDENT  WIDTH  EDIT
 ---  -----------------------------------    -------   ------  -----  ----
   1  City                                    BREAK1      3       8     C
   2  Supplier                                OMIT        3       8     C
   3  Part                                    GROUP       3       4     C
   4  Quantity                                SUM         3       8     L


PAGE:    HEADING ===> Shipments by Supplier City - Date: &DATE
         FOOTING ===> Page: &PAGE
FINAL:   TEXT ===> *** Grand Total
BREAK1:  NEW PAGE FOR BREAK? ===> NO
         FOOTING ===> * Total for &1
BREAK2:  NEW PAGE FOR BREAK? ===> NO
         FOOTING ===>
OPTIONS:  OUTLINE? ===> YES            DEFAULT BREAK TEXT? ===> YES

1=Help      2=Check    3=End        4=Form.Columns  5=Form.Options  6=Query
7=Backward  8=Forward  9=Form.Page  10=Form.Final   11=Form.Break1  12=Report

COMMAND ===> OK, cursor positioned.                  SCROLL ===> PAGE
```

Fig. 19.8 Form for displaying a bar chart

DISPLAY CHART with this form will create the bar chart shown in Fig.
19.9.

The rules used by QMF for constructing charts are as follows:

- For report forms without any GROUP or BREAK*n* columns, the X-
  axis data is taken from the leftmost data column. For report forms that
  include one or more GROUP or BREAK*n* columns, as in our example,
  the X-axis data is taken from those columns.

- The Y-axis data is taken from the remaining *numeric* columns of the
  report—i.e., the Quantity column, in our example.

- The legend Quantity comes from the column heading of the Y-axis data
  column.

- The chart heading is the same as the report heading.

It is important to realize that these four aspects of the chart format
are completely defined by the QMF report form; they can be temporarily
modified in the ICU for some specific purpose, but any such modifications
will not be reflected in the chart when it is next displayed from QMF. Other
aspects of the chart format, such as chart size, axis titles, data color, and
the position, color, and size of the legend and titles, can be permanently

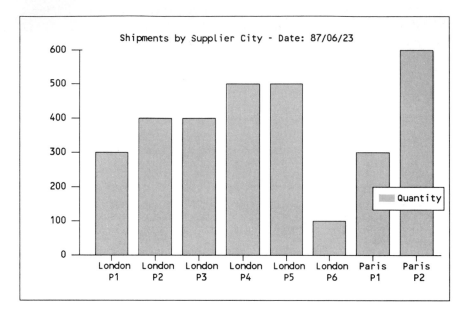

Fig. 19.9 Sample bar chart

modified, by making the desired changes and saving the modified format in the ICU under a new name. The modified format can then be used by specifying that new name in the QMF DISPLAY CHART command. If a QMF-provided chart format is used and not modified in any way, it does not have to be saved in the ICU.

Charts can be printed using the PRINT CHART command. For example, the command

```
PRINT CHART ( ICUFORM=PIE UNITS=PERCENT CWIDTH=80 CLENGTH=80 )
```

will print the current chart as a pie chart occupying 80 percent of the printed page. Other options allow the user to specify the horizontal and vertical positioning of the chart on the page and support the routing of the output to a printer other than the default one in the user's QMF profile.

19.5 COMMANDS AND PROCEDURES

Commands

So far in this chapter we have shown the use of QMF commands to create, execute, and save queries, and to display and print reports and charts. Many additional commands are also available. For purposes of reference, we present below a summary of all the main QMF commands (including those already discussed):

- CMS: Enter a CMS command or execute a QMF application (see Section 19.6).
- CONNECT: Change the user ID under which you are running QMF (see Chapter 11).
- DISPLAY: Display a query, form, report, chart, procedure, profile, or table. The table option provides a quick way to display some specified table (it is shorthand for coding and executing the SQL statement "SELECT * FROM table").
- DRAW: Create a skeleton query.
- EDIT: Edit a QMF procedure or SQL query, using an editor of the user's choice instead of the builtin QMF editor.
- ERASE: Erase a query, form, procedure, or table from the system (the table option is shorthand for coding and executing the SQL statement "DROP TABLE table").
- EXPORT: Transfer data, a query, form, procedure, or chart to a CMS file (see Section 19.6).
- EXTRACT: Invoke DXT from the QMF environment (see Section 19.7).
- HELP: Get online information about using QMF.
- IMPORT: Transfer data, a query, form, or procedure from a CMS file into QMF (see Section 19.6).
- ISPF: Invoke ISPF/PDF (see Section 19.7).
- LIST: List saved QMF items.
- PRINT: Print a query, form, report, chart, procedure, profile, or table.
- RESET: Clear the current QMF item.
- RETRIEVE: Retrieve and redisplay previously entered QMF commands.
- RUN: Execute a query or procedure.
- SAVE: Save the current query, form, procedure, profile, or data for future use (the data option is equivalent to executing the SQL statement "CREATE TABLE," followed by a statement to populate that newly created table).
- SET: Change the user profile without first displaying it.

Procedures

There will frequently be situations in which the same set of QMF commands needs to be executed repeatedly on some regular basis. In such a situation, it is obviously convenient to be able to execute the complete set via a single command. QMF therefore allows commands to be grouped together to form a QMF *procedure*. Such a procedure can be invoked by means of the QMF RUN command. Like queries, procedures are created using an editor; they can be saved for later reuse using the SAVE command, and—again like queries—can contain variables (i.e., parameters), values for which must be supplied when the procedure is executed.

Procedures must contain QMF commands only, and have no branching capability. They can optionally be run in batch, freeing the terminal for other work. The sample procedure below contains several of the commands discussed earlier in this chapter. *Note:* Lines beginning with a double hyphen are comment lines.

```
-- Run the stored query called CITYQUERY;
-- CITYNAME is a variable contained in CITYQUERY;
-- other variables are for use with the procedure itself:
--
RUN CITYQUERY ( FORM = &FORMN  &&CITYNAME = &CITY )
--
-- Create a new table containing the result data:
--
SAVE DATA AS &NEWTAB
--
-- Print report using a page length of 55 lines:
--
PRINT REPORT ( LENGTH = 55 )
```

The procedure can be saved by executing a SAVE command—for example:

```
SAVE PROC AS CITYPROC
```

—and can be executed using a RUN command. For example:

```
RUN CITYPROC ( &FORMN=CITYFORM &CITY='London' &NEWTAB=CITYDATA )
```

See also the discussion of QMF applications and the QMF Command Interface in Section 19.6.

19.6 APPLICATION SUPPORT FACILITIES

In addition to all of the end-user facilities discussed in this chapter so far, QMF also provides a set of facilities specifically intended for the professional programmer. Those facilities, known collectively as the *QMF application support facilities,* consist of:

- The QMF *Command Interface,* which allows application programs and CMS EXECs to pass commands to QMF for execution. Those commands are executed in a similar fashion to those entered from the QMF command line or QMF procedures.

- *Installation-Defined Commands,* which make it possible for user-written applications to act as an extension of the QMF command set. Such commands can be invoked just like other QMF commands—i.e., from the QMF command line, from within QMF procedures, or through the QMF Command Interface.

- *PF Key Customization,* which can be used to reassign QMF commands to different PF keys and to add installation-defined commands to PF keys.

- *Application Support Commands,* which are a special set of commands for use by application programs. These commands make it possible for applications to behave just like QMF commands in their style of interaction with the end-user.

- *Externalized Items,* which allow applications to manipulate QMF items (e.g., QMF queries and forms) outside the QMF environment, using the QMF EXPORT and IMPORT commands.

We now briefly describe each of these facilities in turn.

The Command Interface

The Command Interface is a QMF-supplied program (DSQCCI) that can be invoked from a CMS EXEC or from a program written in APL, Assembler Language, COBOL, FORTRAN, or PL/I. Applications using the QMF Command Interface are initially invoked from QMF (interactive or batch) using the QMF CMS command. They can then in turn invoke the Command Interface, passing it a string representing the QMF command to be executed (see Fig. 19.10).

The Command Interface is particularly useful in EXECs, because EXECs offer the branching and looping constructs not available in QMF procedures. For example, the EXEC statement

```
ADDRESS ISPEXEC "SELECT PGM (DSQCCI),
        PARM (RUN CITYQUERY (FORM=CITYFORM &CITYNAME='London'))"
```

invokes the Command Interface and requests QMF to execute the query CITYQUERY using the form CITYFORM (and the CITYNAME "London"). *Note:* ISPF services are used (ISPEXEC) because (as explained above) the application—i.e., the EXEC—is invoked from QMF, and QMF runs under ISPF.

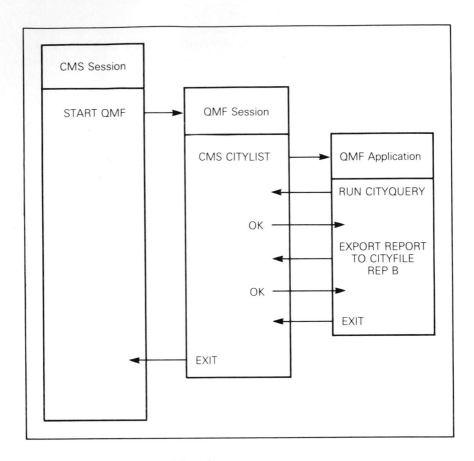

Fig. 19.10 QMF Command Interface

The only information returned to the application is an indication of whether the command executed successfully; in the example above, the result of the query is not returned to the EXEC but is instead stored in the DATA workarea of the QMF session that invoked that EXEC (nor is any information displayed during the execution of the query at the QMF terminal that called the EXEC, incidentally). To access the output report from within the EXEC, it must be exported to a CMS file and then read back from that file. For example, the command

```
ADDRESS ISPEXEC "SELECT PGM (DSQCCI),
       PARM (EXPORT REPORT TO CITYFILE REP B)"
```

exports the report to a file called "CITYFILE REP B," which can now be read in the normal manner (the formats of exported QMF items are all fully documented in the QMF manuals). *Note:* Of course, there is no point in writing an application to execute a query unless further processing is to be done on the result of that query. As an illustration, the EXEC discussed above might go on to perform a more detailed analysis of the data in CITYFILE or produce a more complex report from that data.

QMF applications can also display ISPF information and data-entry panels during execution. Such panels can be made to have a similar appearance to the standard QMF panels.

As already stated, applications using the QMF Command Interface are invoked from QMF (interactive or batch), using the QMF CMS command. If the EXEC application discussed above is named CITYLIST, it can be invoked by means of the command

```
CMS CITYLIST
```

This command can be made more memorable (i.e., more user-friendly) by giving it an appropriate *command synonym*. See the next subsection below.

Installation-Defined Commands

The process of invoking QMF procedures (via the RUN command) and applications (via the CMS command) can be considerably simplified by the introduction of *command synonyms*. Such synonyms constitute *installation-defined commands;* entries describing them are kept by QMF in a *command synonym table*. The specific synonym table to be used during a specific QMF session is defined in the user's QMF profile.

Each row in the synonym table consists of three components: verb, object (optional), and corresponding QMF command. For example:

Verb   *Object*   *Command*

```
COMPUTE   SHIPMENTS     CMS CITYLIST PARM ('&ALL')
```

"COMPUTE SHIPMENTS" is a synonym for the indicated command; the verb is COMPUTE, and the object is SHIPMENTS. "PARM ('&ALL')" means that any additional information coded when entering the synonym is to be passed to the EXEC (i.e., CITYLIST). For example, if the user enters

```
COMPUTE SHIPMENTS ( FORM = CITYFORM  CITYNAME = 'London' )
```

the EXEC called CITYLIST is invoked and is passed the text between the parentheses. This ability to pass text is useful for passing parameter values to an application that executes parameterized QMF queries.

Several synonyms can exist with the same verb, provided each has a different object. QMF's order of search for commands is:

1. Look in the synonym table for a verb/object match; if no match is found, or if no object was specified, then
2. Look in the synonym table for a verb match; if no match is found, then
3. Assume it is a QMF-supplied command.

Synonyms can be assigned to PF keys (see the next subsection).

PF Key Customization

Users can customize the PF key settings on QMF panels: Existing settings can be changed, and unassigned keys can be set, so that (in general) any key can be used for any QMF command or command synonym. The specific settings to be used during a specific QMF session are specified by an appropriate PF key table, which is defined in the user's QMF profile.

Application Support Commands

There are four special commands—INTERACT, MESSAGE, QMF, and STATE—that are specifically intended for use in QMF applications. They enable the application to carry out operations such as interrogating the QMF profile or passing a message out to the end-user via QMF.

- INTERACT

    Normally, as mentioned earlier, when a command is executed through the QMF Command Interface, no interactive communication takes place with the end-user. However, if the application is in fact being executed interactively (i.e., not in QMF batch), it can use the INTERACT command to perform such interactive communication. INTERACT invokes some other QMF command (such as EXPORT) and causes that command to display help, prompt, and status information to the end-user exactly as if it had been executed directly. For example, the following command—

```
ADDRESS ISPEXEC "SELECT PGM (DSQCCI),
        PARM (INTERACT EXPORT REPORT TO CITYFILE REP B)"
```

—will not only execute the specified EXPORT command, but will also cause status information regarding that command to be displayed to the QMF end-user.

- MESSAGE

QMF applications can issue their own messages to the QMF user by executing the MESSAGE command. This command can also be used in a QMF procedure. At the end of the EXEC application CITYLIST, for example, we might issue the command

```
ADDRESS ISPEXEC "SELECT PGM (DSQCCI),
        PARM (MESSAGE (TEXT='EXPORT COMPLETE'))"
```

to inform the user that the query was executed and the data exported successfully.

- QMF

Normally, as explained earlier, when a command is issued, QMF searches the synonym table first to see if the command is installation-defined, before assuming it is QMF-supplied. There may be situations (to be avoided whenever possible) where an installation-defined command and a QMF-supplied command have the same name. To execute the QMF-supplied command in such a case, the synonym table search must be bypassed. The QMF command is provided for this purpose. For example, the command

```
QMF RUN CITYPROC
```

will execute the QMF-supplied RUN command, even if "RUN CITYPROC" is in fact a valid installation-defined command also.

- STATE

The STATE command is used by a QMF application to retrieve information about the state of the current QMF session. The command is executed through the Command Interface. It has no operands.

Externalized Items

The EXPORT and IMPORT commands let users transfer QMF items to and from CMS files. EXPORT allows DATA, FORM, PROC, QUERY, REPORT and CHART items to be exported; it is useful for transferring items to other products for further analysis and/or modification outside the QMF environment. The IMPORT command allows DATA, FORM, PROC, and QUERY items to be imported; it is useful for importing externally created items, and for reimporting items that have been previously exported and then modified. In particular, EXPORT and IMPORT allow items to be moved from one QMF system to another. *Note:* In addition to its own export/import file formats (see the QMF manuals for details), QMF also supports the transfer of data into and out of Integration Exchange Format (IXF) files. See Section 18.4 for a brief discussion of IXF.

QMF-Supplied Applications

The facilities described in the body of this section permit DP professional users to build their own customized QMF applications. QMF also provides a number of *builtin* applications. We conclude this section by briefly summarizing the purposes of those applications:

- BATCH: Allows queries and procedures to be run in batch mode (QMF batch), rather than interactively.
- BUILDQ: Lets users build queries using prompt screens.
- DPRE: Displays reports as they would appear on a printer.
- ISPF: Invokes ISPF (see Section 19.7 for more details).

19.7 INTERFACING TO OTHER PRODUCTS

We have already seen in Section 18.6 how QMF can interface to other IBM products using the EXPORT and IMPORT commands. In this section we will look at additional ways of communicating with other products. The products in question are:

- Data Extract (DXT)
- Interactive System Productivity Facility/Program Development Facility (ISPF/PDF)
- Document processors such as Professional Office System (PROFS) or the Document Composition Facility (DCF)

Accessing DXT

As mentioned in Chapter 18, DXT is IBM's copy management tool for extracting data from operational files (VSAM or sequential) or databases (IMS, DB2, or SQL/DS-VM only) for loading into DB2 or SQL/DS tables. DXT provides a set of *end-user dialogs* for defining, modifying, and submitting extract requests for execution. These dialogs can be invoked from QMF using the QMF EXTRACT command. There are two ways of coding this command:

1. If the command is entered with no operands, the DXT end-user dialogs menu will be displayed. The user can then interactively create and/or edit a DXT request.
2. Alternatively, the command can include the name of an existing DXT extract request. For example, the command

    `EXTRACT PART1`

will cause DXT to submit the extract request called PART1. In this case, there is no question of creating or editing the request before it is executed; the user is simply told that the request has been sent to DXT.

DXT is discussed in more detail in Chapter 23.

Using ISPF/PDF

ISPF/PDF is an application development tool for the VM/CMS environment. Entering the QMF command

```
ISPF
```

will display the ISPF/PDF main menu, from which any of the ISPF/PDF options can be executed. Specific option panels can be invoked directly by entering the appropriate option number with the ISPF command as in the following example:

```
ISPF 3
```

Using the Document Interface

It is possible to embed a QMF report in a conventional text file by means of a special command (actually a macro) called GETQMF, which can be invoked from the appropriate text editor environment (e.g., the XEDIT environment). As an example, the command

```
GETQMF ASIS FILE MYFILE REP B
```

causes the report stored in the FILE "MYFILE REP B" to be embedded in the text file currently being edited. The ASIS option causes the report to be embedded "as is" (the alternative to ASIS is PROFS or DCF—see below).

Here is another example:

```
GETQMF PROFS USEQMF
```

The USEQMF option causes QMF to be invoked, thereby enabling the user to create the required report dynamically. The PROFS option causes PROFS control words to be placed at the start and end, at each page eject, and at the heading and footing of each page in the generated report before it is embedded in the text file. The alternative DCF option could be used in place of the PROFS option to perform the analogous function for the Document Composition Facility.

It is also possible to invoke an editor from QMF (via the EDIT command—see Section 19.5), use that editor to edit a file, and, as part of that editing process, invoke GETQMF to embed a QMF report in that file. In this case the GETQMF command must specify an existing QMF procedure to be executed to generate the report. For example:

```
GETQMF ASIS USEQMF MYPROC
```

The procedure MYPROC will be invoked (via the QMF Command Interface) to produce the required report.

19.8   CONCLUSION

In this chapter, we have presented a comprehensive survey of the capabilities of QMF. QMF provides a set of easy-to-use facilities by which end-users can create their own queries and produce reports and charts (graphs) from the results of those queries. It also provides a set of application support facilities and a set of interfaces to certain other IBM products, all of which can be useful to the DP professional in constructing highly customized applications that make use of the features of QMF. However, QMF is not a complete solution to the application development problem; it does not include any decision support tools or end-user application generation facilities, and its report-writing capabilities are fairly unsophisticated. If the installation has more demanding requirements—requirements that cannot be satisfied by QMF—then a product such as IBM's Application System (AS) must be used instead. AS is covered in the next chapter.

◆

Application System

20.1 INTRODUCTION

Application System (AS) is an end-user query, decision support, and application development tool. Like QMF, it operates with both SQL/DS (under VM/CMS) and DB2 (under MVS/TSO); it also supports VSAM and CMS files, as well as "AS tables," i.e., files stored in AS's own format.* We focus in this book on the use of AS with SQL/DS.

As shown in Fig. 20.1, AS consists of a central file system, an integrated

---

*Throughout this chapter we will take the unqualified term "table" to mean an AS table specifically. We will use the explicitly qualified term "SQL/DS table" when we need to refer to a table in a SQL/DS database.

337

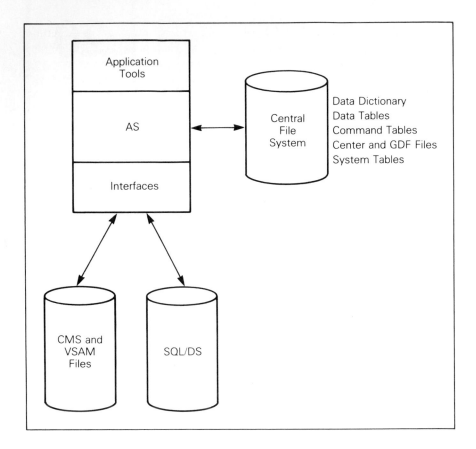

Fig. 20.1 AS structure

set of application tools, and interfaces to external files and databases. The central file system, in turn, consists of:

- The AS data dictionary, which contains descriptions of all AS tables;
- AS data tables;
- User-created "command tables" containing AS commands or language statements;
- Print tables ("center files") and Graphics Data Format (GDF) files containing print and graphic output; and
- Temporary system tables used to hold data and commands created during the user session.

AS operation is controlled by commands or statements in the AS command language. Each individual AS tool has its own set of specialized commands; in addition, AS provides a set of generalized commands for common functions, such as exporting and importing data to and from other IBM products. The main AS tools and their functions are as follows:

Compose — to create text files and documents

Draw — to build customized charts

Edit — to create procedures for validating data

Image — to define screens for data entry and display

Memo — to write memos

Model — to build company and financial models

Network — to manage a project plan

Procedure — to create canned AS procedures

Query — to create AS or SQL queries

Report — to format customized reports

Statistics — to perform statistical and forecasting functions

Tabulate — to perform data analysis

Update — to update AS or SQL/DS tables

In general, the user can interact with an individual AS tool in three different modes, namely Command Mode, Conversational Mode, and Interactive Mode (though not all tools support all three).

1. In *Command Mode,* the user enters commands in the AS *command area.* The command area is located near the bottom of the terminal screen and is identified by a question mark ("?").

2. In *Conversational Mode,* AS conducts a dialog with the user to generate the required commands. These commands can then be modified, executed, or saved for later use.

3. In *Interactive Mode,* AS uses windowing facilities and PF keys to perform the required functions. Most tools that support this mode of operation will optionally produce an equivalent set of AS commands as output, which can then be modified, executed, or saved for later use.

Examples in this chapter show the use of all three modes.

Commands can be stored in command tables, which are created and modified using the AS language editor; this facility permits sets of commands to be saved for later use. All commands are checked by the language editor for syntax errors as they are entered (with the sole exception of SQL

SELECT statements entered via the AS Query tool; such statements are not checked until they are executed).

The command for invoking an AS tool has the general form

```
tool  input-table, output-table
```

where:

- "tool" is the tool to be invoked;
- "input-table" identifies an existing input command table (an asterisk means no input); and
- "output-table" identifies an output command table (either an existing table whose contents are to be replaced or a new table to be created).

For example, the command

```
QUERY  *,CITYQRY
```

invokes the Query tool and causes a new output command table to be created called CITYQRY. The user can now create and store a SQL/DS query (SQL SELECT statement) in that table. If no output table is specified (second argument left blank), AS will create a "system table" automatically, assigning it a system-generated name. At the end of the session, AS will ask the user which system tables are to be kept (if any).

The plan of the rest of the chapter is as follows.

- First, we consider the use of SQL with AS. (*Note:* To access SQL/DS, the user can use either AS commands or SQL statements. If AS commands are used, AS will convert them into corresponding SQL statements. In this chapter we concentrate on SQL, for reasons of familiarity.) SQL statements can be entered and executed in AS by means of the AS QUERY and SQL commands:

  - The QUERY command invokes the Query tool, which is used to enter and execute SQL SELECT statements (only). Once the required data has been retrieved, the Report and Draw tools can be used to produce tailored reports and charts from the retrieved data. Sections 20.2, 20.3, and 20.4 contain detailed discussions of query creation and execution, report formatting, and chart creation, respectively.

  - SQL statements other than SELECT are entered and executed using the SQL command. Section 20.5 shows how this command can be used to perform data modification, data definition, and authorization operations.

- As already mentioned, AS commands can be stored in command tables. A command table can be regarded as a "canned" application or procedure that can be run on a regular basis, via the AS RUN command. Such procedures can vary in complexity considerably; simple procedures might be constructed by an end-user, but more complicated ones would typically be created by a person with programming skills. Sections 20.6 and 20.7 discuss the use of basic procedures and more complex procedures, respectively. Section 20.7 also looks at other AS application development facilities, including the AS Image and Edit tools, which are used to build data entry and validation applications.

- There are several ways of interfacing AS to other IBM products. For example, AS provides commands to allow the AS user to communicate with IBM's DXT and QMF products. Also, the IMPORT and EXPORT commands allow data to be transported between AS systems, and between AS and any other product that supports IBM's Integration Exchange Format (IXF). This subject is discussed in Section 20.8.

- Finally, AS also provides a variety of additional facilities: data analysis and statistics tools, a business planning facility, a project management feature, text processing tools, and an application preparation facility. A brief overview of these facilities is presented in Section 20.9.

20.2 CREATING AND EXECUTING A QUERY

After logging on to CMS and invoking AS, the user is presented with the AS Application Code screen (Fig. 20.2), which lists the "application codes" currently available to this user. An application code is really just shorthand for a list of AS table names; it identifies the set of tables that can be accessed under this particular code. From the Application Code screen, the user can either select one of the existing codes or create a new one. In the example, the code PART has been selected ("PART" has been typed in the command area). Any AS tables created during the AS session will now be associated with this application code.

In order to access SQL/DS from AS, the user must first issue an appropriate ATTACH command—for example:

```
ATTACH SQL(CJWHITE)
```

This command will connect AS to the SQL/DS database using "CJWHITE" as the necessary SQL/DS user ID. If an asterisk ("*") is specified in place of the user ID, the CMS sign-on ID will be used by default. Options on the ATTACH command permit the specification of such matters as the DBspace in which new SQL/DS tables are to be created, whether SQL LABELS are to be used as column titles in reports, and so forth. (One option in particular, DEFAULT, allows the user to specify that

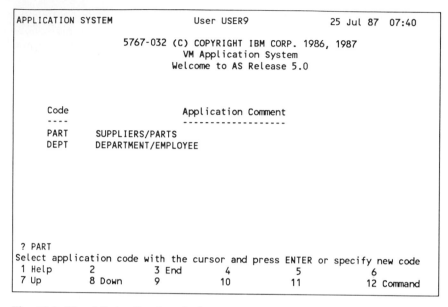

```
APPLICATION SYSTEM              User USER9              25 Jul 87  07:40

                 5767-032 (C) COPYRIGHT IBM CORP. 1986, 1987
                            VM Application System
                          Welcome to AS Release 5.0



      Code                       Application Comment
      ----                       -------------------
      PART       SUPPLIERS/PARTS
      DEPT       DEPARTMENT/EMPLOYEE






 ? PART
Select application code with the cursor and press ENTER or specify new code
 1 Help       2            3 End        4            5            6
 7 Up         8 Down       9            10           11           12 Command
```

Fig. 20.2 The AS Application Code screen

input tables are to be found, and output tables stored, in a certain default location if no other location is specified explicitly. For example, DEFAULT (SQL) means the default location is the SQL/DS database. DEFAULT(AS) is assumed if nothing else is specified.)

Once AS has been connected to the SQL/DS database, the user can perform SQL/DS operations—in particular, SQL SELECT statements. SELECT statements are created and executed via the AS Query tool, which is invoked via the QUERY command. For example:

```
QUERY *,CITYQRY
```

This command creates an output command table called CITYQRY and invokes the AS full-screen editor. The user can now use that editor to create a SELECT statement and save it in the CITYQRY table. *Note:* The AS editor provides a set of edit commands for modifying statements in command tables, merging in other command tables, searching for particular substrings, and so forth. Commands are also available for inserting, deleting, and moving blocks of text on the screen.

A sample SQL query entered via the AS editor is shown in Fig. 20.3.

```
QUERY *,CITYQRY                        Origin 1                    4 Lines

SELECT     S.CITY, S.S#, SP.P#, SP.QTY                             00001
FROM       S, SP                                                  00002
WHERE      S.S# = SP.S#                                           00003
ORDER BY   S.CITY, S.S#, SP.P#                                    00004




?
1                 2 Run       3 End        4 Print     5 Recall    6 Origin
7 Up              8 Down      9 Switch     10 Left      11 Right    12 Command
```

Fig. 20.3 Sample AS query (SQL)

Once the query has been created and saved in the output command table,* the user can validate and execute it by issuing the RUN and VIEW commands; RUN passes the query to SQL/DS for validation and preparation (dynamic SQL PREPARE, etc.), VIEW causes the data to be retrieved. For example (assuming that the query has been saved in CITYQRY):

```
RUN CITYQRY
VIEW
```

The result is shown in Fig. 20.4.

Note: The AS VIEW command typically does *not* retrieve the entire set of result rows all at once. Instead, what happens is the following. Initially, enough rows are fetched to fill the terminal screen; those rows are also kept in an internal file (in main storage if possible, otherwise in an AS table). Backward scrolling merely redisplays rows already retrieved. Forward scrol-

---

*The query can be saved in the output command table by means of PF key 3. (It can also be saved and then immediately RUN by means of PF key 2.) A saved query can be made available to other users via the AS SHARE command; such privileges can subsequently be revoked via the AS WITHDRAW command.

```
VIEW      QUERY(CITYQRY)                              25 Jul 87   07:55
                                                                   1/1
CITY          S#     P#              QTY                        Action
London        S1     P1              300
London        S1     P2              200
London        S1     P3              400
London        S1     P4              200
London        S1     P5              100
London        S1     P6              100
London        S4     P2              200
London        S4     P4              300
London        S4     P5              400
Paris         S2     P1              300
Paris         S2     P2              400
Paris         S3     P2              200




?
1                2 Input      3 End       4 Print      5 Recall      6 Top
7 Up             8 Down       9 Switch    10 Left      11 Right      12 Command
```

Fig. 20.4 Output for the query of Fig. 20.3

ling retrieves more result rows if necessary and adds them to the internal file. (In contrast to the VIEW command, other AS commands do retrieve the entire set of result rows all at once.)

Parameters are permitted in saved queries. For example, if the query

```
SELECT S#, SNAME
FROM   S
WHERE  CITY = @1
```

is saved in the command table CITYQRY, it can be executed later using the commands

```
RUN CITYQRY, @PASS(''London'')
VIEW
```

Saving Query Results

The result of a query can be stored in an AS or SQL/DS table using the OUT and COPY commands in place of the VIEW command. For example, the commands

```
RUN CITYQRY
OUT CITYFILE
COPY
```

will create an AS table named CITYFILE and store the data in that table. (If the OUT command is omitted, the data will be stored in a system-generated table, and the user will be asked at the end of the session whether that table is to be kept.) Alternatively, the commands

```
RUN CITYQRY
OUT (SQL) CITYFILE
COPY
```

will create a SQL/DS table named CITYFILE and store the data there.

Query results can also be used as input to other AS tools such as Report, Draw, etc. (see Sections 20.3 and 20.4).

AS Language Queries

As stated in Section 20.1, the user can access SQL/DS using either AS commands or SQL statements. By way of example, we show an AS command version of the SQL query of Fig. 20.3:

```
IN (SQL) S
INCLUDE (SQL) SP(S#)
SEQUENCE CITY, S#, P#
VIEW CITY, S#, P#, QTY
```

The IN command identifies the SQL/DS suppliers table (table S) as the primary input table; the INCLUDE command joins the SQL/DS shipments table (table SP) to that primary table over matching supplier numbers; the SEQUENCE command defines the result row order; and the VIEW command defines the result columns and displays the result table.

Additional search conditions can be specified by means of the AS SELECT command (not the SQL SELECT statement!). For example, if we had specified

```
SELECT QTY > 300
```

between the INCLUDE and SEQUENCE commands (see above), the effect would have been to restrict the result to just those rows with a shipment quantity greater than 300. Alternatively, we could execute the IN–INCLUDE–SEQUENCE–VIEW statements as previously shown (to produce the result shown in Fig. 20.4), and then execute a SELECT and another VIEW—for example,

```
SELECT QTY > 300
VIEW S#, P#, QTY
```

—in which case the effect would be to produce a new set of output rows, derived from the previous output in accordance with the specified SELECT and VIEW statements.

Using AS commands instead of SQL statements does have a number of advantages:

1. The same commands can be used regardless of the type of table or file being accessed (SQL/DS, VSAM, etc.).

2. The commands can be entered directly into the command area (it is not necessary to create a command table).

3. The AS SELECT statement supports *data browsing*. That is, the user can issue one query, look at the result, issue a SELECT (and VIEW) to refine the result further, etc. SQL does not provide a comparable facility.

20.3   CREATING A REPORT

Reports are defined and created by means of the AS Report tool. The data to be reported on can be an existing AS or SQL/DS table (identified by an IN command), or it can be the result of an AS query (produced by a RUN command). The report format is defined via one of the following:

1. AS language editor Report statements (Command Mode)
2. The conversational Report facility (Conversational Mode)
3. The interactive Report facility (Interactive Mode)

We briefly consider each in turn.

Command Mode

The AS language editor is invoked via the REPORT command. Report statements are entered and modified in a manner similar to that discussed in Section 20.2 for the Query component. For example, if the command sequence

```
RUN CITYQRY
REPORT *,CITYREP
```

is issued, AS will run the query stored in CITYQRY (as discussed in the previous section), then create an output command table called CITYREP. The user can now define a report to be produced from the result of the query by entering Report language statements into the CITYREP table, using the AS editor. (Some examples of Report language statements are discussed in the next subsection below.) The report can then be generated and displayed at the terminal using the RUN command:

```
RUN CITYREP
```

Conversational Mode

The Conversational Mode of operation is invoked by the ?REPORT command. For example, the command

```
?REPORT CITYREP
```

will start a question and answer dialog about the format of the required report. When the dialog is complete, AS will create a command table called CITYREP containing the required Report language statements. Those statements can then be executed by means of the RUN command in the usual way; alternatively, the statements can be edited, using Command Mode, to create a more customized report definition (in other words, Conversational Mode provides an easy way of generating an initial report definition for subsequent tailoring).

Fig. 20.5 shows an example of the use of Conversational Mode to define a simple report using the data retrieved via the query of Fig. 20.3. We have requested a display title (note that the title will include the page number and the current date and time); we have also requested AS to calculate subtotals (for numeric fields) each time the CITY value changes. The resulting report is shown in Fig. 20.6.

```
APPLICATION SYSTEM                                25 Jul 87  07:57

AS Conversational Report

Enter display title.
Shipments by Supplier City
Which fields do you want displayed ?
CITY, S#, P#, QTY
Which field(s) should control sub-totalling ?
CITY
Do you want subtotals only ?
NO
Generating specifications.

   OUT    36  Lines  - Lang  File CITYREP




? RUN CITYREP
1 Help       2 Run       3              4 Print     5 Recall      6
Press ENTER to execute specifications, or give next command.
```

Fig. 20.5 Defining a report using Conversational Mode

```
Page    1                    Shipments by Supplier City        25 Jul 87  08:03

CITY           S#    P#         QTY

London         S1    P1         300
               S1    P2         200
               S1    P3         400
               S1    P4         200
               S1    P5         100
               S1    P6         100
               S4    P2         200
               S4    P4         300
               S4    P5         400
                               -------
London                         2200

Paris          S2    P1         300
               S2    P2         400
               S3    P2         200
                               -------
Paris                           900
                               =======
                               3100
```

Fig. 20.6 Formatted report for the query of Fig. 20.3

    The Report language statements created by AS in response to the dialog of Fig. 20.5 are shown in Fig. 20.7. The *format statements* F1, F2, etc., define the format of the report lines. When the report is run, the report lines will be filled with data and displayed at the terminal as directed by the Report language PRINT statements. Observe that those PRINT statements include references to the format statements; for example, line 00025 includes a reference to the format statement F7.

    Note: Output can be sent to an AS "center file" instead of to the terminal by replacing each PRINT statement by a CENTER statement (CENTER here meaning "DP Center"). Alternatively, the RUN command itself can specify that all PRINT statements are to be (logically) replaced by CENTER statements for the duration of this run only. For example:

```
RUN CITYREP,PRINT=CENTER
```

AS center files are printed using standard VM facilities.

    The reader is referred to the AS manuals for a more detailed discussion of AS Report statements.

```
REPORT CITYREP                    Origin 1                36 Lines

HEADING @PAGE                                               00001
  PRINT F(1,0,'WHITE'),@PAGE,'Shipments by Supplier City',@DATE,@RUN TI 00002
ME
  PRINT SKIP(1)                                            00003
  PRINT F(2,0,'GREEN')                                     00004
*                                                          00005
HEADING CITY,@PAGE                                         00006
  PRINT SKIP(1)                                            00007
  DEFINE !HEAD(A5)='PRINT'                                 00008
*                                                          00009
DETAIL                                                     00010
  IF !HEAD='PRINT'                                         00011
    LET !HEAD=' '                                          00012
    PRINT F(4),CITY,S#,P#,QTY                              00013
  IF NOT                                                   00014
    PRINT F(5)       ,S#,P#,QTY                            00015
*                                                          00016
TOTAL CITY                                                 00017
  PRINT F(6)                                               00018
  PRINT F(8),LAST(CITY),TOTAL(QTY)                         00019
*                                                          00020
TOTAL                                                      00021
  PRINT SKIP(1)                                            00022
  PRINT F(7)                                               00023
  PRINT F(8),' '         ,TOTAL(QTY)                       00024
  PRINT F(7)                                               00025
*                                                          00026
TOTAL @END OF PAGE                                         00027
  PRINT SKIP(-1)                                           00028
*                                                          00029
F1: Page ####              &&&&&&&&&&&&&&&&&&&&&&&&&&     DD MMM YY 00030
  #####
F2:CITY              S#     P#     QTY                     00031
F4:&&&&&&&&&&&&&&& &&&&&& &&&&&& &&&&&&                    00032
F5:              &&&&&& &&&&&& &&&&&&                      00033
F6:                        -------                         00034
F7:                        =======                         00035
F8:&&&&&&&&&&&&&&&           &&&&&&&                       00036
                                                          00037
1          2 Run       3 End       4 Hardcopy  5 Recall    6 Origin
7 Up       8 Down      9 Switch   10 Left     11 Right    12 Command
```

Fig. 20.7 Generated report statements

Interactive Mode

Interactive Mode is a more powerful alternative to Conversational Mode. It allows many more formatting options and will frequently eliminate the need to use Report language statements entirely. As in Conversational

Mode, a command table is generated to allow the user to modify the generated Report statements should such modification be required.

The user selects full-screen mode by issuing the command

```
ENVIRONMENT REPORT(INTERACTIVE)
```

before entering the REPORT command. A sample screen from Interactive Mode is shown in Fig. 20.8.

The big advantage of Interactive Mode is that users immediately see the effects of their actions. When the Report tool is invoked, the input data is displayed at the terminal. Pressing PF key 6 will display an option list, which can be used to display option windows to control the format of the report. Fig. 20.8 shows a *Column Detail* window, which can be used to modify such things as the column heading and width. In the example, we assume that a number of such modifications have already been made (compare the displayed report, partially visible behind the Column Detail window, with the earlier version shown in Fig. 20.6).

The option windows permit the user to specify:

- the overall layout and structure of each page

- the content and position of the top and bottom titles

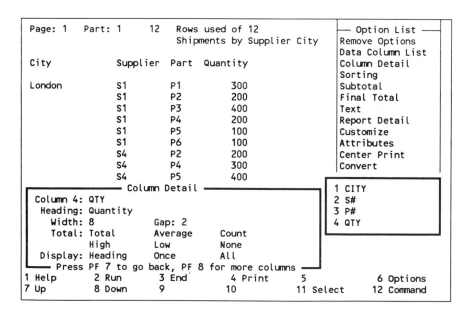

Fig. 20.8 Defining a report using Interactive Mode

- the columns required, their headings, width, and layout
- how data is to be totaled, subtotaled, and ordered
- the format, color, and font of any report component
- whether the report is to be printed on a system printer

More detailed formatting, to add procedural logic, for example, can be done by editing the generated command table. Again, the reader is referred to the AS manuals for further information.

20.4   CREATING A CHART

Section 20.3 explained what is involved in creating an AS report. Another way of presenting data is to use the AS Draw tool to create a chart or graph. The Draw tool uses the Presentation Graphics Facility (PGF) of the IBM Graphic Data Display Manager (GDDM) to display charts. The chart types supported by AS are TOWER, MAP, RADAR, PIE, SCATTER, LINE, SURFACE, HISTOGRAM, and MIXED (as with the analogous feature of QMF, these names are supposed to be self-explanatory). *Note:* The Interactive Chart Utility (ICU) of GDDM can also be used to construct and display charts. It is invoked using the AS ICU command. However, we do not discuss this latter facility here; instead, we restrict our attention to the AS Draw tool specifically.

Fig. 20.9 shows the Draw tool primary screen, which is displayed by means of the AS DRAW command. The user must enter the names of the input and output specification tables. These tables are a special type of command table used to store chart specifications; they cannot be edited by the AS language editor, but can be modified by the Draw tool. Other information entered on the primary screen includes the type of chart being produced—a bar chart (histogram) in our example—and the information (X- and Y-variables) to be plotted on the chart. Once this data has been entered, a "default chart" can be displayed by pressing PF key 2.

The default chart can be tailored using option windows in a manner similar to that discussed in Section 20.3 for tailoring AS reports (Interactive Mode). The option list is displayed by pressing PF key 6. Various option windows can then be selected to do the tailoring. Fig. 20.9 shows an example of a *Chart Options* window, which has been used to modify the spacing of the bars in the chart and to label the bars with Y-variable values. The resulting chart is shown in Fig. 20.10. This chart can be saved by first pressing the Enter key to display the PF key legends and then pressing PF key 5. Chart output is stored in AS Graphics Data Format (GDF) tables. These tables can be displayed using the AS REVIEW command. Chart output can also be directed to a printer by pressing PF key 4.

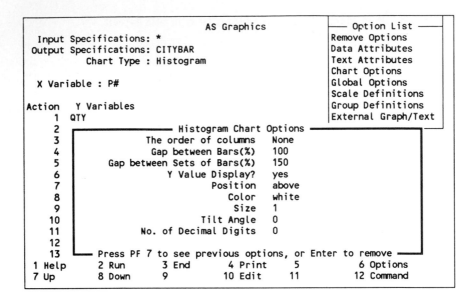

Fig. 20.9 Defining a bar chart

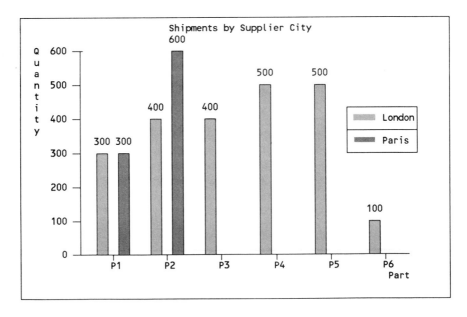

Fig. 20.10 Sample bar chart

20.5 USING SQL STATEMENTS OTHER THAN SELECT

We have seen in Section 20.2 that the AS Query tool can be used to enter and execute SQL SELECT statements. For SQL statements other than SELECT, AS provides the SQL command. This command supports the use of SQL data modification, data definition, and authorization definition statements.

There are three ways to enter SQL statements with the SQL command:

1. Using the AS command screen

   If the SQL command is entered without any parameters, an empty screen is displayed (the AS command screen), which can be used to enter a single SQL statement. Once the statement has been entered, pressing PF key 3 will pass it to SQL/DS for execution.

2. From the AS command line

   In this mode the user types in the SQL statement as a parameter of the SQL command. The statement is executed immediately. To create an index on column S# of the SQL/DS shipments table (table SP), for example, we could enter

   ```
   SQL CREATE INDEX XSPS ON SP ( S# )
   ```

   on the AS command line.

3. From an AS procedure

   AS commands can be embedded in AS procedures. Therefore, any SQL command (and hence any SQL statement supported by AS) can be included in such a procedure. Procedures are discussed in more detail in the next section.

AS provides several commands of its own that can be used in place of SQL statements. We have already seen (in Section 20.2) how the OUT and COPY commands can be used to create and populate a SQL/DS table. A brief summary of the AS commands that generate SQL statements other than SELECT is presented below (the SQL statements generated are also shown in each case):

- SHARE   —   grant authority (GRANT)
- WITHDRAW   —   remove authority (REVOKE)
- OUT/COPY   —   create and populate a table (CREATE TABLE plus INSERT . . . SELECT)
- CLEAR   —   delete all rows (DELETE)

- PURGE   — delete a table (DROP)
- UPDATE   — insert, update, or delete data (see below)

The commands are all basically self-explanatory, except for the last one, UPDATE. The UPDATE command invokes the Update tool. We explain that tool by means of an example. Suppose we have an AS table SNEW containing a set of new supplier rows to be added to the SQL/DS suppliers table (table S). Suppose also that an AS command table called UPDSTMT already exists, containing Update language statements that specify exactly how the AS table SNEW is to be used to update the SQL/DS table S (see below for more details). That table will have been created via the UPDATE command, which invokes the AS editor and permits the creation and/or modification of Update language statements. Now consider the following AS commands:

```
IN (SQL) S, SNEW
MERGE S#
OUT (SQL) S
RUN UPDSTMT
```

These four AS commands have the following effect:

- The IN command specifies the SQL/DS table to be updated (table S) and the table that contains the updating information (SNEW). *Note:* SNEW is an AS table in our example, but in general it too could be a SQL/DS table.
- The MERGE command is used to pair the rows of the two tables based on matching values of column S.S# and column SNEW.S#.
- The OUT command indicates where the output is to be written.
- Finally, the RUN command causes the Update statements in the command table UPDSTMT to be executed. The effect is as follows:
  - AS reads each row of the SNEW table and uses it to access the S table.
  - For each SNEW row, if a match is found, it sets a special variable called @MATCH; if not, it sets a variable called @DETAIL.
  - These variables will be used in Update statements in the UPDSTMT command table to control the update process. For example, the statement

```
WHEN @MATCH
     PRINT 'Error :', S#, ' supplier already exists'
```

tests the variable @MATCH; if it is set, the statement then displays an error message informing the user that the supplier number of the SNEW row already exists in the suppliers table.

Update language statements can also be used to perform UPDATE and DELETE operations. In this case, the table that contains the updating information must include a column whose values indicate the rows to be UPDATEd or DELETEd. This column is referenced by Update language statements to control the UPDATE or DELETE operation. The reader is referred to the AS manuals for a more detailed discussion of the Update language.

20.6   PROCEDURES

A procedure—more precisely, a procedure table—consists of a named set of *generalized* AS commands (as opposed to the specialized AS commands used with each individual AS tool; refer back to Section 20.1 if you need to refresh your memory regarding the distinction between the two). Such procedures can be invoked by means of the AS RUN command. In this section we introduce the basic ideas of AS procedures; the next section then discusses some of the more sophisticated aspects of this facility.

Like other command tables, procedures are created using the AS language editor. To create a procedure called CITYPROC, for example, the user would enter the command

```
PROCEDURE *,CITYPROC
```

The statements constituting the procedure can now be created, using the AS editor. Here is a simple example:

```
/* CITYPROC procedure
*
* run the query called CITYQRY
RUN CITYQRY
*
* run the report called CITYREP
* redirect the output to an AS print file
RUN CITYREP,PRINT=CENTER
*
/* end of CITYPROC
```

Note: All lines in this procedure except the two RUN commands are comment lines. Comments prefixed by "*" are displayed at the terminal when the procedure is executed, comments prefixed by "/*" are not.

20.7   APPLICATION SUPPORT FACILITIES

In addition to its standard end-user tools, AS provides a set of *application support facilities* for extending its capabilities in a variety of ways:

- *AS Procedures:* The AS procedure language provides facilities for building complex applications.

- *Image Tool:* The Image tool is used to build tailored screens for data entry and display.
- *Edit Tool:* The Edit tool provides statements to validate data read from terminals and input tables.
- *Command Interface:* The command interface allows application programs to invoke AS facilities.

We briefly describe each of these facilities in turn.

AS Procedures

The previous section showed how simple AS procedures can be created and executed. More complex procedures can be created using the full AS procedure language (which is in effect a full-function programming language). Facilities provided include:

- arithmetic and logical expressions
- constants
- user and system variables
- branching and looping
- nested procedures
- arguments and parameters
- screen displays
- prompting
- PF key definition

Image Tool

Data entry screens are built using the Image tool. As with most AS tools, Image statements are entered using the language editor, invoked in this case by the IMAGE command. Facilities are provided to support the definition of screen attributes, field data types and lengths, default values, validity checks, and so forth, for data entered via the screen. *Note:* The Edit tool can be used to perform more extensive data validation (see below).

Edit Tool

The Edit tool uses procedural language statements for performing data validation checking. These checks can be made against data retrieved from both AS and SQL/DS input tables, also against data entered using AS Image screens. The validated data is stored in an AS or SQL/DS output table. The Edit tool is invoked using the EDIT command.

Command Interface

The AS command interface permits an application program to call AS to perform some AS operation and return the result(s) to the application. Such applications can be written in a conventional programming language such as COBOL or PL/I or in the CMS REXX command language.

20.8 INTERFACING TO OTHER PRODUCTS

In this section, we take a brief look at how AS can interface to three specific IBM products:

- Data Extract (DXT)
- Query Management Facility (QMF)
- Interactive System Productivity Facility (ISPF)

We also briefly describe the AS EXPORT and IMPORT commands, which can be used to exchange data between AS systems and between AS and other products.

Accessing DXT

The AS facilities for interfacing with DXT directly parallel the analogous QMF facilities (see Section 19.7). Thus, the DXT end-user dialogs, which support the definition, modification, and submission of data extract requests, can be invoked from AS using the AS EXTRACT command (directly comparable to the QMF EXTRACT command). There are two ways of coding this command:

1. If the command is entered with no operands, the DXT end-user dialogs menu will be displayed. The user can then interactively create and/or edit a DXT request.

2. Alternatively, the command can include the name of an existing DXT extract request. For example, the command

   ```
   EXTRACT PART1
   ```

   will cause DXT to submit the extract request called PART1.

Using QMF

As explained in Chapter 18 (and amplified in Chapter 19), QMF is an end-user query and report writing tool for the SQL/DS and DB2 environments. The report-writing facilities of QMF are quite user-friendly but are not as sophisticated as those of AS. There may therefore be situations where the user wants to use QMF to do some initial work and then transfer the results into AS for more detailed processing. The AS QMF command is intended to support this style of operation. It uses the QMF Command Interface (see Section 19.6) to pass a command to QMF for execution. For example, the AS command

```
QMF RUN CITYQUERY
```

will request QMF to execute a QMF query named CITYQUERY.

The procedure for executing QMF commands and moving result data from QMF to AS is as follows:

1. Start QMF.
2. Use the QMF CMS command to start AS under QMF.
3. Execute the QMF command from AS to produce the required data—for example:

```
QMF RUN CITYQUERY
```

   QMF will execute the requested operation (RUN CITYQUERY in the example), but will not display the results at the terminal. Instead, it will hold the data in a QMF work area.
4. When QMF has completed execution of the command, AS will tell the user if the command ran successfully or not. If it failed, appropriate diagnostic information will be displayed at the terminal.
5. Execute the QMF command from AS to export the data from the QMF work area to an IXF file (see Section 18.4 for a brief discussion of IXF)—for example:

```
QMF EXPORT DATA TO TEMP DATA A (DATA FORMAT = IXF,
                                OUTPUT MODE = BINARY)
```

6. Execute an AS IMPORT command to import the IXF file into an AS data table:

```
IMPORT TEMP DATA A, FORMAT(IXF), RENAME (ASDATA)
```

   The AS data table named ASDATA can now be used by any of the normal AS application tools.

The foregoing procedure may appear somewhat complex; in practice, however, most of the required AS commands could be stored in an AS command table and invoked via a single AS RUN command. Also, we assumed above that the entire procedure had to be performed from AS, and so made use of the AS QMF command; in practice, again, the user may well choose to perform Steps 3 and 5 in QMF, before invoking AS using the command shown above as Step 2.

Using ISPF

ISPF is a dialog manager for the CMS environment. If AS is started from ISPF, the AS user can invoke any ISPF dialog (using ISPEXEC), set and retrieve ISPF dialog variables, and use ISPF tables (using the AS IN and OUT commands).

IMPORT and EXPORT Commands

AS supports the export and import of IXF files, also files in AS "transportable format." For an illustration of the IXF case, see the discussion above of moving data from QMF into AS. AS transportable format is used to transfer information between AS systems. To export the AS table CITYDATA into a file named "CITYTEMP DATA A," the following command could be used:

```
EXPORT CITYDATA, FILE(CITYTEMP DATA A) FORMAT(ASTRAN)
```

The keyword ASTRAN indicates that the exported file is to be in AS transportable format (the keyword IXF could be used instead to create a file in IXF format). The ASTRAN-format CITYTEMP file can then be reimported using the command:

```
IMPORT CITYTEMP DATA A, REPLACE, FORMAT(ASTRAN), RENAME(CITYDATA)
```

20.9 ADDITIONAL AS FACILITIES

As indicated in Section 20.1, AS provides an extensive set of additional facilities to assist with the following functions:

- data analysis and statistics
- business planning
- project management
- text processing
- application preparation

Each of these facilities is briefly described below.

Data Analysis and Statistics

SQL aggregate functions (SUM, AVG, etc.) can be used to perform very simple statistical analysis of data in SQL/DS tables. AS augments those functions with its Tabulate and Statistics tools.

1. The Tabulate tool is invoked by the TABULATE command. It performs various arithmetic functions in one, two, or three dimensions (e.g., it could analyze the distribution of parts by supplier city). The functions supported are total, percentage, average, low, high, and count.

2. The Statistics tool is invoked by the STATISTICS command. It provides a broad range of statistical and forecasting functions, including:

   - descriptive statistics
   - correlations
   - regression
   - time series analysis
   - parametric and nonparametric statistics
   - analysis of variance
   - cluster analysis
   - component analysis

   The tool can operate in Command, Conversational, and Interactive Mode. An interface is provided to the AS Draw tool for displaying results, doing curve-fitting, etc. AS or SQL/DS tables can be used for both input and output to the Statistics tool. Results from the analysis can also be used as input to other AS tools.

Business Planning

The AS business planning facility provides capabilities similar to those provided by PC spreadsheet tools. Models are constructed using AS Model language statements or by the Interactive Mode of operation similar to that available with the AS Report and Chart tools. Data entered into such models can be supplied from the terminal, read from an AS or SQL/DS table, or explicitly defined in the model. Output can be stored in an AS or SQL/DS table for use by other AS tools. There is also a direct linkage into the AS Chart tool.

Project Management

Project planning is performed using the AS Network and Project Management Cost tools. These tools can handle numerous planning functions, in-

cluding time and risk analysis, progress reporting, project costing, and resource allocation. The project plan can be displayed as an arrow diagram
or a precedence diagram. Both AS and SQL/DS tables can be used for
input and output.

Text Processing

AS provides the Memo and Compose tools for text processing. The Memo
tool is intended for small documents such as letters and memos. Document
formatting is done using the WYSIWYG ("What You See Is What You
Get") mode of operation common in most PC word processors. Formatting
parameters, such as page width, color attributes, font type, etc., can be
changed dynamically at any time. AS tables can also be used to substitute
data into memo variables.

 Longer and more complex documents can be created using the Compose tool. This tool uses language statements similar to those of IBM's Document Composition Facility (DCF). It supports the building of indexes and
tables of contents, box drawing, figure lists, conditional processing, and so
forth. Data from AS tables and tools can also be included in a document.

Application Preparation

The Application Preparation Facility (APF) is a simple application generator—i.e., it is a menu-driven tool that allows inexperienced users to build
simple AS applications without having to learn AS commands. It uses a
full-screen interface to prompt the user for the necessary application specifications: the screens to be used (e.g., for data entry), the tables to be accessed, the reports and charts to be produced, etc. However, the generated
application cannot use the AS decision support facilities (statistics, business
planning, etc.) discussed earlier in this section.

Cross System Product

21.1 INTRODUCTION

Cross System Product (CSP) consists of a set of DP professional tools for interactive application development and execution. It is called *Cross System Product* because it permits applications to be developed in one environment for execution in another; for example, a CSP SQL/DS application could be developed under VM/CMS and executed under VSE with CICS. The environments supported by CSP are MVS (CICS, TSO), VM/CMS, and VSE (CICS), also PC/DOS (for application execution only, not for application development).

CSP is really several products, not just one:

- Cross System Product/Application Development (CSP/AD)
- Cross System Product/Application Execution (CSP/AE)

- EZ-PREP and EZ-RUN
- Cross System Product/Query (CSP/Q)

CSP applications are developed and tested using CSP/AD, and then executed under CSP/AE (see Fig. 21.1). Applications (more accurately, application *specifications*) are stored during development in a file called the *Member Specification Library* (MSL), which can be thought of as a data dictionary for CSP. When the application has been fully developed, tested, and debugged, it must be "generated" for use in the relevant target environment. The generated form of the application is stored in another file called the *Application Load File* (ALF). Export and import utilities exist to migrate MSL and ALF files from one CSP environment to another.

The EZ-PREP and EZ-RUN products support the generation and execution (but not development) of CSP applications for use on IBM PCs. Development of such applications must have been performed previously using CSP/AD in one of the mainframe environments mentioned above.

The last product in the set, CSP/Q, is a query and report-writing tool for VSAM and CMS data. Definitions of the files to be queried are kept in CSP/AD libraries. Queries are coded using language statements whose syntax is similar to that of SELECT in SQL; they can be saved for later reuse.

CSP applications can access a variety of different databases and files—SQL/DS databases, VSAM files, and so forth. However, EZ-PREP, EZ-RUN, and CSP/Q do not support SQL/DS; we will therefore make no further mention of those components in this book, but will instead concentrate on the use of CSP/AD and CSP/AE specifically.

21.2 DEVELOPING CSP APPLICATIONS

CSP applications are built and tested using CSP/AD, which supports both DB2 and SQL/DS. Creating an application for DB2 is very similar to creating one for SQL/DS; in fact, an application can be built and tested under SQL/DS (e.g., using VM/CMS) for execution under DB2 and vice versa. Fig. 21.2 illustrates the main components of a CSP application, namely record, map, and process definitions. *Note:* Each component has its own name and is stored as a separate member in the Member Specification Library.

- *Record definitions* specify the data to be retrieved and manipulated by the application. A record definition for processing SQL/DS data consists of fields from one or more SQL/DS tables and is defined using CSP/AD's Record Definition screens. Existing SQL/DS definitions (for both base tables and views) can be retrieved from the SQL/DS catalog to help with the record definition process.

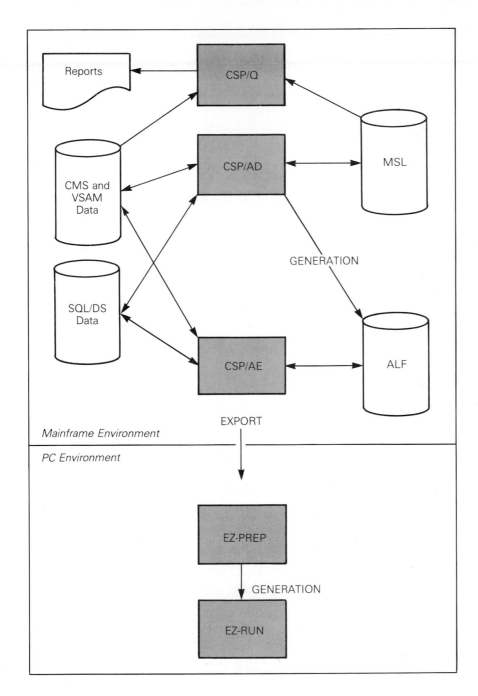

Fig. 21.1 CSP structure

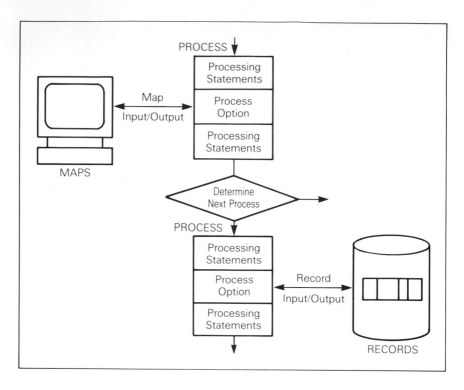

Fig. 21.2 CSP application components

- *Map definitions* specify the screen and printer formats to be used by the application. The CSP/AD *screen painter* provides a set of Map Definition screens for defining such formats and for defining data "edit rules." Edit rules are used to validate data entered by the application user or to format data displayed to the application user (such data will be entered or displayed at execution time via the maps). For example, we might define a rule to verify that any value entered for a shipment quantity is greater than 99 (say).

- *Process definitions* specify the application processing logic. Among other things, they control the display of maps and the reading and writing of records. Processes are defined by means of the CSP/AD Application Definition and Application Process Definition screens. A process definition consists of:

  - A *process option,* which specifies the major task (data access or map display) to be performed by the process, and

- A set of *processing statements,* which perform computations, control the execution flow from one process to the next, etc.

- CSP/AD provides several process options for operating on SQL/DS data (most of which correspond to SQL operations in a fairly obvious manner). It also provides a wide range of processing statements.

Once the application definition is complete, testing can begin. During testing, access to SQL/DS data is performed using dynamic SQL or, optionally, extended dynamic SQL (see Chapter 15). Trace information about the processing of SQL statements can be displayed to the application developer for debugging purposes.

When the application has been fully tested and debugged, it can be generated for execution under CSP/AE. At this time, the developer should decide whether the application is to execute in "dynamic mode" or "extended dynamic mode" (i.e., whether the application is to use dynamic SQL or extended dynamic SQL); the latter is more efficient, but requires an access module to be created and saved. Creating an access module (if required) can be done either during the generation process or at a later time by means of a CSP utility. When generation is complete (and the access module created, if necessary), the application is ready for execution under CSP/AE (except that, if the CSP/AD and CSP/AE operating environments are not the same, utilities will have to be used to move the generated application to the target system).

We have now summarized all of the major tasks involved in developing CSP applications. Before we move on to discuss those tasks in detail, we briefly describe the layout of CSP/AD screens and indicate what is involved in communicating with CSP/AD via such screens. The Record Definition screen (see Fig. 21.3 for an example) can be regarded as typical of CSP/AD screens in general, and we will use it as the basis for our discussion.

The various parts of the screen have the following meanings and uses.

- Line 1 is the title line.

- Line 2 is used for messages from CSP/AD (diagnostics, etc.).

- Line 3 is the *command line* (strictly, *sub*command line). This is where the application developer enters CSP/AD commands to control the CSP/AD session. The CANCEL command, for example, cancels the current function, and the EXIT command exits from the current function.

- Line 4 specifies the PF (and other) keys that can be used to exit from the current display.

```
EZEM11                        RECORD DEFINITION
EZE000087I New definition being created
==>
                PF3 = Exit  (or continue if new definition)
                      Record Name = SHIPREC
      ..................... RECORD SPECIFICATION ...........................

   Organization  => 7
     1  Indexed
     2  Relative
     3  Serial              Default Key Item        =>
     4  Working Storage
     5  Redefined Record
     6  DL/I Segment
     7  SQL Row             Alternate Specification for =>


   ....Total Lines 00003  ..SQL Table Names(s)............................
      CREATOR ID:        TABLE NAME:     TABLE LABEL:
   ***                      TOP OF LIST
   001 cjdate             s               T1
   002 cjdate             sp              T2
   003 cjdate             p               T3
   ***                      END OF LIST
```

Fig. 21.3 Sample CSP/AD Record Definition screen

- Line 5 includes an identification of the object defined via the rest of the screen (where applicable).

- The rest of the screen is divided into a *fixed area* and a *scrollable area* (in general, though not all screens have both). Generally speaking, the fixed area is used to respond to CSP/AD prompts, and the scrollable area (from "TOP OF LIST" to "BOTTOM OF LIST") is used for entering record, map, and process definitions (etc.). The CSP/AD editor supports standard line-oriented editing commands for editing text within this latter area. The editor is context-sensitive, in that it recognizes invalid processing statements, unclosed IF statements, etc.

We now proceed to show what is involved in using CSP to build a SHIPMENT application that will use the suppliers-and-parts database to display information about part shipments for a given supplier. The input to the application is a supplier number; the output consists of the supplier number and city, plus part number, part city, and shipment quantity for all parts supplied by that supplier. We begin by examining the record definition for this application (Section 21.3).

21.3 RECORD DEFINITION

The process of defining a CSP application starts with the CSP/AD *Facility Selection* screen (not illustrated). Selecting option 2 ("Definition") on that screen brings us to the *Definition* screen (Fig. 21.4). That screen in turn permits us to invoke specific screens to define the various components—records, maps, and processes—that go to make up a CSP application. The normal procedure is to define the records first, then the maps, and finally the processes. In our example, therefore, we begin by selecting option 1 ("Record") on the Definition screen and entering a name, say SHIPREC, for the record we intend to define. This option leads us to the Record Definition screen already discussed briefly in the previous section (refer back to Fig. 21.3).

As indicated at the end of the previous section, the SHIPMENT application needs data from all three of the database tables S, SP, and P (S#, P#, and QTY from SP, S.CITY from S, and P.CITY from P). On the Record Definition screen, therefore, we specify option 7 ("SQL Row"), and enter the qualified names of these three tables (owner name plus table name) in the scrollable area created by selecting that option. The "labels" T1, T2,

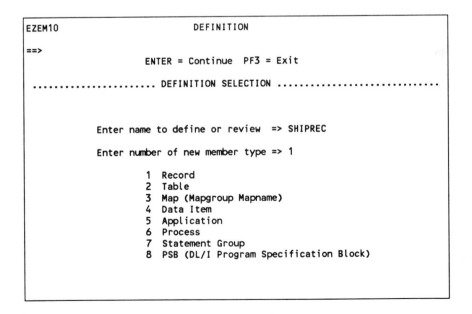

```
EZEM10                        DEFINITION
==>
                    ENTER = Continue   PF3 = Exit

  .................... DEFINITION SELECTION ........................


          Enter name to define or review  => SHIPREC

          Enter number of new member type => 1

                    1  Record
                    2  Table
                    3  Map (Mapgroup Mapname)
                    4  Data Item
                    5  Application
                    6  Process
                    7  Statement Group
                    8  PSB (DL/I Program Specification Block)
```

Fig. 21.4 CSP/AD Definition screen

and T3 are generated automatically by CSP/AD; references to the tables on subsequent screens (e.g., in generated SQL statements) will use these unique labels instead of the qualified names.

One other entry on the Record Definition screen is relevant to SQL/DS applications (in general, though we do not use it in our example)— "Default Key Item." From the entries on the Record Definition screen, CSP/AD builds a set of SQL statements for accessing the required data. The field name specified in the Default Key Item entry (if any) is used to build a default search condition for those statements. We did not specify any such field name in our example because the search condition will be defined explicitly in a later stage of the record definition process (see below).

Once the required tables have been specified via the Record Definition screen, CSP/AD displays the SQL Row Definition screen (Fig. 21.5). This screen allows the developer to indicate which specific fields of those tables are needed. Most of the information displayed on this screen is obtained by CSP from the SQL/DS catalog. The READ ONLY specification is set to YES for every field, because multiple tables are involved (SHIPREC involves a join) and SQL/DS does not permit joins to be updated. *Note:* CSP/AD automatically creates a set of host variables with the same names as the DB2 fields (S#, SNAME, etc.). These variables are used in (e.g.) INTO clauses in generated SQL SELECT statements.

The following editing has been performed in Fig. 21.5:

- The "d" line editor command has been used to remove the fields not required for SHIPREC.

- The field names for S.CITY and P.CITY have been changed to SCITY and PCITY, respectively, to avoid ambiguity.

The developer is free to make other changes on the Row Definition screen—fields can be added or deleted, field definitions can be modified, and so forth. To ensure that everything matches the appropriate SQL/DS definitions, PF key 4 can be pressed to request a comparison with the SQL/DS catalog entries. Any discrepancies found will be displayed on a separate screen.

Finally, CSP/AD needs to know the SQL SELECT statement to be used to retrieve SHIPREC data from the database. This information is specified by means of the *SQL Row Record Definition* screen (see Fig. 21.6). CSP/AD generates a candidate SQL statement automatically, with appropriate SELECT and FROM clauses; if SHIPREC had been drawn from a single underlying table and if we had supplied an entry for the "Default Key Item" on the Record Definition screen, CSP/AD would also generate an appropriate WHERE clause. As it is, however, SHIPREC involves

```
EZEM15                    SQL ROW DEFINITION

==>
  PF3 = Exit   PF4 = SQL Compare   PF10 = Scroll Left    PF11=Scroll Right
                            Record Name = SHIPREC
Total lines 0012 ........ DATA ITEM DEFINITION .........................

*** NAME       TYPE  LENGTH DEC BYTES  READ SQL COLUMN NAME
***                                    ONLY
***                      TOP OF LIST
001 S#         CHA   00005     00005   YES  T1.S#
d02 SNAME      CHA   00020     00020   YES  T1.SNAME
d03 STATUS     BIN   00004     00002   YES  T1.STATUS
004 scity      CHA   00015     00015   YES  T1.CITY
d05 S#         CHA   00005     00005   YES  T2.S#
d06 P#         CHA   00005     00005   YES  T2.P#
007 QTY        BIN   00009     00004   YES  T2.QTY
008 P#         CHA   00006     00006   YES  T3.P#
d09 PNAME      CHA   00020     00020   YES  T3.PNAME
d10 COLOR      CHA   00006     00006   YES  T3.COLOR
d11 WEIGHT     BIN   00004     00002   YES  T3.WEIGHT
012 pcity      CHA   00015     00015   YES  T3.CITY
***                      END OF LIST
```

Fig. 21.5 CSP/AD SQL Row Definition screen

```
EZEM16              SQL ROW RECORD DEFINITION
EZE00642I SQL syntax check has completed successfully
==>
 PF3 = File and exit PF4 = Reset to default statement PF5 = SQL syntax check
 Record  = SHIPREC
                                    Modified clause = YES
Total lines 0011 .... DEFAULT SELECTION CONDITIONS DEFINITION ..............

***                      TOP OF LIST
*** SELECT
***    T1.S#, T1.CITY,
***    T2.QTY,
***    T3.P#, T3.CITY
*** FROM
***    cjdate.s T1,
***    cjdate.sp T2,
***    cjdate.p T3
*** WHERE
010    t1.s# = t2.s# and
011    t2.p# = t3.p#
***                      END OF LIST
```

Fig. 21.6 CSP/AD SQL Row Record Definition screen

a join, and therefore we must enter the WHERE condition (the *selection condition*) explicitly. In the example, we have specified the "obvious" join of tables S, SP, and P over supplier numbers and part numbers.

21.4 MAP DEFINITION

Note: Maps in CSP have little to do with SQL/DS per se—they are concerned with operations on the terminal, not operations on the database. We therefore present only a very brief overview of the map definition process.

Maps provide the medium of communication between the CSP application and the user of that application (i.e., the end-user). They permit

(a) the application to display information to the end-user (typically information retrieved from the database), and

(b) the end-user to submit information to the application (typically information to be used for updating the database or for controlling retrieval from the database).

All the maps used in a given application are considered to belong to the same *mapgroup*. We will assume that the maps in our SHIPMENT example are called SHIP001, SHIP002, etc., and that together they constitute a mapgroup called SHIP. SHIP001 will be used to request a supplier number from the user; SHIP002 will be used to display corresponding output information back to the user. Let us consider what is involved in defining one of these maps, say SHIP002. We go through the following steps:

■   Starting—as always—with the CSP/AD *Definition* screen (refer back to Fig. 21.4), we select option 3 ("Map"), specifying mapgroup SHIP and map SHIP002.

■   We define the device or devices to be used to display the map on the *Map Definition–Device Selection* screen (not illustrated).

■   We define the size of the map and its position on the display using the *Map Definition–Map Specification* screen (not illustrated).

■   We use a series of *Map Definition* screens to define the map appearance, map variables, and associated edit rules (if any). The rest of this section describes the use of these Map Definition screens in more detail. For the sake of the example, we assume that the map we are defining (SHIP002) is to appear as shown in Fig. 21.7.

To define the SHIP002 layout, we use the CSP/AD screen painter and the Map Definition screen shown in Fig. 21.8. *Note:* The fields that make up a map are divided into constant fields and variable fields. Constant fields contain fixed text data; variable fields contain data that can be modified by

```
                    Shipment Information


        Supplier:                    Supplier City:

        Part:                        Part City:

        Quantity:
```

Fig. 21.7 Map SHIP002

```
EZEM22                      MAP DEFINITION

==>
                PF3 = Exit (or continue if new definition)
Total positions 079      Map Name = SHIP SHIP002      Positions 001 to 079
Total lines     024 ...       C(#) V(~) S(/)      ... Lines     001 to 014


                      Shipment Information


      #Supplier:~    #              #Supplier City:~           #

      #Part:   ~     #                #Part City:~             #

      #Quantity: ~   #

   ~                                                           #
```

Fig. 21.8 CSP/AD Map Definition: using the screen painter

the user or by the application. Fields are delimited in the map definition by special code or attribute bytes, which indicate properties of the field such as color, brightness, whether constant or variable, etc.

We explain Fig. 21.8 as follows.

- The application developer has entered the values for constant fields (the "Shipment Information" heading, etc.) and has used the "#" code to mark the position of those fields.

- The developer has also used the "~" code* to mark the position of variable fields (to be used for data entry and display).

A code of "/" can also be used to left or right justify or center text on the map. Various screen painter commands can be entered on the subcommand line (Line 3 on the screen) to specify field attributes (color, protection, brightness, etc.), field positioning, text copying and modification, and so forth. For example, the screen painter command TEST displays (the current version of) the map as it would appear during execution.

Having defined the map layout, the developer must now specify names for the variable fields so that they can be referenced from within the application (see Fig. 21.9). CSP/AD automatically numbers each variable field and displays an area for the developer to assign names corresponding to those numbers. In our example, we have specified field names MSNO, MSCITY, . . ., and MQTY (respectively) for the five variable fields labeled Supplier, Supplier City, . . ., and Quantity on the map. (The sixth field, EZEMSG, allows the application to display messages to the application user.)

Finally, the developer can specify edit rules for variable fields, using the screen shown in Fig. 21.10. Such rules are used to constrain the set of values that can legally be entered by the end-user and to control the format of values that are displayed to the end-user. Examples are shown in Fig. 21.10. A detailed discussion of all possible edit rule options is beyond the scope of this book, but most of them should be self-explanatory.

21.5 PROCESS DEFINITION

As explained in Section 21.2, a CSP application contains one or more named processes (refer to Fig. 21.11). The processes define the processing logic for the application. Processing logic involves displaying maps, reading

---

*We remind the reader that in this book we use the tilde (~) in place of the PL/I-style "not" symbol, for typographic reasons.

```
EZEM24                     MAP DEFINITION


==>
                 PF3 = Exit (or continue if new definition)
0001 <= Number of first field to name        Map Name = SHIP SHIP002
.................... VARIABLE FIELD NAMING .........................
     NAME                      NAME                         NAME
  1  MSNO                   2  MSCITY                   3   MPNO
  4  MPCITY                 5  MQTY                     6   EZEMSG

Total positions 079                    Positions 001 to 079
Total lines     024 ........................... Lines    007 to 014
      Supplier: 1               Supplier City: 2

      Part:    3               Part City: 4

      Quantity: 5


6


```

Fig. 21.9 CSP/AD Map Definition: variable field naming

```
EZEM26                     MAP DEFINITION


==>
      ENTER = Edit changes ( or go to next variable field)   PF3 = Exit
  Field Name = MQTY      Map Name = SHIP SHIP002      Occurs =   Length = 4
  .................... VARIABLE FIELD EDIT DEFINITION ....................
  Data Type        => NUM       Description => number of parts shipped
   Justify         => LEF  Decimal Positions=>     Sign(NO,TRA,LEA) => NO
  Fill Character   =>       Zero Edit       => NO  Numeric Separator=> NO
  Fold             => NO   Currency Symbol  => NO  Date Edit(1->11) =>
                                                   Edit Error Message Numbers:
  Input Required   => NO                           Input Required Error=>
  Edit Routine     =>                              Edit Routine Error  =>
  Minimum Input    =>                              Minimum Input Error =>
  Minimum Value    =>                              Value Error         =>
  Maximum Value    =>                              Data Type Error     =>
Total positions 079                            Positions 001 to 079
Total lines     024 ........................... Lines    001 to 015

      Supplier: _____           Supplier City: _____

      Part:    _____           Part City: _____

      Quantity: ****
```

Fig. 21.10 CSP/AD Map Definition: variable field edit definition

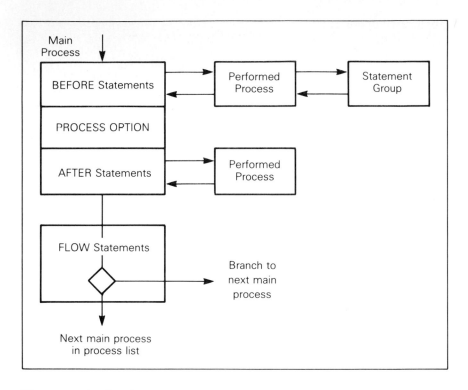

Fig. 21.11 Application process structure

and writing database data, performing computational operations, etc. A process consists of:

(a) A single *process option,* which performs some specific task, typically involving a CSP record (database access) or a CSP map (terminal I/O); together with

(b) Zero or more *processing statements,* which perform various computational or flow-of-control functions.

Processing statements can appear *before* or *after* a process option (or both) and/or in a *flow section.* Statements appearing before the process option are typically used to clear fields on a map, or to specify data to be read from the database. Statements appearing after the process option are typically used to check data entered by the user, or to check return codes after performing database access. Statements appearing in a flow section are used to control the execution flow between the main processes of an application. *Note:* A main process can also invoke other processes by means of the PERFORM statement (see Fig. 21.11); a PERFORMed process can include BEFORE and AFTER statements, but no FLOW statements.

Processing statements can also be used to build common subroutines called *statement groups*. A statement group is invoked simply by specifying its name. Statement groups do not contain a process option.

In order to give some idea as to what is involved in process definition, let us first assume that the logical structure of our SHIPMENT application is as indicated by the following pseudocode:

```
do initialization ;
get supplier number from user using map SHIP001 ;
set up for database read loop ;
do until no more SHIPREC records for this supplier ;
   retrieve next SHIPREC record from database ;
   display SHIPREC record using map SHIP002;
end ;
```

The SHIPMENT application will use:

- A main process called MAIN001 to control the overall logic of the application;
- Processes GETSNUM and DISPDATA to get the supplier number and to display SHIPREC records at the terminal;
- Processes READIT and GETNEXT to set up for the database read and to read the SHIPREC records from the database.

As usual, the starting point for definition is the CSP/AD Definition screen (refer back to Fig. 21.4). This time, we choose option 5 ("Application"), specifying the application name SHIPMENT. After we have defined the type of application we are building (batch or online, for example), the *Application Definition* screen shown in Fig. 21.12 will be displayed. We then use this screen to define the main processes (known as the *process list*) for the application. The process list contains the name of each process, its processing option, the CSP map or record ("object") to be used by the processing option (if any), and a description of what the process does. We enter the name of the single main process, MAIN001, which will be invoked using the EXECUTE processing option. No object name is entered because MAIN001 does not use any CSP maps or records.

We can now enter the "s" Select Definition option on line 001 under the SEL column to display screens for entering the BEFORE, AFTER, and FLOW processing statements for MAIN001. After we have defined these statements (see the subsection "Processing Statements" below for the details), we use the "l" option to display the *Structure List* screen shown in Fig. 21.13. This screen shows the structure of SHIPMENT defined so far.

```
┌──────────────────────────────────────────────────────────────────────────┐
│ EZEM36                    APPLICATION DEFINITION                           │
│                                                                            │
│ ==>                                                                        │
│            ENTER = File and continue     PF3 = File and exit               │
│           PF4 = Display application structure                              │
│                     Application Name = SHIPMENT                            │
│ Select Definition:  S = P+F+L   P = Processing   F = Flow   E = Edit Object│
│                     O = Object Selection         L = Structure List        │
│ Total lines 0001 ...... APPLICATION PROCESS LIST ......................... │
│                                                                            │
│ SEL PROCESS    OPTION      OBJECT     ERROR    DESCRIPTION                  │
│ ***                   TOP OF LIST                                          │
│ 001 MAIN001    EXECUTE                         main process                │
│ ***                   END OF LIST                                          │
│                                                                            │
│                                                                            │
│                                                                            │
│                                                                            │
│                                                                            │
│                                                                            │
└──────────────────────────────────────────────────────────────────────────┘
```

Fig. 21.12 CSP/AD Application Definition screen

```
┌──────────────────────────────────────────────────────────────────────────┐
│ EZEM37                       STRUCTURE LIST                                │
│                                                                            │
│ ==>                                                                        │
│      ENTER = File and continue     PF3 = File and exit    PF4 = Refresh    │
│                    Member Name = SHIPMENT                                  │
│ Select Definition:  S = P+F      P = Processing   F = Flow   E = Edit Object│
│                     O = Object Selection      Maximum Level => 002         │
│ Total lines 0005 ....... PROCESS AND GROUP LIST ..............             │
│                                                                            │
│ SEL NAME     LVL OPTION    OBJECT    ERROR    DESCRIPTION                   │
│ ***                 TOP OF LIST                                            │
│ 001 MAIN001  001 EXECUTE                      main process                 │
│ 002 GETSNUM  002 CONVERSE  SHIP001            get supplier number from user│
│ o03 READIT   002 SETINQ    SHIPREC            set up for data retrieval     │
│ 004 GETNEXT  002 SCAN      SHIPREC            read a row                    │
│ 005 DISPDATA 002 CONVERSE  SHIP002            display row data              │
│ ***                 END OF LIST                                            │
│                                                                            │
│                                                                            │
│                                                                            │
│                                                                            │
└──────────────────────────────────────────────────────────────────────────┘
```

Fig. 21.13 SHIPMENT application Structure List

It shows that MAIN001 invokes the lower level (LVL 002) processes GETSNUM, READIT, GETNEXT, and DISPDATA. The processing options, object names, and process descriptions for these lower level processes can now be entered on the screen as shown. Once this has been done, the "p" Select Definition option can be entered alongside each process name in turn to define the processing statements for the selected process. *Note:* Option "p" is used instead of option "s" because lower level processes do not have a flow section.

We are returned to the Structure List screen after defining the statements for each process. Pressing the PF 4 key on this screen will cause the screen to be refreshed with the latest process structure for the application.

To explain the process options and statements in more detail we will consider the process called READIT.

Process Options

The process option for READIT, namely SETINQ, corresponds in SQL terms to declaring a cursor for some specified query. This query will access the object of the process option, which we have specified as SHIPREC (see Fig. 21.13). In general, the process option can be any of the following (by way of explanation, we give an approximate SQL equivalent in each case):

- INQUIRY — retrieve a single table row (DECLARE CURSOR–OPEN–FETCH–CLOSE)
- UPDATE — retrieve a single row for update (DECLARE CURSOR FOR UPDATE–OPEN–FETCH)
- SETINQ — define a set of rows to be retrieved (DECLARE CURSOR)
- SETUPD — define a set of rows to be retrieved and updated (DECLARE CURSOR FOR UPDATE)
- SCAN — retrieve a row from a defined set (FETCH)
- REPLACE — update a retrieved row (UPDATE CURRENT)
- DELETE — delete a retrieved row (DELETE CURRENT)
- CLOSE — terminate processing of defined set (CLOSE)
- ADD — insert a single row (INSERT)
- EXECSQL — execute the specified SQL statement (any SQL statement other than SELECT)

In addition there are three process options that have no SQL equivalents (i.e., that have nothing to do with database access at all):

- EXECUTE   — execute the specified process
- CONVERSE   — display a map and edit the response from the user
- DISPLAY   — display a map (no response from user)

As already stated, the object of the SETINQ process option in our example is SHIPREC. The SQL statement generated by CSP/AD for this combination of process option and object can be displayed and subsequently edited by means of the CSP/AD Application Definition screen shown in Fig. 21.14. This screen is displayed by entering the option "o" alongside the READIT process name on the Structure List screen for the SHIPMENT application (refer to Fig. 21.13).

The SQL statement is initially generated by CSP/AD using the SHIPREC record defined earlier; we have tailored it for the READIT process by adding an extra search condition and an ORDER BY clause. The purpose of the extra search condition is to ensure that SHIPREC records are retrieved for the required supplier only.

Processing Statements

The CSP/AD *Application Process Definition* screen shown in Fig. 21.15 is displayed as a result of selecting the "p" option on the Structure List screen (refer back to Fig. 21.13). The Application Process Definition screen allows us to specify the processing statements for the process under consideration. In the simple example shown, the BEFORE processing consists of a single MOVE statement to copy the supplier number entered by the user (via the map SHIP001) into the S# field of the SHIPREC record. The process option SETINQ will use the S# field to retrieve shipment information using the SHIPREC record. There are no AFTER processing statements.

A more complex example appears in Fig. 21.16. That figure shows the processing statements for the MAIN001 process of the SHIPMENT application. This process has a processing option of EXECUTE, which simply causes the statements in the process to be executed (no map or record processing is performed). There are no BEFORE processing statements. The AFTER processing statements control the flow of the lower level processes. *Note:* The example of Fig. 21.16 is intended to illustrate process definition in general terms, not to represent a totally realistic application. The statements shown are intended to be more or less self-explanatory.

CSP processing statements fall into the following general categories:

- Computational statements:
  - arithmetic operations ($+$, $-$, $*$, $/$, rounding, remainder)
  - MOVE (move data between CSP objects and working storage)

```
EZEM3M                    APPLICATION DEFINITION
EZE005901 You may edit lines preceded by line numbers
==>
 PF3 = File and exit PF4 = Reset to default statement PF5 = SQL syntax check
 Process = READIT    Description = set up for data retrieval
 Option = SETINQ    Object      = SHIPREC      Modified statements = YES
Total lines 0012 ... OBJECT SELECTION: SQL STATEMENT DEFINITION ............
***                          TOP OF LIST
*** SELECT
002    T1.S#, T1.CITY,
003    T2.QTY,
004    T3.P#, T3.CITY
*** INTO
006    :S#, :SCITY, :QTY,
007    :P#, :PCITY
*** FROM
***    cjdate.s T1,
***    cjdate.sp T2,
***    cjdate.p T3
*** WHERE
010    t1.s# = t2.s# and
011    t2.p# = t3.p# and t1.s# = :s#
012 order by t3.p#
***                          END OF LIST
```

Fig. 21.14 SELECT statement for the READIT process

```
EZEM39                    APPLICATION PROCESS DEFINITION

==>
        PF3 = File and exit  (or file and continue if more selected )
   Process = READIT    Description = set up for data retrieval
    Option = SETINQ         Object = SHIPREC
Total lines 0001 ...    STATEMENT DEFINITION ............................
***                          TOP OF LIST
001 MOVE SHIP001.SNUM TO SHIPREC.S#;
***    ------------------- PROCESS OPTION -----------------------
***                          END OF LIST
```

Fig. 21.15 READIT process definition

```
 EZEM39                    APPLICATION PROCESS DEFINITION

 ==>
         PF3 = File and exit  (or file and continue if more selected )
    Process = MAIN001    Description = set up for data retrieval
     Option = EXECUTE          Object =
 Total lines 0010 ...     STATEMENT DEFINITION ..........................
 ***                      TOP OF LIST
 ***  ------------------- PROCESS OPTION ----------------------
 001 PERFORM GETSNUM ;      GET SUPPLIER NUMBER
 002 SET SHIP002 ;          CLEAR DISPLAY
 003 PERFORM READIT ;       SET UP FOR DATABASE READ
 004 PERFORM GETNEXT ;      READ FIRST ROW
 005 IF SHIPREC IS NRF ;    SUPPLIER NOT FOUND TELL USER
 006   MOVE "INVALID SUPPLIER" TO EZEMSG;
 007 ELSE
 008   WHILE SHIPREC NOT NRF ;
 008    PERFORM DISPDATA ; DISPLAY ROW
 009    PERFORM GETNEXT ;  READ NEXT ROW
 009   END ;
 010 END ;
 ***                       END OF LIST
```

Fig. 21.16 MAIN001 process definition

- RETRIEVE (retrieve data from CSP edit/reference tables)
- SET (set a map, record, or field to a specific value)

■ Conditional statements:

- FIND (search for a matching value in a CSP edit/reference table and execute the associated statement group)
- IF/ELSE/END (perform processing based on comparisons)
- WHILE/END (conditionally repeat processing)
- TEST (check status after map and record processing and execute appropriate processing statement group)

■ Application linkage statements:

- CALL (invoke another CSP or user-written application and return to the next statement in the calling process)
- TRANSFER (transfer control to another CSP or user-written application)

■ Unconditional statements:

- PERFORM (invoke the next lower level process and return to the next statement in the calling process or [optionally] to the flow section of a main process)

- *statement group name* (invoke the named statement group)
- *process name* (used in the flow section to transfer control to the named main process; by default, processing is performed in the order of the processes in the process list)
- *function name* (invoke the specified CSP function)

21.6 TESTING AND GENERATING THE APPLICATION

The CSP/AD test facility is entered by selecting option 3 ("Test") on the main CSP Facility Selection screen. Two principal testing functions are provided:

- *Preprocessor:* Checks the syntax of the CSP processing statements used by the application.

- *Run:* Allows the developer to test application execution. A statement-level trace of the test run can be provided at the terminal. Also, stop points can be defined at which the test run is to pause.

As explained in Section 21.2, processing during testing is performed using either dynamic SQL or extended dynamic SQL. Usually dynamic SQL would be used. After the application is tested and debugged, it can be generated for production execution under CSP/AE by selecting option 4 ("Generation") on the main CSP Facility Selection screen. At this point, a choice should be made between extended dynamic SQL and dynamic SQL. In a production environment, at least, extended dynamic SQL would normally be chosen, for reasons of efficiency.

21.7 CSP UTILITIES

CSP provides many utilities to assist in the building and maintenance of CSP applications. From a SQL/DS perspective, the most important ones are the *MSL and ALF utilities* and the *CSP List Processor.*

- The MSL (Member Specification Library) utilities consist of a set of facilities for manipulating and backing up MSL members (record definitions, map definitions, and process definitions), as follows:
  - *Export and Import:* Move MSL members to and from external files. These functions are used to move applications from one environment to another.
  - *Print:* List the components of a specified application, together with a cross-reference listing.
  - *Copy/Rename/Delete:* Copy, rename, and delete MSL members.

- The ALF (Application Load File) utilities include analogous functions for manipulating ALF objects.

- The CSP List Processor produces a full screen listing of selected MSL members and allows any of the MSL utility functions (except Import) to be executed for a given member or list of members. It also produces a where-used list showing where members are used, allows a global change of all references to a specific member name, and permits individual members to be viewed and edited. The List Processor also supports application testing and application generation.

◆

Data Extract

22.1 INTRODUCTION

Data Extract (DXT) is a program for extracting data from operational databases and files. The extracted data is in a suitable format for loading (via
the appropriate load utility—the DBS utility, in the case of SQL/DS) into
a DB2 or SQL/DS table on the same or a different computer system. DXT
users can use either or both of the following:

- Relational Data Extract Feature (VM, MVS)
  —for extracting data from SQL/DS or DB2 databases
- General Data Extract Feature (MVS only)
  —for extracting data from IMS databases, VSAM or sequential files,
  or nonIBM data sources (e.g., nonIBM SQL databases)

In this chapter we first present an overview of both features; we then go on to discuss the relational feature in more depth. Details of the general feature are beyond the scope of this book; the reader is referred to the IBM manuals for more information.

The main components of DXT are as follows (refer to Fig. 22.1):

- End User and Administrative Dialogs
- Relational Extract Manager (REM)
- User Input Manager (UIM)
- Data Extract Manager (DEM)

Of these components, the End User and Administrative Dialogs constitute the DXT base product, the Relational Extract Manager constitutes the Relational Data Extract Feature, and the User Input Manager and the Data Extract Manager constitute the General Data Extract Feature.

End User and Administrative Dialogs

- The *End User* Dialogs allow users to submit existing extract requests or construct new ones. (*Note:* QMF and AS each provide commands to invoke these dialogs directly.) In the case of a new request, prompt screens allow the user to specify the source of the data, the specific data required (i.e., the selection criteria), and the target SQL/DS or DB2 table into which the extracted data is to be loaded. The data source is identified by selecting the required item(s) from a list of tables and "DXTVIEWs" (a DXTVIEW is a "flat file" view of fields that may be accessed from nonrelational files and databases). The source data and target table do not have to reside on the system where the dialog is executed.

- The *Administrative* Dialogs are used to define and maintain extract requests, to create DXTVIEW and other data descriptions, and to build information about the SQL/DS and DB2 tables accessible by individual users.

Relational Extract Manager (REM)

The REM is the component that performs the actual data extraction when the source is a SQL/DS or DB2 database. Thus, it extracts data from SQL/DS and DB2 tables in accordance with SQL extract requests generated by the DXT End User Dialogs. The extracted data is written to a sequential file or an IXF file or is placed in a spool file for routing back to the submitting location. The extract request can optionally invoke a batch job to load

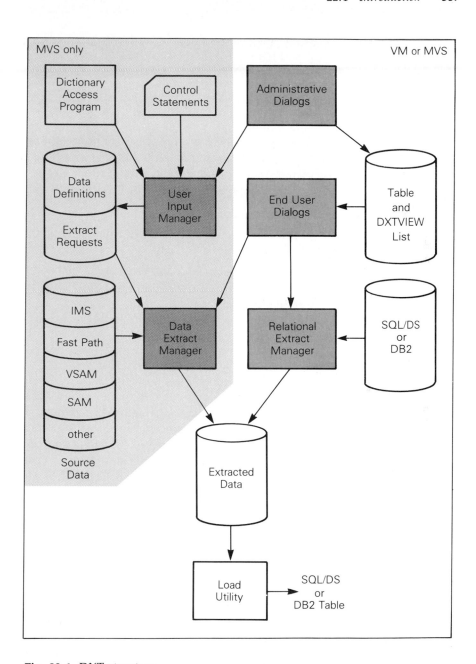

Fig. 22.1 DXT structure

the extracted data into a SQL/DS or DB2 table, using the applicable load utility.

User Input Manager (UIM)

The UIM maintains data descriptions and extract requests for nonrelational files and databases. Data descriptions are stored in the File Description Table Library (FDTLIB); extract requests are stored in the Extract Request Library (EXTLIB). There are three possible sources for UIM input:

1. A card image file of control statements
2. The DXT Administrative Dialogs, which allow the equivalent of the card image input file to be created interactively
3. Output from the DXT Dictionary Access Program (DAP), which creates data descriptions from existing information stored in the IBM DB/DC Data Dictionary

Data Extract Manager (DEM)

The DEM is the component that performs the actual data extraction when the source is something other than a SQL/DS or DB2 database. In other words, the DEM extracts data from IMS databases, VSAM or sequential files, or nonIBM data sources, using extract requests stored in the Extract Request Library (EXTLIB). (*Note*: In the case of nonIBM data sources, the required data is extracted by means of user-supplied exit routines, which are specified by means of the *Generic Data Interface,* GDI.) The DEM can either process all outstanding requests and then terminate, or it can execute continuously, processing requests as they appear in the EXTLIB. Facilities exist to process a batch of requests in a single pass and to control the priority in which requests are processed. (By contrast, the REM simply executes each request as it is submitted.) Extracted data is handled exactly as with the REM.

So much for the basic components of DXT. In the rest of this chapter, we consider in some detail what is involved in using DXT to extract data from a SQL/DS table, basing our discussion (as usual) on the suppliers-and-parts database. We will first show how the End User Dialogs can be used to create and execute an extract request (Section 22.2), and then go on to discuss the facilities provided by the Administrative Dialogs for maintaining the DXT system (Section 22.3). Section 22.4 presents a brief conclusion.

22.2 CREATING AND EXECUTING AN EXTRACT REQUEST

In this section we consider what is involved in creating and executing a DXT request. By way of example, we create a request to extract supplier number, name, and city information for suppliers with status greater than 5. We begin with the main *DXT End User Dialogs* screen shown in Fig. 22.2. The options on that screen lead us to further screens which allow us to specify all aspects of the request in detail. In general, to create a request we must do all of the following (refer to the figure):

- Select the names of the tables or DXTVIEWs from which data is to be extracted (Option 1, TABLES)

- Specify the columns to be extracted (Option 2, COLUMNS)

- Specify the search criteria to be used (Option 3, CONDITIONS)

- Specify the joining condition when extracting data from multiple tables or DXTVIEWs (Option 4, JOIN)

- Identify the target SQL/DS or DB2 table and the system on which it resides (Option 5, TARGET)

- Specify control information for the source and target systems (Option 6, DB ACCESS)

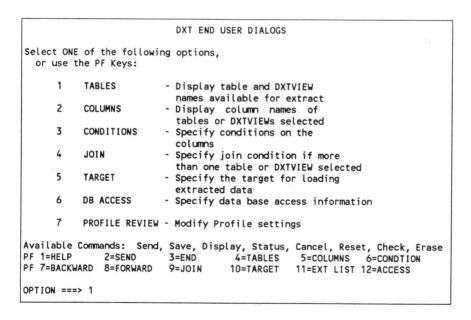

```
                        DXT END USER DIALOGS

Select ONE of the following options,
   or use the PF Keys:

      1      TABLES        - Display table and DXTVIEW
                            names available for extract
      2      COLUMNS       - Display column  names  of
                            tables or DXTVIEWs selected
      3      CONDITIONS    - Specify conditions on the
                            columns
      4      JOIN          - Specify join condition if more
                            than one table or DXTVIEW selected
      5      TARGET        - Specify the target for loading
                            extracted data
      6      DB ACCESS     - Specify data base access information

      7      PROFILE REVIEW - Modify Profile settings

Available Commands:  Send, Save, Display, Status, Cancel, Reset, Check, Erase
PF 1=HELP      2=SEND       3=END      4=TABLES    5=COLUMNS   6=CONDTION
PF 7=BACKWARD  8=FORWARD    9=JOIN     10=TARGET   11=EXT LIST 12=ACCESS

OPTION ===> 1
```

Fig. 22.2 Main DXT End User Dialogs screen

If the request already exists, we can execute it by selecting its name from the "extract list" obtained by pressing PF key 11. In our example, however, we want to create a new request, so we choose Option 1 (TABLES). That choice leads us to the *Select Tables/DXTVIEWs for Extract* screen (Fig. 22.3), which displays the name of each table or DXTVIEW we are allowed to access, the ID of its creator, the name of the system (i.e., node ID) on which it is located, its type, and a short description of its use. (All of this information is maintained by the *DXT administrator* using the DXT Administrative Dialogs. See Section 22.3.)

According to Fig. 22.3, we are allowed to extract data from any or all of the suppliers (S), shipments (SP), and parts (P) tables, also from a DXTVIEW called EDUC (introduced purely for the sake of the example). We enter an "S" ("select") alongside the suppliers table name. Pressing PF key 5 will now display the *Select Columns and Specify Functions* screen (Fig. 22.4), which is used to specify the columns we want to extract. In our example, the screen contains a list of the columns of the supplier table. We select the S#, SNAME, and CITY columns by entering an "S" alongside those column names, and press PF key 6 to display the *Specify Conditions* screen (Fig. 22.5).

The screen in Fig. 22.5 lists the columns of the suppliers table with their

```
          SELECT TABLES/DXTVIEWS FOR EXTRACT              ROW 1 OF 3

Enter an S under SELECT to select table(s) or dxtview(s) you wish to extract
from. Remember to select items from the same LOCATION and of the same TYPE.


SELECT  TABLE/DXTVIEW     CREATOR   LOCATION   TYPE      DESCRIPTION
  S          NAME

=> S    S                 CJDATE    SANJOSE1   SQLDS     SUPPLIERS TABLE
=>      SP                CJDATE    SANJOSE1   SQLDS     SUPPLIERS/PARTS TABLE
=>      P                 CJDATE    SANJOSE1   SQLDS     PARTS TABLE
=>      EDUC              DXT       SANJOSE2   DXT       IMS EDUCATION DB
***************************** BOTTOM OF DATA  *******************************




PF 1=HELP       2=SEND      3=END       4=TABLES    5=COLUMNS   6=CONDTION
PF 7=BACKWARD   8=FORWARD   9=JOIN      10=TARGET   11=EXT LIST 12=ACCESS

COMMAND ===>                                         SCROLL ===> HALF
```

Fig. 22.3 DXT Select Tables/DXTVIEWs for Extract screen

```
              SELECT COLUMNS AND SPECIFY FUNCTIONS              ROW 1 OF 7

Do you wish to select ALL columns for extract, Yes or No?    ===> N


If not, enter an S under SELECT to select specific columns for extract
and enter any FUNCTIONs for the columns. Press HELP for a list of functions.

SELECT  FUNCTION COLUMN              TABLE              CREATOR
  S              NAME               NAME

=> S   =>       S#                  S                  CJDATE
=> S   =>       SNAME               S                  CJDATE
=>     =>       STATUS              S                  CJDATE
=> S   =>       CITY                S                  CJDATE
***************************** BOTTOM OF DATA *******************************




PF 1=HELP      2=SEND     3=END       4=TABLES    5=COLUMNS   6=CONDITION
PF 7=BACKWARD  8=FORWARD  9=JOIN      10=TARGET   11=EXT LIST 12=ACCESS

COMMAND ===>                                        SCROLL ==> HALF
```

Fig. 22.4 DXT Select Columns and Specify Functions screen

```
                      SPECIFY CONDITIONS                      ROW 1 OF 7

Specify the CONDITION field as operator followed by value(s). You may also use
the lines below for free formatted conditions. Press HELP key for syntax.

==>
==>

COLUMN                COLUMN   COLUMN    CONDITION
  NAME                TYPE     LENGTH

S#                    CHAR         5 =>
SNAME                 CHAR        20 =>
STATUS                SMALLINT       => >5
CITY                  CHAR        15 =>
***************************** BOTTOM OF DATA *******************************




PF 1=HELP      2=SEND     3=END       4=TABLES    5=COLUMNS   6=CONDTION
PF 7=BACKWARD  8=FORWARD  9=JOIN      10=TARGET   11=EXT LIST 12=ACCESS

COMMAND ===>                                        SCROLL ===> HALF
```

Fig. 22.5 DXT Specify Conditions screen

data type and length. (The DXT Administrative Dialogs—again, see Section 22.3—allow the DXT administrator to obtain this information from the catalog tables for the SQL/DS source system, thereby making it possible for DXT to build the screen.) We want suppliers with status greater than 5, so we enter the appropriate search condition against the STATUS column; we then press PF key 10, which takes us to the *Name Target for Extract Output* screen. See Fig. 22.6.

To specify the extract target, we first give the "nickname" (CJW1 in our example) for the target system. Nicknames are intended to make it easy for the user to identify individual (source or target) systems. They are maintained by the DXT administrator. In general, a nickname is a shorthand for the combination of all of the following:

- System node ID
- File name: name of a file containing the DXT control statements to be used in building the extract job stream
- File type: DXTVIEW (source systems only), SQL/DS, DB2, or IXF

  After entering the nickname we specify:

- The target table name (SNEW)

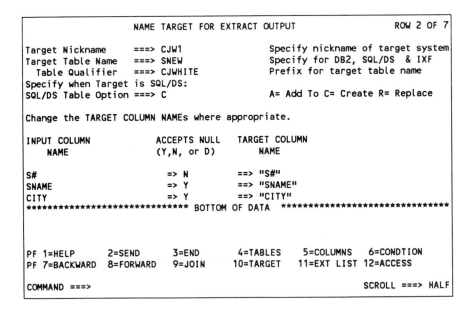

```
                   NAME TARGET FOR EXTRACT OUTPUT                ROW 2 OF 7

Target Nickname    ===> CJW1              Specify nickname of target system
Target Table Name  ===> SNEW              Specify for DB2, SQL/DS  & IXF
  Table Qualifier  ===> CJWHITE           Prefix for target table name
Specify when Target is SQL/DS:
SQL/DS Table Option ===> C                A= Add To C= Create R= Replace

Change the TARGET COLUMN NAMEs where appropriate.

INPUT COLUMN                ACCEPTS NULL    TARGET COLUMN
    NAME                    (Y,N, or D)         NAME

S#                            => N          ==> "S#"
SNAME                         => Y          ==> "SNAME"
CITY                          => Y          ==> "CITY"
**************************** BOTTOM OF DATA  ******************************




PF 1=HELP      2=SEND     3=END      4=TABLES   5=COLUMNS   6=CONDTION
PF 7=BACKWARD  8=FORWARD  9=JOIN     10=TARGET  11=EXT LIST 12=ACCESS

COMMAND ===>                                         SCROLL ===> HALF
```

Fig. 22.6 DXT Name Target for Extract Output screen

- The target table owner (CJWHITE)
- Option "C" (create a new table)
- The mapping of source columns to target columns
- Whether nulls are allowed in the target columns (in the example, we have specified "nulls not allowed" for the S# column)

Once all this information has been entered, we press PF key 12 to reach the *Data Base Access* screen shown in Fig. 22.7.

The Data Base Access screen is in two parts. The top part is used to specify necessary control information to be used to access the source system (node ID, user ID, and password); this information will be used in constructing the data extract job stream. The bottom part (required only if the source system is SQL/DS) specifies similar information for the target system. (Remember that, in general, the source system, target system, and system running the DXT dialogs can all be different.) In practice, most of the information on the Data Base Access screen will be completed automatically using information supplied by the DXT administrator.

Our extract request is now complete. If we press PF key 2 the extract job will be submitted for execution. DXT will route the extract job to the

```
                              DATA BASE ACCESS


Source information:

Location    ===> SANJOSE1              Location of table(s) to be extracted
User ID     ===> CJDATE                User ID to access source table(s).
Password    ===>                       Access password of above User ID.


Target information when source is SQL/DS:

User ID           ===> CJDATE          User ID to execute the job which
                                       processes the extracted output.
Network ID        ===> RSCS            Net ID to route extracted output.
Target Node ID    ===> SANJOSE3        Location for extracted output.


Press ENTER to save the required information.

PF 1=HELP      2=SEND      3=END      4=TABLES    5=COLUMNS   6=CONDTION
PF 7=BACKWARD  8=FORWARD   9=JOIN    10=TARGET   11=EXT LIST 12=ACCESS

COMMAND ===>
```

Fig. 22.7 DXT Data Base Access screen

source system, extract the data, and then route the extracted data to the target system. On the target system it will invoke the appropriate load utility and load the extracted data into the table specified. We will be notified when the data extract job completes and when the load of the target table is finished.

22.3   USING THE ADMINISTRATIVE DIALOGS

The main DXT *Administrative Dialogs* screen is shown in Fig. 22.8. The dialogs support six different administration tasks:

- Build and maintain extract requests (Option 1, EXTRACT)

    This option allows the DXT administrator to build, maintain, and submit DXT requests. Facilities exist to check the status of submitted requests and to cancel them if required.

- Build and maintain data descriptions (Option 2, DESCRIPTION)

    The formats of files and databases to be accessed via the General Data Extract Feature are defined to DXT using this dialog. The dialog is also used to create DXTVIEWs for such files and databases.

```
                     DXT ADMINISTRATIVE DIALOGS
SELECT OPTION ===>



        1    EXTRACT        Build and maintain extract requests.

        2    DESCRIPTION    Build and maintain data description requests.

        3    JCL            Build and maintain Job Control Language.

        4    PROFILE        Specify Dialogs processing options.

        5    ADMINISTER     End User Dialogs Administration.

        6    DXTA           Bridge to DXT Assist.




Press:   ENTER to select   END key to exit   HELP key for information
```

Fig. 22.8 Main DXT Administrative Dialogs screen

- Build and maintain job control statements (Option 3, JCL)

  The job streams to execute the Data Extract Manager, the Relational Extract Manager, and the SQL/DS and DB2 load utilities are created and maintained using this dialog.

- Specify dialog processing options (Option 4, PROFILE)

  Many of the options used in constructing extract job streams are obtained from the user's DXT profile. The DXT administrator uses this dialog to create and maintain such profiles.

- End User Dialogs administration (Option 5, ADMINISTER)

  The administrator uses this option to build the list of nicknames for each user and to construct a DXT table containing the table names and DXTVIEWs the user is allowed to access. A third option permits a job to be submitted to access the system catalog tables of SQL/DS and DB2. This job extracts the data required to build the table and column information used by the End User Dialogs.

- Bridge to DXT Assist (Option 6, DXTA)

  As explained in Section 22.1, it is possible to extract data from nonrelational sources such as IMS for loading into a relational system such as SQL/DS, using the DXT General Data Extract Feature (available for MVS only). The DXTA product ("DXT Assist") helps in building DXT descriptions of nonrelational source files and databases, in creating the definitions of the tables used to store extract results, and in creating the DXT control statements needed for the extract job streams.

22.4 CONCLUSION

Copy management is a complex task, particularly when extracting data from nonrelational files and databases. End-users will typically not set up and maintain their own copy management schemes, but will instead rely on the DP department to perform this function for them. The DXT Administrative Dialogs are designed to assist the DP department in this task. End-users can use the DXT End User Dialogs to code and submit extract requests to extract both relational and nonrelational data for loading into SQL/DS and DB2 tables. However, strict management of this process is required in practice.

23

♦

Micro-to-Mainframe Links

23.1 INTRODUCTION

It is widely recognized that, from the end-user's perspective, microcomputers tend to be much more responsive and much easier to use than their mainframe counterparts. This is why an increasing number of users prefer to use the PC for analyzing data, producing reports and graphs, etc. Frequently, however, the data to be analyzed or reported on resides in some central or departmental database on some other machine. The purpose of a micro-to-mainframe link product is to allow the user to extract the required data from that other machine and copy it down into a PC file or database (a process known as "downloading"), thereby making the data available for subsequent processing by a variety of PC tools.

A micro-to-mainframe link product involves two components, a requester program on the PC and a server program on the other machine (the "host"). The requester receives extract requests entered by the PC user and passes them to the server for processing. The server extracts the required host data and passes it back to the requester. Conversion to the appropriate PC file format can be done either on the host or on the PC.

There are many micro-to-mainframe link products on the market that support access to SQL/DS on a VM host. In this chapter we describe two such products (both from IBM), namely Host Data Base View (HDBV) and Enhanced Connectivity Facilities (ECF). Each of these products allows data to be extracted from both VM and MVS hosts. For obvious reasons, however, we concentrate on the case where the host is running VM (and SQL/DS), and the data to be extracted resides in a SQL/DS database.

Note: As mentioned in Chapter 18, we generally take the term "PC" to include the IBM Personal System/2 (PS/2) as well as the original PC machine. Currently, HDBV and ECF both support PS/2 systems running PC/DOS but not OS/2. However, (a) OS/2 (Extended Edition) does include support for IBM's standard Server-Requester Programming Interface protocols (see Section 23.3), which means that micro-to-mainframe link systems can be written to run under OS/2, and (b) IBM has stated that it does intend to produce a version of ECF for the OS/2 environment (date of availability unknown at the time of writing).

23.2 HOST DATA BASE VIEW

Host Data Base View (HDBV) runs as a requester program on a standard IBM PC. The server function at the host is provided by a regular IBM host product such as QMF (see below). Communication between the PC and the host is performed using standard IBM PC communication facilities (details beyond the scope of this book); however, a User Communication Exit is also provided to allow the use of other (nonIBM) communication products. *Note:* The primary purpose of HDBV is of course to download data from the host to the PC. However, it does also permit files to be copied from the PC to the host ("uploading"), and it also allows the PC user to invoke procedures (e.g., CMS EXECs or TSO CLISTs) on the host.

As just mentioned, the server function (i.e., the data extraction process) is performed at the host by a regular IBM host product. That product can be any of the following:

- Query Management Facility (QMF)
- Application System (AS)
- The Information Facility (TIF)
- Info Center/1 (IC/1)

HDBV also permits data files created by Data Extract (DXT) to be downloaded to the PC.

In order to explain how HDBV works, we will consider an example of extracting data via QMF from the suppliers-and-parts database. (Refer to Chapter 19 if you need to refresh your memory regarding QMF.) When HDBV is first invoked, the HDBV *Main Menu* is displayed (Fig. 23.1). That menu allows us to:

- Extract data from host files and databases
- Reformat extracted data into several popular PC file formats (DIF, SYLK, WRK, WKS, SDF, etc.)
- Execute other PC programs (e.g., dBase III, Lotus 1-2-3) to process the reformatted data
- Add programs to the list of PC programs that can be invoked from HDBV
- Modify values in the HDBV profile (e.g., change the host operating system)

We wish to extract data from the host, so we select "Access host data," which causes the HDBV *Host Services Menu* (not shown) to be displayed.

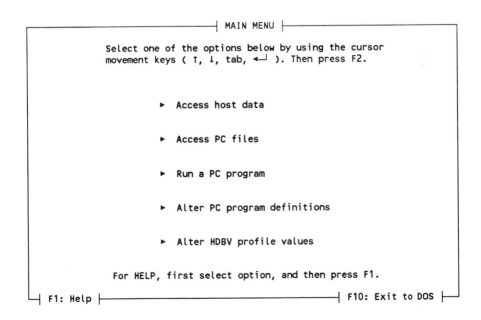

```
────────────────┤ MAIN MENU ├──────────────────

      Select one of the options below by using the cursor
      movement keys ( ↑, ↓, tab, ◄┘ ). Then press F2.



                ►  Access host data


                ►  Access PC files


                ►  Run a PC program


                ►  Alter PC program definitions


                ►  Alter HDBV profile values


         For HELP, first select option, and then press F1.

┤ F1: Help ├────────────────────────────┤ F10: Exit to DOS ├
```

Fig. 23.1 HDBV Main Menu

That menu allows us to choose the host product to be used for extracting the data. Choosing QMF brings us to the HDBV *QMF Services Menu* (Fig. 23.2), which offers three different ways of using QMF:

1. QMF procedure:

    The user can invoke a predefined QMF procedure already existing on the host. This method is useful if the user is not familiar with QMF or SQL. HDBV will display a list of available procedures on request.

2. SQL statement:

    The user can create and execute his or her own SQL statements directly. Those statements can be saved and later reused, with or without subsequent modification.

3. Guided SQL:

    HDBV can guide the user through a series of prompts and menus and hence create SQL statements on the user's behalf. From a displayed list of table names, the user selects the table (possibly a view) from which data is to be extracted. Further options allow the user to specify the columns required, the search criteria, and the order in which data is to

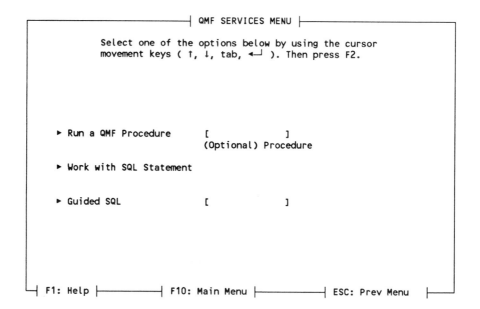

Fig 23.2 HDBV QMF Services Menu

be returned. This method suffers from the limitation that the generated SQL statement cannot extract data from more than one table (though the table in question can be a view and might therefore involve multiple tables indirectly).

In our example, we will create our own SQL statement. Choosing "Work with SQL Statement" on the HDBV QMF Services Menu leads us to the HDBV *QMF SQL Entry Menu* (Fig. 23.3). We then enter the SQL request shown to extract supplier numbers, names, and cities for suppliers with status greater than 5. (*Note:* By entering a name in the "Statement Name" field and pressing PF key 6, we could save the statement for later use.) Then we press PF key 2 and HDBV passes the statement to QMF for execution.

HDBV will inform us when the query has finished and the data has been downloaded to the PC. We can then use the "Access PC files" option on the HDBV Main Menu (refer back to Fig. 23.1) to display the data for browsing or to reformat the extracted data. If we select the browse option, the result shown in Fig. 23.4 will be displayed. This screen can be used to remove headings and unwanted blocks of data before reformatting the data into the required PC file format. (Note that the data returned to HDBV by

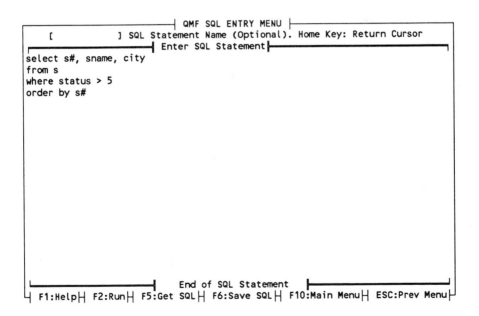

Fig. 23.3 HDBV QMF SQL Entry Menu

```
BROWSING : C:SUPPLIER.RPT                  Line 1    of  7   Column 1    of 35
COMMAND ====>

    S#          SNAME       CITY
    --          -----       ----
    S1          Smith       London
    S2          Jones       Paris
    S3          Blake       Paris
    S4          Clark       London
    S5          Adams       Athens












1:Help 2:Cmd 3:◄ 4:► 5:Block 6:Row 7:Col 8:Hide 9:Fields 10:Reform ESC:Exit
```

Fig. 23.4 HDBV listing of extracted data

QMF is in fact a QMF report. That report should preferably not include
any editing characters such as embedded commas or decimal points, because such material cannot be removed by HDBV.)

23.3 ENHANCED CONNECTIVITY FACILITIES

Enhanced Connectivity Facilities (ECF) is a family of products that allow
PC users to access host (VM and MVS) data, resources, and services. It
consists of:

- A PC requester program (the ECF Requester)
- TSO and CMS server programs (ECF Servers)
- The Server-Requester Programming Interface (SRPI)

The SRPI provides a set of standard protocols for handling communications between a requester on the PC and a server on the host. The protocols are independent of the underlying communications environment; in
fact, they are a subset of IBM's Advanced Program-to-Program Communications (APPC) architecture. The SRPI is provided with VM/SP and
TSO/E on the host and with IBM 3270 emulation programs on the PC.

ECF provides three major sets of functions:

1. *Access to host data:* Data can be downloaded from SQL/DS and DB2 databases and from VSAM and sequential files.
2. *Access to host resources:* Host disks, files, and printers can be accessed by PC users as though they were directly connected to the PC.
3. *Access to host services:* PC users can directly invoke host EXECs, CLISTs, commands, and programs.

In order to facilitate a direct comparison with HDBV, we will first look at the ECF host data access functions. We will then move on to describe the ECF facilities for using host resources and services.

Accessing Host Data

Unlike HDBV, ECF has its own server program and does not require a separate product on the host to access host data. The PC user interacts with the ECF Requester using either commands or menus to specify extract requests. The ECF Requester routes those requests via the SRPI to the ECF Server on the host, which extracts the required data. The extracted data is then either stored in a host file or downloaded to the PC (whichever is specified by the user).

Consider what is involved in using ECF to perform the SQL extract request from Section 23.2: "Extract supplier number, name, and city for all suppliers with status greater than 5" (we deliberately use the same example as we did in our HDBV discussion). When ECF is first invoked, the *Cooperative Processing Services* menu is displayed (Fig. 23.5). From that menu, we can reach any of the services provided by ECF. We wish to extract host data, so we choose the "Use Database Services" option, which opens up the *Use Database Services* window shown in Fig. 23.6. *Note:* That figure also shows the *Use SQL Services* window, to be discussed below.

The *Use Database Services* window provides a menu offering two choices, "Use SQL Services" and "Use DXT Services." If DXT is chosen, the extract request must already have been created on the host; the ECF Requester can display a list of existing DXT requests from which one can be selected for batch execution. In our example, however, we wish to use SQL, so we choose the "Use SQL Services" option. A second window appears on the screen, as shown in Fig. 23.6. That window provides options to:

- Create and execute SQL queries directly (much as with HDBV)
- Create and execute SQL queries using prompts (see below)

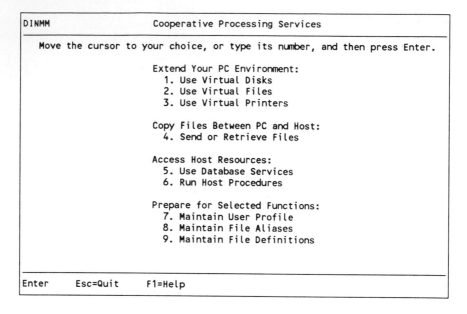

Fig. 23.5 ECF Requester: Cooperative Processing Services menu

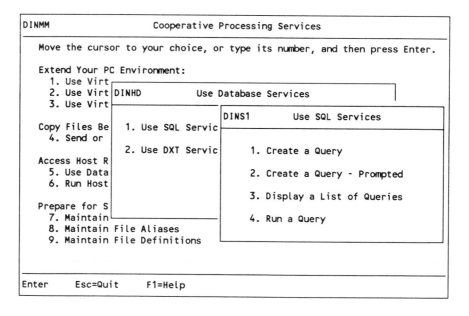

Fig. 23.6 ECF Requester: Database Services and SQL Services menus

- Display saved SQL queries and select one for editing
- Execute a saved SQL query

For the sake of the example, we choose Option 2, which takes us to the *Create a Query—Prompted* menu (Fig. 23.7). We enter the name of the table from which data is to be extracted, namely table S. *Note:* We could alternatively have entered an asterisk ("*"), which would cause ECF to access the SQL/DS catalog and display a list of tables we are allowed to use.

The Requester now displays a list of the columns in table S (see Fig. 23.8); this information is also obtained from the SQL/DS catalog. We can now indicate the columns to be extracted (S#, SNAME, and CITY), together with appropriate search criteria (STATUS > 5). If the data is to be returned in a particular sequence, pressing PF key 5 will open up a window to permit ordering criteria to be specified; we have not shown this step, but let us assume that ordering by S# is requested.

The Requester now generates the required SQL statement and automatically displays it for review. At this point we can modify, save, or execute the generated statement. Requesting execution will cause the *Run a Query* menu (Fig. 23.9) to be displayed. This menu allows the user to limit the

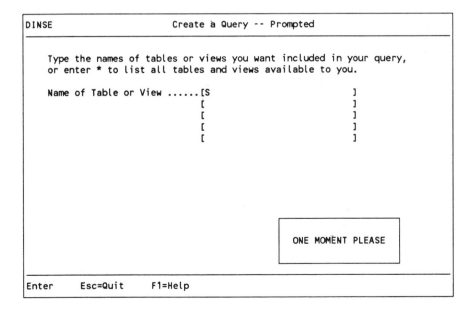

Fig. 23.7 ECF Requester: Create a Query—Prompted menu

```
DINSC                    List of Columns with Tables              18 Lines

    Do any of the following, and then press Enter:
    - to view detailed column information, type V to the left of column names
    - to select columns, specify output sequence numbers to the left
    - to omit columns from this list, type O to the left of column names
    - to limit the query results, type selection criteria

    When finished, press F4 to create the query statement


        Column Name        Owner   Name of Table/View Sort  Selection Criteria
   ─────────────────────────────────────────────────────────────────────────
   [1  ] S#                CJDATE  S                        [                 ]
   [2  ] SNAME             CJDATE  S                        [                 ]
   [o  ] STATUS            CJDATE  S                        [ > 5             ]
   [3  ] CITY              CJDATE  S                        [                 ]




   ─────────────────────────────────────────────────────────────────────────
   Enter     Esc=Quit    F1=Help    F4=Create Query     F5=Sort Sequence  PgUp
                                     F6=Expand Criteria                    PgDn
```

Fig. 23.8 ECF Requester: List of Columns with Tables menu

```
DINS3                           Run a Query
   ─────────────────────────────────────────────────────────────────────────

   Name for Default File Values [                     ]

   Maximum Number of Lines
   To Be Extracted
   From the Database ..........[     ]


   Action on Query Results .... Display on PC Screen
                                Save in PC file using ECF format
                                Save in PC file using format other than ECF
                                Save in host file using ECF format
                                Save in host file using IXF format

   Enter More File Values? .... No    Yes

                                          ┌──────────────────────┐
                                          │                      │
                                          │  ONE MOMENT PLEASE    │
                                          │                      │
                                          └──────────────────────┘

   ─────────────────────────────────────────────────────────────────────────
   Enter     Esc=Quit    F1=Help    F3=List Query Names
```

Fig. 23.9 ECF Requester: Run a Query menu

number of records to be retrieved from the host and also to tell the ECF Server where to place the result. Result data can be

- Displayed on the screen

- Saved in a PC file (like HDBV, ECF supports most popular PC file formats)

- Saved in an IXF file on the host (see Chapter 18 for a discussion of IXF)

- Saved in an ECF file on the host for later copying to the PC

The result of our request will of course contain the same data as in our HDBV example (refer back to Fig. 23.4). However, there is one very important difference between data retrieved via HDBV and data retrieved via ECF:

- For HDBV, extracted data is always in the form of a report. In other words, the data has been formatted at the host by the query product doing the extract.

- For ECF, on the other hand, extracted data is a copy of the data as extracted at the host; it does *not* contain any extraneous information such as headers, embedded punctuation marks, or the like.

So much for the host data access functions of ECF. We conclude this section by briefly describing the other two major ECF functions, namely the host resources and host services access functions.

Accessing Host Resources

Using ECF, PC users can use certain host resources—specifically, certain host devices and files—as if they were directly connected to the PC. Three types of such resources are supported:

- *Virtual disks* are used to store PC files (in PC format) on the host. This facility gives the PC user access to larger capacity (and more reliable) disk storage. Most PC/DOS file and disk commands can be used with virtual disks.

- *Virtual printers* allow host printers to be used in the same manner as a PC printer.

- *Virtual files* are host files (in host format) that appear to the PC user as if they were stored on a PC disk. This facility allows PC users and programs to access host files without having to download them to the PC. It also allows the PC to share data with the host and/or other PCs.

Many PC/DOS commands can be used to manipulate such files; ECF handles all necessary data and field conversions automatically.

Accessing Host Services

This ECF facility permits a PC user to execute CMS EXECs, TSO CLISTs, and CMS and TSO commands and programs. Output results can be displayed on the PC screen or stored in PC files. Host functions requiring prompted input or full-screen output are not supported, however.

23.4 CONCLUSION

This completes our description of IBM's two micro-to-mainframe link products, HDBV and ECF. Each has its own particular strengths and weaknesses. HDBV provides a simple interface to IBM's mainframe query products (QMF, AS, etc.) to download data from host files and databases. It has the advantage that PC users can use tools and interfaces they may already have become familiar with on the host. ECF, on the other hand, contains a more general and more extensive set of functions; it provides a general architecture for cooperative processing between IBM PC and mainframe computers, and hence can be used as the basis for a variety of more specialized micro-to-mainframe link products. In fact, as mentioned in Chapter 3, HDBV itself can use the ECF facilities to access the host (though ECF is only one of several possible underpinnings for HDBV). ECF is likely to become increasingly important over the next few years.

CHAPTER

24

◆

Data Base Relational
Application Directory

24.1 INTRODUCTION

As explained in Chapter 9, descriptive information concerning SQL/DS objects such as base tables, views, etc., is recorded in the SQL/DS catalog. However, the SQL/DS catalog describes SQL/DS objects *only;* it does not contain any information about the use of such objects by application programs, nor about such programs themselves. In other words, it is not a full-function data dictionary. The subject of this chapter, Data Base Relational Application Directory/VM (DBRAD/VM, or DBRAD for short), is not a full-function data dictionary either, but it does go further than the SQL/DS catalog in its support for dictionary-type functions. In particular, it provides a set of tables (logically an extension to the SQL/DS catalog) called the *DBRAD directory,* which allows administrators and application developers to record and manage information about applications—especially CSP applications—and their use of SQL/DS (and other) objects.

DBRAD supports SQL/DS in the VM/CMS environment. (A separate version of the product supports DB2 in the MVS environment.) The main components of the VM version are as follows (refer to Fig. 24.1):

- *Catalog Dialogs* (for querying and displaying SQL/DS catalog information)

- *Import Facilities* (for importing descriptors into the DBRAD directory from the SQL/DS catalog, COBOL and PL/I structure libraries, and CSP applications)

- *Directory Dialogs* (for querying, displaying, and updating DBRAD directory information)

- *Reports* (for reporting on DBRAD directory objects and their interrelationships)

- *Model Generator* (for creating "model" SQL statements, COBOL and PL/I structures, and various other definitions from SQL/DS catalog and DBRAD directory information)

- *Application Program Interface* (for updating DBRAD directory information from an application program)

- *Umbrella Dialogs* (for invoking other IBM tools such as QMF, DBEDIT, and CSP)

Before we can describe the components of DBRAD in more detail, it is necessary to introduce a few basic concepts. First, every DBRAD object is uniquely identified by a 3-part name or "key" consisting of the name of the library the object belongs to, the type of the object, and the name of the object itself.* For example, a certain PL/I structure might be identified by the combination MYPLILIB (library name) plus RECORD (object type) plus EMPREC (object name). Note that every object is required to belong to some library. Libraries are used to group together objects that are logically related in some manner. For example, the set of all structures used in the same PL/I application would typically all belong to the same DBRAD library.

The library concept in DBRAD serves among other things as an access control mechanism: Specific users or groups of users—for example, a specific development team or a specific department—can be granted access

---

*An object can also be given an *alias* in addition to its 3-part library/type/name key. Such aliases can be user-defined or generated by the various directory import functions (see Section 24.4).

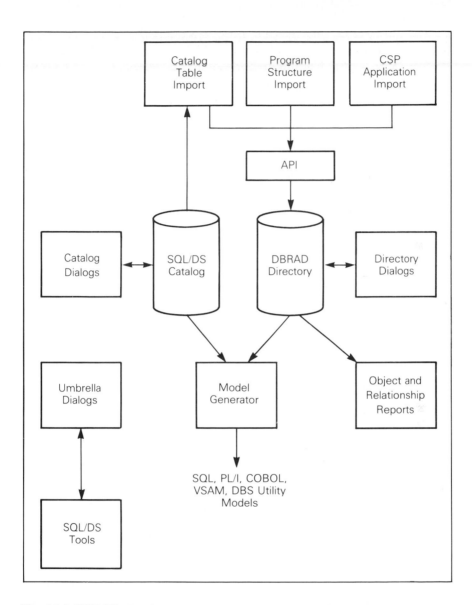

Fig. 24.1 DBRAD structure

(read or write) to a specific library. Also, each library can be assigned a specific status (e.g., test or production). DBRAD directory searches can be restricted to specific libraries. *Note:* A DBRAD library does not necessarily have to correspond to a library in the usual VM sense, although in practice it often will. The reader is referred to the IBM manuals for further discussion of this point.

DBRAD supports a number of predefined object types (TABLE, COLUMN, RECORD, LIBRARY, etc.). It also allows users to define their own object types. The DBRAD directory includes a predefined table for each predefined type, which is used to record attributes for objects of that type. For objects of user-defined type, the directory contains a text description only.

Next, certain objects can have one or more *component* objects; for example, a TABLE object will have a set of component COLUMN objects. In general, the components of a given object are the objects that are immediately subordinate to that given object. DBRAD supports a set of predefined component relationship types (TABLEs contain COLUMNs, etc.), which, like predefined object types, are represented by predefined tables in the DBRAD directory. Users can also define their own relationship types.

One last piece of terminology: If object *B* is a component of object *A*, then object *A* is said to be an *associate* of object *B*. An associate relationship is thus the inverse of a component relationship. However, associate relationships are not separately maintained in the DBRAD directory—the component relationship tables are obviously sufficient to represent the relationships in both directions.

We now move on to discuss each of the DBRAD components in turn.

24.2 CATALOG DIALOGS

The DBRAD Catalog Dialogs provide an easy way to explore the contents of the SQL/DS catalog. They are invoked by selecting the CD option on the DBRAD *Primary Option Menu* shown in Fig. 24.2. Selecting that option causes the DBRAD *Catalog Dialogs Home Panel* to be displayed. See Fig. 24.3. By way of illustration, we have included appropriate entries in that figure to request information for tables created by user CJDATE. *Note:* For SQL/DS tables, the DBRAD "library name" is usually just the SQL/DS user ID.

The effect of this request is to cause a list of all relevant tables to be displayed. From that list, we can request information about an individual table. In Fig. 24.4, we show the result of a request for information about table CJDATE.P (the parts table).

The panel displayed in response to our table request (i.e., Fig. 24.4) offers options ("commands") to display information about other related objects. Using the C command, for example, we could display details about each column of the table. The panel (not shown) used to display such detailed column information offers a *Column Homonym Search* facility,

```
---------------------- DBRAD/VM PRIMARY OPTION MENU ----------------------
OPTION  ===>
Data Base Relational Application Directory for VM/System Product  5798-FAP
  VMUSERID:  DBRAD      Data Base Name:  TSQLDS     SQL/DS USER ID: CJDATE

Dialogs                             Application Development
DD  Directory Dialogs               AD  CSP Application Development
CD  Catalog Dialogs                 AE  CSP Application Execution
                                    AU  CSP ALF Utility
Data Base                           MU  CSP Message File Utility
D   Data Base Interactive           MG  Model Generator
DE  Data Base Edit (DBEDIT)

Reporting & Queries                 Importing
OR  Object Reports                  SI  CSP Source Interface Utility
RR  Relationship Reports            AI  CSP Application Import
I   Interactive SQL                 PI  Program Structure Import
Q   Query & Reporting Facility (QMF) CT  Catalog Table Import
QB  QMF Batch Procedure             FI  File Import

Other                               Program Development ( PD )
PA  System Parameters               0-7 ISPF/PDF Functions

                                    (c) Copyright IBM Corporation 1987
```

Fig. 24.2 DBRAD Primary Option Menu

```
---------------------- DBRAD/VM CATALOG FACILITY -------------------------
COMMAND ===> T
                                         RETRIEVE LIMIT ===> 0100
ENTER ONE OF THE FOLLOWING COMMANDS:               LEVEL : 01

     D  DBSPACE
     T  TABLE/VIEW
     V  VIEW
     S  SYNONYM
     I  INDEX
     C  COLUMN
     H  COLUMN HOMONYMS (requires NAME)
     P  PROGRAM
     A  AUTHORIZATIONS
     L  REVOKE OF AUTHORIZATIONS - Impact List

ENTER/MODIFY THE REQUIRED INFORMATION BELOW:

     CREATOR ===> CJDATE              (AUTHID/USERID/GRANTEE)
        NAME ===>
          IN ===>                     (Table Name - for COLUMN only)
```

Fig. 24.3 DBRAD Catalog Dialogs Home Panel

```
------------------------------------- TABLE ---------------------- ROW 1 OF 16
                                                      SCROLL ===> PAGE
COMMAND ===>                                   RETRIEVE LIMIT ===> 0100
                                                          LEVEL : 03
ENTER ONE OF THE FOLLOWING COMMANDS:
   A - AUTH    C - COLUMN    S - SYNONYM   I - INDEX    U - UPDATEAUTH
   V - VIEW    P - PROGRAM   D - DBSPACE   B - BTABLE   X - ACCESS MODULE
   CREATOR: CJDATE      NAME: P
-------------------------------------------------------------------------
Table Type                  : TABLE
DBSPACE Name                : CJDATE
DBSPACE Number              : 18
Number of Columns           : 5
Indexed                     : Y
Default High Value ID       : 37167
Number of Pages (%)         : 1 (2)
Number of Rows              : 6
Average Row Length          : 39
Number of Rows Overflowed   : 0
Table Identifier            : -32763
Label                       :
LFD Table Identifier        : 0
LFD Link Identifier         : 0
LFD DBSPACE Identifier      : 0
Remarks:
```

Fig. 24.4 Table listing for table P

which produces a list of all tables that contain a column with the same name as the specified column. Fig. 24.5 shows a homonym listing for column name P#. The homonym search facility could be useful for (e.g.) checking consistency of column definitions across tables.

Returning to the table listing panel (Fig. 24.4), we see that another command option is A ("authorization"). If that option is selected, DBRAD will display a list of privileges held on the table, who granted them, and who holds them. DBRAD can also be requested to show the impact of revoking a particular privilege. Fig. 24.6 shows the effect of revoking ALL PRIVILEGES on the parts table from user CJWHITE. The report shows that CJWHITE has authorized USER1 and USER2 to access the parts table and that the revoke would remove these privileges.

24.3 IMPORT FACILITIES

DBRAD provides three facilities for importing object information into the DBRAD directory:

1. Catalog Table Import
2. Program Structure Import
3. CSP Application Import

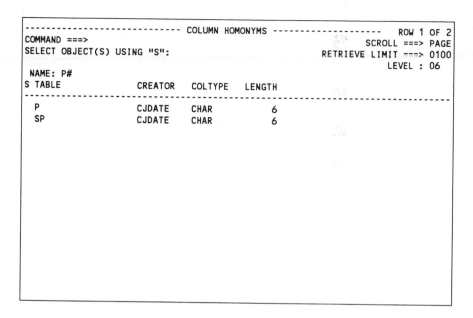

```
----------------------------- COLUMN HOMONYMS -------------------- ROW 1 OF 2
COMMAND ===>                                                SCROLL ===> PAGE
SELECT OBJECT(S) USING "S":                          RETRIEVE LIMIT ===> 0100
                                                                LEVEL : 06
  NAME: P#
S TABLE              CREATOR   COLTYPE   LENGTH
---------------------------------------------------------------------------
  P                  CJDATE    CHAR         6
  SP                 CJDATE    CHAR         6
```

Fig. 24.5 Column homonym listing for column name P#

```
------------------------------ REVOKE IMPACT LIST ---------------- ROW 1 OF 2
COMMAND ===>                                                SCROLL ===> PAGE
                                                     RETRIEVE LIMIT ===> 0100
ENTER ONE OF THE FOLLOWING COMMANDS:                            LEVEL : 07
  REVOKE - REVOKE PRIVILEGE BELOW    GRANT - GRANT PRIVILEGE BELOW

 REVOKE: ALL    ON: CJDATE.P              FROM: CJWHITE   BY: ALL
 GRANTEE   GTYPE    GRANTOR   DATE    TIME     (TARGET VIEW)
----------------------------------------------------------------------------
USER1     USER     CJWHITE   870916  19072981
USER2     USER     CJWHITE   870916  19075061
***************************** ((BOTTOM OF DATA)) ****************************
```

Fig. 24.6 DBRAD Revoke Impact List

Each of these facilities is invoked from the DBRAD Primary Option Menu (see Fig. 24.2). We discuss each in turn.

1. The DBRAD Catalog Table Import facility extracts table information from the SQL/DS catalog and stores it in the DBRAD directory as a TABLE object and a set of COLUMN objects. The component relationships between that table and its columns are also recorded.

Note: SQL/DS definitions must be imported into the DBRAD directory before the Directory Dialogs can be used to report on them. Analogous requirements apply to other definitions also, of course (e.g., CSP application definitions). This fact illustrates the important point that *the DBRAD directory is a passive information source, not an active one;* i.e., there is no guarantee that it contains the most recent version of the information. In particular, note the distinction between the Catalog Dialogs and the Directory Dialogs. The Catalog Dialogs do always operate in terms of the current state of the SQL/DS catalog. The Directory Dialogs, however, operate in terms of the current state of the DBRAD directory, which reflects the state of the SQL/DS catalog (and other information sources) *as of a specific time*—namely, the time when the information was imported into the directory.

2. The Program Structure Import facility is used to import COBOL and PL/I structures into the DBRAD directory from program source libraries. The facility creates RECORD and ITEM objects in the directory, but does not create any relationships between those objects and SQL/DS objects. Instead, such relationships must be created by means of the Directory Dialogs (see Section 24.4). Relationships can be created between records and their corresponding SQL/DS tables, and between items and their corresponding SQL/DS columns.

3. Finally, the CSP Application Import facility is (of course) used to import CSP application information. Surprisingly, the input to the import facility is not CSP's own "dictionary" (i.e., the Member Specification Library or MSL—see Chapter 21), but rather the output from the MSL Print utility. An advantage of this approach is that it allows the installation to consolidate MSLs. Usually, when developing CSP applications, all programmers have their own MSL, and library control and maintenance can become cumbersome. DBRAD helps solve such problems.

CSP Application Import creates the following DBRAD objects:

- APPLICATION object for each CSP application
- PROCESS object for each CSP process or statement group
- RECORD object for each CSP record, table, or SQL row
- MAP object for each CSP map
- ITEM object for each field in a CSP map or record

All these objects are related together in the directory via appropriate component relationships. The Directory Dialogs can be used to relate the CSP objects to the appropriate SQL/DS objects (tables, columns, etc.).

Having discussed how objects are created by the various import functions, we can now move on to outline the facilities provided by DBRAD to query and report on such objects.

24.4 DIRECTORY DIALOGS

The DBRAD Directory Dialogs are used to query, display, and update information in the DBRAD directory. The dialogs are invoked by selecting the DD option on the DBRAD Primary Option Menu (refer back to Fig. 24.2). The DBRAD *Directory Dialogs Home Panel* shown in Fig. 24.7 is then displayed.

Five commands are available from the home panel:

- *Object Search:* Display a list of objects that satisfy some specified search condition
- *Object Details:* Display the attributes of some object
- *Object Components:* Display the components of some object

```
----------------------- DBRAD/VM DIRECTORY DIALOGS -----------------------
COMMAND ===> A
                                                RETRIEVE LIMIT ===> 0100
ENTER ONE OF THE FOLLOWING COMMANDS:                        LEVEL : 01
  S - OBJECT SEARCH    C - OBJECT COMPONENTS    A - OBJECT ASSOCIATES
  O - OBJECT DETAILS   R - RELATIONSHIP DETAILS

ENTER/MODIFY THE REQUIRED INFORMATION BELOW

OBJECT:
    LIBRARY ===> CJDMSL
       NAME ===> P#                ALIAS =>
       TYPE ===> ITEM              (RECORD,ITEM,FILE,PSB,TABLE,COLUMN)
                                   (PROGRAM,APPL,PROCESS,MAP,REPORT)
                                   (SYSTEM,JOB,TRAN,INCLUDE,ALF)
                                   (LIBRARY OR OTHER USER TYPES)

RELATIONSHIPS ===>                 (C,A,B count Components, Associates, Both)

RELATED:
    LIBRARY ===>
       NAME ===>
       TYPE ===>
        SID ===>
```

Fig. 24.7 DBRAD Directory Dialogs Home Panel

- *Relationship Details:* Display relationship information for some object
- *Object Associates:* Display the associates of some object

Space does not permit us to discuss all of these commands in detail here. We content ourselves with a single example, namely a query to produce a "where-used" listing for a specified object. As shown in Fig. 24.7, we enter the "A" command ("object associates"), specifying the object as type ITEM, name P#, in library CJDMSL. The result of the query is shown in Fig. 24.8. The result shows that only one object, the SHIPREC record, uses the specified item.

In general, directory queries can be specified using a full or partial object key (library name, object type, object name). Partial keys can be specified in the same way as the argument to the SQL LIKE predicate (see Chapter 6)—the special characters "%" and "–" can be used to represent any sequence of zero or more characters and any single character, respectively. Queries can also be performed on the basis of object aliases.

As well as retrieving information, the Directory Dialogs can also be used to insert, delete, and update individual objects and relationships. The details are beyond the scope of this book.

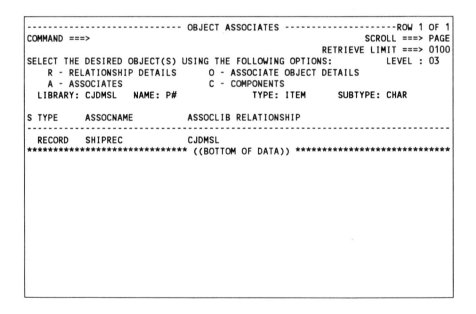

Fig. 24.8 Where-used listing for the P# item

24.5 REPORTS

The DBRAD reporting facilities produce reports from directory information. Two types of report can be produced:

- *Object Reports,* which show the attributes of specified objects
- *Relationship Reports,* which show the associates and components of specified objects

These reporting facilities are invoked directly from the DBRAD Primary Option Menu (see Fig. 24.2 again).

24.6 MODEL GENERATOR

The DBRAD Model Generator uses table definitions in the SQL/DS catalog, or table and record objects in the DBRAD directory, to create "model" statements of various kinds—for example, model SQL SELECT statements. Such model statements can then easily be edited to fit the requirements of some specific application. The following models can be produced, among others:

- Model SQL data definition statements (CREATE TABLE, CREATE VIEW, CREATE INDEX, etc.)
- Model SQL data manipulation statements (SELECT, INSERT, UPDATE, DELETE, DECLARE CURSOR, OPEN, FETCH, etc.)
- Model COBOL and PL/I structure declarations
- Model DATALOAD utility control statements (see Chapter 17)

The Model Generator is invoked from the DBRAD Primary Option Menu (refer to Fig. 24.2 once again). The DBRAD *Model Generator Panel* is then displayed (see Fig. 24.9). We have specified options on that panel to request the generation of a model SQL SELECT statement against the parts table (P), suitable for embedding in a PL/I program. We have also specified that the SQL/DS catalog (rather than the DBRAD directory) should be used as the source for the necessary descriptor information. *Note:* The DBRAD directory might be used for tables that have been dropped from SQL/DS but not deleted from the DBRAD directory. Indeed, the directory might be used in such a case to construct a model CREATE statement that would permit the dropped table to be created again.

The generated SELECT statement corresponding to the specifications of Fig. 24.9 is shown in Fig. 24.10. As that figure indicates, one interesting feature of the model generator is that it will include comments in the generated statements regarding any available indexes on the referenced table(s).

```
-------------------- DBRAD/VM MODEL GENERATOR ----------------------------
COMMAND ===>

ENTER/MODIFY THE REQUIRED INFORMATION BELOW

  SOURCE      ===> C          (D,C - Details from the Directory or SQL/DS Catalog)
  OUTPUT      ===> CJDATE DDL A

  QUALIFIER   ===> CJDATE     (LIBRARY or AUTHID)
  NAME        ===> P
  TYPE        ===>            (REC or TAB - for Directory Object)
  SYSTEM      ===> SQLDS
  MODEL       ===> SELECT     MODEL TYPE:
                              Records - STRUCT,VSAM
                              Tables  - DML WHENEVER,CONNECT,CURSOR,FETCH,SELECT,
                                            INSERT,UPDATE,DELETE,COMMIT,ROLLBACK
                                        ALL SQLCA,HOSTVAR,and DML List
                                        DDL SPACE,TABLE,LABELS,INDEX,VIEW
                                        LOAD
  LANGUAGE    ===> P     (C,P,S - COBOL,PLI,SQL)
  INDICATORS  ===> N     (Y,N - Indicator Variables)
  QUALIFIED   ===> N     (Y,N - Variables qualified by structure name)
  GLOBALS     ===> N     (Y,N - Variables in Global pool)
  TABLE TYPE  ===> A     (A,T,V - Select Table Type - ALL, TABLE, VIEW)
```

Fig. 24.9 DBRAD Model Generator Panel

```
EDIT ---- CJDATE DDL A1 ------------------------------------ COLUMNS 001 072
COMMAND ===>                                                 SCROLL ===> HALF
****** ************************** TOP OF DATA ********************************
000001      /************************************************************/
000002      /* SELECT FOR CJDATE.P                                      */
000003      /************************************************************/
000004        SELECT_P: PROCEDURE;
000005          EXEC SQL
000006            SELECT
000007              P#,PNAME,COLOR,WEIGHT,CITY
000008            INTO
000009              :P#,:PNAME,:COLOR,:WEIGHT,:CITY
000010            FROM CJDATE.P
000011      /*  ** NOTE: THE WHERE COLUMNS MUST BE CHECKED */
000012      /*  FOR APPLICATION CONTEXT SUITABILITY.    */
000013      /*  INDEXED BY CJDATE.XP                    */
000014      /*  RULES  CLUSTERED UNIQUE                 */
000015            WHERE
000016              P#=:P#
000017          ;
000018          END SELECT_P;
```

Fig. 24.10 Model SQL SELECT statement for the parts table

24.7   APPLICATION PROGRAM INTERFACE

DBRAD provides an Application Program Interface (API) to allow user application programs to update information in the DBRAD directory. The interface does not, however, support read access. Read access could be achieved by direct use of SQL SELECT statements against the directory tables.

Several DBRAD functions use this interface. One example is the DBRAD *File Import* facility, which allows most of the online functions we have discussed in this chapter so far to be executed from a CMS EXEC.

24.8   UMBRELLA DIALOGS

The DBRAD Umbrella Dialogs constitute the last major set of DBRAD facilities. They permit the DBRAD user to invoke other IBM tools, such as QMF, CSP, and DBEDIT, without leaving the DBRAD environment. The Primary Option Menu in Fig. 24.2 shows several options for invoking such tools. *Note:* That menu can be tailored to suit the tools installed on a particular SQL/DS system.

24.9   CONCLUSION

As we have seen, the DBRAD directory extends the SQL/DS catalog to allow more application-oriented information to be recorded and tracked. It consolidates much of the information used by many of the separate IBM products that support SQL/DS (most notably CSP; DBRAD allows CSP users to consolidate distinct MSL libraries and to relate MSL information to the SQL/DS objects used by CSP applications). Although intended primarily as a tool to help integrate SQL/DS and CSP, it offers significant function for nonCSP users as well.

PART

IV

◆

SUMMARY
AND CONCLUSIONS

Whither SQL/DS?

25.1 INTRODUCTION

In the preceding three parts of this book we have presented a detailed description of SQL/DS, a state-of-the-art relational DBMS, and some of its major companion products. Our description has been at the level of SQL/DS Version 2, Release 2. The following topics have been covered (among others):

- system structure
- operating environments
- basic objects and operators
- data definition
- data manipulation
- the catalog

- views
- security and authorization
- integrity
- application programming
- transaction management
- storage structure
- SQL/DS tools (ISQL, DBS utility, etc.)
- end-user tools (QMF, AS)
- DP professional tools (CSP, DBRAD)
- data extract (DXT)
- PC link products (HDBV, ECF)

In the next (and final) section of the book, we offer some opinions regarding possible future developments in connexion with SQL/DS. A word of warning: Please understand that this material is necessarily some-what speculative in nature. Other writers may disagree with any or all of the opinions expressed. Also, much of the discussion is fairly general and is applicable to any relational DBMS, not just to SQL/DS.

25.2 FUTURE DEVELOPMENTS

Relational systems such as SQL/DS stress, to a much greater degree than nonrelational systems, the distinction between externals and internals, or (equivalently) between the logical and physical levels of the system. At the logical level, the emphasis is on *usability:* The system provides a simple data structure and simple operators for manipulating that structure, and that simplicity leads to high user productivity (see Appendix A). At the physical level, the emphasis is on *freedom:* The decoupling of the two levels means that the installation is free to make nontrivial changes at the physical level without affecting the user at all (other than in performance, of course).

Turning to SQL/DS specifically, we can expect to see significant devel-opments at both levels in the near future. At the physical level, new kinds of access mechanism (hashing, pointer chains, etc.) are likely to be provided as alternatives to the existing index mechanism, and the optimizer will be enhanced to exploit those new structures. (Of course, such new mechanisms should not be directly visible at the logical level.) At the logical level, exten-sions to the SQL language to provide direct support for such functions as outer join are likely to be implemented (see the book *Relational Database: Selected Writings,* by C. J. Date, Addison-Wesley, 1986).

Still in the near term, there are some obvious trends of a more directly commercial and competitive nature. SQL/DS has clearly established itself as a leader in the database marketplace. As a result, we can expect to see (and indeed are already beginning to see) commercial developments in a number of areas:

- Other vendors will build products to plug gaps in IBM's own product line—for example, products to assist in SQL/DS security management, SQL/DS performance monitoring and tuning, and SQL/DS database design.

- Other vendors will also build interfaces from their own proprietary DBMSs, application generators, etc., to SQL/DS. Again, several such interfaces already exist.

- Application packages for specialized application areas—for example, human resource management—will be produced to run on SQL/DS. Such packages will be available from both IBM and other vendors.

More far-reaching developments can be expected in the longer term. In order to get some idea as to what those longer-term developments might look like, we can take a look at the activities currently under way in university laboratories and similar research establishments. There are in fact a large number of such activities, all of them building on a relational foundation. They include:

- distributed database systems
- shared database machines
- semantic modeling
- integration of new kinds of data (e.g., text, images)
- expert database systems
- new kinds of interface, including natural language
- engineering and scientific database systems

and others. Of course, some of these expected developments are much less "long-term" than others; for example, database machines are available in the marketplace today, and so are natural-language systems; but the point is that research is continuing on all of these topics, and nearly all of it is relational-based. Moreover, the fact that these activities are built on a relational base is significant in itself: Much of the research would scarcely even be feasible on any other kind of foundation.

On the question of distributed systems specifically, it is interesting to note that a distributed version of the old System R prototype called R* (pronounced "R star") has been operational for some time in the IBM research laboratories. It is therefore not unlikely that the technology of R* will someday be incorporated into distributed versions of both SQL/DS and DB2, especially as some of IBM's competitors have already produced distributed versions of their own proprietary relational products. In some respects, in fact, the emergence of true distributed systems in the market-place is likely to be the most significant event since the (long-awaited) emergence of true relational systems.

The fact that all of this research is based on a relational foundation is of course an indication of the general acceptance of relational ideas in the academic world.* By now, of course, relational ideas have become generally accepted in the commercial world also. In support of this claim, we can point to the enormous number of recent product announcements; it is a fact that just about every announcement these days is either for a brand-new relational system or for "relational" enhancements to one of the older, nonrelational systems ("relational" in quotes because it is by no means always clear that those enhancements are in fact relational; see Appendix B for a discussion of this point). At a conservative count, there are now well over 100 relational systems on the market (including a significant number for microcomputers), and no doubt that number will have increased considerably by the time this book appears in print. And the success of SQL/DS can do nothing but strengthen the influence of relational technology in the commercial world. Nobody can now deny that, so far as database management is concerned, relational systems are the way of the future.

---

*Further evidence of that acceptance is provided by the fact that the Association for Computing Machinery (ACM) presented its 1981 Turing Award to Dr. Codd, the original architect of the relational model, for his work on relational theory. The Turing Award is presented annually for significant and fundamental contributions to the field of computer science. It is generally recognized as the most prestigious award in the entire field.

APPENDIXES

Advantages of SQL/DS

A.1 INTRODUCTION

If the advantages of a relational system such as SQL/DS must be summed up in a single word, that word is *simplicity*—where by "simplicity" we mean, primarily, simplicity for the user. Simplicity, in turn, translates into *usability* and *productivity*. Usability means that even comparatively unskilled users can use the system to do useful work; that is, end-users can frequently obtain useful results from the system without having to go through the potential bottleneck of the DP department. Productivity means that both end-users and DP professionals can be more productive in their day-to-day activities; as a result, they can between them make significant inroads into the well-known application backlog problem (see Section A.7 below). In this appendix we discuss the advantages of a system like SQL/DS in some detail.

A.2   SOUND THEORETICAL BASE

The first point is that relational systems are based on a formal theoretical foundation, the *relational model* (discussed in detail in Appendix B). As a result, they behave in well-defined ways; and (possibly without consciously realizing the fact) users have a simple model of that behavior in their mind that enables them to predict with confidence what the system will do in any given situation. There are (or should be) no surprises. This predictability means that the user interfaces are easy to document, teach, learn, use, and remember.

Note: It cannot be denied that most systems today, even relational systems, do nevertheless display rather ad hoc and unpredictable behavior in some areas. As an example, consider the treatment of view updating in SQL/DS, which does display a certain amount of unpleasant arbitrariness (see Section 10.4). But such arbitrariness tends to occur precisely at those points where the implementation has departed from the underlying theory. For example, a crucial component of the relational model is the concept of *primary key* (see Appendix B). However, SQL/DS does not fully support that concept, and it is that omission that is the direct cause of the arbitrariness just referred to. SQL/DS is not the sole offender in this regard, of course—similar criticisms apply to most other systems at the time of writing—but it does serve to illustrate the undesirable consequences of disregarding the prescriptions of the underlying model.

Incidentally, we remark in passing that many critics of relational systems in the past have actually objected to the fact that it is based on theory! The objection seems to be that only theoreticians are capable of understanding, or need to understand, something that is based on theory. Our own position is exactly the opposite: Systems that are not based on theory are usually very difficult for *anyone* to understand. It cannot be stated too strongly that "theoretical" does *not* mean "not practical." On the contrary, considerations that are initially dismissed as being "only theoretical" [sic] have a nasty habit of becoming horribly practical a few years later on.

A.3   SMALL NUMBER OF CONCEPTS

The relational model is notable for the small number of concepts it involves. As pointed out in Section 8.5, all data in a relational database is represented in one and only one way, namely as column values within rows of tables, and hence only one operator is needed for each of the four basic manipulative functions (retrieve, change, insert, delete). For exactly the same reason, fewer operators are also needed in a relational system for all the other functions—data definition, security and authorization control, storage mapping, etc.—that are required in a general-purpose DBMS. In the case of authorization specifically, it is the simplicity and regularity of the data structure that makes it possible to define such a sophisticated data protection mechanism (one in which, as was shown by the examples of Chapter 11, value-dependent, value-independent, context-dependent, and other constraints can be easily defined and conveniently enforced).

A separate but related point is the following: In the relational model, distinct concepts are cleanly separated, not bundled together. By contrast, the parent-child (or owner-member) link construct found in hierarchic and network systems bundles together several fundamentally distinct notions: It is simultaneously a representation of a one-to-many relationship, an access path (or collection of access paths), a mechanism for enforcing certain integrity constraints, and so on. As a result, it becomes difficult to tell exactly what purpose a given link is serving (and it may be used for a purpose for which it was not intended). For example, a program may come to rely on an access path that is really a side effect of the way the database designer chose to represent a certain integrity constraint. If that integrity constraint needs to be changed, then the database will have to be restructured, with a strong likelihood that the program will then have to be rewritten—even if that program is completely uninterested in the integrity constraint per se.

A.4 SET-LEVEL OPERATORS

Relational data manipulation operations (such as SELECT, UPDATE, etc., in SQL) are *set-level* operations. This fact means that users simply have to specify *what* they want, not *how* to get to what they want. For example, a user needing to know which parts are supplied by supplier S2 can simply issue the SQL query:

```
SELECT  P#
FROM    SP
WHERE   S# = 'S2'
```

SQL/DS decides how to "navigate" through the physical storage structure on the disk in order to respond to this query. (For this reason, as mentioned in Chapter 1, systems such as SQL/DS are frequently described as "automatic navigation" systems. By contrast, systems in which users have to do that navigation for themselves are described as "manual navigation" systems.) By taking this burden off the user's back, SQL/DS is freeing the user to concentrate on solving the real problem—i.e., on finding an answer to the query, in the case at hand, and using that information for whatever purpose it is needed in the outside world. In the case of end-users, in fact, it is automatic navigation that makes it possible for the user to use the system in the first place. It is not difficult to find a simple SQL/DS query for which an equivalent COBOL program would be ten or twenty pages long, and writing such a program would be out of the question for most users (and maybe not worth the effort involved even when not).

Furthermore, application programmers can take advantage of the automatic navigation feature of the system as well, just as end-users can. Application programmers too can be more productive in a system like SQL/DS.

A.5 THE DUAL-MODE PRINCIPLE

In SQL/DS the same language, namely SQL, is used for both programming and interactive access to the database. This fact has two immediate consequences:

1. Different categories of user—database administrators, application programmers, end-users from any number of different backgrounds—are all "speaking the same language" and are thus better able to communicate with one another. It is also easy for one person to switch between categories—e.g., to perform data definition (administrative) functions on one occasion and ad hoc query (end-user) functions on another.

2. Application programmers can easily debug the database portions of their programs (i.e., embedded SQL statements) through one of the SQL/DS interactive interfaces (e.g., ISQL or QMF). Those interfaces thus serve as a powerful and convenient program debugging aid.

A.6 DATA INDEPENDENCE

Data independence is the independence of users and user programs from details of the way the data is stored and accessed. It is critically important for at least two reasons:

1. It is important for application programmers because, without it, changes to the structure of the database would necessitate corresponding changes to application programs. In the absence of such independence, one of two things happens: Either it becomes almost impossible to make required changes to the database because of the investment in existing programs, or (more likely) a significant portion of the application programming effort is devoted purely to maintenance activity— maintenance activity, that is, that would be unnecessary if the system had provided data independence in the first place. Both of these factors are significant contributors to the application backlog problem mentioned in the introduction to this appendix.

2. It is important for end-users because, without it, direct end-user access to the database would scarcely be possible at all. Data independence and very high level languages such as SQL go hand in hand.

Of course, data independence is not an absolute—different systems provide it in differing degrees. To put this another way, few systems, if any, provide no data independence at all; it is just that some systems are more data-dependent than others. Furthermore, the term "data independence" really covers two somewhat distinct notions, namely physical data independence (i.e., independence of the physical arrangement of the data on the storage medium) and logical data independence (i.e., independence of the logical structure of the data as tables and fields). SQL/DS is fairly strong on both aspects, though there is undoubtedly still room for improvement in both areas (for example, it is unfortunate that the logical notion of enforcing uniqueness is bundled with the physical notion of an index). Basically, SQL/DS provides physical data independence by virtue of its automatic navigation and automatic recompilation features (see Section 2.5 if you need to refresh your memory concerning the latter), and logical data independence by virtue of its view mechanism (see Section 10.5 for details).

A.7 EASE OF APPLICATION DEVELOPMENT

SQL/DS facilitates the application development process in a variety of significant ways:

1. First, as discussed in Chapter 18, the availability of the SQL/DS front-end products—QMF, AS, IC/1, etc.—means that it may not be necessary to develop an application program (in the traditional sense of the term) at all. The importance of this point can scarcely be over-emphasized.

2. Second, the availability of CSP (see Chapter 21) means that if specialized applications are needed, then they can be developed quickly and easily, still without any programming in the conventional sense.

3. Third, the high degree of data independence provided and the high level of the SQL/DS application programming interface (embedded SQL) together mean that when it *is* necessary to write a conventional program, then that program is easier to write, requires less maintenance, and is easier to change when it does require maintenance, than it would be in an older, nonrelational system.

4. Last, and largely as a consequence of the previous three points, the application development cycle can involve a great deal more *prototyp-*

ing than it used to: A first version can be built and shown to the intended users, who can then suggest improvements for incorporation into the next version, and so on. As a result, the final application should do exactly what its users require it to. The overall development process is far less rigid than it used to be, and the application users can be far more involved in that process, to the benefit of all concerned.

A.8   DYNAMIC DATA DEFINITION

We have already discussed the advantages of dynamic data definition at some length in Chapter 5 (Section 5.5), and we will not repeat the arguments here. However, we make one additional point: The ability to create new definitions at any time without having to bring the system to a halt is really only part of a larger overall objective, which is to eliminate the need for *any* planned system shutdown. Thus, for example, utilities can be invoked from an online terminal, and they can run in parallel with production work; it is possible, for example, to take an image copy of the database even while transactions are simultaneously updating it. Ideally, the system should have to be started exactly once, when it is first installed, and should then run "forever." (We are not claiming that this objective has yet been fully achieved.)

A.9   EASE OF INSTALLATION AND EASE OF OPERATION

SQL/DS is designed to be as easy to install and easy to operate as possible. Various features of the system, some of them touched on in previous sections of this appendix, contribute to the achievement of this objective. Details of such features (other than details already given in the body of the text) are beyond the scope of this book, but it is worth pointing out explicitly one very important consequence of them, namely the following: It requires only a comparatively small population of DP professionals (database administrators, system programmers, console operators) to provide SQL/DS services to a very large population of users (application programmers and end-users). SQL/DS is an extremely cost-effective system.

A.10   SIMPLIFIED DATABASE DESIGN

Database design in a relational system is easier than it is in a nonrelational system for a number of reasons (though it may still involve some difficult decisions in complex situations).

- First, the decoupling of logical and physical levels means that logical and physical design problems can be separately addressed.

- Second, at the logical level, the data structure is just about as simple as it can possibly be.

- Third, there are some sound principles (basically the principles of *normalization*) that can be brought to bear on the logical design problem.

- Last, the dynamic data definition feature and the high degree of data independence (again) mean that it is not necessary to do the entire design all at once, and neither is it so critical to get it right first time.

A comprehensive logical design methodology that uses a combination of the principles of normalization with a top-down (entity-based) approach is described in the book *Relational Database: Selected Writings,* by C. J. Date (Addison-Wesley, 1986).

A.11 INTEGRATED CATALOG

As explained in Chapter 9, the SQL/DS catalog is completely integrated with the rest of the data, in the sense that it is represented in the same way (as tables) and can be queried in the same way (via SQL). In other words, there is no artificial and unnecessary distinction between catalog data and other data, or between data and "data about the data" (or "metadata," as it is sometimes called). This integration brings with it a number of benefits, among them the following:

1. Looking something up in the database and looking something up in the catalog are one and the same process. To see the advantage here, consider the analogy of looking something up in a book and looking something up in the table of contents for that book. It would be very annoying if the table of contents appeared somewhere other than in the book itself, in a format that required some different manner of access (for example, if the table of contents was in Spanish and was stored on a set of 3-by-5 cards, while the text of the book itself was in English). The role of the catalog with respect to the database is precisely similar to that of the table of contents with respect to a book.

2. The process of creating generalized (i.e., metadata-driven) application programs is considerably simplified. For example, suppose it is required to write a program that checks that every supplier number value appearing anywhere in the database also appears in the S# column of the suppliers table S—in itself a reasonable requirement—without making any prior assumptions about the structure of the database (i.e., the program must not rely on any builtin knowledge as to what tables exist or what their columns are). More generally, suppose it is required to write a program to check that every value of type X appearing anywhere in

the database also appears in some specified column *Y* of some specified table *Z* (where *X, Y,* and *Z* are parameters), again without making any prior assumptions about the structure of the database. In both of these examples, the integrated catalog is crucial.

A.12 SQL SUPPORT

SQL/DS supports (a dialect of) the industry standard relational language SQL. SQL can be used:

- For data definition, data manipulation, and data control operations
- For ad hoc query access to the database (ISQL, QMF, AS)
- For defining the data to be reported on (QMF, AS)
- For defining the data to be graphed (QMF, AS)
- For defining the data to be downloaded to a PC (HDBV, ECF)
- For programmed access to the database via one of the SQL/DS-supported programming languages (APL, BASIC, COBOL, FORTRAN, PL/I, Prolog, REXX, or Assembler Language)

As the industry standard, SQL provides a potential base for intersystem communication: A SQL/DS site might one day be able to communicate across a communications network, not only with other SQL/DS sites (partially supported already via database switching), but with any site that supports a system of any kind that supports the same SQL interface. Such intersystem communication in turn could provide the basis for true distributed database support. Finally, SQL/DS support for SQL also raises the possibility of running third-party, SQL-based applications software on top of the SQL/DS DBMS.

A.13 PERFORMANCE

Critics of relational systems have traditionally always focused on the performance question. Ever since the first prototypes were built in the early 1970s, relational systems have suffered from the stigma of being (allegedly) poor performers. The fact is, however, that (contrary to popular belief) performance is actually a strength of relational systems like SQL/DS.

Of course, it is difficult to make definitive statements regarding the performance of any given DBMS; performance depends on so many variables, including machine type and size, operating system, buffer parameters, number of users, and of course transaction mix. But one general point that can be made is the following: Performance in a relational system is *critically* dependent on the quality of the system optimizer; performance in a nonrelational system, by contrast, is critically dependent on the quality of the application programmer. In some ways, in fact, the optimizer can be regarded as an embodiment and mechanization of the skills of a good human programmer. Given that not all human programmers are "good," therefore, it is surely obvious that in the long run (and at least on average) a good relational system will *out*perform a typical nonrelational system. There are at least three reasons for this state of affairs:

1. The optimizer has a wealth of information available to it that a human programmer typically would not have. To be specific, it has certain statistical information, such as the size of each table, the number of distinct values in each column (though in SQL/DS this latter statistic is an estimate merely), the percentage of pages in a given tablespace occupied by a given table, and so on. As a result, the optimizer is able to make a more accurate assessment of the efficiency of any given strategy for implementing a particular request, and is thus more likely to choose the most efficient implementation.

2. Furthermore, if the database statistics change significantly, then a different choice of strategy may be desirable; in other words, reoptimization may be required. In a relational system, reoptimization is trivial— it simply involves a reprocessing of the request by the system optimizer (i.e., a SQL recompilation, in the case of SQL/DS). In a nonrelational system, by contrast, reoptimization involves a rewrite of the program, and will probably therefore not be done at all.

3. Finally, the optimizer is a *program,* and is therefore by definition much more patient than a typical application programmer. The optimizer is quite capable of considering literally hundreds of different implementation strategies for a given request, whereas it is extremely unlikely that a human programmer would consider more than three or four.

Thus it can be argued with some justification that a relational system with a good optimizer is quite likely to outperform a nonrelational system (on average). And the evidence is that the SQL/DS optimizer is indeed quite good—and, of course, it is likely to improve from release to release.

A.14 EXTENDABILITY

As pointed out in Section 25.2, almost all research in database systems is founded upon a relational base. As a consequence, users of today's relational systems should be in a better position to take advantage of the fruits of that research as and when they appear (where by "better" we mean, of course, "better than if they were users of some other kind of system").

The Relational Model

B.1 INTRODUCTION

SQL/DS is a relational DBMS ("relational system" for short). The purpose of this appendix is to explain exactly what that statement means. Basically, a relational system is a system that is constructed in accordance with the relational *model* (or at least the major principles of that model); and the relational model is *a way of looking at data*—that is, a prescription for how to represent data and how to manipulate that representation. More specifically, the relational model is concerned with three aspects of data: data *structure,* data *integrity,* and data *manipulation.* We examine each of these in turn (in Sections B.2, B.3, and B.4, respectively), and then consider the question of what exactly it is that constitutes a relational *system* (in Section B.5).

Note: In this appendix we will (for the most part) be using formal rela-

Formal relational term	Informal equivalents
relation	table
tuple	record, row
attribute	field, column
primary key	unique identifier

Fig. B.1 Some terminology

tional terminology. For convenience, Fig. B.1 repeats from Chapter 1 the major relational terms and their informal equivalents.

B.2   RELATIONAL DATA STRUCTURE

The smallest unit of data in the relational model is the individual data value. Such values are considered to be *atomic*—that is, they are nondecomposable so far as the model is concerned. A *domain* is the set of all possible data values of some particular type. For example, the domain of supplier numbers is the set of all valid supplier numbers; the domain of shipment quantities is the set of all integers greater than zero and less than 10,000 (say). Thus domains are *pools of values,* from which the actual values appearing in attributes (columns) are drawn. The significance of domains is as follows: If two attributes draw their values from the same domain, then comparisons—and hence joins, unions, etc.—involving those two attributes probably make sense, because they are comparing like with like; conversely, if two attributes draw their values from different domains, then comparisons (etc.) involving those two attributes probably do not make sense. In SQL terms, for example, the query

```
SELECT P.*, SP.*
FROM   P, SP
WHERE  P.P# = SP.P#
```

probably does make sense, whereas the query

```
SELECT P.*, SP.*
FROM   P, SP
WHERE  P.WEIGHT = SP.QTY
```

probably does not. (SQL/DS, however, has no notion of domains per se. Both of the foregoing SELECT statements are legal in SQL/DS.)

Note that domains are primarily conceptual in nature. They may or may not be explicitly stored in the database as actual sets of values. But they should be specified as part of the database definition (in a system that supports the concept at all—but most systems currently do not); and then each attribute definition should include a reference to the corresponding domain. A given attribute may have the same name as the corresponding domain or a different name. Obviously it must have a different name if any ambiguity would otherwise result (in particular, if two attributes in the same relation are both based on the same domain; see the definition of relation below, and note the phrase "not necessarily all distinct").

We are now in a position to define the term "relation." A *relation* on domains D1, D2, . . ., Dn (not necessarily all distinct) consists of a *heading* and a *body*. The heading consists of a fixed set of *attributes* A1, A2, . . ., An, such that there is a one-to-one correspondence between the attributes Ai and the underlying domains Di (i = 1,2,. . .,n). The body consists of a time-varying set of *tuples,* where each tuple in turn consists of a set of attribute-value pairs (Ai:vi) (i = 1,2,. . .,n), one such pair for each attribute Ai in the heading. For any given attribute-value pair (Ai:vi), vi is a value from the unique domain Di that is associated with the attribute Ai.

As an example, let us see how the supplier relation S measures up to this definition (see Fig. 1.2 in Chapter 1). The underlying domains are the domain of supplier numbers (D1, say), the domain of supplier names (D2), the domain of supplier status values (D3), and the domain of city names (D4). The heading of S consists of the attributes S# (underlying domain D1), SNAME (domain D2), STATUS (domain D3), and CITY (domain D4). The body of S consists of a set of tuples (five tuples in Fig. 1.2, but this set varies with time as updates are made to the relation); and each tuple consists of a set of four attribute-value pairs, one such pair for each of the four attributes in the heading. For example, the tuple for supplier S1 consists of the pairs

```
( S#      : 'S1'      )
( SNAME  : 'Smith'   )
( STATUS : 20         )
( CITY   : 'London'  )
```

(though it is normal to elide the attribute names in informal contexts). And of course each attribute value does indeed come from the appropriate underlying domain; the value S1, for example, does come from the supplier number domain D1. So S is indeed a relation according to the definition.

Note carefully that when we draw a relation such as relation S as a table, as we did in Fig. 1.2, we are merely making use of a convenient method for representing the relation on paper. A table and a relation are not really the same thing, though for most of this book we have assumed that they are. For example, the rows of a table clearly have an ordering (from top to bottom), whereas the tuples of a relation do not (the body of a relation is a mathematical *set,* and sets do not have any ordering in mathematics). Likewise, the columns of a table also have an ordering (from left to right), whereas the attributes of a relation do not.

Notice also that the underlying domains of a relation are "not necessarily all distinct." Many examples have already been given in which they are not; see, e.g., the result relation in Example 6.3.1 (Chapter 6), which includes two attributes both defined on the domain of city names.

The value *n* (the number of attributes in the relation, or equivalently the number of underlying domains) is called the *degree* of the relation. A relation of degree one is called *unary,* a relation of degree two *binary,* a relation of degree three *ternary,* . . ., and a relation of degree *n n-ary.* In the suppliers-and-parts database, relations S, P, and SP have degrees 4, 5, and 3, respectively. The number of tuples in the relation is called the *cardinality* of that relation; the cardinalities of relations S, P, and SP of Fig. 1.2 are 5, 6, and 12, respectively. The cardinality of a relation changes with time, whereas the degree does not.

B.3   RELATIONAL DATA INTEGRITY

One important consequence of the definitions in the previous section is that *every relation has a primary key.* Since the body of a relation is a set, and sets by definition do not contain duplicate elements, it follows that (at any given time) no two tuples of a relation can be duplicates of each other. Let R be a relation with attributes A1, A2, . . ., A*n*. The set of attributes K = (A*i*,A*j*,. . .,A*k*) of R is said to be a *candidate key* of R if and only if it satisfies the following two time-independent properties:

1. *Uniqueness:*
   At any given time, no two distinct tuples of R have the same value for A*i,* the same value for A*j,* . . ., and the same value for A*k*.
2. *Minimality:*
   None of A*i,* A*j,* . . ., A*k* can be discarded from K without destroying the uniqueness property.

Every relation has at least one candidate key, because at least the combination of all of its attributes has the uniqueness property. For a given relation, one candidate key is designated as the *primary* key; the remaining candidate keys (if any) are called *alternate* keys. *Note:* The rationale by which one candidate key is chosen as the primary key (in cases where there is a choice) is outside the scope of the relational model per se. In practice the choice is usually straightforward.

Example: Suppose that supplier names and supplier numbers are both unique (at any given time, no two suppliers have the same number or the same name). Then relation S has two candidate keys, S# and SNAME. We choose S# as the primary key; SNAME then becomes an alternate key.

Continuing with the example, consider attribute S# of relation SP. It is clear that a given value for that attribute, say the supplier number S1, should be permitted to appear in the database only if that same value also appears as a value of the primary key S# of relation S (for otherwise the database cannot be considered to be in a state of integrity). An attribute such as SP.S# is said to be a *foreign key.* In general, a foreign key is an attribute (or attribute combination) of one relation R2 whose values are required to match those of the primary key of some relation R1 (R1 and R2 not necessarily distinct). Note that a foreign key and the corresponding primary key should be defined on the same underlying domain.

We can now state the two integrity rules of the relational model. *Note:* These rules are *general,* in the sense that any database that conforms to the model is required to satisfy them. However, any specific database will have a set of additional specific rules that apply to it alone. For example, the suppliers-and-parts database may have a specific rule to the effect that shipment quantities must be in the range 1 to 9999, say. But such specific rules are outside the scope of the relational model per se.

1. *Entity integrity:*
   No attribute participating in the primary key of a base relation is allowed to contain any nulls.

2. *Referential integrity:*
   If base relation R2 includes a foreign key FK matching the primary key PK of some base relation R1, then every value of FK in R2 must either (a) be equal to the value of PK in some tuple of R1 or (b) be wholly null (i.e., each attribute value participating in that FK value must be null). R1 and R2 are not necessarily distinct.

(A couple of asides: First, a *base relation* corresponds to what we have been calling a base table in the body of this book; i.e., it is an autonomous, named relation. See Chapter 5 for further discussion. Second, although the two rules are framed in terms of nulls, we do not necessarily assume the rather peculiar kind of null that is found in SQL today.)

The justification for the entity integrity rule is as follows:

1. Base relations correspond to entities in the real world. For example, base relation S corresponds to a set of suppliers in the real world.

2. By definition, entities in the real world are distinguishable—i.e., they have a unique identification of some kind.

3. Primary keys perform the unique identification function in the relational model.

4. Thus, a primary key value that was null would be a contradiction in terms—in effect, it would be saying that there was some entity that had

no known *id*entity. An entity that cannot be identified is a contradiction in terms. Hence the name "entity integrity."

To put it another way: *In a relational database, we never record information about something we cannot identify.*

As for the second rule ("referential integrity"), it is clear that a given foreign key value must have a matching primary key value in some tuple of the referenced relation if that foreign key value is nonnull. Sometimes, however, it is necessary to permit the foreign key to accept nulls. (We remark, however, that nulls in a foreign key position are likely to be of the "property does not apply" variety, rather than the "value unknown" variety.) For example, suppose that in a given company it is legal for some employee to be currently assigned to no department at all. For such an employee, the department number attribute (which is a foreign key) would have to be null in the tuple representing that employee in the database.

B.4   RELATIONAL DATA MANIPULATION

The manipulative part of the relational model consists of a set of operators known collectively as the *relational algebra,* together with a relational assignment operator which assigns the value of some arbitrary expression of the algebra to another relation. We discuss the algebra first.

Each operator of the relational algebra takes either one or two relations as its input and produces a new relation as its output. Codd originally defined eight such operators, two groups of four each: (1) the traditional set operations union, intersection, difference, and Cartesian product (all modified slightly to take account of the fact that their operands are relations, as opposed to arbitrary sets); and (2) the special relational operations select, project, join, and divide. The eight operations are shown symbolically in Fig. B.2. We give a brief definition of each operation below; for simplicity, we assume in those definitions that the left-to-right order of attributes within a relation *is* significant—not because it is necessary to do so, but because it simplifies the discussion.

Traditional Set Operations

Each of the traditional set operations takes two operands. For all except Cartesian product, the two operand relations must be *union-compatible*— that is, they must be of the same degree, n say, and the ith attribute of each ($i = 1,2,. . .,n$) must be based on the same domain (they do not have to have the same name).

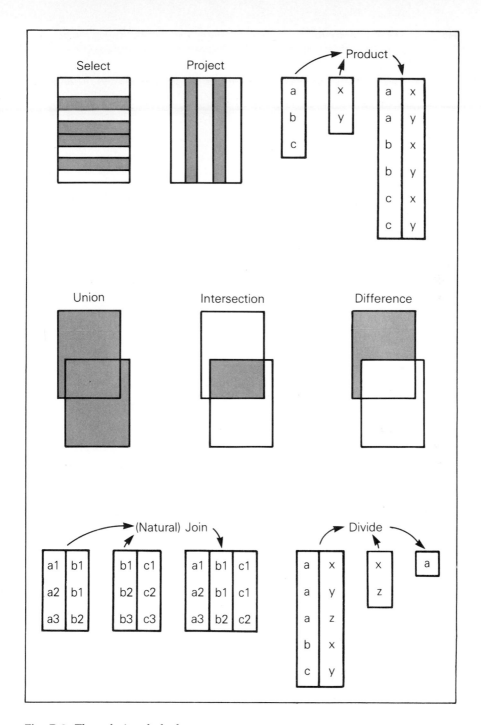

Fig. B.2 The relational algebra

- Union

The union of two (union-compatible) relations A and B is the set of all
tuples *t* belonging to either A or B (or both).
    SQL example:

```
SELECT S.S# FROM S
UNION
SELECT SP.S# FROM SP
```

- Intersection

The intersection of two (union-compatible) relations A and B is the set of
all tuples *t* belonging to both A and B.
    SQL example:

```
SELECT S.S# FROM S
WHERE   EXISTS
      ( SELECT SP.S# FROM SP
        WHERE  SP.S# = S.S# )
```

- Difference

The difference between two (union-compatible) relations A and B—in that
order—is the set of all tuples *t* belonging to A and not to B.
    SQL example:

```
SELECT S.S# FROM S
WHERE   NOT EXISTS
      ( SELECT SP.S# FROM SP
        WHERE  SP.S# = S.S# )
```

- Product

The product of two relations A and B is the set of all tuples *t* such that *t* is
the concatenation of a tuple *a* belonging to A and a tuple *b* belonging to
B.
    SQL example:

```
SELECT S.*, SP.*
FROM   S, SP
```

Special Relational Operations

- Selection

Let *theta* represent any valid scalar comparison operator (for example, =,
~=, >, >=, etc.). The theta-selection of relation A on attributes X and
Y is the set of all tuples *t* of A such that the predicate "*t*.X *theta t*.Y"
evaluates to *true*. (Attributes X and Y should be defined on the same domain, and the operation *theta* must make sense for that domain.) A constant value may be specified instead of attribute Y. Thus, the theta-selection

operator yields a "horizontal" subset of a given relation—that is, that sub-set of the tuples of the given relation for which a specified predicate is satis-fied. *Note:* "Theta-selection" is often abbreviated to just "selection." But note that "selection" is not the same as the SELECT operator of SQL.

SQL example:

```
SELECT  S.*
FROM    S
WHERE   CITY ~= 'London'
```

- Projection

The projection operator yields a "vertical" subset of a given relation—that is, that subset obtained by selecting specified attributes and then eliminating redundant duplicate tuples within the attributes selected, if necessary.

SQL example:

```
SELECT  DISTINCT P.COLOR, P.CITY
FROM    P
```

- Join

Let *theta* be as defined under "Selection" above. The theta-join of rela-tion A on attribute X with relation B on attribute Y is the set of all tuples *t* such that *t* is the concatenation of a tuple *a* belonging to A and a tuple *b* belonging to B and the predicate "*a*.X *theta b*.Y" evaluates to *true*. (Attri-butes B.X and B.Y should be defined on the same domain, and the opera-tion *theta* must make sense for that domain.)

SQL example:

```
SELECT  S.*, P.*
FROM    S, P
WHERE   S.CITY > P.CITY
```

If *theta* is equality, the join is called an equijoin. It follows from the definition that the result of an equijoin must include two identical attri-butes. If one of those two attributes is eliminated (which it can be via pro-jection), the result is called the *natural* join. The unqualified term "join" is usually taken to mean the natural join.

- Division

In its simplest form (which is all that we consider here), the division opera-tor divides a relation of degree two (the dividend) by a relation of degree one (the divisor), and produces a result relation of degree one (the quo-tient). Let the dividend (A) have attributes X and Y, and let the divisor (B) have attribute Y. Attributes A.Y and B.Y should be defined on the same domain. The result of dividing A by B is the relation C, with sole attribute X, such that every value *x* of C.X appears as a value of A.X, and the pair of values (*x*,*y*) appears in A for *all* values *y* appearing in B.

SQL example:

```
SELECT DISTINCT SPX.S# FROM SP SPX
WHERE   NOT EXISTS
      ( SELECT P.P# FROM P
        WHERE   NOT EXISTS
              ( SELECT SPY.* FROM SP SPY
                WHERE  SPY.S# = SPX.S# AND SPY.P# = P.P# ) )
```

Here we are assuming for simplicity that (a) relation SP has only two attributes, namely S# and P# (we are ignoring QTY), and (b) relation P has only one attribute, namely P# (we are ignoring PNAME, COLOR, WEIGHT, and CITY). We divide the first of these two relations by the second and obtain a result, namely a relation with one attribute (S#) that lists supplier numbers for suppliers that supply all parts.

It is worth mentioning that, of these eight operations, only five are primitive, namely selection, projection, product, union, and difference. The other three can be defined in terms of those five. For example, the natural join is a projection of a selection of a product. In practice, however, those other three operations (especially join) are so useful that a good case can be made for supporting them directly, even though they are not primitive.

Turning now to the relational assignment operation, the purpose of that operation is simply to allow the value of some algebraic expression—say a join—to be saved in some more or less permanent place. It can be simulated in SQL by means of the INSERT . . . SELECT operation. For example, suppose relation XYZ has two attributes, S# and P#, and suppose also that it is currently empty (i.e., contains no tuples). The SQL statement

```
INSERT INTO XYZ ( S#, P# )
       SELECT S.S#, P.P#
       FROM   S, P
       WHERE  S.CITY = P.CITY
```

assigns the result of the SELECT (namely, a projection of a join) to the relation XYZ.

By way of conclusion, Fig. B.3 summarizes the major components of the relational model.

B.5 RELATIONAL SYSTEMS

We are now (at last) in a position to define exactly what we mean by a *relational database management system* (relational DBMS, or relational system for short). The point is, *no* system today supports the relational model in its entirety (several come close, but most systems fall down on some detail or another—on domains if nowhere else). On the other hand, it would be unreasonable to insist that a system is not relational unless it

```
Data Structure
    domains (values)
    n-ary relations (attributes, tuples)
    keys (candidate, primary, alternate, foreign)
Data integrity
    1. primary key values must not be null
    2. foreign key values must match primary key values (or be null)
Data manipulation
    relational algebra
        union, intersection, difference, product
        select, project, join, divide
    relational assignment
```

Fig. B.3 The relational model

supports every last detail of the model. The fact is, not all aspects of the model are equally important; some of course are crucial, but others may be regarded merely as features that are "nice to have" (comparatively speaking). We therefore define a system as relational—*minimally so*—if and only if it supports at least the following:

- Relational databases (i.e., databases that can be perceived by the user as tables, and nothing but tables);

- At least the operations select, project, and join of the relational algebra (without requiring any predefinition of physical access paths to support those operations).

Note carefully that a system does not have to support the select, project, and join operators *explicitly* in order to qualify as relational by this definition. It is only the functionality of those operators that we are talking about here. For example, SQL/DS provides the functionality of all three of those operators (and more besides) within the SELECT operator of SQL. More important, note that a system that supports relational databases but not these three operators does not qualify as a relational system under our definition. Likewise, a system that allows (say) the user to select tuples according to values of some attribute X only if that attribute X is indexed also does not qualify, because it is requiring predefinition of physical access paths.

We justify our definition as follows:

1. Although select, project, and join are less than the full algebra, they are an extremely useful subset. There are comparatively few practical

problems that can be solved with the algebra that cannot be solved with select, project, and join alone.

2. A system that supports the relational data structure but not the relational operators does not provide the productivity of a genuinely relational system.

3. To do a good job of implementing the relational operators *requires* the system to do some optimization. A system that merely executed the exact operations requested by the user in a comparatively unintelligent fashion would almost certainly not have acceptable performance. Thus, to implement a system that realizes the potential of the relational model in an efficient manner is a highly nontrivial task.

SQL/DS is a relational system according to our definition (even though there are certain aspects of the relational model that it does not support). But there are a number of products on the market today that do not meet the criteria defined above. As we have tried to suggest, those criteria are useful as a means of drawing a sharp line between systems that are indeed genuinely relational and systems that are merely "relational-like." "Relational-like" systems do not truly provide the full benefits of the relational model. The distinction is thus worth making, as it ensures that the label "relational" is not used in misleading ways.

Note: For further discussion of what it means for a system to be relational, the reader is referred to a more recent paper by E. F. Codd, "Is Your DBMS Really Relational?", also to the series of Codd and Date Database Product Reports (see Appendix H).

Date and Time Support

C.1 INTRODUCTION

The date and time support in SQL/DS is quite extensive (and quite complicated—unduly so, in this writer's opinion). Rather than discussing that support in full detail in the main part of the text, therefore, and thereby interfering with the overall flow of the presentation, it seemed better to relegate any such discussion to some less obtrusive position in the book; hence this appendix. *Note:* In order to make the appendix reasonably self-contained, we do repeat some of the details (regarding, e.g., "date/time constants" and date/time functions) from the body of the book.

One preliminary note on terminology: Throughout this appendix, we use the term "date/time" to mean "date or time or timestamp." For example, the expression "date/time data types" means the three data types DATE and TIME and TIMESTAMP, considered collectively.

C.2 DATA TYPES

As indicated at the end of the previous section, there are three date/time data types in SQL/DS:

DATE	Date, represented as a sequence of eight unsigned packed decimal digits (*yyyymmdd*), occupying four bytes; permitted values are legal dates in the range January 1st, 1 A.D., to December 31, 9999 A.D.
TIME	Time, represented as a sequence of six unsigned packed decimal digits (*hhmmss*), occupying three bytes; permitted values are legal times in the range midnight to midnight, i.e., 000000 to 240000
TIMESTAMP	"Timestamp" (combination of date and time, accurate to the nearest microsecond), represented as a sequence of 20 unsigned packed decimal digits (*yyyymmddhhmmssnnnnnn*), occupying ten bytes; permitted values are legal timestamps in the range 00010101000000000000 to 99991231240000000000

By the term "legal dates" in the foregoing, we mean that SQL/DS will not permit invalid dates such as 19840431 ("April 31st, 1984") or 19870229 ("February 29th, 1987"). Similarly for times and timestamps, of course.

C.3 CONSTANTS

As explained in Chapter 4, strictly speaking there is no such thing as a date/time constant. Instead, there are *interpreted character string constants*. If a character string constant appears in a context that requires a date/time value,* then that character string will be interpreted as a date/time value, provided of course that it is of the appropriate form (a conversion error will occur if it is not). We will use the term "date/time string" to refer to a character string that represents a legal date/time value.

"Date/time string" constants, then, take the following forms (except as noted below):

---

*More generally, of course, any character string *expression* can appear in such a context (see Section C.6).

date string	Written as a character string constant of the form *mm/dd/yyyy*, enclosed in single quotes

Examples: `'1/18/1941'`
`'12/25/1989'`

time string	Written as a character string constant of the form *hh:mm* AM or *hh:mm* PM, enclosed in single quotes

Examples: `'10:00 AM'`
`'9:30 PM'`

timestamp string	Written as a character string constant of the form *yyyy-mm-dd-hh.mm.ss.nnnnnn*, enclosed in single quotes

Examples: `'1990-4-28-12.00.00.000000'`
`'1944-10-17-18.30.45'`

Note: Actually, several different date/time string formats are supported: U.S. style (USA), European style (EUR), International Standards Organization style (ISO), Japanese Industrial Standard Christian Era style (JIS), and installation-defined (LOCAL). A variety of methods (installation options, preprocessor options, etc.) are available for specifying the particular style to be used in any particular context. In this appendix we will always assume U.S. style, barring any explicit statement to the contrary. As pointed out in Chapter 4, a peculiarity of U.S.-style time string constants is that they do not include a seconds component. Nevertheless, the internal representation of a time value always does include such a component.

To repeat some syntactic details from Chapter 4: Leading zeros can be omitted from the month and day portions of a date or timestamp string constant and from the hours portion of a time or timestamp string constant. The seconds portion (including the preceding colon or period) can be omitted entirely from a time string constant (in fact, it must be so omitted in U.S. style); an implicit specification of zero is assumed. Trailing zeros can be omitted from the microseconds portion of a timestamp string constant; the microseconds portion (including the preceding period) can also be omitted entirely, in which case an implicit specification of zero is assumed.

C.4   COLUMN DEFINITIONS

Date/time column definitions of course use the conventional SQL/DS syntax—

```
column data-type [ NOT NULL ]
```

—where "data-type" is DATE or TIME or TIMESTAMP. As mentioned in Section C.2, date/time values are represented internally as unsigned sequences of packed decimal digits, 2 digits to a byte, with a width of 4 bytes (DATE), 3 bytes (TIME), or 10 bytes (TIMESTAMP).

C.5 DURATIONS

SQL/DS supports the notion of a *duration*. A duration is an interval of time, such as "3 years" or "90 days" or "5 minutes 30 seconds." For example, subtracting the time "9:00 AM" from the time "10:15 AM" yields the duration "1 hour 15 minutes." *Note carefully, however, that there is no duration data type.* Instead, durations are *interpreted decimal integers.* For example, suppose we are given the following data definition:

```
CREATE TABLE T
     ( ... ,
        START_TIME   TIME,
        ... ,
        WAIT_TIME    DECIMAL(6),
        ... )
```

Now consider the expression:

```
START_TIME + WAIT_TIME
```

If START_TIME and WAIT_TIME happen to have the values "9:00 AM" and 50000, respectively, then this expression will evaluate to "2:00 PM"; in other words, the value 50000 will be interpreted to mean "5 hours." Likewise, if they have the values "9:00 AM" and −50000, respectively, then the expression will evaluate to "4:00 AM."

It follows from the foregoing that durations can be stored in the database, but only in the form of DECIMAL values. SQL/DS is not aware that the column in question (i.e., WAIT_TIME, in the example) is really being used to hold duration values.

Durations are of two basic kinds, date durations and time durations. A third kind, "microsecond durations," also exists but seems to have no official classifying name; see the discussion of "labeled durations" below.*

- A date duration is a signed decimal integer of 8 digits (5 bytes) of the form *yyyymmdd,* where *yyyy* is the number of years (0–9999), *mm* is the number of months (0–99), and *dd* is the number of days (0–99).

---

*Note that there is no such thing as a "timestamp duration." This omission is due to the following combination of facts: (a) Durations are intended primarily for use in date/time arithmetic; (b) timestamps are represented as 20-digit decimal numbers with an assumed decimal point six digits from the right; (c) SQL/DS cannot perform DECIMAL(20,6) arithmetic.

- A time duration is a signed decimal integer of 6 digits (4 bytes) of the form *hhmmss,* where *hh* is the number of hours (0–99), *mm* is the number of minutes (0–99), and *ss* is the number of seconds (0–99).
- A "microsecond duration" is a signed decimal integer of 6 digits (4 bytes) of the form *nnnnnn,* representing *nnnnn* microseconds.

Note that a duration such as "90 days" or "25 hours" is legal; i.e., "days" is not restricted to a maximum of 31, nor "hours" to a maximum of 23 (etc.). To return to the example discussed earlier: If START_TIME and WAIT_TIME have the values "9:00 AM" and 250000, respectively, then the expression

```
START_TIME + WAIT_TIME
```

evaluates to "10:00 AM"; the overflow in the hours position is ignored (see Section C.8).

Since "duration" is not really a data type but is instead just an interpreted decimal integer, there is strictly speaking no such thing as a "duration constant." Instead, decimal integers (of the appropriate format) can be used, as in (e.g.) the expression

```
START_TIME + 050000.
```

Note that the decimal value must have *exactly* the right precision and scale.

However, SQL/DS does also include the notion of a *labeled duration* (also known as a "simple duration"). Labeled durations are a special kind of scalar expression, whose value is a decimal integer that is to be interpreted as a duration (date or time or "microsecond"). Such expressions can be used to play the role of "duration constants" (among other things). Labeled durations take the form "n units", where "n" is any numeric expression (it is converted to a decimal integer if necessary), and "units" is any of the following:

```
YEAR[S]
MONTH[S]
DAY[S]
HOUR[S]
MINUTE[S]
SECOND[S]
MICROSECOND[S]
```

Examples:

```
3 YEARS
90 DAYS
1 MINUTE
47 MICROSECONDS
```

Of the seven possible "units" specifications listed above, the first three identify the duration as a date duration, the next three as a time duration, and the last one as a "microsecond duration" (not an official SQL/DS term). *Note:* Observe that date durations in general involve years *and* months *and* days, but *labeled* date durations involve years *or* months *or* days (not a mixture). Similarly, time durations in general involve hours *and* minutes *and* seconds, but labeled time durations involve hours *or* minutes *or* seconds, not a mixture.

Note: The IBM manuals classify durations differently, into date, time, and labeled durations (i.e., a labeled duration is not the same thing as either a date duration or a time duration). This classification is somewhat counter-intuitive, however, since a labeled duration clearly does represent a "duration" (in the ordinary English sense) of years or days or hours or . . . (etc.). In this appendix we will stay with our own classification.

Here are some examples of the use of labeled durations:

```
UPDATE T
SET    START_TIME = START_TIME + 15 MINUTES
WHERE  ...

SELECT ...
FROM   T
WHERE  END_TIME < START_TIME + 1 HOUR + 30 MINUTES

UPDATE SCHEDULE
SET    FINISH = FINISH + :SLIPPAGE MONTHS
WHERE  ...
```

SLIPPAGE here is a (numeric) host variable.

Note finally that the *only* context in which a labeled duration can appear is in an expression involving infix " + " or " − ", in which one operand is the labeled duration in question and the other is a date/time value. See Section C.8 for further discussion.

C.6 CONVERSIONS

SQL/DS includes a number of scalar builtin functions for performing explicit conversions involving date/time data.

Extraction of Date/Time Components:

- YEAR, MONTH, DAY

   Convert the year or month or day portion (as applicable) of a specified date or timestamp or date duration to a binary integer.

- HOUR, MINUTE, SECOND

   Convert the hours or minutes or seconds portion (as applicable) of a specified time or timestamp or time duration to a binary integer.

- MICROSECOND

  Converts the microseconds portion of a specified timestamp to a binary integer.

  Examples:

  ```
  MONTH ( END_DATE )
  DAY ( DEPART - ARRIVE )
  SECOND ( CURRENT TIME )
  ```

Conversions to/from Other Data Types:

- DATE, TIME, TIMESTAMP

  Convert a specified scalar value to a date or time or timestamp (as applicable). In the case of TIMESTAMP, the scalar value can be specified as a pair of values, representing a date and a time respectively.

- CHAR

  Converts a specified date/time value to its character string representation in USA, EUR, ISO, JIS, or LOCAL format (as specified by an argument to the function).

- DAYS

  Converts a specified date or timestamp to a binary integer, representing the number of days since December 31st, 1 B.C. (Note that there is no "0 B.C."; December 31st, 1 B.C., is immediately followed by January 1st, 1 A.D.)

  Examples:

  ```
  DATE ('6/7/87')
  TIME ( CURRENT TIMESTAMP )
  CHAR ( START_DATE, USA )
  DAYS ( '1/18/1941' )
  ```

Implicit Conversions:

In certain circumstances SQL/DS will also perform implicit date/time conversions:

(a) If a character string value occurs in a position where the language requires a date/time value, then the string will be interpreted as a date/time if possible.

(b) If a decimal value occurs in a position where the language requires a duration, then the decimal value will be interpreted as a duration if possible.

(c) If a date/time value occurs in a position where the language requires a character string value, then the date/time will be converted to its character string representation.

Examples:

```
1.  UPDATE  T
    SET     START_DATE = :XMDY
    WHERE   ...
```

Here XMDY is a character string variable of eight characters, to be interpreted as a date string.

```
2.  UPDATE  T
    SET     START_TIME = START_TIME + 050000.
    WHERE   ...
```

In this example the decimal value is interpreted as a time duration of 5 hours.

```
3.  SELECT  START_DATE
    INTO    :HOST_CHAR_FIELD
    FROM    T
    WHERE   ...
```

Here START_DATE will be converted to its character string representation.

Note, however, that SQL/DS does not always permit a date/time value to appear in place of a character string value (Case (c) above). For example, the argument to LIKE is required to be a string—it cannot be a date/time value. On the other hand, the converse situations (Cases (a) and (b)) are apparently always legal—that is, a character string or decimal value can always appear in place of a date/time value or duration, respectively—although actually even this is not totally clear from the documentation. In fact, the precise rules as to exactly what is permitted do not seem to be very well defined. On the whole, the best practice would seem to be to avoid implicit conversions by always using the explicit functions DATE (etc.). We refer the reader to the IBM manuals for further clarification.

There are no implicit conversions between dates and timestamps, or times and timestamps, or dates and times.

C.7 SPECIAL REGISTERS

SQL/DS supports a number of date/time "special registers" (as explained in Chapter 4, this is the DB2 term; SQL/DS does not appear to have a term of its own for the concept). The date/time special registers are CURRENT TIMEZONE, CURRENT DATE, CURRENT TIME, and CURRENT

TIMESTAMP. A reference to one of these registers returns a scalar value, as follows:

- CURRENT TIMEZONE

  Returns a time duration representing (typically) the displacement of the local time zone from Greenwich Mean Time (GMT).* The value returned by each of CURRENT DATE, CURRENT TIME, and CURRENT TIMESTAMP (see below) is based on a reading of the CPU clock, incremented in each case by the value of CURRENT TIMEZONE. In the case of Pacific Standard Time, for example, if the CPU clock is set to GMT and CURRENT TIMEZONE to "−8 hours," then CURRENT DATE, CURRENT TIME, and CURRENT TIMESTAMP would each return the true local value. If, on the other hand, the CPU clock is in fact set to the local value, then CURRENT TIMEZONE should probably be set to zero.

- CURRENT DATE

  Returns the current date, i.e., the date "today" (but see CURRENT TIMEZONE above).

- CURRENT TIME

  Returns the current time, i.e., the time "now" (but see CURRENT TIMEZONE above).

- CURRENT TIMESTAMP

  Returns the current timestamp, i.e., the date "today" concatenated with the time "now" (but see CURRENT TIMEZONE above).

When any given SQL data manipulation statement is executed, all references to CURRENT DATE and/or CURRENT TIME and/or CURRENT TIMESTAMP are based on a single reading of the local clock. Thus, for example, the WHERE clause "WHERE CURRENT TIME = CURRENT TIME" is always guaranteed to evaluate to *true*.

C.8 EXPRESSIONS

The infix arithmetic operators " + " and " − " (only) can be used with date/times. For example, a date and a date duration can be added to yield another date. The reader is warned, however, that not all operations that

---

*The actual value of CURRENT TIMEZONE is established by an installation-defined system parameter.

would appear to make sense are in fact permitted. Here is a complete list of the legal possibilities in SQL/DS:

First operand	Operator	Second operand	Result
date	+	date duration	date
date duration	+	date	date
date	−	date	date duration
date	−	date duration	date
time	+	time duration	time
time duration	+	time	time
time	−	time	time duration
time	−	time duration	time
timestamp	+	duration	timestamp
duration	+	timestamp	timestamp
timestamp	−	duration	timestamp

In other words:

■ For addition (infix "+")

  ▪ if one operand is a date, the other must be a date or date duration

  ▪ if one operand is a time, the other must be a time or time duration

  ▪ if one operand is a timestamp, the other must be a duration

■ For subtraction (infix "−")

  ▪ if the first operand is a date, the second must be a date or date duration

  ▪ if the first operand is a time, the second must be a time or time duration

  ▪ if the first operand is a timestamp, the second must be a duration

  ▪ if the second operand is a date, the first must be a date

  ▪ if the second operand is a time, the first must be a time

Note in particular that it is not legal to subtract one timestamp from another. It might reasonably be argued that such an operation does make sense and should yield a timestamp duration, but—as explained in Section C.5—SQL/DS does not support timestamp durations.

Labeled durations are subject to an additional (major) constraint, namely as follows: They are permitted *only* as operands of infix "+" or "−", and *only* if the other operand is a date/time value—*not* another duration (labeled or otherwise). Thus the following operations are all ★★★ ILLEGAL★★★ if either of the duration operands is labeled (the "Result" column thus shows what might be expected in each case, *not* what SQL/DS will actually produce).

First operand	*Operator*	*Second operand*	*"Result"*
date duration	+	date duration	date duration
date duration	−	date duration	date duration
time duration	+	time duration	time duration
time duration	−	time duration	time duration
microsec duration	+	microsec duration	microsec duration
microsec duration	−	microsec duration	microsec duration

The aggregate functions COUNT, MAX, and MIN (but not SUM or AVG) can be applied to date/time arguments; the result is an integer for COUNT, a date/time value of the appropriate type for MAX and MIN.

Examples:

Note that some of the following expressions are not legal. We leave it as an exercise for the reader to determine why not.

```
DATE ('8/17/1972') - DATE ('10/28/1969')
DATE ('8/17/1972') -      '10/28/1969'
     '8/17/1972'   - DATE ('10/28/1969')
     '8/17/1972'   -      '10/28/1969'          *** ILLEGAL ***

START_DATE +   1 YEAR   +  6 MONTHS
1 YEAR     +   6 MONTHS +  START_DATE           *** ILLEGAL ***
               1 YEAR   +  6 MONTHS             *** ILLEGAL ***
( START_DATE +  1 YEAR ) +  6 MONTHS
START_DATE + ( 1 YEAR   +  6 MONTHS )           *** ILLEGAL ***
START_DATE +   6 WEEKS                          *** ILLEGAL ***
START_DATE +   4 HOURS                          *** ILLEGAL ***

START_TIME + WAIT_TIME
START_TIME + HOUR(WAIT_TIME) HOURS
START_TIME + 120000.
TIME('9:00 AM')  + 120000.
'9:00 AM'  + 120000.                            *** ILLEGAL ***
9 HOURS    + 120000.                            *** ILLEGAL ***

CURRENT TIMESTAMP + 1 SECOND + 500000 MICROSECONDS
CURRENT TIME - CURRENT TIMEZONE
ETA - ( CURRENT TIME - CURRENT TIMEZONE )
```

Date/time arithmetic is performed in accordance with the calendar and permissible date/time values. Thus, for example, the expression

```
DATE('5/31/1988') + 1 MONTH
```

yields the result "6/30/1988" (*not* "6/31/1988"—i.e., "June 30th, 1988," not "June 31st, 1988"). On the other hand, the expression

```
DATE('6/30/1988') - 1 MONTH
```

yields the result "5/30/1988" (*not* "5/31/1988"—i.e., "May 30th, 1988," not "May 31st, 1988"). In other words, the expression

```
DATE('5/31/1988') + 1 MONTH - 1 MONTH
```

does not yield "5/31/1988"! More generally, if we add a date duration *d* to some date and then subtract that same duration *d* from the result, we are not guaranteed to end up with the date we started with. By contrast, the expression

```
DATE('5/31/1988') + 30 DAYS - 30 DAYS
```

will indeed yield "5/31/1988"—i.e., we do end up with the date we started with in this case.

Another potential trap for the unwary is illustrated by the following example: What is the value of each of the following two expressions? We leave the details as an exercise for the reader. (Hint: Which value is the greater?)

```
TIME('9:00 AM') + 000100.
TIME('9:00 AM') + 000099.
```

Date/time arithmetic can cause overflow or underflow. The rules are as follows (for brevity, we use the term "overflow" to include both overflow and underflow):

- For dates:
  - overflow in the days position affects the months
  - overflow in the months position affects the years
  - overflow in the years position is an error
- For times:
  - overflow in the seconds position affects the minutes
  - overflow in the minutes position affects the hours
  - overflow in the hours position is ignored
- For timestamps:
  - same as above, except that overflow in the hours position affects the days

C.9 ASSIGNMENTS

Assignments occur on database update and retrieval operations. We consider the DATE data type first. On update:

- If the source is of type DATE, the target must be either of type DATE or of type character string. In the latter case, the date is implicitly converted to its string representation (a date string).

- If the target is of type DATE, the source must be either an expression that evaluates to a date or a character string that can legally be interpreted as a date (a date string). In the latter case, the string is implicitly converted to a date.

On retrieval:

- If the source is of type DATE, the target must be of type character string. The date is implicitly converted to its string representation (a date string).

Analogous rules apply to TIMEs and TIMESTAMPs, of course.

The fact that character strings are considered to be compatible with date/times for assignment purposes permits us to transfer date/time values to and from and programs written in languages such as PL/I that do not support any date/time data types.

Note that it is not possible to assign a value to an individual component (such as the days portion) of a date/time value. Note too that there are no explicit assignment rules for durations, because there is no duration data type; a "duration assignment" is merely a special kind of numeric assignment.

Examples:

```
SELECT  START_DATE
INTO    :HOST_CHAR_FIELD
FROM    T
WHERE   ...

INSERT
INTO    T ( ..., START_TIME, ... )
VALUES  ( ....., '10:30 AM', ... )

UPDATE  T
SET     START_TIME = :HOST_CHAR_FIELD + 25 MINUTES
WHERE   ...
```

An example of a "duration assignment":

```
UPDATE  T
SET     WAIT_TIME = 030000.
WHERE   ...
```

Note that in this example no harm would result if the leading zero and the decimal point were dropped from the constant; SQL/DS's ordinary numeric conversion rules would take care of everything satisfactorily.

C.10 COMPARISONS

Comparisons can be performed between

(a) a DATE, TIME, or TIMESTAMP value, on the one hand, and

(b) either another value of the same type or a character string that can legally be interpreted as a value of the same type (i.e., an appropriate date/time string), on the other.

Comparisons are performed in accordance with chronologic ordering. Note that the fact that character strings are considered to be compatible with date/times for comparison purposes permits us to compare date/time values with values from programs written in languages such as PL/I that do not support any date/time data types. Note too that there are no explicit comparison rules for durations, because there is no duration data type; a "duration comparison" is merely a special kind of numeric comparison.

Examples:

```
SELECT ...
FROM    T
WHERE   START_TIME > '9:00 AM'
AND     END_TIME   < '5:00 PM'

SELECT ...
FROM    FLIGHTS
WHERE   ETA > CURRENT TIME - CURRENT TIMEZONE
```

Here is an example of a "duration comparison":

```
SELECT ...
FROM    T
WHERE   START_TIME - END_TIME < 080000.
```

And here are two examples involving date/time functions:

```
SELECT ...
FROM    T
WHERE   MINUTE ( START_TIME ) = 0


SELECT ...
FROM    T
WHERE   HOUR ( START_TIME ) NOT BETWEEN 9 AND 17
```

One possible surprise that can occur in connexion with TIME and TIMESTAMP comparisons is the following: A time value (*hhmmss*) of 240000 is considered to be greater than a time value of 000000, even though logically they both represent the same time (i.e., midnight). Note that these two representations are both legal; refer back to Section C.2.

Syntax of SQL Data Manipulation Operations

D.1 INTRODUCTION

We present a simplified BNF grammar for the four data manipulation operations of SQL (SELECT, INSERT, UPDATE, and DELETE) described in this book. The grammar makes use of the following convenient shorthand:

- If "xyz" is a syntactic category, then "xyz-commalist" is a syntactic category consisting of a list of one or more "xyz"s in which each pair of adjacent "xyz"s is separated by a sequence of characters consisting of zero or more spaces, followed by a comma, followed by zero or more spaces.

We also make use of some simplifying abbreviations, namely "exp" for expression, "ref" for reference, and "spec" for specification. The following are terminal categories with respect to this grammar (i.e., they are not defined further in the production rules):

```
identifier
constant
integer
```

Note: Aspects of the four statements not described in the body of the book (e.g., the comparison operators > ANY, = ALL, etc.) are ignored. In the interests of clarity and brevity, moreover, the grammar does not accurately reflect all of the syntactic limitations of SQL but is instead rather permissive, in the sense that it allows the generation of certain constructs that are not legal in SQL. For example, it allows the argument to an aggregate function such as AVG to consist of a reference to another such function, which SQL does not permit (see Chapter 7, Section 7.4). It also makes no attempt to distinguish between the different types of scalar expression (numeric expressions, character string expressions, etc.). See Chapter 4, also Appendix C, for the details of such distinctions. (Our reason for making these simplifications is that SQL is a very context-sensitive language, and attempts to reflect context sensitivity in BNF tend to lead to a rather unwieldy set of production rules.)

D.2 BASIC ELEMENTS

```
table-spec
    ::=     table-ref [ range-variable ]

table-ref
    ::=     base-table | view

base-table
    ::=     [ user . ] identifier

user
    ::=     authorization-identifier

authorization-identifier
    ::=     identifier

view
    ::=     [ user . ] identifier

range-variable
    ::=     identifier

column-ref
    ::=     [ column-qualifier . ] column

column-qualifier
    ::=     table-ref
          | range-variable

column
    ::=     identifier
```

D.3 SCALAR EXPRESSIONS

```
scalar-exp
    ::=     scalar-term
       |    scalar-exp  +    scalar-term
       |    scalar-exp  -    scalar-term
       |    scalar-exp "||" scalar-term
```

Note: We show the concatenation operator "‖" in quotes to avoid confusion with the vertical bar "|" which is used to separate alternatives in the grammar. The quotes are not part of the operator.

```
scalar-term
    ::=     scalar-factor
       |    scalar-term * scalar-factor
       |    scalar-term / scalar-factor

scalar-factor
    ::=   [ + | - ] scalar-primary

scalar-primary
    ::=     constant
       |    labeled-duration
       |    column-ref
       |    special-register
       |    scalar-function-ref
       |    aggregate-function-ref
       |    ( scalar-exp )

labeled-duration
    ::=     scalar-exp units

units
    ::=     YEAR[S]
       |    MONTH[S]
       |    DAY[S]
       |    HOUR[S]
       |    MINUTE[S]
       |    SECOND[S]
       |    MICROSECOND[S]

special-register
    ::=     USER
       |    CURRENT TIMEZONE
       |    CURRENT DATE
       |    CURRENT TIME
       |    CURRENT TIMESTAMP

scalar-function-ref
    ::=     scalar-function ( scalar-exp-commalist )
```

```
scalar-function
    ::=     CHAR    | DATE        | DAY    | DAYS      | DECIMAL
       |    DIGITS  | FLOAT       | HEX    | HOUR      | INTEGER
       |    LENGTH  | MICROSECOND | MINUTE | MONTH     | SECOND
       |    STRIP   | SUBSTR      | TIME   | TIMESTAMP | TRANSLATE
       |    VALUE   | VARGRAPHIC
```

Note: Each of these scalar functions takes just a single scalar-expression argument, except (a) CHAR and TIMESTAMP, which take two, (b)

DECIMAL, STRIP, and SUBSTR, which take three, and (c)
TRANSLATE, which takes four, and (d) VALUE, which takes an arbitrary
number (at least two).

```
aggregate-function-ref
   ::=    COUNT ( * )
       |  aggregate-function ( [ ALL ] scalar-exp )
       |  aggregate-function ( DISTINCT column-ref )

aggregate-function
   ::=    COUNT | SUM | AVG | MAX | MIN
```

D.4   SELECT-EXPRESSIONS

```
select-exp
   ::=     select-clause
           from-clause
         [ where-clause ]
         [ grouping-clause ]
         [ having-clause ]

select-clause
   ::=     SELECT [ ALL | DISTINCT ] select-spec

select-spec
   ::=     * | selection-commalist

selection
   ::=     table-ref . *
         | scalar-exp

from-clause
   ::=     FROM table-spec-commalist

where-clause
   ::=     WHERE predicate

grouping-clause
   ::=     GROUP BY column-ref-commalist

having-clause
   ::=     HAVING predicate
```

D.5   PREDICATES

```
predicate
   ::=     predicate-term
         | predicate OR predicate-term

predicate-term
   ::=     predicate-factor
         | predicate-term AND predicate-factor

predicate-factor
   ::=     [ NOT ] predicate-primary
```

```
predicate-primary
    ::=     condition
          | ( predicate )

condition
    ::=     compare-condition
          | between-condition
          | like-condition
          | in-condition
          | test-for-null
          | existence-test

compare-condition
    ::=     scalar-exp comparison scalar-exp
          | scalar-exp comparison ( column-select-exp )

comparison
    ::=     = | ~= | <> | < | <= | > | >=

column-select-exp
    ::=     column-select-clause
            from-clause
          [ where-clause ]
          [ grouping-clause ]
          [ having-clause ] ]

column-select-clause
    ::=     SELECT [ ALL | DISTINCT ] scalar-exp

between-condition
    ::=     column-ref [ NOT ] BETWEEN scalar-exp AND scalar-exp

like-condition
    ::=     column-ref [ NOT ] LIKE constant

in-condition
    ::=     scalar-exp [ NOT ] IN ( set-of-scalars )

set-of-scalars
    ::=     constant-commalist
          | column-select-exp

test-for-null
    ::=  column-ref IS [ NOT ] NULL

existence-test
    ::=     EXISTS ( select-exp )
```

D.6   STATEMENTS

```
statement
    ::=     select-statement
          | insert-statement
          | update-statement
          | delete-statement

select-statement
    ::=     union-exp [ ordering-clause ]
```

```
union-exp
   ::=      union-term
         |  union-exp UNION [ ALL ] union-term

union-term
   ::=      select-exp
         |  ( union-exp )

ordering-clause
   ::=      ORDER BY order-item-commalist

order-item
   ::=      ordering-column [ ASC | DESC ]

ordering-column
   ::=      column-ref | integer

insert-statement
   ::=      INSERT INTO table-ref [ ( column-commalist ) ]
                       source-values

source-values
   ::=      VALUES ( insert-item-commalist )
         |  select-exp

insert-item
   ::=      constant | NULL | special-register

update-statement
   ::=      UPDATE table-spec
            SET column-assignment-commalist
         [ where-clause ]

column-assignment
   ::=      column = scalar-exp
         |  column = NULL

delete-statement
   ::=      DELETE FROM table-spec [ where-clause ]
```

E

♦

Some Differences between SQL/DS and the SQL Standard

E.1 INTRODUCTION

In this appendix we present a summary (almost certainly incomplete) of differences between the SQL/DS Version 2 Release 2 dialect of SQL and the official ISO/ANSI standard dialect. For a thorough description of the standard version, the reader is referred to the book *A Guide to the SQL Standard,* by C. J. Date (Addison-Wesley, 1987).

In an attempt to structure the discussion, we divide what follows into three main sections: "Standard Features Not Supported in SQL/DS," "SQL/DS Features Not Supported in the Standard," and "Incompatibilities" (features included in both but treated differently). However, the assignment of topics to sections is sometimes a little arbitrary.

E.2   STANDARD FEATURES NOT SUPPORTED IN SQL/DS

- The standard allows annotation (i.e., embedded comments, introduced by a double hyphen "--" and terminated by end-of-line) to appear within SQL statements. SQL/DS does not.

- SQL/DS does not support the NUMERIC data type.

- In SQL/DS, if the argument to an aggregate function such as SUM includes DISTINCT, then the function reference must appear in isolation—i.e., it cannot be an operand in a larger arithmetic expression such as SUM(DISTINCT F) + 3. This restriction does not exist in the standard.

- The standard includes a CHECK option on CREATE VIEW, specifying that INSERTs and UPDATEs to the view are to be checked to ensure that the newly inserted or updated record satisfies the view-defining condition. SQL/DS does not support this option.

- The standard separates data definition operations from data manipulation operations. CREATE TABLE and CREATE VIEW (and GRANT) operations are specified as part of a "schema" by means of the *schema definition language.* All other standard SQL operations are specified as part of a "module" by means of the *module language.* SQL/DS has no notion of schemas or modules (in the sense of the standard) at all.

E.3   SQL/DS FEATURES NOT SUPPORTED
   IN THE STANDARD

- The standard does not allow any characters to appear in identifiers other than the uppercase letters A–Z, the digits 0–9, and the underscore character. SQL/DS allows the characters #, @, and $ to appear in an identifier wherever a letter can appear. SQL/DS also supports "delimited identifiers" (see the IBM manuals for details).

- The DROP PROGRAM statement is not supported in the standard.

- The following SQL/DS data types are not supported in the standard:

```
VARCHAR (and LONG VARCHAR)
GRAPHIC
VARGRAPHIC (and LONG VARGRAPHIC)
DATE
TIME
TIMESTAMP
```

  The concept of "durations" also does not exist in the standard.

- The standard does not include any primary or foreign key support at all. Thus everything discussed in Chapter 12 of this book is a SQL/DS extension. (*Note:* The SQL/DS support for primary or foreign keys is broadly but not totally compatible with the standards committee's longer-term proposals for extending the standard in this area.)

- SQL/DS allows a value of approximate numeric type (FLOAT) to be assigned to an object of exact numeric type (SMALLINT, INTEGER, or DECIMAL). The standard does not.

- The standard does not include any date/time support at all. Thus everything discussed in Appendix C of this book is a SQL/DS extension.

- SQL/DS supports hexadecimal constants.

- SQL/DS supports a concatenate operator ($\|$).

- The standard does not include any scalar builtin functions. Thus the functions discussed in Section 4.4 of this book (SUBSTR, LENGTH, etc.) are all SQL/DS extensions.

- The standard SELECT statement is strictly a singleton SELECT—i.e., it retrieves a single row. Multiple-row retrieval must be done by means of a cursor. (The standard, not unnaturally, is oriented towards the use of SQL in application programs, rather than interactive SQL.)

- SQL/DS supports the scalar comparison operator $\sim =$ as an alternative representation of $< >$.

- SQL/DS allows qualified references of the form "R.*" (where R is a range variable) in a SELECT clause. SQL/DS also allows references of the form "*" (or "R.*") in a SELECT clause to appear in conjunction with other items. Both of these possibilities are prohibited in the standard.

- UNION (with or without ALL) is strictly a binary operation in the standard. That is, an expression such as x UNION y UNION z is not permitted; it must be replaced by one of the two expressions (x UNION y) UNION z or x UNION (y UNION z).

- SQL/DS supports the use of explicitly defined range variables in UPDATE and DELETE as well as in SELECT.

- The standard does not include any definition of catalog tables (SYSCATALOG, SYSCOLUMNS, etc.).

- The standard does not support the COMMENT or LABEL statements.

- The standard does not support synonyms (CREATE SYNONYM, DROP SYNONYM).

- The standard does not support the CONNECT statement.

- The only privileges defined in the standard are SELECT, INSERT, UPDATE (possibly column-specific), DELETE, and ALL. SQL/DS supports several additional privileges, and ALL has different semantics (see Chapter 11 for details). SQL/DS also allows privileges to be REVOKEd (the standard does not include a REVOKE statement).

- SQL/DS's rules regarding view updatability (see Section 10.4) are slightly more permissive than those of the standard, as follows:

  (a) In SQL/DS, if a column of the view is derived from a constant or an expression that does not involve an aggregate function, then INSERT operations are not allowed, and UPDATE operations are not allowed on that column, but DELETE operations are allowed, and so are UPDATE operations on other columns. In the standard, such a view cannot be updated at all.

  (b) In SQL/DS, if the WHERE clause in the view definition includes a subquery *and the FROM clause in that subquery refers to the base table on which the view is defined,* then the view is not updatable. In the standard, a view cannot be updated if its definition involves any subquery whatsoever.

- The FOR UPDATE clause on a cursor definition is not included in the standard.

- The SQLWARNING condition on WHENEVER and the STOP action are not supported in the standard.

- The standard does not allow a cursor to be declared for INSERT and hence does not support the PUT statement either.

- The SQL Communication Area (SQLCA) is not included in the standard, except for the single feedback parameter SQLCODE; there is therefore no INCLUDE SQLCA statement in the standard either. SQLCODE values are explicitly stated in the standard to be implementation-defined, except for the special values 0 and +100, so SQL/DS does conform to the standard in this respect even though other implementations will generate different SQLCODEs.

- The standard does not support an explicit LOCK statement.

- All dynamic SQL features—the statements PREPARE, DESCRIBE, and EXECUTE, the SQL Descriptor Area (SQLDA), the special INCLUDE statement for incorporating the SQLDA into host programs, the miscellaneous associated facilities (special form of OPEN, etc.)—are excluded from the standard.

- All extended dynamic SQL features—the statements CREATE PROGRAM and DROP STATEMENT and the extended versions of the statements PREPARE, DESCRIBE, EXECUTE, DECLARE

CURSOR, OPEN, FETCH, PUT, and CLOSE—are excluded from the standard.

- The standard does not include any ALTER or DROP statements at all. Therefore, the statements ALTER TABLE, DROP TABLE, and DROP VIEW are all SQL/DS extensions.

- The standard does not include any of the more "physical" data definition statements that are supported in SQL/DS—CREATE/DROP INDEX and ACQUIRE/ALTER/DROP DBSPACE. In fact, the standard says nothing at all about physical storage constructs such as indexes and DBspaces, and hence does not support the "IN dbspace" operand on CREATE TABLE either.

- As stated in Section E.2, SQL/DS has no notion of a schema per se. SQL definitional statements (like all other SQL statements) can be executed in SQL/DS both interactively and—in the form of embedded SQL—from within a program.

- The standard does not support the EXPLAIN and UPDATE STATISTICS statements.

- The standard defines host language interfaces for COBOL, FORTRAN, Pascal, and PL/I (only). It also restricts the range of data types accessible from each of those languages; for example, INTEGER data is not accessible from PL/I in the standard (of course, this is probably an error in the standard). SQL/DS does not have such restrictions.

E.4 INCOMPATIBILITIES

- The standard and SQL/DS have different sets of reserved words.

- The standard requires UNIQUE constraints to be specified on CREATE TABLE instead of on CREATE INDEX (in fact, as mentioned in Section E.3, the standard does not support indexes at all).

- UNIQUE columns or column combinations are required to be NOT NULL in the standard.

- String constants are varying length in SQL/DS but fixed length in the standard.

- String comparisons in the standard are always performed by padding the shorter with blanks to the length of the longer. The same rule applies to SQL/DS, except in the case where both strings are varying length (see Chapter 4 for details).

- Indicator variables can be used in WHERE and HAVING clauses in the standard but not in SQL/DS.

- The SQL/DS concept that there is an implicit WHENEVER statement for each condition—NOT FOUND, SQLERROR, also SQLWARNING —at the start of the program text, specifying CONTINUE in each case, is not supported in the standard.

- The SQL/DS rules determining the binding of range variables to their corresponding table are not identical to those of the standard. The details are beyond the scope of this appendix; we merely observe that the behavior of SQL/DS may be unpredictable (and in some cases is certainly incorrect) if a FROM clause (a) mentions the same table twice and introduces an explicit range variable in one of the two mentions only (e.g., FROM S, S SX), or (b) mentions two tables and introduces explicit range variables for both, each having the same name as the other table (e.g., FROM S P, P S). The standard handles these cases (and all others like them) correctly.

- (Another illustration of the preceding point.) Suppose for the sake of the example that fields S.CITY and P.CITY (supplier city and part city) of the suppliers-and-parts database are renamed as S.SCITY and P.PCITY. Consider the following SELECT statement:

```
SELECT  S#
FROM    S
WHERE   NOT EXISTS
      ( SELECT *
        FROM    P
        WHERE   PCITY = SCITY )
```

This SELECT is valid in the standard but not in SQL/DS (the standard recognizes that the reference to SCITY is implicitly qualified by table name S, but SQL/DS does not; "correlated references" in SQL/DS are never unqualified).

- The standard requires all concurrent executions of interleaved transactions to be serializable (i.e., equivalent to some serial execution of those same transactions, running them one at a time). SQL/DS cannot provide such a guarantee if any of the transactions in question executes under CS isolation level.

F

◆

Some Differences between SQL/DS and DB2

F.1 INTRODUCTION

In this appendix we summarize some—not all—of the differences between the dialects of SQL supported by SQL/DS Version 2 Release 2 and DB2 Version 2 Release 1. For a thorough description of the DB2 version, the reader is referred to the authors' book *A Guide to DB2* (3rd edition, Addison-Wesley, to appear).

In an attempt to structure the discussion, we divide what follows into three main sections: "DB2 Features Not Supported in SQL/DS," "SQL/DS Features Not Supported in DB2," and "Incompatibilities" (features included in both but treated differently). However, the assignment of topics to sections is sometimes a little arbitrary.

F.2   DB2 FEATURES NOT SUPPORTED IN SQL/DS

▪ DB2 supports self-referencing tables (referential cycles of length 1).

▪ DB2 supports multilevel cascade delete.

▪ DB2 supports nonnull default values.

▪ DB2 has slightly fewer restrictions than SQL/DS on the use of long strings.

▪ DB2 supports the scalar comparison operators $\sim <$ and $\sim >$ as alternative representations of $> =$ and $< =$, respectively.

▪ In DB2, the list of constants in an IN condition (first format—see Example 6.2.8) must include at least one constant; in SQL/DS, it must include at least two. DB2 also allows the argument to IN to be a single scalar expression, in which case the IN is interpreted as " $=$ ".

▪ DB2 defines union-compatibility much more flexibly than SQL/DS. Basically, two values are union-compatible in DB2 if they are compatible in the sense of Section 4.5.

▪ In DB2, GRANT and REVOKE allow a list of table names (not necessarily just one) to be specified in the ON clause, and allow that list to be optionally preceded by the noiseword TABLE.

▪ DB2 supports numerous privileges (SYSADM and many others) that SQL/DS does not.

▪ In DB2, users can read the catalog only if they have been explicitly authorized to do so. In SQL/DS, everyone can read the catalog (except for password information).

▪ DB2 performs retrievals successfully against a much wider class of views than SQL/DS does.

▪ DB2 supports a CHECK option on CREATE VIEW, specifying that INSERTs and UPDATEs to the view are to be checked to ensure that the newly inserted or updated record satisfies the view-defining condition. SQL/DS does not support this option.

▪ SQL/DS requires declarations of host variables that are to be referenced in embedded SQL statements to appear within a "declare section" (bounded by BEGIN and END DECLARE SECTION statements). DB2 does not.

▪ SQL/DS does not support the DECLARE TABLE statement.

▪ DB2 supports a "declarations generator" facility (DCLGEN). SQL/DS does not.

▪ DB2 allows host variables to be elements of a structure. DB2 also allows a structure to be used as shorthand for a list of scalars (e.g., in the VALUES clause of INSERT).

- DB2 allows the leading colon to be omitted from host variable references in contexts where no ambiguity can result (e.g., in INTO clauses). SQL/DS permits such omission only in PREPARE, EXECUTE, and DESCRIBE statements.

- The keyword WORK in COMMIT and ROLLBACK WORK is optional in DB2 but required in SQL/DS.

- DB2 supports a lock wait timeout feature. SQL/DS does not.

- DB2 allows COMMIT and ROLLBACK WORK statements to be PREPAREd. SQL/DS does not.

- SQL/DS does not support the DECLARE STATEMENT statement.

- SQL/DS does not support databases in the DB2 sense. The DB2 statements CREATE and DROP DATABASE are not supported.

- SQL/DS does not support tablespaces. The DB2 statements CREATE, ALTER, and DROP TABLESPACE are not supported.

- SQL/DS does not support storage groups. The DB2 statements CREATE, ALTER, and DROP STOGROUP are not supported.

- SQL/DS does not support an ALTER INDEX statement.

- DB2 supports partitioned tables. SQL/DS does not.

- DB2 supports edit, field, and validation procedures (EDITPROC, FIELDPROC, and VALIDPROC on CREATE TABLE, and VALIDPROC on ALTER TABLE).

- DB2 supports authorization groups, together with a current SQLID special register and a SET statement to assign a value to that special register.

- DB2 supports an audit facility.

F.3 SQL/DS FEATURES NOT SUPPORTED IN DB2

- SQL/DS automatically creates an index on the primary key. DB2 does not.

- SQL/DS allows primary and foreign key checking to be ACTIVATEd and DEACTIVATEd. DB2 does not.

- SQL/DS supports a REFERENCES privilege (DB2 uses the ALTER privilege to provide a similar capacity).

- SQL/DS allows hexadecimal constants to be used to represent graphic values. DB2 does not.

- SQL/DS supports an ESCAPE clause on the LIKE predicate to permit the special interpretation given to the percent and underscore characters to be disabled. DB2 does not support this clause.

- SQL/DS allows indicator variable references to be immediately preceded by the optional keyword INDICATOR. DB2 does not.

- DB2 does not support the CONNECT statement. In particular, it does not support database switching (in the sense that a local application can access a remote database).

- DB2 does not support the SQL/DS RUN, CONNECT, DBA, or RESOURCE privileges.

- In SQL/DS, a user with DBA authority is allowed to perform direct INSERTs, UPDATEs, and DELETEs on the catalog. No user is ever allowed to perform such operations in DB2.

- SQL/DS supports Prolog. DB2 does not.

- SQL/DS supports REXX. DB2 does not.

- DB2 does not allow a cursor to be declared for INSERT and hence does not support the PUT statement either.

- The STOP action on WHENEVER is not supported in DB2.

- SQL/DS supports COMMIT and ROLLBACK WORK in all environments. DB2 supports those statements only under TSO.

- SQL/DS supports nonrecoverable data (i.e., nonrecoverable DBspaces). All data is recoverable in DB2.

- SQL/DS supports single-user mode. DB2 does not.

- SQL/DS supports private data (i.e., private DBspaces); users never wait for a lock on such data. In DB2, all data is at least potentially public, and any lock request can lead to a wait.

- SQL/DS supports true record-level locking. DB2 does not.

- SQL/DS allows a program to set its own isolation level (RR or CS) dynamically. DB2 does not.

- DB2 does not support extended dynamic SQL at all, and hence does not support the statements CREATE PROGRAM and DROP STATEMENT, nor the extended versions of the statements PREPARE, DESCRIBE, EXECUTE, DECLARE CURSOR, OPEN, FETCH, PUT, and CLOSE.

- DB2 does not support DBspaces, and hence does not support the ACQUIRE, ALTER, DROP, and LOCK DBSPACE statements either.

- DB2 does not support the UPDATE STATISTICS statement.
- The only form of EXPLAIN supported by DB2 is EXPLAIN PLAN.
- DB2 does not support the DROP PROGRAM statement.

F.4 INCOMPATIBILITIES

- DB2 and SQL/DS have different sets of reserved words.
- Foreign key names are up to 8 characters in DB2 but up to 18 characters in SQL/DS.
- The rules for assigning default foreign key names are different in the two products.
- If a DECIMAL column is defined with even precision p, SQL/DS rounds that precision up to the next odd number $P + 1$. DB2 does not.
- String comparisons in DB2 are always performed by padding the shorter with blanks to the length of the longer. The same rule applies to SQL/DS, except in the case where both strings are varying length (see Section 4.5 for details of this case).
- The number, names, and contents of catalog tables are completely different in the two products. The catalog "creator" is SYSTEM in SQL/DS but SYSIBM in DB2.
- Dropping a table (base table or view) causes all synonyms on that table to be dropped in DB2 but not in SQL/DS.
- Operations such as adding a foreign key to an existing nonempty table· cause an immediate integrity check in SQL/DS but set a "check pending" condition (and the data is unavailable) in DB2.
- The semantics of "GRANT ALL PRIVILEGES" are different in the two products. In DB2, the statement means "Grant all privileges for which the grantor holds the grant option." In SQL/DS, it means "Grant all privileges that apply to base tables." (In consequence, the statement cannot be applied to a view in SQL/DS, because some base table privileges—e.g., ALTER—do not apply to views.)
- Most SQLCODEs are different, except for the values 0 and +100.
- The SQLWARNING condition is defined differently in the two products.
- If cursor C is positioned on record R and record R is deleted, C goes into the "before" state in DB2 but the "between" state in SQL/DS.
- The DB2 and SQL/DS PLAN_TABLEs (used with EXPLAIN PLAN) are different in the two products.

G

♦

Query-By-Example

G.1 INTRODUCTION

As stated in Chapter 19, the Query Management Facility product (QMF) provides a Query-By-Example interface as well as a SQL interface. Query-By-Example (QBE) is a relational query language that is in some respects more "user-friendly" than SQL, at least for users who have no training in DP professional skills.* It is certainly true that SQL is more user-friendly than older languages such as DL/I, but it still assumes a certain amount of

---

*As explained in Chapter 19, the QBE language was previously supported by IBM as the interface to an "Installed User Program" product (confusingly also called QBE) running on the VM operating system. The reason for supporting the QBE language in QMF was presumably to wean away users of the old QBE product on to the new (and fully supported) QMF product.

programming expertise; it is still basically a programming language in the traditional sense, albeit one at a very high level. QBE, by contrast, is a language in which all operations are formulated simply by *making entries in empty tables on the screen*—in effect, by filling in forms. This "fill-in-the-blanks" style is very easy to learn and understand, and is frequently more attractive than the SQL style to users who have received little or no formal DP training. In this appendix, therefore, we present a short tutorial on QBE.

QBE (at least, the dialect of QBE supported by QMF) supports analogs of the SQL data manipulation operations SELECT, UPDATE, DELETE, and INSERT (but no others—data definition and data control operations, such as CREATE and GRANT, can be issued only via the SQL interface).* The operations available in QBE are P., U., D., and I., corresponding respectively to the SQL operations SELECT, UPDATE, DELETE, and INSERT. *Note:* "P." stands for "print," but it does not actually cause any printing to occur. The QMF PRINT command is provided for that purpose, as explained in Chapter 19.

The basic idea behind QBE is very simple, and is illustrated by the following example. Consider the query "Get supplier numbers for suppliers in Paris with status > 20" (Example 6.2.5 from Chapter 6). This query can be represented in QBE as follows:

```
S    | S#  | SNAME  | STATUS   | CITY    |
-----|-----|--------|----------|-------- |
     | P.  |        | > 20     | Paris   |
```

Explanation: First, by issuing the command DRAW S, the user causes QMF to display a blank version of table S (i.e., a version showing the table name and column names only, without any data values). Then the user constructs the query by typing entries in three positions in the body of that table, namely "P." in the S# position (to indicate the target of the query, i.e., the value(s) to be "printed" or displayed), and "> 20" and "Paris" in the STATUS and CITY positions (to indicate the condition(s) that those target values must satisfy).

It is also possible to specify "P." against the entire row, e.g., as follows:

```
S    | S#  | SNAME  | STATUS   | CITY    |
-----|-----|--------|----------|-------- |
P.   |     |        | > 20     | Paris   |
```

---

*It is worth mentioning that some of the SQL features added to SQL/DS in Version 2 were exposed in the SQL interface of QMF but not the QBE interface. Examples of features omitted from the QBE interface are the new scalar functions (e.g., DATE) and date/time arithmetic operations. These omissions suggest that IBM now regards the QBE interface to QMF as a "second-class citizen."

which is equivalent to specifying "P." in every column position in the table:

```
S    | S#  | SNAME | STATUS  |  CITY    |
---- |---- |-------|---------|----------|
     | P.  | P.    | P. >20  | P.Paris  |
```

Note, incidentally, that character string values such as Paris can be specified without being enclosed in quotes. It is never wrong to supply the quotes, however, and sometimes they are required (e.g., if the string includes any blanks).

In the rest of this appendix we illustrate some of the highlights of the QBE interface by showing a number of further examples. For convenience we give references (where applicable) to the SQL versions of the examples in Chapters 6, 7, and 8. We do not, however, go into as much detail as we did with SQL. Before we get started, a couple of preliminary remarks:

- As stated in Chapter 19, the user's QMF profile specifies whether queries will be formulated in SQL or QBE. It is possible to switch dynamically between the two within a single QMF session.

- Editing commands are available to tailor blank tables on the screen by the addition or removal of columns and rows and by the widening and narrowing of columns. Tables can thus be edited to fit the requirements of whatever operation the user is trying to formulate; in particular, columns that are not needed for the operation in question can be eliminated. For example, in the first of the sample queries shown earlier, the SNAME column could have been eliminated:

```
S    | S#  | STATUS  |  CITY    |
---- |---- |---------|----------|
     | P.  |  > 20   |  Paris   |
```

We shall usually not bother to show such details in what follows. However, we will frequently omit columns that are not needed to formulate the query under consideration.

G.2   RETRIEVAL OPERATIONS

G.2.1   Retrieval with Duplicate Elimination.   Get part numbers for all parts supplied, with redundant duplicates eliminated. (Example 6.2.2)

```
SP   | S#  | P#  | QTY   |
---- |---- |---- |-------|
UNQ. |     | P.  |       |
```

"UNQ." stands for "unique" (corresponds to DISTINCT in SQL).

G.2.2 *Retrieval with Ordering.*   Get supplier numbers and status for suppliers in Paris, in ascending supplier number order within descending status order. (Extended version of Example 6.2.6)

```
S    |    S#     | SNAME | STATUS    |  CITY
-----|-----------|-------|-----------|--------
     | P.AO(2).  |       | P.DO(1).  | Paris
```

"AO." stands for ascending order, "DO." for descending order. The integers in parentheses indicate the major-to-minor sequence for ordering columns; in the example, STATUS is the major column and S# the minor column.

G.2.3 *Retrieval Involving OR.*   Get supplier numbers and status for suppliers who either are located in Paris or have status > 20 or both. (Modified version of Example 6.2.5)

Conditions specified within a single row are considered to be "ANDed" together, as the examples so far have illustrated. To "OR" two conditions, they must be specified in different rows, as here:

```
S    | S#  | SNAME | STATUS  |  CITY
-----|-----|-------|---------|--------
     | P.  |       |         | Paris
     | P.  |       | > 20    |
```

Note: If a given supplier satisfies both of the conditions in this example, the corresponding supplier number will still appear only once in the output.

Another approach to this query makes use of what is known as a *condition box.* A condition box allows the specification of conditions of any degree of complexity. For example:

```
S    | S#  | SNAME | STATUS  |  CITY
-----|-----|-------|---------|--------
     | P.  |       | _ST     | _SC
```

```
|          CONDITIONS          |
|------------------------------|
|  _SC = Paris OR _ST > 20     |
```

Explanation: _ST and _SC are "example elements." In fact, they are really *variables,* standing for the status and city, respectively, of some potential target supplier. The condition box specifies a predicate that those variables must satisfy in order that the corresponding target supplier appear among those retrieved. The name of an example element is arbitrary, except that it must begin with an underscore character.

Another editing command, DRAW COND, is provided to cause QMF to display a blank condition box. Conditions in a condition box can involve AND, OR, NOT, IN (the simple list-of-values form only), LIKE, and NULL, very much as in SQL. (*Note:* IN, LIKE, and NULL can also be

used in entries in a blank table as well as in a condition box.) But it is frequently just as easy to formulate queries without making use of a condition box, and we shall usually ignore the possibility from this point on.

G.2.4 Retrieval Involving Multiple Conditions on the Same Column ANDed Together.
Get parts whose weight is in the range 16 to 19 inclusive. (Example 6.2.7)

P	P#	PNAME	COLOR	WEIGHT	WEIGHT	CITY
	P.			>= 16	<= 19	

Editing commands are used to add another column to the blank table and to name it WEIGHT before the query is formulated.

G.2.5 Retrieval of Computed Values.
For all parts, get the part number and the weight of the part in grams. Weights are given in table P in pounds. (Example 6.2.3)

P	P#	WEIGHT		
	P.	_PW	P. 'Weight in grams ='	P. _PW * 454

G.2.6 Retrieving (Specified Fields from) a Join.
Get all supplier-number/part-number combinations such that the supplier and part concerned are "colocated." (Example 6.3.4)

S	S#	CITY		P	P#	CITY				
	_SX	_CX			_PX	_CX		P.	_SX	_PX

Explanation: Three blank tables are needed for this query, one each for S and P (only relevant columns shown) and one for the result (no table name or column names may be specified). Notice how example elements are specified to link these three tables together. The entire query can be paraphrased:

"Display supplier-number/part-number pairs, SX/PX say, such that SX and PX are both located in the same city CX."

G.2.7 Joining a Table with Itself.
Get all pairs of supplier numbers such that the two suppliers concerned are colocated. (Example 6.3.6)

S	S#	CITY				
	_SX	_CZ		P.	_SX	_SY
	_SY	_CZ				

A condition box can be used to specify the additional condition _SX < _SY, if desired (see Chapter 6 for a discussion of this point).

G.2.8 Retrieval Involving Existential Quantification. Get supplier names for suppliers who supply part P2. (Example 7.3.1)

```
S   | S#  | SNAME   |     SP   | S#  | P# |
----|-----|---------|     ----|-----|----|
    | _SX | P.      |         | _SX | P2 |
```

The row in table SP is *implicitly* quantified by the existential quantifier "there exists." The query can be paraphrased:

> "Display supplier names for suppliers SX such that there exists a shipment showing supplier SX supplying part P2."

QBE thus (implicitly) includes an analog of EXISTS in SQL. Note, however, that it does *not* include any analog of NOT EXISTS. Thus, for example, a query such as "Get supplier names for suppliers who do *not* supply part P2" cannot be formulated in QBE, at least in the dialect implemented in QMF. The QMF dialect of QBE is therefore (unfortunately) strictly less powerful than the QMF dialect of SQL.*

G.2.9 Retrieval Involving an Aggregate Function. Get the total quantity of part P2 supplied. (Example 7.4.4)

```
SP | S# | P# | QTY |
---|----|----|-----|--------------
   |    | P2 | _QX | P.SUM._QX
```

The following aggregate functions are supported: "CNT." (or "COUNT."), "SUM.", "AVG.", "MAX.", and "MIN.".

G.2.10 Retrieval Involving an Aggregate Function, with Grouping. For each part supplied, get the part number and the total shipment quantity for that part. (Example 7.4.7)

```
SP | S# | P#   | QTY |
---|----|------|-----|--------------
   |    | G.P. | _QY | P.SUM._QY
```

"G." causes grouping (corresponds to GROUP BY in SQL).

G.2.11 Retrieval Involving an Aggregate Function, with Grouping and a Condition. Get part numbers for all parts supplied by more than one supplier. (Example 7.4.9)

```
SP | S#  | P#   |     CONDITIONS
---|-----|------|     -------------
   | _SX | G.P. |     CNT._SX >1
```

---

*This statement is true quite apart from the fact that (as mentioned earlier in this appendix) certain SQL/DS Version 2 features, such as date/time arithmetic, have been exposed in SQL but not in QBE.

The condition box can be used to formulate both WHERE-type conditions and HAVING-type conditions (in SQL terms).

G.2.12 Retrieval Involving Union. Get part numbers for parts that either weigh more than 16 pounds or are supplied by supplier S2 or both. (Example 7.5.1)

P	P#	WEIGHT		SP	S#	P#			
	_PX	> 16			S2	_PY		P.	_PX
								P.	_PY

G.3 UPDATE OPERATIONS

G.3.1 Single-Record Insert. Add part P7 (city Athens, weight 24, name and color at present unknown) to table P. (Example 8.2.1)

P	P#	PNAME	COLOR	WEIGHT	CITY
I.	P7			24	Athens

Note that "I." applies to the entire row and so appears beneath the table name.

G.3.2 Single-Record Update. Change the color of part P2 to yellow, increase its weight by 5, and set its city to null. (Example 8.3.1)

P	P#	PNAME	COLOR	WEIGHT	WEIGHT	CITY
	P2		U.Yellow	_WT	U._WT + 5	U.NULL

G.3.3 Multiple-Record Update. Set the shipment quantity to zero for all suppliers in London. (Example 8.3.3)

SP	S#	QTY		S	S#	CITY
	_SX	U.0			_SX	London

G.3.4 Multiple-Record Delete. Delete all shipments with quantity greater than 300. (Example 8.4.2)

SP	S#	P#	QTY
D.			> 300

"D.", like "I.", appears beneath the table name.

This concludes our short tutorial on QBE. By way of practice, the reader is recommended to try producing QBE solutions to some of the exercises in Chapters 6–8.

Bibliography

We present a short list of selected further reading (over and above the official SQL/DS, QMF, etc., manuals, which are available from IBM).

M. M. Astrahan et al.: "System R: Relational Approach to Database Management." *ACM Transactions on Database Systems 1,* No. 2 (June 1976).

The paper that first described the overall architecture of System R, the prototype forerunner of SQL/DS (and DB2).

M. W. Blasgen et al.: "System R: An Architectural Overview." *IBM Systems Journal 20,* No. 1 (February 1981).

Describes the architecture of System R as it became by the time the system had been fully implemented.

D. D. Chamberlin et al.: "A History and Evaluation of System R." *Communications of the ACM 24,* No. 10 (October 1981).

Discusses the lessons learned from the System R prototype.

D. D. Chamberlin, A. M. Gilbert, and R. A. Yost: "A History of System R and SQL/Data System." *Proceedings of the 7th International Conference on Very Large Data Bases* (September 1981). Obtainable from ACM, IEEE, and INRIA.

Includes a description of the major differences between System R and SQL/DS (and, by extension, DB2).

E. F. Codd: "A Relational Model of Data for Large Shared Data Banks." *Communications of the ACM 13,* No. 6 (June 1970). Reprinted in *Communications of the ACM 26,* No. 1 (January 1983).

This was the paper that (apart from some internal IBM documents) first proposed the ideas of the relational model.

E. F. Codd: "Relational Database: A Practical Foundation for Productivity." *Communications of the ACM 25,* No. 2 (February 1982).

The paper that Codd presented on the occasion of his receiving the 1981 Turing Award. The definition of "relational system" in Appendix B of this book is taken from this paper.

E. F. Codd: "Is Your DBMS Really Relational?" (*Computerworld,* October 14, 1985); "Does Your DBMS Run by the Rules?" (*Computerworld,* October 21, 1985).

These two papers include proposals for a more stringent definition of what it means for a system to be relational in the mid to late 1980s.

Codd and Date Consulting Group: *Database Product Reports* (to appear).

An in-progress series of reports on commercially available relational products, including of course SQL/DS.

American National Standards Institute: *Database Language SQL,* Document ANSI X3.135–1986. Also available as International Standards Organization Document ISO/TC97/SC21/WG3 N117.

The official SQL standard definition.

C. J. Date: *An Introduction to Database Systems: Volume I* (4th edition, Addison-Wesley, 1985); *Volume II* (1st edition, Addison-Wesley, 1983).

These two books between them provide the basis for a comprehensive education in most aspects of database technology. In particular, they include a very detailed treatment of the relational approach.

C. J. Date: *Relational Database: Selected Writings* (Addison-Wesley, 1986).

A collection of papers on various aspects of relational technology, including several on the SQL language and one (rather long) on a relational database design methodology that is directly applicable to SQL/DS.

C. J. Date (with Colin J. White): *A Guide to DB2* (2nd edition, Addison-Wesley, 1988).

The book on which the present book is based.

C. J. Date: *A Guide to INGRES* (Addison-Wesley, 1987).

A companion to the present book, describing another important relational product—INGRES, from Relational Technology Inc. (RTI).

C. J. Date: *A Guide to the SQL Standard* (Addison-Wesley, 1987).

An indepth discussion of the official standard version of the SQL language.

C. J. Date: "Dates and Times in IBM SQL: Some Technical Criticisms." *InfoDB* *3,* No. 1 (Spring 1988).

An analysis and critical evaluation of the date and time support in SQL/DS (and DB2).

C. J. Date: "Referential Integrity and Foreign Keys. Part I: Basic Concepts; Part II: Further Considerations." To appear.

Abbreviations
and Acronyms

We list below some of the more important abbreviations and acronyms introduced
in the text, together with their meanings.

ALF	Application Load File (CSP)
ANSI	American National Standards Institute
API	application programming interface
AS	Application System
BNF	Backus-Naur Form
CICS	Customer Information Control System
CMS	Conversational Monitor System (VM)
CS	cursor stability (isolation level)
CSP	Cross System Product
CSP/AD	CSP/Application Development
CSP/AE	CSP/Application Execution
DB/DC	database/data communications

DBA	database administrator
DBMS	database management system
DBRAD	Data Base Relational Application Directory
DBS	Data Base Services (SQL/DS utility)
DBSS	Data Base Storage System (SQL/DS)
DB2	IBM DATABASE 2
DCF	Document Composition Facility
DEM	Data Extract Manager (DXT)
DOS DL/I	Disk Operating System Data Language/I (VSE)
DSC	Data System Control (SQL/DS)
DXT	Data Extract
DXTA	DXT Assist
ECF	Enhanced Connectivity Facilities
GDDM	Graphic Data Display Manager
HDBV	Host Data Base View
I/O	input/output
IC/1	Info Center/1
ICCF	Interactive Communication Control Facility (VSE)
ICU	Interactive Chart Utility
ISO	International Standards Organization
ISPF	Interactive System Productivity Facility
ISQL	Interactive SQL (SQL/DS)
IXF	Integration Exchange Format
PF key	program function key
PROFS	Professional Office System
QBE	Query-By-Example (QMF)
QMF	Query Management Facility
RDS	Relational Data System (SQL/DS)
REM	Relational Extract Manager (DXT)
RID	record ID
RR	repeatable read (isolation level)
S lock	shared lock
SAA	Systems Application Architecture
SQL	Structured Query Language
SQL/DS	Structured Query Language/Data System
SQLCA	SQL Communication Area
SQLDA	SQL Descriptor Area
SRPI	server-requester programming interface
TID	tuple ID (= RID)
TIF	The Information Facility
TSAF	Transparency Services Access Facility (VM)
UIM	User Input Manager (DXT)
VSAM	Virtual Storage Access Method (VSE)
WYSIWYG	what you see is what you get
X lock	exclusive lock

Index